JOURNAL FOR THE STUDY OF THE OLD TESTAMENT SUPPLEMENT SERIES
214

Sheffield Academic Press

New Visions of Isaiah

Roy F. Melugin &
Marvin A. Sweeney (eds.)

Journal for the Study of the Old Testament
Supplement Series 214

To

Ronald E. Clements

Published by Sheffield Academic Press Ltd
Mansion House
19 Kingfield Road
Sheffield S11 9AS
England

Printed on acid-free paper in Great Britain
by Bookcraft Ltd
Midsomer Norton, Bath

British Library Cataloguing in Publication Data

A catalogue record for this book is available
from the British Library

ISBN 1-85075-584-1

CONTENTS

Part I
IS MEANING LOCATED IN 'AUTHOR' OR TEXT?

ACKNOWLEDGMENTS

This volume is born in debt. The essays herein are a result of the lively discussions of the Formation of the Book of Isaiah Seminar of the Society of Biblical Literature. The editors of this volume are grateful to the members of the Seminar for having stimulated the debate, much of which is reflected in these papers. We are also grateful to David Lull and the SBL Program Committee for their assistance to the Seminar and for their encouragement of its scholarly work. We are especially appreciative of the invitation by David Clines to produce this volume and for his patient guidance during its preparation. Hearty thanks go to Paula Jonse for her skill, hard work, and good humor in preparing the manuscript to be sent to the printer.

A special debt is owed to Ronald Clements, whose writings have been important in the Seminar's discussions and whose leadership in the founding of the Seminar was invaluable. We dedicate these essays to him as a sign of our respect and affection.

Marvin A. Sweeney
Roy F. Melugin

ABBREVIATIONS

AB	Anchor Bible
AcOr	*Acta orientalia*
AnBib	Analecta biblica
ANET	J.B. Pritchard (ed.), *Ancient Near Eastern Texts*
AOAT	Alter Orient und Altes Testament
ATANT	Abhandlungen zur Theologie des Alten und Neuen Testaments
ATD	Das Alte Testament Deutsch
BASOR	*Bulletin of the American Schools of Oriental Research*
BBB	Bonner biblische Beiträge
BDB	F. Brown, S.R. Driver and C.A. Briggs, *Hebrew and English Lexicon of the Old Testament*
BETL	Bibliotheca ephemeridum theologicarum lovaniensium
BHT	Beiträge zur historischen Theologie
Bib	*Biblica*
BibRev	*Bible Review*
BibOr	Biblica et orientalia
BKAT	Biblischer Kommentar: Altes Testament
BN	*Biblische Notizen*
BR	*Biblical Research*
BWANT	Beiträge zur Wissenschaft vom Alten und Neuen Testament
BZAW	Beihefte zur *ZAW*
CBC	Cambridge Bible Commentary
CBQ	*Catholic Biblical Quarterly*
CBQMS	*Catholic Biblical Quarterly*, Monograph Series
ConBOT	Coniectanea biblica, Old Testament
CRINT	Compendia rerum iudaicarum ad Novum Testamentum
CTA	A. Herdner, *Corpus des tablettes en cunéiformes alphabétiques découvertes à Ras Shamra-Ugarit de 1929 à 1939*
EBib	Etudes bibliques
ETL	*Ephemerides theologicae lovanienses*
ETR	*Etudes théologiques et religieuses*
FB	Forschung zur Bibel
FOTL	The Forms of the Old Testament Literature
FRLANT	Forschungen zur Religion und Literatur des Alten und Neuen Testaments
FzAT	Forschung zum Alten Testament
HKAT	Handkommentar zum Alten Testament
HSM	Harvard Semitic Monographs
HTR	*Harvard Theological Review*

HUCA	*Hebrew Union College Annual*
IB	*Interpreter's Bible*
ICC	International Critical Commentary
IDB	G.A. Buttrick (ed.), *Interpreter's Dictionary of the Bible*
Int	*Interpretation*
ITC	International Theological Commentary
JBL	*Journal of Biblical Literature*
JPS	Jewish Publication Society
JQR	*Jewish Quarterly Review*
JSOT	*Journal for the Study of the Old Testament*
JSOTSup	*Journal for the Study of the Old Testament*, Supplement Series
JSS	*Journal of Semitic Studies*
KTU	M. Dietrich, O. Lonetz, and J. Sanmartín (eds.), *Die keil–alphabetischen Texte aus Ugarit*
NCB	New Century Bible
NICOT	New International Commentary on the Old Testament
OBO	Orbis biblicus et orientalis
OBT	Overtures to Biblical Theology
OTL	Old Testament Library
OTS	*Oudtestamentische Studiën*
RB	*Revue biblique*
SBL	Society of Biblical Literature
SBLDS	SBL Dissertation Series
SBLSP	SBL Seminar Papers
SBS	Stuttgarter Bibelstudien
SBT	Studies in Biblical Theology
SJT	*Scottish Journal of Theology*
SPB	Studia postbiblica
SSN	Studia semitica neerlandica
TB	Torch Bible Commentaries
TBS	The Biblical Seminar
TBü	Theologische Bücherei
TDNT	G. Kittel and G. Friedrich (eds.), *Theological Dictionary of the New Testament*
THAT	E. Jenni and C. Westermann (eds.), *Theologisches Handwörterbuch zum Alten Testament*
ThWAT	G.J. Botterweck and H. Ringgren (eds.), *Theologisches Wörterbuch zum Alten Testament*
TLZ	*Theologische Literaturzeitung*
UUÅ	Uppsala universitetsårsskrift
VT	*Vetus Testamentum*
VTSup	*Vetus Testamentum*, Supplements
WBC	Word Biblical Commentary
WMANT	Wissenschaftliche Monographien zum Alten und Neuen Testament
ZAW	*Zeitschrift für die alttestamentliche Wissenschaft*
ZBK	Zürcher Bibelkommentare
ZTK	*Zeitschrift für Theologie und Kirche*

LIST OF CONTRIBUTORS

Mark E. Biddle
Associate Professor of Religion
Carson-Newman College

David M. Carr
Associate Professor of Hebrew Bible
Methodist Theological School of Ohio

Edward W. Conrad
Reader in Studies in Religion
University of Queensland

Katheryn Pfisterer Darr
Associate Professor of Hebrew Bible
Boston University School of Theology

Chris A. Franke
Associate Professor of Theology
College of St Catherine

Roy F. Melugin
Gould H. and Marie Cloud Professor of Religion
Austin College

Rolf Rendtorff
Professor of Old Testament, Emeritus
Ruprecht-Karl Universität, Heidelberg

Gerald T. Sheppard
Professor of Old Testament Literature and Exegesis
Emmanuel College of Victoria University, and
Toronto School of Theology at the University of Toronto

Benjamin D. Sommer
Assistant Professor of Religion
Northwestern University

Gary Stansell
Professor of Religion
St Olaf College

Marvin A. Sweeney
Professor of Hebrew Bible, School of Theology at Claremont, and
Professor of Religion, Claremont Graduate School

Roy D. Wells, Jr
Professor of Religion
Birmingham-Southern College

INTRODUCTION

Roy F. Melugin

I

In today's world there is a mind-boggling array of fundamentally different interpretations of the book of Isaiah. There are indeed so many different understandings of Isaiah that a person untrained in biblical studies might well wonder whether they are all interpretations of the same book. The Formation of the Book of Isaiah Seminar of the Society of Biblical Literature, co-chaired by Marvin Sweeney and myself, has more of a shared vision, for all of us (as far as I can tell) have been greatly influenced by the earlier work of scholars such as Peter Ackroyd, Ronald Clements and Rolf Rendtorff in an effort to interpret the entire sixty-six chapter book holistically.[1]

The members of our seminar are nevertheless by no means of one mind as to how to interpret Isaiah. As Rolf Rendtorff, himself a member of the seminar, has recently written, one of the most important items on our agenda must be the relationships between synchronic and diachronic approaches to the text.[2] Indeed, although our seminar seems united

---

1. See P.R. Ackroyd, 'Isaiah I–XII: Presentation of a Prophet', in J.A. Emerton *et al.* (eds.), *Congress Volume: Göttingen 1977* (VTSup, 29; Leiden: Brill, 1978), pp. 16-48, and 'Isaiah 36–39: Structure and Function', in W.C. Delsman *et al.* (eds.), *Von Kanaan bis Kerala* (Festschrift J.P.M. van der Ploeg; Neukirchen–Vluyn: Neukirchener Verlag, 1982), pp. 3-21; R.E. Clements, 'The Unity of the Book of Isaiah', *Interpretation* 36 (1982), pp. 117-29, and 'Beyond Tradition History: Deutero-Isaianic Development of First Isaiah's Themes', *JSOT* 31 (1985), pp. 95-113; R. Rendtorff, 'The Composition of the Book of Isaiah', 'Isaiah 6 in the Framework of the Composition of the Book', and 'Isaiah 56.1 as a Key to the Formation of the Book of Isaiah', in *idem*, *Canon and Theology* (trans. and ed. M. Kohl; Minneapolis: Fortress Press, 1993), pp. 146-69, 170-80, 181-89.

2. R. Rendtorff, 'The Book of Isaiah: A Complex Unity', E.H. Lovering, Jr (ed.), *Society of Biblical Literature 1991 Seminar Papers* (Atlanta: Scholars Press, 1991), pp. 8-20. An updated version of Rendtorff's essay appears in this volume.

about the importance of synchronic analysis, there is more disagreement about the need for asking diachronic questions. Ronald Clements, Marvin Sweeney and Christopher Seitz, for example, are committed to a redaction-*historical* approach.[3] Edgar Conrad, at the opposite pole, refuses to locate meaning in author or redactor *or* in an actual historical community's reception of the text. He deliberately chooses instead to focus on the text's 'implied reader'; that is, fictive audiences as 'theoretical constructs encoded in the text'.[4] Katheryn Pfisterer Darr also employs the concept of an implied reader and, like Conrad, develops an interpretation of the book of Isaiah which is almost entirely synchronic.[5]

Why these differences? In my judgment, they are the result of different reading strategies.[6] By this I mean that the understandings which we acquire in the reading of texts are the result of interaction between the reader and the text. What we call 'meaning' is in no way independent of the strategies which we bring to the reading of a text.[7] *We* decide what questions to ask; *we* decide which methods of analysis to employ; *we* determine what is appropriate to consider or leave out of consideration. Whether one believes that meaning is 'in' texts or thinks instead that meaning is inherently a construct which is in no small measure the creation of the reader, one must surely agree that *in practice* the interpreter and the interpreter's biases do affect the way a text is actually read.

Many of the reader's decisions about how to address the text will not be consciously made. Many of our reading strategies are unconscious because they are widely shared in communities of readers.[8] For example, historical criticism of the Bible is an approach to reading which has a long history in the scholarly community. Yet it is an approach which once was not, and it now enjoys widespread credibility because it has extensive support in a particular social group. Moreover, it represents an

---

3.   Clements, 'Unity', pp. 117-29, and 'Beyond Tradition History', pp. 95-113; Sweeney, *Isaiah 1–4 and the Post-Exilic Understanding of the Isaianic Tradition* (BZAW, 171; Berlin and New York: de Gruyter, 1988); Seitz, *Zion's Final Destiny* (Minneapolis: Fortress, 1991).

4.   E. Conrad, *Reading Isaiah* (Minneapolis: Fortress Press, 1991), p. 31.

5.   K.P. Darr, *Isaiah's Vision and the Family of God* (Louisville: Westminster John Knox, 1994).

6.   Conrad, *Reading Isaiah*, pp. 3-33.

7.   S. Fish, *Is there a Text in this Class? The Authority of Interpretive Communities* (Cambridge: Harvard University Press, 1980), pp. 1-17.

8.   Fish, *Is there a Text in this Class?*, pp. 318-321.

approach to the text whose conventions change as the reading community itself becomes different.

What I am saying here can be seen in the history of Isaiah studies over the past century. Isaiah scholarship was once preoccupied with recovering original creative prophetic traditions—the words of the eighth-century Isaiah and the towering unnamed prophetic genius whom we conventionally call 'Second Isaiah'. The reading community generally considered redactors to be inferior and to be mechanistic in their approach. Since that time, however, conventions in the community of scholars have changed. Redactors are now commonly understood to have had author-like creativity and to have possessed important theological insights. These more recent developments did not come about primarily because of a discovery of a body of information hitherto unknown but because of changing ways of conceptualizing how texts could grow and develop as the community of scholars transformed its own hermeneutical conventions.

Ronald Clements exhibits quite well some of the newer developments in historical criticism. In an article in the April 1982 edition of *Interpretation*, he proposed a view of the unity of the book of Isaiah based on the relationships between the prophecies of the historical Isaiah and their later interpretation after the destruction of Jerusalem.[9] Within chs. 1–39 there are references to Babylon (13.21–14.23; 39), so that the supposed distinction between First and Second Isaiah is not razor sharp. Instead, we find that the book as a whole deals with the political fortunes of Israel from the eighth all the way to the fifth centuries BCE.[10] This leads Clements to conclude that 'the overall structure of the book shows signs of editorial planning and that, at some stage in its growth, attempts were made to read and interpret the book as a whole'.[11]

According to Clements, a Josianic redaction[12] was supplemented by the addition of Isaiah 36–39, which built a bridge joining this Josianic redaction to some of the material in chs. 40–55 which had already been included as a part of the developing book of Isaiah. In the late sixth and early fifth centuries under Persian rule, chs. 56–66 were added to

9. Clements, 'Unity', pp. 117-29.
10. Clements, 'Unity', p. 120.
11. Clements, 'Unity', p. 120.
12. H. Barth, *Die Jesaja-Worte in der Josiazeit: Israel und Assur als Thema einer produktiven Neuinterpretation der Jesajasuberlieferung* (WMANT, 48; Neukirchen–Vluyn: Neukirchener Verlag, 1977).

'highlight the way in which the promises and rich assurances given by the exilic prophet of chapters 40–55 began to take effect'.[13]

The Isaianic prophecies of the overthrow of the Assyrians, expanded upon by the anti-Assyrian Josianic redaction, were used and alluded to by the 'great unnamed prophet of Isaiah 40–55' in developing a larger message of prophecy and fulfillment in which the themes of 'former things' and blindness and deafness are prominent (6.9-10; 32.3; 35.5; 42.18-20; 43.8).[14] The prophecies of Isaiah had given insight into the judgments which befell Israel and Judah, although a Davidic ruler had remained on the throne. Once Jerusalem was overthrown, the temple destroyed, and the Davidic monarchy removed from power, a 'renewed urgency and severity attached to Isaiah's prophecies which had warned of judgment even upon the city of Jerusalem itself.[15] In Clement's judgment, there are quite good reasons 'for concluding that the prophecies of Isaiah came to be used and interpreted by the survivors of 587 BC in order to understand the reasons for what had befallen them'.[16]

I find Clement's essay to be wondrously compelling. Yet it is the product of his own subtle and sophisticated imagination through which he has created a picture of what these redactors did. There are no marginal notes in the manuscripts explaining that this is how the text came to be; we have only the *text*. Clements's fertile imagination has created for us an almost psychological portrayal of the thought processes of these exilic and post-exilic redactors. We might ask whether Clements has discovered a past reality or whether he has created it. Surely the picture he has painted is very useful; I would perhaps not want him to retract a single word. But I also think we should recognize that he has chosen a way of reading—a way of reading which, in many of today's reading communities, will surely strike chords of appreciative response.

Christopher Seitz is also a historical-critical interpreter. Yet his approach is not as much focused on the social and psychic needs which precipitated additions to the earliest forms of Isaiah as it is on the text itself and the literary history of the *text*. In his *Reading and Preaching the Book of Isaiah*, Seitz uses the analogy of a farmhouse in North

---

13. Clements, 'Unity', p. 123.
14. Clements, 'Unity', p. 125.
15. Clements, 'Unity', p. 127.
16. Clements, 'Unity', p. 127.

Carolina as a clue for understanding the redaction of texts.[17] The farmhouse was a 'redacted' building. When one entered the central hall, one could see that the right side of the house had settled lower than the left side. Moreover, a main section of a rear interior wall was covered with exterior siding, and a full sash window—surely originally on an outside wall—faced out into the interior of the house. It was possible to deduce that the house exhibited a definite unity of form that made sense only if an original house had been added to with concern for its final shape rather than having been a merger of several originally independent houses.

Such is the case with the book of Isaiah, according to Seitz. There were earlier Isaianic traditions which existed independent of the book as it now is. But Isaiah 40–55 and 56–66 were never literary complexes which once existed apart from chs. 1–39. Isaiah 40–55 contains no call narrative of its own; 40.1-8 is not truly a commissioning of the prophet 'Second Isaiah' but rather a transition between traditions concerning the epoch of Isaiah to a new time following the exile of Babylon.[18] Indeed, a message of comfort to Jerusalem, with the announcement that her 'time of service' had come to an end (40.1-2), makes no sense apart from Jerusalem's having already fallen. And the fall to Babylon is accounted for in ch. 39, which in turn connects the punishment by Babylon with the reprieve given to Hezekiah in the days of Sennacherib's invasion (chs. 36–38).[19] Because of Hezekiah's obedience, Yahweh's plan of old (the 'former things') came to include a new epoch ('new things') long after the time of Isaiah himself. The later seventh and sixth-century traditions reinterpret the earlier Isaianic traditions by continuing and extending the expectation of the ultimate deliverance of Zion.[20]

Seitz's preoccupation with redaction history leads him always to remember the 'unwieldiness in form' in the book of Isaiah; that is, 'how the different redactional layers make it sometimes 'difficult to get from room to room' in the present book of Isaiah.[21] Yet he never undertakes a detailed analysis of the structure of the book. That task has been taken

17. C. Seitz, 'Isaiah 1–66: Making Sense of the Whole', in *idem* (ed.), *Reading and Preaching the Book of Isaiah* (Philadelphia: Fortress Press, 1988), pp. 108-109.

18. C. Seitz, 'The Divine Council: Temporal Transition and New Prophecy in the Book of Isaiah', *JBL* 109 (1990), pp. 229-47.

19. Seitz, 'Isaiah 1–66', pp. 110-11.

20. Seitz, *Zion's Final Destiny*, pp. 197-99.

21. Seitz, 'Isaiah 1–66', p. 109.

on by Marvin Sweeney.[22] Along with his mentor Rolf Knierim, Sweeney appears to have recognized that no history of redaction can be reconstructed until one has first of all recovered the structure and intention of the text as formulated by its final redactor.[23] Only after the text in its final form is accounted for can one identify earlier stages of development within the text. Therefore, Sweeney presents a sophisticated analysis of the structure of the book of Isaiah in its completed form. Then he attempts to reconstruct the redaction history of the first four chapters of Isaiah.

Sweeney's approach, firmly located in the extended family of form and redaction critics though it is, nevertheless exhibits a reading strategy which is distinctive among interpreters of Isaiah. He presents structure in Isaiah as a series of blocks of text—a linear progression of units which are hierarchically interrelated. As Gerald Sheppard has pointed out, Sweeney's construal of structure as linear progression by no means exhausts the possibilities for the conceptualization of structure.[24] What we should conclude from this is not necessarily that Sheppard proposes a truer representation of structure than Sweeney but rather that Sweeney *decided* how he would represent structure. One may indeed ask whether Sweeney has 'discovered' the structure of the book of Isaiah or whether he has instead created a particular way of doing structural analysis. Moreover, if meaning is thought to be related to structure, one may ask to what extent Sweeney's interpretation of the intentions of the final redactor of Isaiah is a discovery of a past meaning or to what extent it is a creation of Sweeney the interpreter.

Rolf Rendtorff's studies on the unity of the book of Isaiah focus on the text itself rather than diachronic considerations about the redactional process by which the book was given its form. For example, he mentions correlation between chs. 1 and 40: 'Woe to the sinful nation, a people laden with guilt' (1.4) and 'Speak to the heart of Jerusalem and cry to her that her time of service is ended, that her guilt is pardoned' (40.2). He also contends that all three parts of the book of Isaiah

---

22. Sweeney, *Isaiah 1–4.*

23. R. Knierim, 'Old Testament Interpretation Reconsidered', *Interpretation* 27 (1973), pp. 435-70.

24. G. Sheppard, 'The Book of Isaiah: Competing Structures according to a Late Modern Description of its Shape and Scope', E.H. Lovering, Jr (ed.), *Society of Biblical Literature 1992 Seminar Papers* (Atlanta: Scholars Press, 1992), pp. 555-57.

manifest language about the 'comfort' supplied by Yahweh: 'I will give thanks to thee, YHWH; yes, thou wast angry with me, but let thy anger be turned away, that thou mayst comfort me' (12.1); 'Comfort, comfort my people' (40.1); 'As one whom his mother comforts, so I will comfort you' (66.13). Furthermore, Rendtorff observes that language about God's 'glory' unifies the book: 'Holy, holy, holy is YHWH Sabaoth, what fills the earth is his glory' (6.3); 'The glory of YHWH shall be revealed' (40.5); 'Arise, shine, for your light is coming, and the glory of YHWH is rising upon you' (60.1); Yahweh will bring together 'all nations and all tongues and they shall come and see my glory' (66.18).[25] I have space to mention only these few examples of connections across the entire book as seen by Rendtorff in his insightful essays on the unity of Isaiah. He is of course well aware that the book of Isaiah grew into its present form over a long period of time, but he has chosen to interpret the book as a unity by synchronic rather than diachronic analysis.

Edgar Conrad's *Reading Isaiah* provides us with a hermeneutic which locates meaning in the reader instead of in the author or text. Conrad rehearses with approval the contention of Stanley Fish that meaning is the result of what interpreters do and is therefore not something which resides *in* texts. Different approaches to interpretation are theories of meaning developed by readers in various communities of interpretation.

Conrad therefore does not reconstruct the intentions of author or redactor, nor does he make claims about a meaning inherent in the text. Instead he speaks of 'implied reader' and 'implied audience', which are fictive constructs that our reading of Isaiah leads us to imagine.[26] The 'we' who reflect upon what would have happened if Yahweh had not left a few survivors (1.9) are construed by Conrad as an imaginary audience which the text presents to its reader rather than as a real historical community. Indeed, Conrad reads the entire book of Isaiah as revolving around an implied community who continue to refer to themselves in the first person; for example, 'behold you were angry and we sinned' (64.4); 'you hid your face from us' (64.6); 'why do you make us err from your ways and harden our heart?' (63.17). Conrad reads the entire book of Isaiah synchronically as addressed to and by an implied community of survivors who have experienced judgment and who wait for justice and righteousness (chs. 1–5; 40–66).[27] The larger

25. Rendtorff, 'Composition', pp. 149-152.
26. Conrad, *Reading Isaiah*, p. 31.
27. Conrad, *Reading Isaiah*, pp. 87-110.

block of text which opens and closes with narratives about the historical Isaiah (chs. 6–39) functions as 'vision' and 'testimony' from the past,[28] to support the implied community wrestling with its own experience of judgment and hope.

Whether Conrad's apparent commitment to Stanley Fish and the hermeneutic which Conrad actually employs are completely consistent lies beyond the scope of these introductory remarks. What is important just now is for us to recognize in Conrad the presence of someone who is postmodern and reader-centered among the different voices in the Formation of the Book of Isaiah Seminar. Katheryn Pfisterer Darr, also a member of the seminar, focuses upon the reader as well. In her *Isaiah's Vision and the Family of God* she reads the book of Isaiah synchronically through the eyes of a fourth-century Israelite reader whom she has created.[29] This hypothetical reader reads the text holistically from beginning to end in sequential fashion without concern for identifying different layers of redaction.

Because the implied reader is Darr's creation, she can exercise a certain freedom in choosing how this reader will read the book. She can decide that her reader will focus on metaphors and other tropes. She can decide who the reader is and what the reader knows. Presumably she could decide *how* her reader will interpret the tropes encountered in the text. Just how boldly or how conservatively Darr portrays her reader need not be resolved here. Whether (or to what extent) her reader is the product of discovery by objective historical inquiry or is instead *in toto* a construct is a valid question which I shall not presently try to answer. For the moment, it is enough to be aware that with both Darr and Conrad, reader-response criticism has come to be a major player in the orchestra of Isaiah scholarship.

II

The essays in this volume are diverse in approach. They exhibit the diversity which has always been present in the Seminar. Each essay has a unique perspective and thus extends the frontiers of research on the book of Isaiah. Yet, taken as a group, they tend to fall into the broad typologies which I discussed above. Seven of the essays appear to be 'objective' in their approach to the text; they embrace either historical-

28. Conrad, *Reading Isaiah*, pp. 110-13.
29. Darr, *Isaiah's Vision*, pp. 13-32.

critical method or a synchronic approach in which text rather than reader seems to be the focus. The remaining five essays are 'postmodern' in the sense that meaning is in no small degree located in what the reader does.

Part I: An essay by Rolf Rendtorff heads the entire volume since he shows that recent studies of the shape of the *book* of Isaiah may profitably be distinguished from one another according to the various ways in which scholars interrelate diachronic and synchronic approaches to the text. Some scholars, he reports, depict the form of the book almost entirely in synchronic terms, while others exhibit primarily diachronic methodology. Still others combine synchronic and diachronic approaches, but different scholars interrelate the two in a variety of ways. Rendtorff himself sees considerable value in combining diachronic and synchronic methods, yet he also appears to argue that, in future Isaiah scholarship, there should be a place for studies of the entire book (or even parts of it) that are completely synchronic—sometimes to the exclusion of diachronic questions of redaction or composition.

Rendtorff's essay is helpful in laying a foundation for the subsequent essays in this volume, for all of them are self-conscious about questions of the appropriateness of diachronic and/or synchronic approaches to the analysis of the book of Isaiah. Moreover, most of them, like Rendtorff, are concerned with the form(ation) of the book of Isaiah as a whole, or at least with considerable parts of the book.

An essay by Marvin Sweeney comes next in this volume since it combines synchronic and diachronic method by proposing a structure and historical setting for the whole book of Isaiah. According to Sweeney, the entire book of Isaiah is a prophetic exhortation to Judah and Jerusalem to be faithful to the covenant of Yahweh. The book, as Sweeney understands it, falls into two basic parts: (1) Yahweh's plans for world-wide sovereignty at Zion with judgment against Jerusalem, Judah, Israel and the nations to be followed by restoration once the judgment has taken place (chs. 1–33), and (2) a focus on the actualization of God's plans for world-wide sovereignty once the judgment (at least its beginning stages by means of Assyria and Babylon) has been completed (chs. 34–66).[30] The vision of a new international order of peace is achieved through the teaching role of Yahweh's torah (2.2-4). Indeed,

---

30. For a full argument supporting his macrostructural divisions, see Sweeney's *Isaiah 1–39, with an Introduction to Prophetic Literature* (FOTL, 16; Grand Rapids: Eerdmans, 1996), pp. 39-48.

the entire book of Isaiah, as Sweeney interprets it, is based on an under-standing of torah analogous to the role of the Mosaic torah which underlies the reform program of Ezra and Nehemiah. Indeed, Sweeney argues, the book of Isaiah can best be dated in the fifth century BCE along with the reforms of Ezra and Nehemiah. Although the Mosaic torah of Ezra's reform focuses on internal matters within the Israelite covenant community while Isaiah used torah to define Yahweh's worldwide intentions, both are centered around torah.

Gary Stansell also concerns himself with the structure of the book as a whole. Although Stansell, like Sweeney, is known for historical-critical research, in the essay for this volume he concerns himself with a syn-chronic description of the role of Isaiah 28–33 in the larger book of Isaiah. He considers chs. 28–33 as a subsection of chs. 1–39. Chapters 28–33 are a literary unit with their own structure and themes. Indeed, Stansell argues, in the larger scope of the book of Isaiah chs. 28–33 look both backward and forward. They look backward to themes in chs. 1–12; for example, the pronouncements of woe, the concern for the fate of Zion, the themes of the 'Holy One of Israel', the interest in the northern kingdom. And they must be connected with the apocalyptic 24–27 that immediately precedes. Yet chs. 28–33 also look ahead to the narrative about the righteous king Hezekiah by articulating their own interest in the monarchy (32.1-8; 33.17ff.). The attention to justice and righteous-ness in chs. 28–33 anticipates the appearance of that theme in chs. 40–66. And the promises of salvation to Zion in chs. 28–33 foreshadow the expectation of Zion's restoration of chs. 40–66.

Contributions by Chris Franke and Mark Biddle, like Sweeney and Stansell, undertake synchronic analyses of Isaiah. In contrast with Sweeney's depiction of structure in linear terms, Franke and Biddle concern themselves with reverberations between texts that are separated from one another by many chapters of material in between. Franke compares the poem on the king of Babylon in Isaiah 14 with the taunt against the virgin daughter Babylon in ch. 47. Her comparison of the two texts involves particular attention to similarities in theme and rhetoric; for example, the descent to the dust of Sheol, the elevation of throne or loss of it, the boastful pretensions of both king and virgin daughter and their claims to be divine or nearly divine, the parodied expressions of grief in both texts. Biddle presents literary interrelation-ships among a series of feminine personifications of cities in Isaiah 47–66, four of which are in 47–55 (47.1-15; 49.14-26; 51.17–52.10; 54.1-

17) and four of which are in 56–66 (57.6-13; 60.1-22; 62.1-12; 66.6-13). Biddle undertakes a literary comparison of the four texts in chs. 47–55 and concludes that the Babylon depicted in ch. 47 is the 'polar opposite' of Jerusalem as portrayed in chs. 49, 51–52 and 54. Furthermore, he argues that the four texts in chs. 56–66 are literary parallels of the four texts in chs. 47–55.

Both Franke and Biddle employ literary analyses that remind us in many ways of the rhetorical-critical approach of James Muilenburg and also the concern for tropes that we find in Darr. Particularly noteworthy are the backward-and-forward relationships between texts in their understanding of structure. Though Franke and Biddle would surely not reject the idea that reading is a sequential activity, their vision of structure as involving reading both forward and backward over a considerable expanse of text represents a challenge to the more strictly linear portrayal of structure in the work of Sweeney.

If Franke's and Biddle's comparisons of widely separated texts are largely synchronic and their discussion limited almost entirely to the book of Isaiah, the comparisons between texts undertaken by Roy Wells and Benjamin Sommer are diachronic and their approach allows comparison of texts both inside and outside the book of Isaiah. Wells argues that Isaiah 56.1-8 was composed with other texts in mind, both inside and outside Isaiah. For example, Isaiah 56.2 with its language about 'keep(ing)' the Sabbath, not 'profaning' it, and refraining from 'do(ing)' evil (Isa. 56.2) was formulated through the influence of Exodus 31.12-17. Indeed, Wells contends, the composer of Isaiah 56.1-8 made use of a number of Pentateuchal and Isaianic texts in formulating Isaiah 56.1-8. Sommer moves in a similar direction by proposing that a number of passages in Isaiah 40–66 allude to texts in the first part of Isaiah and to materials in Jeremiah. Earlier texts were reformulated in Isaiah 40–66, Sommer argues, for a variety of purposes; for example, historical recontextualization, confirmation of older prophecies, reprediction. Sommers agrees with Clements and Seitz that Isaiah 40–66 was written to react to or to supplement First Isaiah, but he contends that Deutero-Isaiah made use of Jeremiah in a similar manner. Indeed, he argues, Isaiah 40–66 was not written to be a part of the book of Isaiah but was an independent body of literature which was secondarily incorporated into the emerging book of Isaiah. Surely this claim will precipitate discussion.

Scholars will surely want to consider whether the similarities between texts which Wells and Sommers discuss seem convincing as diachronic relationships. If their arguments persuade their readers, their contribution to the scholarly discussion will be quite obvious. If not, their essays might well be of value to a canonical approach to interpretation. The interrelationships between texts which they postulate *could* be understood as relationships among texts within a canon of scripture, irregardless of their diachronic connections.

Part II: The seven essays just discussed seem to locate meaning either in the producer of the text or in the text itself. The following five place more emphasis on the reader. The essay by David Carr seems to build a bridge between the two. He uses Isaiah 1 and 65–66 to sketch some of the differences between modern readings of the book of Isaiah and how it might have been read in ancient times. He cites the redaction-historical reading of Steck and the synchronic reading by Conrad as illustrative of the methodological pluralism which characterizes biblical studies in our time. Ancient use of Isaiah would not have focused as intently on the book as a whole (as in modern criticism), for the ancients' primary use of the book was oral; therefore, they would have only heard parts of it at a time. Preservation of Isaiah on scrolls made it less amenable for comparison of its various parts. Moreover, Carr argues, ancient readers' interest in Isaiah was less to construct a picture of the literary unity of the individual book as to develop an understanding of legal or theological unity of the larger body of authoritative tradition of which the individual book is a part.

The major part of Carr's essay involves a modern reading of Isaiah 1, 65–66 and an assessment of different possibilities of interpreting the entire book as a unity. In ch. 1, he argues, we have before us a composition in which a disobedient community is summoned to repent (1.10-17)—to repent and eat the good of the land (1.18) or to refuse and be consumed by the sword (1.19-20). Verses 21-31 outline the consequences of continuing disobedience as well as the results of repentance. Isaiah 65–66 exhibit a somewhat different understanding. In response to the remembrance in 63.7-14 of Yahweh's deliverance in the past despite past misdeeds (63.10a) and the following prayer for deliverance despite the recent misdeeds of the community (64.4b-6), chs. 65–66 reject the hope that God would deliver the whole community despite its sins. Yahweh will instead divide the community into two groups, with salvation as the destiny of the righteous and punishment as the inevitable fate of the unrighteous. Isaiah 1 with its emphasis on repentance and chs. 65–66 with their focus on the inevitability of salvation for the righteous and punishment for the wicked do not reflect the same understanding of the future. If we moderns are to read the book of Isaiah as a unity, *we* must construct the reading. We can, with Sweeney, use ch. 1 as the lens and read the whole book as a summons to repentance of a disobedient community. Or we can read the book through the spectacles of chs. 65–66 as reassurance to a group that is already righteous. Whichever we choose—or if we elect still another alternative—it is *we* who will have determined how to read the book as a whole.

The essay by Darr about Hezekiah's proverb, 'Babes are positioned for birth but there is no strength to deliver' (Isa. 37.3), is to be understood as a further example of the reader-response criticism which she employs in her *Isaiah's Vision and the Family of God*. We must see this essay as a synchronic reading performed by the fourth-century Israelite reader that Darr has created. Following a discussion of the social function of proverbs and the construction of a model for proverb analysis, Darr proposes an interpretation of the function of Hezekiah's proverb in Isaiah 36–37. Her reader understands that Hezekiah's inhabitants are compared to endangered babes ('we are trapped and in danger of death') and Hezekiah and his advisors are identified with helpless women ('our babes are stuck fast and we are unable to deliver them'). The reader of this proverb, in the context of chs. 36–37 and the book of Isaiah as a whole, will interpret what Hezekiah says and does against the backdrop of the criticism of the making of alliances with Egypt in Isaiah 30.1-7 and 31.1-3. In sharp disagreement with Seitz, Darr's reader construes Hezekiah as a monarch who repents of his alliances with Egypt (30.1-7; 31.1-3; 36.4-10) and turns to put his trust in Yahweh. Precisely why Seitz and Darr interpret this narrative so differently will surely be of interest to interpreters of Isaiah. Is it true, as Darr claims, that Seitz collapses the story's suspense? Does Darr's greater sensitivity to the literary artistry of the text account for the disagreement with Seitz? Do the differences between her synchronic approach and his inclinations toward redaction history contribute to this important difference in interpretation? Such questions are surely significant.

To what extent Carr and Darr have similar views of the role of the reader and the nature of the activity of reading is a question well worth asking. That question becomes even more interesting when the essay of Gerald Sheppard is introduced into the discussion. Sheppard, in a significantly modified version of an earlier essay,[31] argues that scholarly

31. Sheppard, 'The Book of Isaiah', pp. 549-82.

readers of Isaiah often exhibit significantly different visions of what is taken to be the same text. Derrida has demonstrated, Sheppard argues, that there is no objective structure, no objective 'unity' or 'center' to a text. Readers *postulate* a center; indeed, they cannot function without a center. But the center is a construct of the reader, the consequence of preunderstanding in the activity of interpretation. To demonstrate that readers display different visions of the 'same' text, Sheppard analyzes the different ways of envisioning Isaiah by Marvin Sweeney, Edgar Conrad, H.G.M. Williamson and Christopher Seitz.

Sheppard's 'deconstructionist' arguments are not made simply for the purpose of demonstrating the relativity of textual interpretation. Sheppard's most basic interest lies rather in envisioning Isaiah as Scripture. Indeed, his critiques of Seitz involves a contention that much of Seitz's hermeneutic is 'pre-scriptural' in that it emphasizes pre-scriptural levels of redaction. His criticism of Conrad's arguments for treating the biblical text the way other texts are treated comes from Sheppard's contention that just as there is no objective 'center', no universal 'competent reader' found in some forms of reader-response criticism, there is also no legitimacy for a Schleiermacherian 'general hermeneutic' for all literature. Reading Isaiah as Scripture is a special enterprise which involves a particular way of envisioning the text. To illustrate this claim, Sheppard presents two constructive proposals concerning the reading of Isaiah as a book of Jewish and Christian Scripture. His first proposal presents the argument that the message which the people in Isaiah's day were too blind to see and too deaf to hear—a message which involved not being afraid and refusing to trust Yahweh—is reformulated again and again across the entire book of Isaiah, 'unleashed upon generation after generation of audiences'. His second proposal has to do with the canonical form of Isaiah as a book of torah, even as a book of torah which may well be 'complementary to the Mosaic Torah of Ezra'.

My own essay may easily be put into dialogue especially with the preceding essays by Darr, Carr and Sheppard. Like Darr, my interpretation focuses on the figurative character of the text. Isaiah 1 begins with the metaphor of Yahweh's foolish and rebellious sons whose folly is demonstrated by their persistence in behavior which leads them to continue being smitten, even though their land is being eaten by foreigners. These disobedient sons indeed rebel against God by bringing for God's eating unwanted sacrifices instead of justice. They are given two choices: obey and eat the good of the land or rebel and be eaten by the sword.

The choice of disobedience will result in the punishment of the faithless whore Jerusalem followed by her purification—a purification in which those who repent will be redeemed and those who do not will be punished. The interpretation itself explicitly involves dialogue with Sweeney, Darr, Carr and Conrad.

My essay shares with Sheppard the intent to interpret Isaiah as Scripture. Yet there is a sharp focus in this regard: I preoccupy myself with figurative speech for the express purpose of constructing a symbolic world in which communities of faith can live and undergo the shaping of their identity through being addressed by Scripture. I, in concurrence with Sheppard, employ a special rather than a general hermeneutic. Indeed, it is a hermeneutic grounded in use theory,[32] for what the text is used to *do* is central to the purposes of my interpretation. Finally, as an interpretation geared to use, it is an interpretation rooted in the *interpreter's* vision of the text and its use.

The essay by Edgar Conrad is entirely dedicated to hermeneutics. Part of it can be read with an eye toward an implied dialogue with Sheppard and Melugin, for Conrad considers much of the hermeneutical tradition which we have inherited as appropriate for theological seminaries but not for non-confessional university settings. The German idealistic historiographic tradition, Conrad argues, has imposed an ideology on the study of history which privileges intangibles such as 'ideas' or 'spirit' or Western ideas about God rather than emphasizing the social dimension of reality or considering *all* religions as data for understanding the broad question of what it means to be human. Conrad shows clearly that interpretation is not to be separated from particular reading communities and their purposes (or, in my terms, the *uses* to which the text is put). Conrad's proposals appear to undercut arguments for 'general hermeneutics' because of his understanding of the connections between interpretation and the use of texts in particular interpretive communities.

32. See J.L. Austin, *How to Do Things with Words* (New York: Oxford University Press, 1962), and J.R. Searle, *Speech Acts: An Essay in the Philosophy of Language* (Cambridge: Cambridge University Press, 1970). Austin and Searle were interested, not so much in the truth or falsity of linguistic utterances, but in what language *does* in its *usage* in everyday life. The statement, 'I pronounce you husband and wife', *does* something; it *creates* a marriage. Communities of faith use Scripture to *do* something; e.g., to shape the community's self-identity, to establish precedents for the community's life, to bond the community in fellowship with God and with one another, to exhort the community to action, to criticize the community for its inattention to God's commands, to mention but a few kinds of *uses* for Scripture.

Most of Conrad's essay is concerned with his claim that synchronic and diachronic approaches cannot successfully be blended. If redactors are more like authors than compilers, their work becomes difficult, or even impossible to identify. The 'author' of Isaiah used earlier sources, but the process of the book's growth can indeed be imagined in such fundamentally different ways that the distinctions between 'author' (i.e. 'redactor') and earlier sources cannot be successfully recovered. This view is obviously at odds with those of Clements, Seitz, Sweeney, Wells and Sommer.

All those who wish to dispute Conrad's claims must take into account his arguments (based on theorists such as Hayden White and Dominick LaCapra) that all language—even portrayal of history—constructs reality rather than reflects it. We can never get behind language about the past to apprehend the past itself. Any attempt to penetrate behind a text's depiction of the past results, not in a recovery of the past, but in yet another constructed story of the past. These arguments are of sufficient merit, so it seems to me, that the entire enterprise of historical criticism needs to be re-examined. Even though some scholars might be more persuaded than Conrad of the possibility of historical reconstruction, the questions which he raises cannot lightly be dismissed.

III

Readers of this volume will conclude, no doubt, that there is no new vision of Isaiah but rather a multiplicity of visions. What the differences signify must not be oversimplified. Although I have categorized them in terms of those who locate meaning 'objectively' in authors or in texts as opposed to those who contend that meaning is constructed by readers, these are by no means the only issues which cry out for attention. The possibility or impossibility of diachronic analysis is also at stake, along with more nuanced ways of conceptualizing the problem. Another has to do with what is at issue in a quest for unity. Still another has to do with contexts and/or purposes of usage and the choice of appropriate interpretive strategies.

This volume of essays will hardly produce a consensus in the months and years to come. Marvin Sweeney and I do hope, however, as editors of this collection, that the new visions contained herein will lead to still more new visions. We hope also, as new visions emerge and are tested, that the values to be gained from the uses of these visions can come to be sharply and clearly understood.

Part I

IS MEANING LOCATED IN 'AUTHOR' OR TEXT?

THE BOOK OF ISAIAH:
A COMPLEX UNITY. SYNCHRONIC AND DIACHRONIC READING

Rolf Rendtorff

> Today scholars are beginning to move from analysis to synthesis in the
> interpretation of the Book of Isaiah. The established practice of separating
> the book into several discrete parts, each of which is viewed in isolation
> from the whole, is giving way to exploratory efforts to understand the
> overall unity and the theological dynamic of the Isaiah tradition. Indeed, it
> is an illuminating experience to lay aside most of the commentaries of the
> past and read through in one sitting the Book of Isaiah with a kind of
> 'second naiveté' (Anderson 1988: 17).

This quotation expresses some of the basic elements that built the
starting point of the consultation (now a seminar) on 'The Formation of
the book of Isaiah' in the framework of the Society of Biblical Literature
in which for a number of years scholars have attempted to develop a
new reading of this important book of the Hebrew Bible.[1] As one of the
inaugral papers, Marvin Sweeney presented a lecture on 'The Unity of
the Book of Isaiah in the History of Modern Critical Research' in which
he showed how 'current discussion of the unity of the book is rooted in
earlier discussion of its disunity'. The intention of this essay is first of all
to review the contributions to the ongoing discussion with regard to
their methodological approaches, and to highlight some of the questions
that seem to be the major topics now to be dealt with.

'The question of the unity of the book of Isaiah was reopened by
Brevard Childs's canonical approach in *Introduction to the Old Testament as Scripture*' (Anderson 1988: 35 n. 1), in which book 'Childs's
most spectacular success is with the book of Isaiah' (Brueggemann
1984: 89). Almost at the same time, and independently of Childs, Peter

---

1. This is a revised and updated version of my paper, 'The Book of Isaiah: A
Complex Unity. Synchronic and Diachronic Reading' (SBLSP, 1991; Atlanta:
Scholars Press, 1991), pp. 8-20.

R. Ackroyd's article, 'Isaiah I–XII: Presentation of a Prophet' (1978), appeared which could be characterized as the other fundamental and influential contribution to this newly reopened debate. The comparison of these two works shows important basic agreements between the two scholars, in particular in the pronounced interest in the final form of the text; on the other hand each of them approaches this question in a totally different way. In his powerful claim for the canonical unity of the book of Isaiah, Childs concentrates on the book as a whole and on the canonical interrelation between its three commonly assumed parts. Ackroyd on his part scrutinizes the question, 'Why is there so substantial a book associated with the prophet Isaiah?' (1978: 19) and finds 'the clue…in the actual structure of i–xii' (27) which he elaborates in detail.

Here a number of methodological problems appear which since then have been much more diversified by the contributions of several other scholars. In addition, in retrospect it is apparent that through the years time and again the question of the unity of the book of Isaiah had been raised by individual scholars, some of whose observations and reflections are now taken up in the new broader framework.[2]

I

The common starting point among scholars interested in the formation of the book of Isaiah is the conviction, or at least the assumption, that the present shape of the book is not the result of more or less accidential or arbitrary developments but rather that of deliberate and intentional literary and theological work. Apart from details, the general question arises as to how to define the leading methodological interest in exploring this work and its results. Childs speaks of 'The Canonical Shape of the Book of Isaiah' (1979: 325). Other scholars, too, explicitly use the terms 'canon', 'canon-criticism', 'canonical critical' and the like.

All of them are aware of certain possible misunderstandings or misinterpretations. Ackroyd writes, 'I do not for one moment fear that anyone will suppose that I am thereby disclosing myself as a biblical fundamentalist, though I may have to accept the dubious distinction of being misquoted as having abandoned one of the key points of critical scholarship' (1978: 17). And he later sums up:

2.   I refer in particular to the works of Jones (1955), Liebreich (1955–57), Eaton (1959), Schreiner (1967), Becker (1968), Lack (1973), and Melugin (1976). For the history of research see also Vermeylen 1989: 11-27.

> Canon-criticism, as a distinct area of discussion, involves a sensitive
> appraisal of both the final stages of the according of authority to the
> biblical writings, and the awarness of the different levels at which this has
> operated in the eventual determining of the texts which have come down
> to us, stamped with the hallmark of experiential testing in the life of the
> community to which they belonged (1978: 47-48).

It is indeed of particular importance to emphasize 'the sensitive appraisal
of both' instead of playing off the awareness of the different levels
against the keen interest in the final stage or stages. Childs writes, 'To
hear the different notes within the one book is an essential part of taking
seriously the canonical shape' (1979: 330), and similarly other scholars
using canon terminology are expressing their 'indebtedness to historical
analysis...which seeks to locate the text at prior historical moments'
(Seitz 1988: 105).

Clements raises an objection against this terminology: 'Our problem is
a literary and theological one of redaction-criticism, not the larger and
more problematic one of canon criticism, which we may set aside for
discussion in the realm of hermeneutics' (1985: 97). He argues that 'the
reasons why the book of Isaiah acquired its present shape' have nothing
to do with the final 'canonization' of the Hebrew Bible, and he even
declares that 'it appears to be methodologically wrong to attempt to
resolve these problems [i.e. of the book of Isaiah] by an all-embracing
hermeneutical appeal to the perspective of the canon' (1985: 112 n. 10).
The question raised here has two different aspects. One is the
understanding of the term 'canonical'. In the framework of the current
debate on the book of Isaiah (as well as on other books of the Hebrew
Bible) the term is mainly applied to the final shape of the respective
book in which it eventually became part of the canon as a whole.
Therefore, it might be possible to discuss several aspects of the
formation of the book of Isaiah without using the term 'canonical'. Yet
the more fundamental aspect of the question is that of the intention of
scholars who try to understand the final form of a biblical book, in
particular of such a central one as the book of Isaiah, the entirety of
which is extremely complex. For a number of scholars it is even the
'canonical' question that led them to this kind of exegetical work. For
them it would not make sense to set this question aside and to make
such a strict distinction and even separation between exegesis and
hermeneutics as Clements proposes. Therefore, the relevance and function of the 'canonical' aspect has to be discussed further.

II

The next set of questions concerns the three main parts of the book of Isaiah as they have been accepted by most of the Old Testament scholars of the last century. Even today the exploration of the formation of the book of Isaiah almost always starts from a point where the existence of (Proto-) Isaiah (chs. 1–39), Deutero-Isaiah (chs. 40–55) and Trito-Isaiah (chs. 56–66) is either taken for granted or explicitly discussed. This problem, again, has two major aspects. One is concerned with the prophetic figure behind each of the three parts of the book; the other with the literary unity and independence of the parts. Both aspects are interrelated to each other.

At this point the above mentioned methodological differences between Childs and Ackroyd are particularly obvious. Childs does not question the original existence of the three parts of the book of Isaiah (calling them First, Second and Third Isaiah). With regard to Second Isaiah he assumes that there originally existed certain elements showing the historical context of these prophecies, which later had been eliminated so that these chapters lost 'their original historical particularity'. Here Childs's canonical approach did not touch the classical assumption of the earlier existence of several (at least two) independent parts of the book of Isaiah. Childs sees changes happening only at the level where 'the canonical editors of this tradition employed the material in such a way as to eliminate almost entirely those concrete features and to subordinate the original message to a new role within the canon' (1979: 325-26).[3] Accordingly, he views the canonical editing of First Isaiah as a 'coupling of collections' after which 'a large amount of later material is scattered througout the entire collection. Moreover, both its older and newer elements have been structured into a clear theological pattern which is integrally connected with Second Isaiah' (1979: 330-31).

Ackroyd's approach is different. From the outset he questions the independent existence of chs. 1–39, in particular as a collection of sayings of a prophet of the eighth century who was primarily a prophet of doom. In chs. 1–12 he finds 'a presentation of the prophet', 'the messenger of doom, now fulfilled, as he is also presented as messenger of

3.   I do not fully understand the relation between the above quoted and Childs's question of whether 'the material of Second Isaiah in fact ever circulated in Israel apart from its being connected to an earlier form of First Isaiah' (1979: 329).

salvation' (1978: 45). These chapters are composed of smaller units such as 1.2–2.5; 2.6–4.6; 5.1–11.16 (including 6.1–9.6), each of them containing oracles of doom and salvation. The psalm in ch. 12 'provides an interpretative comment on what precedes, drawing out in a final poetic statement the broadest significance of the prophet's person and message' (1978: 34-40). In his conclusion Ackroyd declares,

> It is not my intention to try to sort out either the genuine from the non-genuine, or the possible situations...to which this or that passage may belong, or in which reapplication has been made...Whether the prophet himself or his exegetes were responsible, the prophet appears to us as a man of judgement and salvation (1978: 44-45).

The comparison of these two approaches shows a basic methodological problem with regard to the formation of the book of Isaiah: Is the final form to be seen as the result of connecting or merging two (or three) originally independent parts (or books) by (one or more) redaction(s)?— or is the originally independent existence of those parts no longer to be taken for granted? Among scholars working towards an understanding of the book of Isaiah as a whole both positions are clearly represented.

With regard to the first position some qualifications are necessary. The question of Trito-Isaiah has again recently become a subject of discussion (see below). Therefore, some scholars would rather speak of relations between chs. 1–39 and 40–66. With regard to the first part, some scholars set aside chs. 36–39 as a later addendum, speaking of chs. 1–35. But also ch. 35 is taken by some scholars as never having been part of the original collection of Proto-Isaiah but added as a redactional bridge between First and Second Isaiah.

The common conviction of these scholars is that a collection of First-Isaiah sayings containing major parts of chs. 1–39 had existed before having been combined with chs. 40–66. For most of them this conviction includes a redactional reworking of certain parts of chs. 1–39, be it in one or more redactional stages, even before their combination with chs. 40–66. Widely accepted is the thesis of one (or two) redaction(s) in the time of Josiah and later after the fall of Jerusalem (Barth 1977; Clements 1980b; Clements 1980c). For Clements this is an important stage in the redactional history of the book of Isaiah:

> Once the connection between the prophecies of Isaiah and the destruction of Jerusalem is recognized as a factor in the way the Book of Isaiah came to be developed, we have the single most essential clue towards

understanding why the prophecies of chapters 40 and following came to
be incorporated into the book (1982: 127).

Steck (1985) identifies ch. 35 as another crucial point for the connection
between the two formerly independent collections. In a scrutinizing
exegesis he shows this chapter's interrelations into both directions,
forward to ch. 40, and backward to chs. 32–34. He concludes that ch.
35 had been formulated in order to be written in 'at the join between
the end of the complex of sayings of First Isaiah (Isa. *1–34) and the
beginning of those of Second Isaiah (Isa. *40–62)'. He emphasizes that
until then both parts had been independent from each other and that
each of them had been formulated in an unalterably fixed form
(1985: 101).[4]

Both scholars represent characteristic examples of an approach to the
book of Isaiah that on the one hand strongly emphasizes the deliberate
formation of the book as a whole, and on the other hand firmly holds to
the original independence of the first and the second part of the book
from each other. From this point of view the final shape of the book is
the result of a redactional process. The original parts are not themselves
touched by a 'canonical' idea.

The most pronounced counterexample is given by Seitz (1988). His
provocative thesis is that 'The whole notion of Second and Third Isaiah
depends in no small part on there being a clear First Isaiah. Such an
Isaiah is not to be found' (1988: 111). He emphasizes that 'Isaiah 1–39
is an extremely complex collection of material, with a diverse background', and he claims that this has already been shown by several
recent studies that 'demand a complete rethinking of the relatively simple
formulation 1, 2, 3 Isaiah' (1988: 125 n. 14). Indeed, the extremely complex character of chs. 1–39 is conceded by almost all exegetes. The
question is whether these divergent materials have been brought together
before and independently from the joining of chs. 1–39 with chs. 40ff.

Steck, for example, declares explicitly that the main corpus of chs. 1–
39 before its connection with the following chapters did exist in a
fixed form whose formulation no longer could be touched ('in der
Formulierung nicht mehr antastbar' [1985: 101]). According to his view,
ch. 35 had been carefully worked in so that it could build the bridge
between the two now preceding and following parts of the book. Some

---

4. Similarly Clements 1982: 121, who calls ch. 35 'a summarized "digest" of
the main content of the prophecies of chapters 40–55'.

more texts share this bridging function with ch. 35, such as Isa. 11.11-16
and 27.13(12) (as well as 62.10-12 in the second part), by expressing
'the same redactional view'.[5]

Clements also mentions texts in chs. 1–39 that express the ideas of
chs. 40ff. Similar to Steck he finds, in addition to ch. 35, in Isa. 11.12-
16; 19.32; 27.12-13 'summarizing assurances of the return of Yahweh's
people to Zion...which are based upon the prophecies from chapter 40
on' (1982: 121). Chapters 36–39, according to Clements, also have been
added to chs. 1–35 'at a time when much of the material of chapters 40
and following had already been joined to this earlier prophetic book'
(1982: 123). Chapters 24–27 are 'a very late section' which should 'not
be...read in isolation from the rest of the book' (1982: 122). Those
observations lead him to the suggestion 'that the linking of the prophecies of chapters 40 and following with the tradition of Isaiah's prophecies
belongs more fundamentally to the structure of the book' (1982: 123).
That means that the junction of chs. 1–39 and 40–66 appears not merely
as one act of redaction at one certain point, but rather as a process by
which elements of an earlier tradition ('Isaiah') had been intertwined
with those of exilic and postexilic traditions.

From this point of view the difference between the positions of
Clements and Seitz seemed to be reduced to the question of whether
there remains an identifiable 'First Isaiah' when it lacks all the elements
that belong to the structure of the book as a whole. Here, of course, the
discussion has to go into detail. In particular, Ackroyd's concept of a
'presentation of the prophet' has to be taken into account as questioning
the existence of a definable 'First Isaiah'.

Another important point in Seitz's argumentation is the fact that 'The
literary boundaries between 1, 2, 3 Isaiah are not marked in any special
way' (1988: 109). Indeed, in Isaiah 40 no hint is given that a new
chapter begins and that it is a different prophet who is speaking from
that point; and there is no evidence of a loss of any superscription or
introduction. This problem is related to the question, Which text had
been read immediately before ch. 40 at the time when the two supposed
collections had been combined? One argument for the presence of a
clear beginning in ch. 40 is the change of tone and content from doom
to comfort. This would appear to be true if ch. 40 was preceded by chs.
36–39. But many scholars believe that these chapters had been inserted
much later into the book of Isaiah, probably as 'one of the latest steps to

5.   See the chart in Steck 1985: 80.

occur in its formation' (Clements 1980: 277), 'thereby separating the different collections' (275). But if it is ch. 35 that has to be read immediately before ch. 40, there is no change in tone and content. The close relationship of ch. 35 to, or even its dependence upon, Deutero-Isaiah has been noted by many scholars. For Clements the argument is reversed: Not the difference, but the similarity between the end of First Isaiah (now ch. 35) and the beginning of Second Isaiah (ch. 40) made the connection possible or even more plausible.

Here again chs. 36–39 have to be taken into account. Ackroyd (1982) has convincingly shown a number of interrelations between these chapters and chs. 1–12, in particular 6.1–9.6. 'Both these narrative or partly narrative sections...are evidently concerned with themes of judgement and of deliverance' (1982: 19). And these sections 'alone in the book provide a full contextual setting for the activity and message of Isaiah' (1982: .19), so that not only chs. 1–12 but also chs. 36–39 could be called 'presentation of a prophet' (16). From ch. 39 it is obvious that God's words of judgment against Israel will not become a reality through the Assyrians in the days of Hezekiah; but the last words of the chapter make it clear to the reader that there will be only a sparing of Hezekiah and his generation and that the judgment will come in the days of the Babylonians.[6] Seitz summarizes his reading of chs. 36–39 as follows:

> A theological and a readership problem are solved in one fell swoop by the inclusion of chapters 36–39. God's word of judgement over Israel's sins, declared in the Assyrian period by Isaiah, is to be fulfilled in the Babylonian period. At the same time, the reader is prepared for the words of comfort that appear in Isaiah 40ff., words that only make sense once the sentence of judgement, the 'time of service' of Isa. 40:2, has been carried out (1988: 111; cf. also Seitz 1990).

In the meantime the connections between chs. 36–39 and other parts of the book have also been studied by Conrad (1988 and 1991) and in more detail by Seitz himself (1991).

III

This discussion shows a changing approach to the question of earlier collections of material now combined in the book of Isaiah. For some scholars the starting point still is the more or less unquestioned existence

---

6. Cf. already Melugin, 1976: 177.

of two or three 'books' that had been brought together by redactional work. With regard to chs. 1–39 this includes a mainly diachronic reading of the texts led by the question at which stage of the redactional history a specific text had been formulated, reformulated, inserted and the like. Other scholars are developing a different approach reading the texts within chs. 1–39 in its given form as parts of the book as a whole (Ackroyd, Seitz).

The latter reading, which I am sympathetic with, does not imply a denial of diachronic questions but a change—and perhaps a reversal—of scholarly priorities. The first and main question is no longer, What was the 'original' meaning of this text?, and also not, When and how had this text been incorporated into its present context?, but, What is the meaning of the text in its given context? This does not exclude the first two questions to be asked for additional information and clarification. But the priority is now clearly given to the interpretation of the text in its given context.

This changed approach in the book of Isaiah has its first and most fundamental influence on the reading of chs. 1–39. Most scholars would agree that 'Isaiah 1–39 is an extremely complex collection of material' (Seitz 1988: 111). Up to now most scholars would try to find out the original words of Isaiah, or the texts that formed the first, original collection of words by Isaiah, and then continue to define the stages of redaction through what other texts had been added to it. But if one reads chs. 1–12 as a deliberately composed 'presentation of a prophet', the direction of view changes. Chapters 1–12 will then be understood as a meaningful composition in itself comprising materials of different types and from different times depicting Isaiah as a prophet of judgment and salvation (Ackroyd 1978: 45). The diachronic question is not at all to be excluded but can help in understanding the interrelations between some of the texts that are now part of this composition.

Another example of results of a changing view is the understanding of the oracles against other nations in chs. 13–23. Particularly important is the fact that this composition begins with an oracle against Babylon in chs. 13–14. This shows that Yahweh's words of judgment spoken in times of the Assyrian rule will be realised by the Babylonians. Thereby, already at this point the borders from the times of First Isaiah to that of Second Isaiah are crossed (cf. Seitz 1988: 112). From now on the reader is aware that the prophetic message of the book of Isaiah is not restricted to the times of Assyrian rule but embraces a time span going beyond that period into the Babylonian era. Then the transition from ch. 39 to ch. 40 does not come as a surprise to the reader. And even the further step from exile to return—that is, from the Babylonian to the Persian era—has now been prepared.

Actually, this reading of the book of Isaiah as embracing a long period of time with changing political events and experiences begins in the first chapters of the book. It has long been observed that ch. 1 forms a composition representing a summary of the prophetical message of 'Isaiah' (Fohrer). This chapter contains elements that—at least by later readers—can be understood as speaking from a point *after* the divine judgment had come on Israel. Verse 1.9 is taken by many interpreters 'to be a late, exilic, addition in which the condition of Jerusalem after 587 was read back into Isaiah's prophecy of 701' (Clements 1980a: 32). It is now a question of approach as to whether this 'reading back' is taken as a late addition or as an integral element of the canonical presentation of the prophet. The same holds for the word on Jerusalem's fate in 1.21-28, in particular for its ending in vv. 27-28 that 'evidently supposes that Jerusalem had suffered severe setbacks' (Clements 1980a: 35); and it holds, of course, for the vision of the eschatological role of Mount Zion in 2.1-5. Ackroyd summarizes his reading of 1.2–2.5 'as an appeal and a promise: Jerusalem the unfaithful and judged city of God, over which the lament of 1.21ff. is pronounced, is to be the true and faithful city, the centre of the religious life of the world' (1978: 42).

These kinds of observations and reflections must necessarily lead to a new definition of 'First Isaiah'. In this context it has to be taken into account that the person of the prophet appears rather rarely and not before ch. 6. Compared with a number of other prophetic books, such as Jeremiah and Ezekiel, but also Amos and Hosea, the person of the prophet Isaiah remains elusive, as 'Second Isaiah' and 'Third Isaiah' do as well (cf. Seitz 1988: 120). The consequences of this peculiarity of the book of Isaiah have to be reflected, together with the other aspects mentioned before.

IV

The impact the changing approach has on interpreting Isa. 40–66 is different from that which it has for chs. 1–39. At first glance, there seems to be no influence from chs. 1–39 on the later parts of the book. Yet already the beginning of 'Second Isaiah' in 40:1ff. poses questions that are not to be answered without looking back to what precedes. The opening of this chapter without any introduction or superscription, and with the call for comfort referring back to Jerusalem's 'service' and her sins, obviously addresses readers that know something of what had been said in the preceding part of the book. In addition, the well-known parallels between Isa. 40.1-8(11) and 6.1-11 have been recently re-examined by different scholars particularly looking for interdependences between these two texts pivotal in either part of the book (Melugin 1976: 83-84; Ackroyd 1982: 5-6; Rendtorff 1989: 79-81 [ET 177-79]; Albertz 1990: 242-48; Seitz 1990). Albertz is mainly interested in the adoption and continuation of Isaianic motifs in Deutero-Isaiah, and he recalls the idea of an 'Isaiah-school' as it had been raised earlier by Mowinckel and others. Other scholars reflect the possibility of a reciprocal influence on the level of composition or redaction (Rendtorff, Seitz). In any case, the opening verses of chs. 40–66 have to be read in the context of the book of Isaiah as a whole.

The same is true for other texts and motifs. Childs emphasizes that the 'former things' in Deutero-Isaiah in the context of the book as a whole 'can now only refer to the prophecies of First Isaiah' (1979: 328-29; cf. Seitz 1988: 110). But then the question arises as to what this expression might have pointed to in an earlier stage when chs. 40–66 had not yet been combined with chs. 1–39. Would the 'former things' then have meant anything different from earlier prophecies of judgment? And if not, which prophecies had they referred to? So the question remains as to whether there could or should be assumed in chs. 40–66 conscious references to chs. 1–39. This question is also dealt with by Clements who mentions several topics by which he wants 'to show that the evidence that the prophecies of "Second Isaiah" reveal a conscious dependence on earlier sayings of Isaiah of Jerusalem is firm and reliable' (1985: 109).

Finally, in the course of looking at the book of Isaiah as a whole the interrelations between 'Second' and 'Third Isaiah' are re-examined under different aspects. The most decisive step has been taken by Steck (1989) who, in the context of broad methodological reflections, denies the existence of a prophet or author 'Trito-Isaiah' and sees chs. 56–66 as literary texts that never existed as a separate collection but have gradually been added to chs. 40–55 (so chs. 60–62) or to a 'Greater Isaiah' (*Großjesaja*); that is, to the now emerging collection that included great parts of chs. 1–39 and of chs. 40–55. The question of the juxta-position of chs. 1–39 and 40–55 is related to Steck's earlier assumption (1985) that ch. 35 had been formulated in order to build the bridge between chs. 1–39 and 40–55 at the time that they were first combined (see above). (The existence of an independent 'Trito-Isaiah' is also denied by Vermeylen [1989: 42-44], though his concept of the history of chs. 40–55 is totally different from Steck's.)

Beuken's approach is different. He is also interested in Third Isaiah's relations to First and Second Isaiah which he describes as 'Isaianic legacy' (1986). But he sees in Trito-Isaiah 'a literary and theological personality in his own right' (1986: 64), who is the successor of Deutero-Isaiah and, in a certain sense, also of Proto-Isaiah, and who 'has used the prophecies of F[irst]I[saiah] and S[econd]I[saiah] for his particular message, in a situation that was quite different' (ibid.). Beuken's conviction of the unity and originality of Trito-Isaiah finds its specific expression in the developing of 'The Main-Theme of Trito-Isaiah', that of 'the servants of Yahweh', that he finds as a 'theme' throughout the whole of chs. 56–66, even where the expression itself does not appear (1990).

These two approaches differ in two respects: 1) the unity of chs. 56–66 and personality of the 'prophetic' author, and 2) the relation of chs. 56–66 to the book of Isaiah as a whole. Beuken's position with regard to the book as a whole is only touched on in his articles, while for Steck this is one of his main concerns. With regard to chs. 56–66 this concern leads him to a principal denial of one of the basic hypotheses of classical *Literarkritik* in the field of prophetical literature: the existence of 'Trito-Isaiah'. Steck's own answer is mainly oriented towards a growth of the book of Isaiah as a whole. The later stages of redaction in chs. 56–66, after the first combination of chs. 1–39 with 40–62, he sees interrelated to certain stages in the redactional history of chs. 1–39.

Here a new and interesting debate is beginning, and we expect further work in this field. With regard to the book of Isaiah as a whole, of particular interest would be the question of how developments in chs. 40–66 are related to those within chs. 1–39. For example, certain inter-relations between chs. 1 and 66 have been observed by several scholars. And could it be possible that 'those responsible for the last forming of the third part also contributed to the composition of the final shape of the book'? (Rendtorff 1984: 319).

V

Several contributions to the topic of the book of Isaiah as a whole have not yet been mentioned in this essay, in particular those which are not built up on questions of the structure of texts but on certain themes, topics, expressions and so on. My own first article in this area (1984) tried to show a number of topics and themes that are characteristic of the book of Isaiah and at the same time appear in all—or at least in more than one—of the different parts of the book. My approach was basically influenced by Melugin and Ackroyd, and many of the observations and questions of that article have been absorbed in the following discussions. My more recent article (1991) discusses the different meanings of the word $ṣ^e dāqâ$ in the context of the book of Isaiah as a whole, including chs. 56–66.

Another contribution to be named here is that of Anderson. He approaches the book of Isaiah as a whole, but writes that 'Instead of reading the Isaiah tradition forward from the standpoint of the seminal preaching of Isaiah of Jerusalem...I propose to consider it from the viewpoint of its final apocalyptic *relecture* or rendering' (1988: 18). This brings texts from all parts of the book in relation to each other in a new and often surprising way. Anderson keeps the diachronic aspects in mind so that his essay easily and fruitfully can be related to questions of the redactional or compositorial history of the texts.

In general, I believe that a changing view on the book of Isaiah should allow, and even require, studies on topics, themes, expressions, and even ideas characteristic of the book as a whole or considerable parts of it, without at the same time discussing questions of redaction or composition. A synchronic reading, if carried out with the necessary sophistication, should have its own rightful place.

VI

In sum, the discussion of the last decade has revealed the unity of the book of Isaiah. Of course, it is not a simple unity but a highly complex one. Yet scholars have now begun to realize the complexity of this unity and to interpret it.[7] The methodological approaches are different, as explained in detail in this essay. But it seemed to me to be remarkable

---

7.　See, for example, Carr 1993.

that nevertheless on certain crucial points a basic agreement can be reached.

In my view, one such crucial point is the question of an independent book or collection of 'First Isaiah', containing major parts of chs. 1–39. The scholarly discussion shows that there is broad agreement on the 'secondary' character of elements like chs. 13–23; 24–27, and also of smaller units like 2.1-5; 4.2-6; 12.1-6 and others. This makes it nearly impossible to read the 'original' parts (in whatever sense) of chs. 1–39 as a continuous 'book'. Nevertheless, some scholars continue to speak of a 'First Isaiah' thereby including some of the 'secondary' elements.[8] Other scholars prefer to read the non-uniform and composed chs. 1–39 from the outset as a part of the book of Isaiah as a whole.

The first mentioned position is led by a consistently diachronic interest. Many of these scholars try to define a number of redactional stages, some of which are to be dated before the combination of chs. 1–39 with chs. 40–66, others after this point. In my view, many of these stages, and in particular their datings, are highly hypothetical. In addition, these scholars have to assume a number of anonymous redactors, editors and so on whose intentions they try to understand. The result is, on the one hand, an extremely complicated hypothetical redactional history, from the prophet Isaiah in the eighth century through to the Hellenistic era. On the other hand, it is no longer possible to read the book of Isaiah in its continuity at any point before the final ('canonical') shape of the text.

The other position reads the book of Isaiah mainly in its given 'canonical' shape, though in full awarness of its (diachronic) complexity. In my view, it is the great advantage of such a sophisticated synchronic reading that the interpreter is able to read the text in its given continuity. To choose one example, Ackroyd (1978) reads chs. 1–12 as a complex

8. The commentary by J.H. Hayes and S.A. Irvine (1987) is one recent example of interpreting almost the whole of Isaiah 1–39 as deriving from the eighth-century BCE prophet. The authors mention explicitly the impact of Y. Gitay's work, 'who has pioneered in the rhetorical analysis of prophetic speeches' (15). In the meantime Gitay's book appeared (1991) in which he presents his view with regard to chs. 1–12. He also holds that Isaiah 1–12 in its entirety derives from the prophet Isaiah and is to be understood as a series of oratorical reflections. Therefore, the problem of how the complex unity of the book of Isaiah came into being, as discussed in this essay, for him does not exist. It would go beyond the scope of this essay to discuss Gitay's rhetorical theories. Future research will have to show whether and how it would be possible to relate these different approaches to each other.

unity, while according to Steck (1985: 80), 4.2-6; 11.11-16 and 12.1-6 were added at different times—12.1-6 only 'after 302/1'. It is the text in its present form which the reader now possesses.

The main difference between these two approaches might be expressed by the following two questions: 1) (Synchronic) What does the text (in all its complexity) mean in its given final shape? 2) (Diachronic) In what stages did the text reach its final form? Certainly, these two questions oversimplify the complex character of the problems. Yet by this simplification I am intending, on the one hand, to point to a crucial difference between these two approaches, on the other hand to stimulate a discussion on the agreements and disagreements between these two positions.

Therefore, I want to give another example in order to show an important agreement between scholars of different positions. Steck's interpretation of Isa. 35 as written with the explicit function to connect chs. 1–39 and 40–66 (in Steck's view, 40–62) with each other, in my view is one of the most important contributions towards an understanding of the book of Isaiah as a whole. As shown above, Steck takes a strictly literary-critical position with regard to chs. 1–39 which seems to be hardly compatible with that of Ackroyd, Seitz and others, including myself. Nevertheless, I believe that his study of Isa. 35 will be appreciated by most scholars as a milestone in the research into the problems of the book of Isaiah as a whole.

By these examples I want to show that there are clearly definable differences between the methodological approaches that should be studied seriously, but that at the same time the common progress in the understanding of the book of Isaiah as a whole as made during the last decade is remarkable and promising.

BIBLIOGRAPHY

Ackroyd, P.R.
  1978 'Isaiah I–XII: Presentation of a Prophet', in J.A. Emerton *et al.* (eds.), *Congress Volume: Göttingen 1977* (VTSup, 29; Leiden: Brill): 16-48 (= P.R. Ackroyd, *Studies in the Religious Tradition of the Old Testament* [London: SCM Press, 1987]: 79-104).
  1982 'Isaiah 36–39: Structure and Function', in J.R. Nellis *et al.* (eds.), *Von Kanaan bis Kerala* (Festschrift J.P.M. Van der Ploeg; AOAT, 211; Neukirchen–Vluyn: Neukirchener Verlag): 3-21 (= Ackroyd, *Studies*: 105-20).

Albertz, R.
  1990 'Das Deuterojesaja-Buch als Fortschreibung der Jesaja-Prophetie', in E. Blum *et al.* (eds.), *Die Hebräische Bibel und ihre zweifache Nachgeschichte* (Festschrift R. Rendtorff; Neukirchen–Vluyn: Neukirchener Verlag): 241-56.

Anderson, B.W.
  1988 'The Apocalyptic Rendering of the Isaiah Tradition', in J. Neusner *et al.* (eds.), *The Social World of Formative Christianity and Judaism* (Festschrift H.C. Kee; Philadelphia: Fortress Press): 17-38.

Barth, H.
  1977 *Die Jesaja-Worte in der Josiazeit* (WMANT, 48; Neukirchen–Vluyn: Neukirchener Verlag).

Becker, J.
  1968 *Isaias—Der Prophet und sein Buch* (SBS, 30; Stuttgart: Katholisches Bibelwerk).

Beuken, W.A.M.
  1986 'Isa. 56.9–57.13—An Example of the Isaianic Legacy of Trito-Isaiah', in J.W. van Henten *et al.* (eds.), *Tradition and Reinterpretation in Jewish and Early Christian Literature* (Festschrift J.C.H. Lebram; Leiden: Brill): 48-64.
  1989 'Servant and Herald of Good Tidings: Isaiah 61 as an Interpretation of Isaiah 40–55', in J. Vermeylen (ed.), *The Book of Isaiah—Le Livre d'Isaïe* (BETL, 81; Leuven: Peeters): 411-42.
  1990 'The Main Theme of Trito-Isaiah "The Servants of YHWH"', *JSOT* 47: 67-87.

Brueggemann, W.
  1984 'Unity and Dynamic in the Isaiah Tradition', *JSOT* 29: 89-107.

Carr, D.
  1993 'Reaching for Unity in Isaiah', *JSOT* 57: 61-80.

Childs, B.S.
  1979 *Introduction to the Old Testament as Scripture* (Philadelphia: Fortress Press).

Clements, R.E.
  1980a *Isaiah 1–39* (NCB; London: Marshall, Morgan, and Scott).
  1980b *Isaiah and the Deliverance of Jerusalem* (JSOTSup, 13; Sheffield: JSOT Press).
  1980c 'The Prophecies of Isaiah and the Fall of Jerusalem in 587 BC', *VT* 30: 421-36.
  1982 'The Unity of the Book of Isaiah', *Int* 36: 117-29.
  1985 'Beyond Tradition History: Deutero-Isaianic Development of First Isaiah's Themes', *JSOT* 31: 95-113.

Conrad, E.W.
  1988 'The Royal Narratives and the Structure of the Book of Isaiah', *JSOT* 41: 67-81.
  1991 *Reading Isaiah* (OBT, 27; Minneapolis: Fortress Press).

Eaton, J.H.
  1959 'The Origin of the Book of Isaiah', *VT* 9: 138-57.

1982   'The Isaiah Tradition', in R. Coggins, A. Phipps, and M. Knibb (eds.), *Israel's Prophetic Tradition* (Festschrift P. Ackroyd; Cambridge: Cambridge University Press): 58-76.

Fohrer, G.

1962   'Jesaja 1 als Zusammenfassung der Verkündigung Jesajas', *ZAW* 74: 251-68.

Gitay, Y.

1991   *Isaiah and his Audience: The Structure and Meaning of Isaiah 1–12* (SSN, 30; Assen/Maastricht: Van Gorcum).

Hayes J.H. and S.A. Irvine

1987   *Isaiah: The Eighth-Century Prophet: His Times and his Preaching* (Nashville: Abingdon Press).

Jones, D.

1955   'The Tradition of the Oracles of Isaiah of Jerusalem', *ZAW* 67: 226-46.

Lack, R.

1973   *La symbolique du livre d'Isaïe* (AnBib, 59; Rome: Biblical Institute Press).

Liebreich, L. J.

1955–57   'The Compilation of the Book of Isaiah', *JQR* 46: 259-77; *JQR* 47: 114-38.

Melugin, R.

1976   *The Formation of Isaiah 40–55* (BZAW, 141; Berlin: de Gruyter).

Rendtorff, R.

1984   'Zur Komposition des Buches Jesaja', *VT* 34: 295-320 (= *Kanon und Theologie: Vorarbeiten zu einer Theologie des Alten Testaments* [Neukirchen–Vluyn: Neukirchener Verlag, 1991]: 141-61 [ET *Canon and Theology* (Minneapolis: Fortress Press, 1993)]: 146-69).

1989   'Jesaja 6 im Rahmen der Komposition des Jesajabuches', in J. Vermeylen (ed.), *The Book of Isaiah—Le Livre d'Isaïe* (BETL, 81; Leuven: Peeters): 73-82 (= *Kanon und Theologie*: 162-71; ET: 170-80).

1991   'Jesaja 56, 1 als Schlüssel für die Komposition des Buches Jesaja', in *Kanon und Theologie: Vorarbeiten zu einer Theologie des Alten Testaments* (Neukirchen–Vluyn: Neukirchener Verlag): 172-79 (ET: 181-89).

Schreiner, J.

1967   *Das Buch jesajanischer Schule: Wort und Botschaft: Eine theologische und kritische Einführung in die Probleme des Alten Testaments* (Würzburg: Echter).

Seitz, C.

1988   'Isaiah 1–66: Making Sense of the Whole', in *idem* (ed.), *Reading and Preaching the Book of Isaiah* (Philadelphia: Fortress Press): 105-26.

1990   'The Divine Council: Temporal Transition and New Prophecy in the Book of Isaiah', *JBL* 109: 229-47.

1991   *Zion's Final Destiny: The Development of the Book of Isaiah—A Reassessment of Isaiah 36–39* (Minneapolis: Fortress Press).

Steck, O.H.

1985   *Bereitete Heimkehr: Jesaja 35 als redaktionelle Brücke zwischen dem Ersten und Zweiten Jesaja* (SBS, 121; Stuttgart: Katholisches Bibelwerk).

1989   'Tritojesaja im Jesajabuch', in J. Vermeylen (ed.), *The Book of Isaiah—Le Livre d'Isaïe* (BETL, 81; Leuven: Peeters): 361-406.

1990   'Zions Tröstung: Beobachtungen und Fragen zu Jesaja 51, 1-11', in E. Blum *et al.* (eds.), *Die Hebräische Bibel und ihre zweifache Nachgeschichte* (Festschrift R. Rendtorff; Neukirchen–Vluyn: Neukirchener Verlag): 257-76.

Sweeney, M.A.

1988   *Isaiah 1–4 and the Post-Exilic Understanding of the Isaianic Tradition* (BZAW, 171; Berlin: de Gruyter).

Vermeylen, J.

1977–78   *Du prophète Isaïe à l'apocalyptique* (2 vols.; EBib; Paris: Gabalda).

1989   'L'unité du livre d'Isaïe', in *idem* (ed.), *The Book of Isaiah—Le Livre d'Isaïe* (BETL, 81; Leuven: Peeters): 11-53.

Watts, J.D.W.

1985   *Isaiah 1–33* (WBC, 24; Waco: Word Books).

1987   *Isaiah 34–66* (WBC, 25; Waco: Word Books).

THE BOOK OF ISAIAH AS PROPHETIC TORAH

Marvin A. Sweeney

I

Perhaps one of the best known passages in the entire book of Isaiah is the magisterial vision in Isa. 2.2-4 of the nations streaming to Zion in the latter days to receive YHWH's Torah:

> It shall come to pass in the latter days that the mountain of the house of the Lord shall be established as the highest of the mountains, and shall be raised above the hills; and all the nations shall flow to it, and many peoples shall come, and say: 'Come, let us go up to the mountain of the Lord, to the house of the God of Jacob; that he may teach us his ways and that we may walk in his paths.' For out of Zion shall go forth the law (*tôrâ*) and the word of the Lord from Jerusalem. He shall judge between the nations, and shall decide for many peoples; and they shall beat their swords into ploughshares and their spears into pruning hooks; nation shall not lift up sword against nation, neither shall they learn war any more (RSV).

This passage is generally understood as the prophet's vision of eschatological peace and co-existence among the nations of the world, and thereby constitutes a vision of a new world order in which YHWH's sovereignty is recognized by all the earth (see Wildberger 1972: 88-90). Furthermore, it is not simply a vision for the nations; Israel, or 'the House of Jacob' as it is called in this context, is invited in v. 5 to join the nations on Zion to walk in the light of YHWH: 'O house of Jacob, come, let us walk in the light of the Lord' (RSV). One of the key terms in this passage is the Hebrew word *tôrâ*, here translated as 'law'. Scholars generally recognize that this translation is incorrect, in that it is heavily influenced by the Greek term *nomos*, 'law' (*TDNT* IV: 1059-85). The polemical intent of such a translation is clear in that *nomos* is employed throughout the New Testament as the Greek equivalent of *tôrâ* in order to contrast the caricatured, rigid and unbending Mosaic 'law' of the Old Testament with the proclamation of God's love and grace in the form of the new gospel. The Hebrew word *tôrâ* is more properly translated as 'instruction' (cf. *TDNT* IV: 1046), as indicated by its derivation from the *hiphil* form of the root *yrh* which means 'to guide' or 'to instruct'.

It is on this basis that exegetes generally interpret Isa. 2.2-4 as a vision that depicts God's 'instruction' of the nations from Zion in the eschatological age (cf. Wildberger 1972: 88-90). Although the word *tôrâ* elsewhere in the Hebrew Bible is employed as a technical term to refer to the Pentateuch or Five Books of Moses, scholars generally presuppose that the prophetic context, which in Christian theology is diametrically opposed to the legal context of the Pentateuch, establishes the meaning of *tôrâ* as 'instruction', which has nothing to do with Mosaic Torah. This mundane understanding of the word *tôrâ* is reinforced by the appearance of the verb *yrh* in Isa. 2.3: 'that he may teach us (*w^eyōrēnû*) his ways and that we may walk in his paths'. Although a legal sense is suggested in v. 4 by the portrayal of YHWH's judging the cases of the nations ('He shall judge [*w^ešāpaṭ*] between the nations, and shall decide [*w^ehôkîaḥ*] for many peoples', there is no suggestion that the term *tôrâ* here refers in any way to Mosaic legislation.

The placement of Isa. 2.2-4 in the context of Isaiah 1–39, often labelled the First Isaiah because of its presentation of the words and actions of the eighth-century prophet Isaiah ben Amoz, likewise reinforces this understanding. Because Isaiah lived and spoke during the eighth century, it is unlikely that he would have been aware of Mosaic Torah, which did not come to prominence in Judah until the fifth century reforms of Ezra. The fact that Isa. 2.2-4 may have been composed by a much later author writing during the time of the exile (Sweeney 1988:134-84) is rarely taken into account. Nevertheless, the sixth-century context for the writing of this passage, and the use of *tôrâ* in Deutero-Isaiah (cf. Isa. 42.4, 21, 24; 51.4, 7) precludes a reference to Mosaic Torah. Not only does Ezra appear a century after this time, but the prophetic context for the writing of this passage and the works of Deutero-Isaiah continues to play a role in the interpretation of the term *tôrâ*.

Recent shifts in the paradigm for reading the book of Isaiah may begin to change this understanding of *tôrâ* in Isa. 2.2-4. The past paradigm of historically-based critical scholarship led scholars to read Isaiah 1–39; 40–55; and 56–66 as separate literary works, based on the conclusion that each of these segments reflected the writings of prophets from the eighth, sixth, and fifth centuries respectively. But more recent scholarship has employed a literary and redactional paradigm to read the book of Isaiah as a literary whole, while at the same time recognizing that it includes material that was composed by various writers over the course of some four hundred years or more (Rendtorff 1991; Sweeney 1993). This leads to the conclusion that the book of Isaiah achieved its full and final form at some point during the fifth century BCE, in conjunction with the reform program of Ezra and Nehemiah (Sweeney 1988; 1996). This conclusion is supported by the observation that Ezra's return to Jerusalem and program of religious reform is presented in part as a fulfillment of prophecy in the book of Isaiah (Koch 1974).

This obviously has implications for the understanding of *tôrâ* in Isa. 2.2-4 and elsewhere in the book of Isaiah. Although it is unlikely that the eighth-century prophet Isaiah, or even any of the other Isaianic writers prior to the time of Ezra, employed the term *tôrâ* in reference to Mosaic Torah, it is likely and even probable that Ezra understood the term in reference to his own reform program that was based explicitly upon Mosaic Torah. Certainly, the invitation to the House of Jacob to come to Zion to learn YHWH's Torah would support his understanding of the need to reconstitute the Jewish community in Jerusalem on the basis of the teachings of Mosaic Torah. On the other hand, the inclusion of the nations in this scenario would seem to contradict Ezra's program which called upon Jewish men to send away their gentile wives and children (Ezra 10). Given the fifth century context for the composition of the final form of Isaiah, one may legitimately ask whether the book of Isaiah supports Ezra's reforms, and if so, how the vision of the teaching of Torah at Zion would relate to that reform.

II

In order to understand the meaning of the term *tôrâ* in the context of the book of Isaiah as a whole, it is first necessary to establish the literary form and setting of the book. A full discussion of this issue is not possible within the limits of the present context, but the reader may turn to the introduction of my recent commentary on Isaiah 1–39 which takes up this issue in detail (Sweeney 1996). The following is a summary of that discussion.

As indicated by the superscription of the book in Isa. 1.1, the book of Isaiah constitutes 'the vision of Isaiah ben Amoz which he saw concerning Judah and Jerusalem in the days of Uzziah, Jotham, Ahaz, (and)

Hezekiah, kings of Judah'. The book is formulated as a prophetic exhortation to Judah and Jerusalem to adhere to YHWH's covenant. This is evident in that parenetic or exhortational material in Isaiah 1 and 55 that calls upon the people to accept YHWH's terms appears at key points in the structure of the book. The placement of this exhortational material in relation to the instructional material that constitutes the balance of the book defines the overall generic character of the book of Isaiah as a prophetic exhortation. In its present form, the exhortational material interacts with the instructional material so that the appeal to adhere to YHWH's covenant in Isaiah 1 and 55 is supported by the instructional material that demonstrates how the people have failed to do so in the past and how adherence will benefit them in the future.

The structure of the book comprises two basic parts that are identified by various features of the text. The first part in Isaiah 1–33 focuses on YHWH's projected plans for world-wide sovereignty at Zion in that these chapters are designed to project judgment against Jerusalem, Judah, Israel and the nations, followed by restoration once the judgment is complete. The second part in Isaiah 34–66 focuses on the realization of YHWH's plans for world-wide sovereignty at Zion in that these chapters presuppose that the judgment (or at least the initial stage of judgment at the hands of Assyria and Babylonia) is over and that the period of restoration is about to begin with the return of the people to Jerusalem.

This structural division is supported by several other factors. The first is the transitional function of Isaiah 36–39 within the structure of the book as a whole. Past scholars have generally concluded that these chapters form the conclusion to the First Isaiah material in Isaiah 1–39, insofar as these chapters portray the statements and activities of Isaiah ben Amoz during the Assyrian siege of Jerusalem in 701 BCE (for example, Eissfeldt 1965: 304). But more recent studies demonstrate that Isaiah 36–39 does not close the material devoted to First Isaiah; instead it introduces the material that appears beginning in Isaiah 40 (Ackroyd 1982; Seitz 1990; Seitz 1991). Thus, Isa. 39.6-7 presents Isaiah's prediction of the Babylonian exile which is presupposed throughout the rest of the book. Likewise, Isaiah 36–39 presents a portrayal of Hezekiah in a time of crisis that is designed deliberately to idealize Hezekiah and to contrast his faithfulness in YHWH's promises of security for Jerusalem and the House of David with Ahaz's faithless rejection of the same promises in a similar time of crisis as portrayed in Isa. 6.1–9.6 (Sweeney

1988: 12-17). The presentation of Ahaz's response to YHWH's promises through the prophet Isaiah demonstrates the behavior and attitudes that lead to the judgment outlined in the prophet's vocation account in Isaiah 6 and that are elaborated upon throughout Isaiah 1–33. The presentation of Hezekiah's response to YHWH's promises delivered through the prophet Isaiah demonstrates the behavior and outlook that lead to the restoration announced in the renewed prophetic commission in Isa. 40.1-11 and that are elaborated upon throughout the balance of the book. By means of this contrast, the portrayal of Hezekiah defines the model of faithful behaviour expected of those who are to be included in YHWH's covenant.

The transitional function of Isaiah 34–35 likewise plays a constitutive role in establishing the structure of the book. Scholars frequently note that these chapters were composed much later than the material in First Isaiah, and many maintain that both chapters, especially Isaiah 35, were written either by Deutero-Isaiah or the prophet's immediate followers (for example, Wildberger 1982: 1330-41, 1355-59; Clements 1980: 271-77). Regardless of the circumstances of their composition, both chapters play a transitional role in that they reflect upon the themes of judgment from Isaiah 1–33 and simultaneously point forward to the new possibility of salvation and restoration articulated in the second half of the book. In this regard, Isaiah 34–35 constitute an introduction to Isaiah 34–66 that is parallel to Isaiah 1 and its introductory role in relation to Isaiah 1–33 (Brownlee 1964; Evans 1988). Both passages begin with a call to attention directed to the world at large to witness respectively YHWH's punishment against Israel in Isaiah 1 and YHWH's punishment against the nations in Isaiah 34. The call to witness Israel's punishment in Isaiah 1 corresponds to the concern with the punishment and purification of Jerusalem, Judah and Israel evident throughout Isaiah 1–33, and the call to witness the nations' punishment in Isaiah 34 corresponds to the concern to establish YHWH's world-wide sovereignty over all the nations evident in Isaiah 34–66. Likewise, Isaiah 35 portrays the return of the exiled Jews through the wilderness to Zion, which takes up the concern for the anticipated return to Zion announced in Isa. 11.11-16 and 27.12-13 and the imminent return to Zion announced in 40.1-11 and 62.10-12 (cf. Steck 1985).

Other factors also establish the two-part structure of the book of Isaiah. Isaiah 1–33 anticipates the punishment and subsequent restoration of Jerusalem, Judah and Israel; Isaiah 34–66 presupposes that this punishment is completed and that the restoration is now taking place. Isaiah 1–33 anticipates the downfall of Jerusalem's enemies, identified as Assyria (Isa. 10.5-34; 14.24-27) and Babylon (Isa. 13.1–14.23); Isaiah 34–66 presupposes the downfall of YHWH's major enemies, identified as Edom (Isa. 34; 63.1-6) and Babylon (Isa. 46–47). Isaiah 1–33 anticipates the reign of the righteous Davidic monarch which will inaugurate an era of peace (Isa. 9.1-6; 11.1-16; 32.1-20); Isaiah 34–66 presupposes the continuing role of the Davidic covenant for Israel (Isa. 55.3), but portrays the rule of Cyrus as the initial manifestation of YHWH's righteous rule in Zion (Isa. 44.24-28; 45.1-7; 60–62; 65–66; cf. Kratz 1991).

Each half of the book displays its own distinct structure which posits an interplay between exhortational and instructional material. The structure of each is determined in part by the interrelationships between the textual blocks that constitute the structural sub-units of the two halves.

Isaiah 1–33 begins with the introductory parenesis in Isaiah 1 that constitutes the prologue for the entire book of Isaiah as well as the introduction for the first half of the book (cf. Fohrer 1962). It is identified by the superscription in Isa. 1.1, and it portrays YHWH's intention to purify and redeem Jerusalem. The instructional material in Isaiah 2–33 constitutes the balance of the first half of the book. It is identified by the superscription in Isa. 2.1, and it announces the projected 'Day of YHWH' as indicated by the frequent references to the 'day' in the first half of the book. Essentially, the 'Day of YHWH' identifies YHWH's plans to establish world-wide sovereignty by punishing and thereby purifying Jerusalem, Israel and the nations in preparation for divine rule. Four major sub-units comprise this portion of the book. Isaiah 2–4 constitutes a prophetic announcement concerning the preparation of Zion for its role as the center for YHWH's world rule; it thereby serves as a key text in identifying the overall concern of the first half of the book. Isaiah 5–12 constitutes prophetic instruction concerning the significance of Assyrian judgment against Israel in that it projects the restoration of righteous Davidic rule over Israel. Isaiah 13–27 constitutes a prophetic announcement concerning the preparation of the nations for YHWH's world rule from Zion. Isaiah 28–33 constitutes prophetic instruction concerning YHWH's plans to establish the royal savior in Jerusalem.

Isaiah 34–66 takes up the realization of YHWH's plans for world-wide sovereignty at Zion. This half of the book begins with prophetic instruction concerning the realization of YHWH's world-wide sovereignty at Zion in Isaiah 34–54. This textual block comprises three major sub-units

defined by their respective generic characters and concerns. Isaiah 34–
35 constitutes prophetic instruction concerning YHWH's power to return
the redeemed exiles to Zion. Isaiah 36–39 constitutes royal narratives
concerning YHWH's deliverance of Jerusalem and Hezekiah that portray
Hezekiah as a model of faithful action for those who would maintain
YHWH's covenant. Isaiah 40–54 constitutes prophetic instruction that
presents a series of arguments designed to prove that YHWH is maintaining the covenant and restoring Zion. The second half of Isaiah 34–66
appears in Isaiah 55–66 which constitutes a prophetic exhortation to
adhere to YHWH's covenant. The exhortation proper appears in Isaiah
55, which defines the generic character of the whole. The substantiation
that supports the exhortation appears in Isaiah 56–66 in the form of
prophetic instruction concerning the character of the reconstituted
covenant community in Zion. These chapters include prophetic instruction concerning the proper observance of the covenant in Isaiah 56–59;
a prophetic announcement of salvation for the reconstituted covenant
community in Isaiah 60–62; and prophetic instruction concerning the
process of selection for the reconstituted covenant community in Isaiah
63–66.

Overall, the final form of the book of Isaiah presents an argument or
exhortation to adhere to YHWH's covenant and thereby to be numbered
among the righteous who will survive YHWH's judgment against the
wicked in preparation for the establishment of the new creation in which
YHWH's rule from Jerusalem will be manifested throughout the world
(see esp. Isa. 65–66). Altogether, the final form of the book of Isaiah is
designed to support the reforms of Ezra in the late fifth century BCE.
Several arguments support this contention.

First, the universal perspective of the book of Isaiah includes the
nations that comprised the Persian empire during the fifth century BCE.
All of the nations listed in the oracles against the nations in Isaiah 13–23,
including Babylon, Assyria, Philistia, Moab, Aram and Israel, Ethiopia
and Egypt, Midbar Yam (the Tigris-Euphrates delta region), Dumah,
Arabia, Jerusalem and Tyre were all incorporated into the Persian
empire. Greece is notably absent, which precludes a later date in the
Hellenistic period. Persia is likewise not listed as one of the nations not
subjected to YHWH's judgment, but Isa. 21.2 identifies Elam and the
Medes as the parties responsible for Babylon's downfall, and Isa. 44.24–
45.7 identifies Cyrus, the Persian monarch, as YHWH's anointed king
and Temple builder. In addition, the importance of the downfall of

Babylon in the book of Isaiah reflects Cyrus's subjugation of the city. This suggests that YHWH's world-wide rule is identified with the rule of the Persian empire.

Secondly, the final form of the book of Isaiah presupposes that the Temple has already been rebuilt (see Isa. 56; 60–62), but the full manifestation of YHWH's rule has not yet occurred (see Isa. 65–66). This corresponds to the situation of the late-fifth century BCE when Nehemiah and then Ezra returned to Jerusalem to begin their work. Nehemiah took measures to restore support for the Temple and to repopulate the city of Jerusalem (Neh. 3–7; 11–13). Ezra's reform measures were designed to establish the Torah or Five Books of Moses as the basic guidelines to establish Jewish identity and life centered around the Temple in Jerusalem (Neh. 8–10; Ezra 7–10). Insofar as the book of Isaiah is designed to re-establish ideal Jewish life in Zion based on Torah (cf. Isa. 2.2-4), it shares the same goal as Ezra's reform.

Thirdly, the final form of the book of Isaiah presupposes a distinction between the righteous and the wicked, and calls upon its readers (or hearers) to identify with the righteous and thereby to avoid the final judgment against the wicked (see Isa. 1.27-28; 65–66). Such a perspective corresponds to the program of Ezra who attempted to define a righteous Jewish community during the course of his reforms. Many see the book of Isaiah in opposition to Ezra's reforms in that Isa. 56.1-8 and 66.8-24 make it quite clear that the righteous include eunuchs and foreigners (for example, Westermann 1969: 312-15). Ezra, on the other hand, required that Jewish men send away their Gentile wives and children, and therefore could not have envisioned the righteous community portrayed in Isaiah. But this view overlooks several important points. The book of Isaiah does not address the issue of intermarriage; it addresses the issue of proper observance of the covenant. The eunuch or foreigner who observes the covenant is acceptable in the Temple. There is no indication that Ezra's reforms exclude the foreigner who adopts the covenant of Judaism; that is, who converts to Judaism. In this regard, the Ezra traditions indicate only that foreign wives and children were banished, not foreign husbands. Scholars tend to assume that Jewish women who married foreign men in this period abandoned Judaism to follow their pagan husbands, but no consideration is given to the possibility that such husbands adopted Judaism or that their children were raised as Jews. If foreign wives of Jewish men raised their children as pagans, so Jewish wives of foreign men would raise their children as

Jews. Hence, there was no need to expel foreign husbands as they would present little threat of apostasy.

Finally, the book of Isaiah and Ezra's reforms share various other points in common. Both employ the term *ḥārēd*, 'one who trembles', to describe those who adhere to YHWH's covenant (Isa. 66.2, 5; Ezra 9.4; 10.3); both polemicize against those who fail to observe the covenant; both emphasize observance of the Sabbath as the cornerstone of the covenant (Isa. 56.1-8; 58.13-14; Neh. 9.14; 10.31; 13.15-22); both emphasize YHWH's Torah; both support the centrality of the Temple; and neither precludes the participation of foreigners or eunuchs who convert to Judaism. Altogether, the book of Isaiah is a book that may well support Ezra's reforms. In this respect, it is no accident that Ezra's reform program is presented as a fulfillment of prophecy in Isaiah (Koch 1974). Thus Ezra refers to the people as the 'holy seed' (Ezra 9.2; cf. Isa. 6.13) and a 'remnant' (Ezra 9.8; cf. Isa. 4.2; 10.20; 37.31-32), and Ezra's return to Jerusalem is presented as a second Exodus in keeping with the new Exodus proclaimed in the book of Isaiah (Koch 1974; cf. McConville 1986). In this regard, the liturgical form of passages such as Isaiah 12 and 35 would suggest that the book of Isaiah might have been read as part of the liturgy of the Temple (Eaton 1982). Certainly Ezra's reading of the Torah to the people during Sukkot in Nehemiah 8–10 constitutes a liturgical occasion. Sukkot stresses the themes of the ingathering of the grape and wine harvest together with the theme of the ingathering of the people of Israel from the Exodus at the end of forty years of wilderness wandering. These themes appear frequently throughout the book of Isaiah (for example, Isa. 11.11-16; 12; 27.12-13; 35.8-10; 40.1-11; 62.10-12), which would facilitate the people's understanding of the Exodus theme of the Torah by pointing out that the experience of exile at the hands of Assyria and Babylon and restoration at the hands of YHWH would constitute a second Exodus and restoration during the Persian period.

III

The term *tôrâ* appears twelve times in the book of Isaiah: 1.10; 2.3; 5.24; 8.16, 20; 24.5; 30.9; 42.4, 21, 24; and 51.4, 7. These texts stem from several different historical settings in relation to the composition of the book of Isaiah, and therefore represent different understandings of the meaning of the term *tôrâ* (cf. Jensen 1973). In order to establish the meaning of the term in the book of Isaiah, each occurrence of the term must first be examined in relation to its immediate literary and historical context. Afterwards, the usage of the term *tôrâ* must be examined in relation to the overall literary context of the book of Isaiah as a whole. Suchstudy will facilitate understanding of both the hermeneutics employed in the composition and development of the book of Isaiah and the meaning of the term *tôrâ* in the final form of the text.

The term *tôrâ* in Isa. 1.10 appears in the larger context of Isa. 1.10-17, which demands that the people heed 'the teaching of our God' (*tôrat ᶜᵉlōhênû*). This text constitutes a prophetic instruction concerning the proper role of sacrifices. It dates to the latter part of the eighth century BCE, during the period of Hezekiah's reforms prior to his revolt against Sennacherib in 705-701 BCE. It apparently represents Isaiah's criticisms against Hezekiah's reform measures by which he cleansed the Temple of foreign or pagan influence and established purified YHWHistic sacrifice as a means to re-establish the Temple as the religious center of the Davidic kingdom. In this scenario, the purified Temple stands as a powerful symbol of Judean independence from Assyrian rule. Isaiah's criticisms are directed against Hezekiah's program and his clear plans for revolt against the Assyrians. He employs standard stereotypical terminology for the criticism of the monarchy that emphasizes the need to do justice and to protect the widow and orphan. Such language and imagery is typically employed to characterize just rule and proper royal policy in the ancient near east (Fensham 1962). The use of the term *tôrat ᶜᵉlōhênû*, 'the teaching of our God', here parallel to *dᵉbar yhwh*, 'the word of YHWH', signifies the normal priestly instruction concerning proper ritual procedure in the Temple in Jerusalem. The prophet employs the term in a satirical manner to demonstrate his point that 'the Torah of YHWH' in this instance does not pertain to correct sacrificial procedure, but to the underlying purpose that the sacrifice serves. In his view, Hezekiah's Temple reform and plans to revolt against Assyria will only lead the nation to ruin.

The term *tôrâ* in Isa. 2.3 appears in the context of Isa 2.2-4, which portrays the nations streaming to Zion to learn the 'teaching' (*tôrâ*) of YHWH that will settle their disputes. This text stems from the sixth-century redaction of the book of Isaiah which portrays the Persian conquest of Babylon, the return of exiled Jews to Jerusalem and the restoration of the Jerusalem Temple as manifestations of YHWH's world-wide rule. The nations are portrayed as subject to YHWH's rule which inaugurates an era of world peace. The term *tôrâ*, again parallel to *dᵉbar yhwh*, 'the word of YHWH', apparently refers to YHWH's instruction on the proper way to conduct international relations. It appears in the context of the legal resolution of disputes between the nations, in which YHWH is portrayed as the typical ancient near eastern monarch who employs his 'Torah' as a means to settle disagreements among his subjects. In this sense, Torah signifies a means to effect world-wide order.

The term *tôrâ* in Isa. 5.24 appears in the context of Isa. 5.8-24, which enumerates instances of the people's rejection of 'the teaching of YHWH Sebaot'. Isa. 5.24 constitutes a concluding summary of the crimes detailed throughout the passage. It presents Isaiah's rationale for the fall of the northern kingdom of Israel to Assyria in 724–21 BCE. The expression *tôrat yhwh ṣᵉbāʾōt*, 'the teaching of YHWH of Hosts', parallel to *ʿimrat qᵉdôš yiśrāʾēl*, 'the word of the Holy One of Israel', apparently refers to the norms of social conduct, especially those that pertain to property rights, that are presupposed throughout Isa. 5.8-24. Apparently, the prophet points to the abuse and violation of these norms as the cause of YHWH's decision to bring the Assyrians to punish the northern kingdom (cf. Isa. 5.25-30).

The occurrences of *tôrâ* in Isa. 8.16 and 8.20 appear in the context of the prophet's command to seal or bind up 'the testimony' (*tᵉʿûdâ*) and 'the teaching' (*tôrâ*) in 8.16–9.6. It apparently refers to the prophet's efforts to put away his teachings until a more propitious time at which they might be understood or realized. The historical context of this passage relates to the Syro-Ephraimitic War of 735–32 BCE in which the Assyrian empire first invaded Israel to protect Judah from a combined Israelite-Aramean assault that was designed to overthrow the Davidic dynasty and to bring Judah into an anti-Assyrian coalition. Isa. 8.16–9.6 expresses Isaiah's view that the Assyrian invasion represents an opportunity for the House of David to re-establish its rule over the former northern kingdom, but King Ahaz's refusal to act on this premise forced the prophet to give up his efforts. The term *tôrâ* appears in parallel with *tᵉʿûdâ*, 'testimony', which apparently refers to the document written by the prophet in Isa. 8.1-4 to name his child symbolically in reference to the anticipated fall of the Syro- Ephraimitic coalition to Assyria. In this instance, *tôrâ* simply refers to the prophet's teachings on this matter insofar as he states that the 'torah' and 'testimony' are to be bound up and sealed among his 'teachings' (*limmudāy*, 'my teachings').

The occurrence of the plural *tôrōt* in Isa. 24.5 appears in the larger context of Isaiah 24–27, which outlines a scenario for the establishment of YHWH's rule over the nations following a period of world-wide upheaval. This text stems from the sixth-century redaction of the book of Isaiah, and portrays the world-wide disruption occasioned by the fall of Babylon to Persia as a manifestation of the establishment of YHWH's sovereignty on earth. The term *tôrōt* is employed in parallel to *ḥōq*, 'statute', and refers to the violation of the 'laws' or 'norms' that constitute the 'eternal covenant' (*bᵉrît ʿôlām*) by which the earth's 'inhabitants' dwell on the land. This appears to be a reference to the laws that govern the structure of creation rather than to any given body of divine teachings. The term *tôrâ* (*tôrōt*) then refers to a cosmic principle of order in the world.

The occurrence of the term *tôrat yhwh*, 'the instruction of YHWH', in Isa. 30.9 appears in the context of Isaiah 30 which expresses the prophet's dissatisfaction with the people for sending an embassy to Egypt to conclude an alliance against Assyria. The passage dates to the latter part of the eighth century BCE, and it was apparently written by Isaiah in conjunction with his polemic against King Hezekiah's efforts to secure support for his planned revolt against the Assyrian empire. The prophet characterizes the people as rebellious in v. 9, and he states that 'they are not willing to hear the Torah of YHWH'. As in Isaiah 8.16–9.6, Isa. 30.8 indicates the prophet's intention to record his words for a later time. In this instance, the term *tôrat yhwh* apparently refers to the prophet's words, which express the teachings of YHWH concerning Hezekiah's projected alliance with Egypt.

The occurrence of *tôrâ* in Isa. 42.4 appears in the context of Isa. 42.1-4, the first of the so-called 'Servant Songs' in the writings of the Second Isaiah. The text is part of the writings of the Second Isaiah, which date to the middle of sixth century BCE. In its present context, it is a part of a larger textual sub-unit in Isa. 41.1–42.13 which contends that YHWH is the master of human events. This supports the overall purpose of Second Isaiah to demonstrate that YHWH maintains the covenant with Israel and that YHWH is restoring Zion. The text presents 'his teaching' (*tôrātô*); that is, the teaching of the Servant, in relation to the 'justice' (*mišpāṭ*) that the Servant will establish among the nations of the earth (Isa. 42.1). Insofar as Second Isaiah contends that YHWH is both creator and ruler of the world, *tôrâ* and *mišpāṭ* apparently refer to the principles by which order will be established among the nations of the earth.

The occurrences of the term *tôrâ* in Isa 42.21, 24 appear in the context of the larger textual sub-unit Isaiah 42.14–44.23, which argues that YHWH is the redeemer of Israel (Sweeney 1988: 72-76). Again, this passage forms a part of the writings of the Second Isaiah from the sixth century BCE. As part of the author's attempt to argue that YHWH is the redeemer of Israel, the text maintains in Isa. 42.21 that YHWH attempted to 'magnify Torah and make (it) glorious' (*yagdîl tôrâ wᵉyaʾdîr*), but that Israel was not willing to accept this teaching as Isa. 42.24 states, 'and they were not willing to walk in his ways, and they did not listen to his Torah (*bᵉtôrātô*)'. The immediate context gives no clues as to the specific meaning of *tôrâ* other than to identify it as the 'teaching' of YHWH that was initially rejected by the Servant Israel (cf. Isa. 42.19), thereby bringing YHWH's punishment upon itself. Despite this rejection, the context makes it clear that YHWH is now prepared to redeem the blind and deaf Servant Israel as an example to the nations of YHWH's power.

Finally, the occurrences of the term *tôrâ* in Isa. 51.4, 7 appear in the larger context of Isaiah 49–54, which contends that YHWH is restoring Zion. Again, this passage is a part of the writings of the sixth-century prophet Second Isaiah. In both cases, the term is employed in a context which calls upon the people of Israel and the nations to listen to YHWH so that they may understand the significance of the restoration of Zion as an act of YHWH. Isa. 51.4 employs the reference to the *tôrâ* that will go forth from YHWH in parallel to YHWH's 'justice' (*mišpāṭ*) that will serve as 'a light for the peoples' (*lᵉʾôr ʿammîm*), and Isa. 51.7 refers to YHWH's Torah (lit., 'my Torah', *tôrātî*) which is in the heart of the people. Again, the context identifies *tôrâ* as a term that refers to the principles of order and justice among the nations of the earth.

IV

When one considers the meaning of the term *tôrâ* in relation to the final form and setting of the book of Isaiah, it becomes apparent that the broader literary context plays a determinative role in defining the interpretation of the term. This is not to say that the immediate literary context no longer serves as an important criterion for establishing the meaning of *tôrâ*. Rather, the broader literary context acts together with the immediate context to incorporate the individual occurrences of the term into an overall conception of *tôrâ* in the book of Isaiah. In this regard, the meaning of *tôrâ* in Isaiah must be considered in relation to the meaning of the other occurrences of the term. Although it is debatable whether the individual authors of Isaiah intended such a comprehensive view of *tôrâ* when they wrote the passages in which the term occurs, the meaning of *tôrâ* takes on a hermeneutical life of its own when it is considered in relation to its full literary and interpretative context in the final form of the book of Isaiah (cf. Sheppard 1992: 578-82).

When the individual occurrences of *tôrâ* are considered in relation to the other instances of the term in Isaiah, several common features begin to emerge that provide criteria for establishing a comprehensive under-standing of the meaning of *tôrâ* in the book of Isaiah. First, although *tôrâ* is clearly understood as the teaching of the prophet in Isa. 8.16, 20, it is very clearly identified in several instances as the 'Torah of our God' (*tôrat ʾelōhênû*, Isa. 1.10); the 'Torah of YHWH of Hosts' (*tôrat yhwh ṣᵉbāʾôt*, Isa. 5.24); the 'Torah of YHWH' (*tôrat yhwh*, Isa. 30.9); 'my (i.e. YHWH's) Torah' (*tôrātî*; 51.7); and 'his (i.e. YHWH's) Torah' (*bᵉtôrātô*, Isa. 42.24). Likewise, Torah proceeds from YHWH (Isa. 2.3; 51.4), and it is identified as the 'word of YHWH' (*dᵉbar yhwh*, Isa. 1.10; 2.3) or the 'saying of the Holy One of Israel' (*ʾimrat qᵉdôš yiśrāʾēl*, Isa. 5.24). Secondly, several occurrences of the term make it clear that *tôrâ* is to be written down and stored away for the future when it will be understood by later generations. Thus, the prophet commands, 'bind up the testimony, seal the Torah among my teachings' in Isa. 8.16 (cf. Isa. 8.20), and 'now, go write it (Torah) before them upon a tablet, and upon a book inscribe it' in Isa. 30.8. Thirdly, it is equated with YHWH's 'justice' (*mišpāṭ*) in Isa. 42.4 and 51.4 or YHWH's 'righteousness' (*ṣedeq*) in Isa. 42.21 and 51.7, in which capacity it serves as a means to establish the norms of proper conduct among nations (Isa. 2.4; 42.4) and within Israel itself (Isa. 2.5; 5.24; 42.24; 51.7). Finally, it refers to a principle of cosmic order which stands at the foundation of the structure of creation (Isa. 24.5).

The sum total of these occurrences identifies *tôrâ* as the teaching of YHWH, expressed by the prophet, which stands as the norm for proper conduct by both Israel and the nations, and which stands as the norm for order in the created world. It is likewise identified as something that is not properly understood in the time of the prophet, but the full signifi-cance of which will be apparent at a future time in which YHWH's world-wide sovereignty is recognized. As such, *tôrâ* signifies YHWH's revelation to both Israel and the world at large.

In this regard, the symbolism of the revelation of YHWH's Torah to the nations and Jacob at Zion in Isa. 2.2-4, 5 becomes especially important in that it establishes an analogy of the revelation of Torah to Israel (and to the nations, represented by Egypt and the Pharaoh) in the Sinai pericope of the Pentateuch (Exod. 19–Num. 10). Just as Mount Sinai serves as the locus of revelation to Israel in the Mosaic traditions, so Zion serves as the locus of revelation to Israel and the nations in the book of Isaiah (cf. Levenson 1985). Just as the revelation of Torah at Mount Sinai provides guidance or instruction in the norms of proper behavior for the people of Israel, so the revelation of Torah at Mount Zion provides guidance or instruction in the norms of proper behavior for the nations as well as for the people of Israel.

The significance of this observation for understanding the book of Isaiah in relation to Mosaic Torah is reinforced by the prominent role played by the motif of the return of the exiles to Zion in the book of Isaiah. Scholars have long noted that the Second Isaiah portrays the return of the Babylonian exiles to Zion as a second or a renewed Exodus analogous to that of the Mosaic period (Anderson 1962; Anderson 1976; Kiesow 1979). Thus, Isa. 40.1-11 portrays the highway through the wilderness that will bring the exiles to Zion in analogy to the 'way of the wilderness' and the 'King's Highway' that brought the Mosaic generation through the wilderness to the promised land (e.g. Exod. 13.17-18; Num. 20.17). Isa. 43.14-21 identifies YHWH as the One who makes a path in the sea and subdues horse and chariot in analogy to the splitting of the sea and the defeat of the Egyptian chariotry in the Exodus from Egypt (Exod. 14–15). Isa. 48.20-21 portrays YHWH's making water flow from the rock in the desert in analogy to the water produced by Moses when he struck the rock in the wilderness (Exod. 17.1-7; Num. 20.2-13). Finally, Isa. 51.10-11 makes it very clear that the goal of the guidance through the wilderness is to bring Israel back to Zion, just as Exod. 15.13-18 identified the goal of Israel's journey through the sea and the wilderness as YHWH's mountain and sanctuary. In this regard, the witness of the nations plays an important role in establishing YHWH's reputation, just as the witness of the nations plays a similar role in Second Isaiah.

But this concern with the return of Israel to Zion as an analogy to the Exodus and Wilderness tradition is not limited only to the writings of Second Isaiah; it permeates the rest of the book of Isaiah as well. Isa. 4.2-6 portrays the sanctuary at Zion covered by a cloud by day and a flaming fire by night in analogy to the pillar of smoke and flame that guided Israel through the wilderness and eventually settled upon the tabernacle which symbolizes the Temple (Exod. 13.21-22; cf. 40.34-38). The motif of YHWH's closing the eyes and ears of the people so that they do not understand and repent in Isaiah 6 calls to mind the hardening of Pharaoh's heart so that he does not thwart YHWH's demonstration of power in the Exodus (Exod. 7.1-5; 14.8), and Isaiah's unclean lips (Isa. 6.5) recall the uncircumcised lips of Moses (Exod. 6.12, 30). Isa. 10.24-26 and 11.11-16 portray YHWH's rod of punishment against Assyria in analogy to the rod of Moses that punished Egypt at the Exodus (Exod. 7–11; 14), and the result is the return of the exiles to Zion along the highway (cf. Isa. 27.12-13; 35.1-10; 62.10-12).

Very clearly, the understanding of *tôrâ* in the final form of the book of Isaiah is presented in relation to a new Exodus instigated by YHWH to return the exiled Jews to Zion and to establish YHWH's world-wide sovereignty.

V

In sum, the book of Isaiah as a whole portrays the revelation of YHWH's Torah to the nations and Israel in analogy to the revelation of Torah to Israel and the nations in the Mosaic tradition. This has obvious implications for understanding the role of the book of Isaiah in relation to the reform and restoration program of Ezra and Nehemiah, based upon Mosaic Torah. Whereas the Mosaic tradition portrays this revelation as a means to establish Israel in its own land, the Isaiah tradition portrays the revelation as a means to demonstrate YHWH's world-wide sovereignty and to re-establish Israel in Zion. Likewise, the Mosaic revelation of Torah establishes the norms of life for the people of Israel insofar as it conveys the laws that govern both community life and sacred worship. But the book of Isaiah focuses on Israel's relationship to the nations of the world insofar as it establishes Israel's role in Zion, the centre for YHWH's world sovereignty where the nations come to recognize YHWH's rule. In short, Mosaic Torah defines Israel's internal relations within its own community; the book of Isaiah defines Israel's relations among the nations. Both define Israel as a holy community. Both therefore serve the ends of Ezra's reforms, insofar as the goal of the program was to re-establish Israel as a holy community in Jerusalem.

Mosaic Torah provides the means for community organization; Isaianic
Torah provides the rationale.

BIBLIOGRAPHY

Ackroyd, P.R.
1982　　'Isaiah 36–39: Structure and Function', in J.R. Nellis *et al.* (eds.), *Von Kanaan bis Kerala* (Festschrift J.P.M. Van der Ploeg; AOAT, 211; Neukirchen–Vluyn: Neukirchener Verlag): 3-21.

Anderson, B.W.
1962　　'Exodus Typology in Second Isaiah', in B.W. Anderson and W. Harrelson (eds.), *Israel's Prophetic Heritage* (Festschrift J. Muilenburg; New York: Harper & Row): 177-95.
1976　　'Exodus and Covenant in Second Isaiah and Prophetic Tradition', in F.M. Cross, Jr, *et al.* (eds.), *Magnalia Dei/The Mighty Acts of G-d* (Festschrift G.E. Wright; Garden City: Doubleday): 339-60.

Brownlee, W.H.
1964　　*The Meaning of the Qumran Scrolls for the Bible* (New York: Oxford University Press).

Clements, R.E.
1980　　*Isaiah 1–39* (NCB; London: Marshall, Morgan & Scott; Grand Rapids: Eerdmans).

Eaton, J.H.
1982　　'The Isaiah Tradition', in R. Coggins *et al.* (eds.), *Israel's Prophetic Tradition* (Festschrift P.R. Ackroyd; Cambridge: Cambridge University Press): 58-76.

Eissfeldt, O.
1965　　*The Old Testament: An Introduction* (trans. P.R. Ackroyd; Oxford: Basil Blackwell).

Evans, C.A.
1988　　'On the Unity and Parallel Structure of the Book of Isaiah', *VT* 38: 129-47.

Fensham, F. C.
1962　　'Widow, Orphan, and the Poor in Ancient Near Eastern Legal and Wisdom Literature', *JNES* 21: 129-39.

Fohrer, G.
1962　　'Jesaja 1 als Zusammenfassung der Verkündigung Jesajas', *ZAW* 74: 251-68.

Jensen, J.
1973　　*The Use of tôrâ by Isaiah: His Debate with the Wisdom Tradition* (CBQMS, 3; Washington: Catholic Biblical Asociation of America).

Kiesow, K.
1979　　*Exodustexte im Jesajabuch* (OBO, 24; Freibourg: Editions Universitaires; Göttingen: Vandenhoeck & Ruprecht).

Koch, K.
1974　　'Ezra and the Origins of Judaism', *JSS* 19: 173-97.

Kratz, R.G.
1991   *Kyros im Deuterojesajabuch: Redaktionsgeschichtliche Untersuchun-
            gen zu Entstehung und Theologie von Jes 40–55* (FzAT, 1; Tübingen:
            Mohr [Paul Siebeck]).

Levenson, J.D.
1985   *Sinai and Zion: An Entry into the Jewish Bible* (New York: Winston
            [Seabury]).

McConville, J.G.
1986   'Ezra-Nehemiah and the Fulfillment of Prophecy', *VT* 36: 205-24.

Rendtorff, R.
1991   'The Book of Isaiah: A Complex Unity. Synchronic and Diachronic
            Reading', in E.H. Lovering, Jr (ed.), *SBL 1991 Seminar Papers*
            (Atlanta: Scholars Press): 8-20.

Seitz, C.R.
1990   'The Divine Council: Temporal Transition and New Prophecy in the
            Book of Isaiah', *JBL* 109: 229-47.
1991   *Zion's Final Destiny: The Development of the Book of Isaiah–A
            Reassessment of Isaiah 36–39* (Minneapolis: Fortress Press).

Sheppard, G.T.
1992   'The Book of Isaiah: Competing Structures According to a Late
            Modern Description of its Shape and Scope', in E.H. Lovering, Jr
            (ed.), *SBL 1992 Seminar Papers* (Atlanta: Scholars Press), pp. 549-82.

Steck, O.H.
1985   *Bereitete Heimkehr: Jesaja 35 als redaktionelle Brücke zwischen dem
            Ersten und dem Zweiten Jesaja* (SBS, 121; Stuttgart: Katholische
            Bibelwerk).

Sweeney, M.A.
1988   *Isaiah 1–4 and the Post-Exilic Understanding of the Isaianic
            Tradition* (BZAW, 171; Berlin: de Gruyter).
1993   'The Book of Isaiah in Recent Research', *Currents in Research:
            Biblical Studies* 1: 141-62.
1996   *Isaiah 1–39, with an Introduction to Prophetic Literature* (FOTL, 16;
            Grand Rapids: Eerdmans).

Westermann, C.
1969   *Isaiah 40–66: A Commentary* (OTL; trans. D.M.G. Stalker; London:
            SCM Press).

Wildberger, H.
1972   *Jesaja 1–12* (BKAT, 10.1; Neukirchen–Vluyn: Neukirchener Verlag).
1982   *Jesaja 28–39* (BKAT, 10.3; Neukirchen–Vluyn: Neukirchener Verlag).

ISAIAH 28–33: BLEST BE THE TIE THAT BINDS (ISAIAH TOGETHER)

Gary Stansell

Introduction

From the beginning of modern critical study of the book of Isaiah, scholars have typically understood chs. 28–32 (33) to form a major section or unit within Isaiah 1–39. B. Duhm's commentary (1892) considers chs. 28–33 to have been a once independently existing *Buchlein* which, although its nucleus originated from Isaiah himself, was given its present shape by later editors. Thus according to Duhm there were originally two separate 'books': chs. 1–12 and 28–33. S. Mowinckel (1933: 267-92) argued that originally there was only one 'book' comprised of smaller collections of prophetic sayings. This book, according to Mowinckel, was later dismantled, rearranged and supplemented with new material. Thus the section chs. 28–35, both its arrangement and placement within the larger work, is traced not to an original 'booklet' but to an editorial process. In either case, these chapters are understood to contain a core of 'genuine' Isaianic prophecies, chiefly seen in chs. 28–31. Other critics are content to speak less of books or booklets and more of collections (Gray 1912: xlvii) or of tradition complexes (Kaiser 1973: 187). Some are still inclined to think that Isaiah himself (Fohrer 1966; Barth 1978) or at least the prophet's disciples (Wildberger 1982) first put the material into written form. In any case, both literary and redaction critical methods have amply demonstrated that chs. 28–33 are composed of various kinds of oracles, redactional pieces and later interpolations, with a complex and long history of growth (Scott 1956; Barth 1977; Clements 1980a). A general consensus has emerged, yet with some continuing debate, on which sayings derive from Isaiah of Jerusalem; namely 28.1-4, 7-22; 29.1-4, 9-10, 13-14, 15-16; 30.1-5, 6-7, 8-11, 12-14, 15-16; 31.1-4. H. Barth, for the most part followed by R. Clements (1980a), assigns a second group of texts to a seventh-century 'Assyrian [Clements 1980a: 'Josianic'] redaction': 28.23-29; 29.5-7 (thus

Clements 1980a; Barth 1977, only v. 8); 30.27-33; 31.5, 8-9 (Barth, 8b-9); 32.1-5, 15-20. Remaining salvation oracles or glosses have generally been assigned a later, exilic/post-exilic date: 28.5-6; 29.17-24; 30.18-26; 31.6-7; 32.9-14 (a lament form); 32.15-20. Chapter 33, a complex of different forms often taken as a 'prophetic liturgy' (Gunkel 1924) is mostly considered to be of late date, containing little if any 'genuine' material, although a few scholars find eighth-century material in this chapter.

While acknowledging that such diachronic approaches to chs. 28–33 have brought enormous gains in reconstructing the message of Isaiah of Jerusalem, the development and growth of the book, the dating of smaller units and so on, the purpose of this essay is neither to carry on such discussions nor to enter into debate with the results as we have them. Rather, in what follows, I shall attempt a reading of chs. 28–33 in terms of a synchronic reading (cf. Rendtorff 1991; Darr 1994: 14-22). The unit will be read as a whole; that is, in its final canonical shape, without regard to its history of growth. My interest will limit itself, however, to three realms of inquiry. First (part I), I shall examine chs. 28–33 as a unit: What structural clues suggest a meaningful arrangement and shaping of the material? Are there major themes or motifs which hold the unit together, lend it cohesion and make it a unity? Secondly (part II), I shall ask about the unit's fundamental connections to other sections of the book: What are the structural, verbal or thematic links which relate it to other major sections of the book, especially, but not only, chs. 1–12? Finally (part III) and more briefly, I shall ask about the function of chs. 28–33 in the present arrangement of the book: How is the unit itself (chs. 28–33) to be understood in its present canonical context?

I

Little consensus exists among critics on the delimitation of the unit. While there is no doubt that it commences with the woe-cry in 28.1, does it end with ch. 31 (Wildberger 1982), 32 (Fohrer 1966; Kaiser 1973), 33 (Duhm 1892; Gray 1912) or 35 (Sweeney 1988a: 54-55)? The crux of the matter is not only the function and placement of ch. 33 (Sweeney: 35 n. 101), but whether the criteria of 'genuineness' (Fohrer 1966) and/or of close literary and redactional connections are in the foreground. Thus, concerning the latter criterion, Sweeney (1988a) takes chs. 28–33 as a part of 28–35, while Seitz's (1993) commentary interprets chs. 28–33 in terms of the larger section of chs. 28–39. For the purposes of the present essay, the literary unit is to be defined as 28–33. This presupposes that the initial 'woe' in 33.1 ties this chapter inseparably to the preceding five 'woes' in chs. 28–31, that the content of ch. 33 is closely linked to the preceding chs. 28–32, that it functions as a conclusion to the section (details below) and that the new addressees and new thematic elements in chs. 34–35 create a major break between chs. 33 and 34.

If chs. 28–33 may be taken as a unit or a sub-section within chs. 1–39, wherein does its *unity* lie? Are there formal, structural or thematic elements which provide inner coherence, or is there a development of theme or progression of thought which can help the interpreter make sense of this unit in its final, canonical shape?

As long as critics focused on the question of which pericopes stem from the primary level of the Isaianic tradition, the date and the general theme of the genuine oracles could be seen to provide a kind of unity. Thus, excluding 28.1-4, the 'Isaianic' kernel within chs. 28–33 is often assigned mostly to the last period of the prophet's activity (705–701 BCE), the time of Hezekiah's rebellion against the Assyrian Empire. The prophet's message here is seen to be essentially addressed to Judah and Jerusalem and their leading circles, who seek help in the political crisis by making alliances with Egypt (Wildberger 1982). But such a broad understanding of the unity of chs. 28–33 leaves much to be desired, not the least because the historical question dominates and also eliminates from consideration at least half of the material in the unit.

Are there not elements of structure and theme which point to a larger unity of the whole of chs. 28–33? The structuring of the material in this section has apparently been made on the basis of the הוי exclamation which recurs six times (28.1; 29.1; 29.15; 30.1; 31.1; 33.1). Duhm thought that chs. 28–33 are held together by the six woes (also Gray and other commentators). Such a pattern of six woes is already familiar to the reader of the book from 5.8, 11, 18, 20, 21, 22. But unlike 5.8-22, the key woe passages in our unit form subsections which are extended by salvation oracles of diverse kinds (28.5-6, 23-28; 29.5-8, 17-24; 30.18-26; 31.5, 8-9; 33.2-6, 17-24) as well as by additional prophetic announcements of judgment (28.7-22; 29.9-10 etc.).

In comparison with the six woe-sayings in 5.8-22, the series here obviously exhibits a more complex structuring principle. The woe oracles, together with other prophecies of judgment in the unit, are joined with words of salvation which establish a basic pattern of doom-salvation that has frequently been observed within various prophetic books. Moreover, each chapter in the unit concludes with a salvation passage, which means that five of the six woe oracles follow immediately upon a word of salvation (excluding 29.15-16, which does not follow a salvation oracle). The point to be stressed here (following Clements 1978:43-44, 49) is the significance of such structures and patterns which 'coordinate' various kinds of prophetic sayings into a 'unified message'. The pattern can be diagrammed in a simple way:

	Woe		*Woe*		*Woe*
Judgment	28.1-4	28.7-22	29.1-4	29.9-14	29.15-16
Salvation	5-6	23-29	5-8		17-24

	Woe	*Woe*			*Woe*
Judgment	30.1-17	31.1-4	32.9-14		33.1
Salvation	18-26	5-8; 32.1-8		15-20	2-24

The pattern is quite consistent but not entirely symmetrical. Nevertheless, it sets off chs. 28–33 from other sections within chs. 1–39 and gives these chapters their own kind of structural unity and pattern.

A somewhat more complex matter is that of the thematic unity in chs. 28–33. Do one or more themes emerge which lend an overarching cohesion to these chapters? Commentators generally note that most sayings exhibit a similar content (Fohrer 1966) or that these passages represent an 'Assyrian cycle' of oracles (denied, for example, by Kaiser 1973 and Wildberger 1982, but for different reasons). Wildberger (1982: 1558) is content with observing that, while chs. 28–31 contain no 'aufdrängende Unterteilung [intrusive subdivision]', the pericopes all belong to the same epoch and present a 'unified theme'. A. Mauchline (1962) entitles chs. 28–32 'The Rule of God and the Plans of Men.' The royal motif his title emphasizes is echoed by M. Sweeney's (1988a: 61) rubric for chs. 28–35; his structural analysis of the unit leads him to the title, 'Announcement of YHWH's Assumption of Kingship in Jerusalem.' C. Seitz (1993), who takes chs. 28–39 as the larger unit, tentatively suggests in his overview of these chapters that the Zion theme 'might rightly be considered a unifying theme or concern for these various chapters' (1993: 205), but he also includes the reign of a righteous king and wisdom/knowledge as other important themes. But let me now turn to a brief analysis of several themes which suggest a broad unity within chs. 28–33. The limits of the essay require some selectivity, so that the aim of what follows is to be suggestive rather than complete. I limit myself to four themes: (1) Zion/Jerusalem; (2) Yahweh's Exaltation; (3) Hearing/Sight/Insight; (4) Foreign Alliances and the Assyrian Threat.

1. *Zion/Jerusalem*

It is well-known that the Zion/Jerusalem theme is dominant in all three parts of the book of Isaiah (chs. 1–39; 40–55; 56–66; cf. Rendtorff 1993a: 156). Its prominence in the smaller section chs. 28–33 is therefore hardly surprising. Although ch. 28 opens with a judgment saying against Ephraim and its leaders (vv. 1-4), the chapter quickly moves to a focus on Jerusalem and its leaders (vv. 7-14) and then on to Yahweh's work of 'laying a foundation-stone in Zion' (v. 16). Jerusalem is referred to again in ch. 29, where it is called 'Ariel' in vv. 1, 2, 7 and is the object of divine punishment. But the doom changes to salvation in vv. 5-8, where the enemy nations who dare 'fight against Mount Zion' will be thwarted (v. 8). Isa. 30.19 addresses 'the people in Zion who dwell in Jerusalem' and in 31.4 it is prophesied that 'Yahweh of hosts will fight upon/against Mount Zion', but Yahweh will 'protect Jerusalem' (v. 5), whose fire is in Zion...Jerusalem' (v. 9). Neither Jerusalem nor Zion is mentioned by name in ch. 32, but in 32.9-14 a prophetic voice summons women/daughters to lament over the 'joyous houses in the joyful *city*' because the palace and the 'populous *city*' will be destroyed (vv. 13-14); indeed, 'the *city* will be utterly laid low' (v. 19). The unnamed city can be none other than Jerusalem. Chapter 33 returns to the specific mention of Zion/Jerusalem. Although 'sinners dwell in Zion' (v. 14), it is to be filled with 'justice and righteousness' (v. 5). Indeed, the community of worshippers will not only see the king, it is summoned to 'look upon Zion, the city of appointed feasts'; their 'eyes will see Jerusalem', a city that is quiet and immovable (v. 20).

Thus within chs. 28–33 the capital city is named no less than nine times (Jerusalem; Zion; Mount Zion; [Mount] Zion//Jerusalem) and referred to as 'Ariel' or 'city' in another six instances. The distribution is somewhat even in that each chapter contains a direct or an indirect mention of the city. The structure is such that the reader is returned again and again to the Zion/Jerusalem theme, whether it be in contexts of judgment (28.14; 29. 1, 2, 7; 31.4; 32.13-14, 19) or salvation (28.16; 29.8; 30.19; 31.5, 9; 33.5, 20). Significantly, the movement is from judgment to salvation, emphasized not only within redactional units (e.g. 29.1-8; 31.1-5, 8-9) but in the section as a whole, for the first word about Jerusalem is judgment against its rulers (28.14-22), while the conclusion to the unit in ch. 33 proclaims Zion's purification (v. 5) and salvation, for 'there' (in Jerusalem) Yahweh 'will be for us' (v. 20) and 'save us' (v. 22).

2. *Yahweh's Exaltation*

The theme of Yahweh's honour and majesty, which must arise, and human pride or power, which must be brought low, is given particular prominence in chs. 28–33; indeed, the unit begins (28.1-6) and ends (33.3, 5, 10, 21) with texts which set it forth. Important terms for pride, exaltation, majesty, honour, lifted up and so on, abound in these passages. The significance of the theme is indicated by the placement of the woe oracle against Ephraim at the very beginning of our unit. In 28.1-4 the root גאה, which occurs in the book of Isaiah no less than twenty-four times (Stähli 1971: 379), initiates the accusation against Ephraim (Samaria) and its haughty leaders, which are metaphorically characterized as a 'garland of pride' (עטרת גאות, 28.1, 3) that will fade like flowers, and their 'glory' (צבי, vv. 1, 4) will be no more. While human pride must thus be humbled, Yahweh's own 'garland of glory' (אטרת צבי, v. 5), a metaphor for his exaltation or majesty, will be established 'in that day' and the result will be a 'spirit of משפט' for Israel's judges and power for her warriors (v. 6), implying a time of peace and salvation.

In the lament (Wildberger 1982) in 33.2-7, the community prays for grace and salvation, and in response Yahweh asserts his honour by 'lifting himself up' (מרוממתך, v. 3). Here Yahweh's exalting of himself, as in 28.5, is associated with the downfall of his opponents (vv. 3-4). The glorification of Yahweh is continued in 33.5, where Yahweh is praised as 'exalted' (נשׂגב) and 'dwelling on high' (מרום) and, again as in 28.5, Yahweh's exaltation is connected with the bringing of משפט; but to the term 'justice' is now also added a host of other key words belonging to the eschatological age: salvation, righteousness, stability, wisdom, knowledge (v. 5). Yahweh's exaltation is mentioned a third time in the 'oracular response' (Clements 1980a) in vv. 10-13, where in the first-person speech form Yahweh announces, 'Now I will arise (אקום), now I will lift myself up (ארומם), now I will be exalted (אנשׂא, v. 10), actions which result in the destruction of the peoples, who must be 'cut down (קוצים) like thorns' (vv. 11-12). Again, Yahweh's exaltation is connected to the humbling of his enemies. In the prophetic promise in vv. 17-24, Yahweh's majesty is affirmed for the fourth and last time in this chapter. The congregation is exhorted to look upon Zion/Jerusalem, a place of quiet and security. Two parallel sentences (vv. 21-22) provide the motivation, each introduced by כִּי: For Yahweh will be there for us 'in majesty' (אַדִּיר; on the textual problem, cf. Wildberger [1982], who reads יְהִיָה instead of יְהוֹה); for Yahweh, our judge, ruler, king, 'will save us' (יוֹשִׁיעֵנוּ). I therefore note that in both the initial and concluding texts in chs. 28–33, Yahweh's majesty must prevail (28.5; 33.3, 5, 10, 21), while his opponents must be brought low and scattered (28.1-4; 33.3, 11-12). Moreover, in both texts, Yahweh's exaltation is connected with justice (מִשְׁפָּט, 28.6; 33.5). Finally, when Yahweh arises, the result is salvation for his people (28.5-6; 33.21-22). Thus the exaltation theme, which initiates and concludes the section, frames it and gives it a further sense of unity.

But these initial and concluding texts are closely linked to yet a third passage which is found roughly in the middle of chs. 28–33; namely, the brief, isolated promise of salvation in 30.18, whose language is reminiscent of the Psalms (Fohrer 1966). Here Yahweh's exaltation of himself (יָרוּם; on the textual problem, cf. Wildberger 1982) is tied to his gracious disposition (חָנַן, רַחֵם) as well as to his justice (מִשְׁפָּט). The exaltation theme in 30.18 recalls Yahweh's 'garland of honour' in 28.5, but the term יָרוּם provides a precise verbal link to the verbs (root רוּם) in 33.3, 5, 10, while the close association of Yahweh's majesty and his justice (מִשְׁפָּט) in 30.18 connects it both to 28.6 and especially to 33.5 (compare 'he exalts himself/Yahweh is a God of justice' [30.18], with 'Yahweh is exalted...dwells on high/fills Zion with justice' [33.5]). Finally, 30.18 exhibits a close connection with 33.2 (cf. Williamson 1994: 231). In both texts there is a 'waiting' (the verbs are different) for grace (חָנַן): Yahweh 'waits to be gracious' (30.18) and his people 'wait for him' (30.18; 33.2), hoping for his 'grace' (33.2).

These three texts, 28.1-6; 30.18; and 33.2-24, occurring at the beginning, middle, and end of the section, exhibit close thematic and linguistic ties which further suggest a thematic unity to the section. The motifs of exaltation and honouring of Yahweh, the humbling of his opponents, and the waiting to give or receive divine grace are like threads which, in their linking together of the three passages, suggest to the reader a coherent arrangement which presents a sense of the section's unity.

3. *Hearing/Sight/Insight*

That Israel has difficulty in 'seeing' and 'hearing' is clear from the entire book of Isaiah. But a particular prominence is given to this theme in chs. 28–33. Early on in the unit, in the first text that turns to the Southern Kingdom (28.7-13), the reader is directed to the troubled 'sight' of the prophets; in a drunken stupor, they 'err in seeing' (בראה v. 7). The passage concludes on an accusatory note in v. 12, with a reproach against 'this people': 'yet they would not hear' (שמוע). The passage underscores the significance of eye and ear in Israel's inability to receive a message from its God. The concluding pericope in ch. 28, the 'wisdom parable' in vv. 23-29, has been prepared for by, and thus looks back to, the 'refusal to hear' in v. 12. The parable begins with the insistent, four-part appeal of the wisdom teacher to listen: 'Give ear to/hear my voice, hearken unto/hear my speech' (v. 23). Those who have refused to listen are now invited not only to hear but to accept instruction, teaching (v. 26), wisdom and counsel (v. 29). The movement of thought within the chapter is from error in seeing/refusal to listen, to the invitation to hear, and then to the gaining of insight. But the further emphasis in the chapter on 'hearing' is not to be overlooked, as is indicated by the prophet's 'summons to hear the word of Yahweh' in v. 14 and his own report of a message of destruction in v. 22: 'I have *heard...*'

The prophets' difficulty in seeing in 28.7 now in 29.9-10 turns into the problem of their blindness (v. 9). The imperative 'blind yourselves' (v. 9) stands in ironic contrast to the imperatives to 'hear' in 28.23. But the reason for the prophets' (taking MT as it stands) blindness is given in v. 10, for a deep sleep, whose source is Yahweh, has closed their eyes: they *cannot* see. A further link between 29.9-10 and 28.7 is seen not only in the reference to drunkenness, which the texts have in common, but in its resultant stumbling and staggering about. This close connection of the two texts has been made even more explicit by the later hand which added the words 'the prophets...the seers' to 29.10.

The seeing/hearing difficulties of prophets and people, associated with debauchery or lack of will in 28.7, 12 and 29.9-10, has prepared the reader for a succinct statement of the blind/deaf theme in 29.18. Here, in the larger context of a prophecy of salvation (vv. 17-21), the spiritual lethargy of the past is to be reversed in the impending future ('yet a little while', v. 17):

> In that day the deaf shall hear
> the words of a book,
> and out of their gloom and darkness
> the eyes of the blind shall see. (RSV, 29.18)

While the theme of blindness/sight thus links chs. 28 and 29 together, 29.18 is also closely connected to its surrounding context in ch. 29 by a play on the word 'to see'. Whereas v. 18 prophesies that 'eyes of the blind will see' (תראינה), in the immediately preceding woe oracle in 29.15-16, those who hide from Yahweh ask, 'Who sees us?' (ראנו). But in the passage following 29.18 in vv. 22-24, a sign of the eschatological age is that Jacob will 'see his children' (בראתו, v. 23), worship God and 'come to understanding (בינה) and accept instruction' (v. 24). Thus the juxtaposition of the two texts 29.17-21 and 29.22-24 and the connection made by the term 'to see' (vv. 18, 23) reinforces the relationship of sight to insight/understanding and recalls the wisdom poem in 28.23-29: he who 'hears' is instructed and comes to understanding, counsel, and wisdom (vv. 26, 29). Similarly, in 29.17-21, 22-24, when the deaf hear and the shall blind see, Yahweh's people will see (v. 23) and achieve 'understanding' (בינה v. 24), that which was formerly hidden from the wise due to divine judgment (root בין twice in v. 14).

Isaiah 30.9-10 combines elements from 29.7 (prophets and seeing) and from 28.12 (refusal to hear) and connects them in an ironic way: the rebels who refuse to hear instruction (30.9) forbid the prophets to see (v. 10). Indeed, their perversity is underscored by the last line of v. 11: 'let us no more hear of the Holy One of Israel'. The blind/deaf theme recurs again in 30.20-21, where it is promised, in an extended prose description of Jerusalem's salvation, that 'your eyes shall see your teacher and your ears shall hear a word...' But in v. 30 it is no longer Yahweh's representative but God himself who is the object of the people's spiritual perception, for Yahweh's voice will be heard and the blow of his arm seen. Even more, in v. 31 the Assyrians will hear his voice as well as the 'sound of timbrels' and be terrified (v. 31).

The theme continues in a text that announces the advent of the righteous king (32.1-5), whose coming will bring sight to the blind and hearing to the deaf (v. 3); to see and to hear means to 'understand (יבין; cf. 29.14, 16, 24). While 32.1-5 is linked most closely to 29.17-18, it introduces a new perspective by connecting the blind/deaf motif with royal ideology. By virtue of this connection, it serves well as a transition to the emphasis on 'sight' in 33.17-24. The close connection between

32.1-5 and 33.17-24 has often been noted (cf. Clements 1980a, who speaks of the influence of 32.1-5 on 33.17-24). It could be argued that in 33.17-24. all the previous passages about 'seeing' are brought to a proper conclusion. The prophet in v. 17 addresses his audience in the second-person singular: 'Your eyes will see the king and behold a land...' While 32.1-5 connects the coming of the righteous king with the opening of eyes and ears, here the *king* himself becomes the object of Israel's vision. To see the king (v. 17) means that 'they will see no more' their enemies, whose obscure tongue will no longer be heard or understood (בינה, v. 19, which makes a verbal link to 28.9, 19; 29.14, 16, 24; 32.4). Finally, in v. 20 we come to the last reference to seeing in the entire unit. The prophet commands, 'Look upon Zion...your eyes will see Jerusalem.' But it is not really the city that they are to behold as much as it is Yahweh, for 'there Yahweh will be for us' (v. 21), the king who will 'save us' (v. 22). Sight thus means salvation.

The theme of blind/deaf, sight/hearing and insight which I have traced throughout chs. 28–33, reveals any number of cross-references and verbal linkages. The many interconnections suggest some continuity as well as development. Prophets stumble in vision (28.7) and people refuse to hear (28.12; 30.9, 11), while forbidding the prophets to see (30.9). Yet those who would listen to the wisdom of the parable gain insight and instruction (28.26, 29). But the new era of salvation which is about to break in will transform the (spiritually) deaf and blind, who will then see and hear (29.18; 30.20, 21; 32.3). Indeed, their ability to see will lead them not only to worship (29.23) but to insight (29.24; 32.4). The new gift of sight and sound belongs to the time when the righteous king appears (32.1, 3), but in the age of salvation (33.5-6) it is God as majestic king (33.17) and his chosen city (33.20) which will become the object of human sight. The many instances of the theme, albeit in a variety of forms and contexts, and their close interrelationships are further indicative of coherence and unity in the present shape of chs. 28–33.

4. *Foreign Alliances and the Assyrian Threat*

A main theme in the unit chs. 28–33, but which is by no means contained in each chapter (only chs. 28–31), is that of Judah's rebellion against Assyria and alliance with Egypt (Kissane 1941; Scott 1956; Clements 1980a). While it cannot be claimed that this theme creates as broad and significant a unity as the previously discussed themes, it nevertheless requires brief explication for our purposes. According to 30.1-5 the league with Egypt, which seeks its counsel and protection, will result only in shame and disgrace for Judah. It accords neither with Yahweh's plan (v. 1) nor counsel (v. 2). The league with Egypt is probably what is meant by the highly ironic (Clements 1980a) words put into the mouths of the scoffers in 28.15 ('We have made a covenant with death'), although Egypt is not named. In 31.1-3 a woe oracle, parallel in many ways to 30.1-5, pronounces doom on those who 'go down to Egypt' and falsely rely and trust (יבטחו // ישענו; cf. 30.12) in their chariots and horsemen; Egypt's help is worth nothing (30.7). The impending doom is to come from Assyria, although the empire is not named in the various announcements of judgment on the nation (28.17-21; 29.2-4, 14; 30.3-5, 13-14, 17; 31.3-4; cf. 32.9-14). The Assyrians are mentioned, however, in texts which speak of their own doom (30.31; 31.8).

II

1. *Chapters 28–33 and 1–12*

These two major sections, chs. 1–12 and chs. 28–33, now separated by the intervening chs. 13–27, are generally considered to be closely associated: each contains a nucleus of 'genuine' sayings; each represents a combination of prophecies of doom and salvation; each has undergone some of the same redactional moves at later stages in the development of the tradition (e.g. Barth 1978) and so on. On the other hand, the tradition did not leave them standing side by side in the book, and thus they form, it is generally held, two different tradition 'complexes' or collections. According to Clements (1980a: 3), chs. (1) 2–12 is the 'primary collection' while 28–31 (33) is 'an important supplementary collection'. How is this to be explained? Do chs. 28–33 simply come, more or less, from a later period of Isaiah's activity (705–701?) and just happen to have been collected into another group, with, in a sense, a life of their own? Are they a supplement or a complement? Or could the editors of chs. 1–12 not find a way to incorporate chs. 28–33 into the first major section of the book? Of course, we will never know. But the more significant question to be asked here is, given these two separate, different collections, In what ways are they connected, interrelated, linked? Are there similarities in structure? As one reads chs. 28–33, are there allusions backward, echoes, or perhaps straight-forward repetitions or new applications which connect the unit to previously occurring themes and motifs in chs. 1–12? Or might there even be some development or refinement of theme to be recognized in a comparison of the two sections? To offer a detailed answer to such questions is not possible in a brief essay, but perhaps what follows might suggest something of the nature of the relationship and linkages between chs. 28–33 and chs. 1–12.

A. First, it will be instructive to consider several structural similarities and dissimilarities. Chs. 28–33 do not have a superscription or title that mark the clear beginning of a new section; there is nothing comparable to 1.1; 2.1 (cf. 13.1; 15.1; 17.1; 19.1; 22.1; 23.1). On the contrary, the 'woe' in 28.1 stands unmediated after 27.13, an eschatological prophecy about the gathering of the people of God to worship on the holy mountain. On the other hand, the closure to chs. 1–12 in 12.1-6 finds a counterpart in 33.2-24. Here I will briefly note (see below for further comparison of chs. 33 and 12) that, with the Psalm-like, liturgical character of both ch. 12 and ch. 33 and their emphasis on the exaltation of Yahweh and his salvation, they both clearly and similarly mark a conclusion to what precedes and serve as a transition to the sections that follow each (chs. 13–23, chs. 34–35). The series of six woes (already discussed above) in chs. 28–33, the structural underpinning of the unit, is surely reminiscent of the series of six in 5.8-22 (Conrad 1991: 124-30; cf. Seitz 1993: 206). But the woe-cry of the brief series in ch. 5.8-22 has become the chief marker of structure in chs. 28–33, where the scaffold-like arrangement suggests that the 'woes' are that on which the other pieces within each chapter depend for the ordering of the material. In any case, the woes in each unit (1–12; 28–33), by virtue of the inter-connection created between the units, can be seen by the reader as pointing forward or backward, thus creating a tie that jumps across chs. 13–27, as it were, putting our two units into a close affinity that cannot be overlooked. The pattern of doom-salvation in chs. 28–33 explored above is of course present in the structure of chs. 1–12, but without the same more tightly organized, alternating structure in chs. 28–33. Thus the promise of salvation in 2.1-5 follows Yahweh's judgment on Jerusalem in 1.24-31; the announcement of salvation in 4.2-6 comes after the judgment on the proud women of Jerusalem in 3.14–4.1; the messianic oracle 9.1-6 (2-7) follows upon judgment pronounced on the mediums and wizards in 8.19-23 (9.1); 10.20-27a promises hope for a remnant after words of doom to Assyria in 10.12-19; the prophecy of a messianic age in 11.1-16 follows upon the punishment expected on Judah from the Assyrians in 10.27b-34. It should further be noted that, while of course chs. 28–33 do not contain any narrative material like the memoirs in 6.1–8.18, the salvation oracles common to both sections appear to be placed intentionally more toward the end of the sections (9.2-6 (7); 11.1-9; 32.1-18; 33.17-24). But here we might pause to ask whether chs. 28–33 contain anything to suggest that they, like chs. 1–12, are shaped in order to make a 'presentation of a prophet', as Ackroyd has argued in his study of chs. 1–12 (Ackroyd 1987a: 80-104). Clearly, the two units differ in their basic structure and ordering of the material. But if close linkages of the two sections suggest that much of what is found in chs. 28–33 mirrors, echoes, parallels or expands chs. 1–12, then the way would be clear to read chs. 28–33 less as a supplementary appendix to chs. 1–12 and more as an extension and completion of these chapters. Put another way, do chs. 28–33 re-present essential themes and interests first met in chs. 1–12, or do they rather, by virtue of the position after chs. 13–27, take the reader further on the journey through the book. Of course, they might do both. But this question can be left open at this point.

B. The very first pericope in 28.1-6, although it is linked to the succeeding chapters by the woe-cry, immediately establishes connections with chs. 1–12. Some critics have considered the passage 'out of place' in that it belongs before or at the time of the fall of Samaria and thus is earlier than the core material in chs. 28–33 and supposedly would have its rightful or original place within chs. 1–12, or perhaps within the section 'Oracles against the Nations', chs. 13–23 (Fohrer 1967; Wildberger 1982). Whatever its original place, 28.1-6 now provides the introduction to the larger unit chs. 28–33. Significantly, the judgment on Ephraim (Samaria) in vv. 1-4 finds no echoes in the rest of chs. 28–33, but it points backward especially to 9.7-20 (Eng. vv. 8-21), a word of judgment against Jacob/Israel and Ephraim/Samaria (cf. 7.8-9; 8.4; 10.9-11; 7.8). In 9.7-20, as in 28.1, 4, the accusation against the Northern Kingdom is associated with their 'pride' (root גאה). The first passage in chs. 28–33 thus forms a connection with a previous, similar announcement of judgment upon Ephraim and an immediate bridge is built between chs. 1–12 and 28–32. The 'first Ephraim then Judah' program is reflected in the structure of ch. 28 (vv. 1-4, judgment on Ephraim; vv. 7-22, judgment on Judah) and recalls the words put into the mouth of Assyria in 10.11: 'Shall I not do to Jerusalem and her idols as I have done to Samaria and her images'; compare as well the structure of 9.7[8]–10.4, where the focus moves from Ephraim/Samaria to the rulers of Jerusalem (10.1-4; cf. the superscription in Mic. 1.1: 'Samaria [then] Jerusalem', and the structure of Mic. ch. 1: judgment comes first to Samaria [1.2-7], but then upon Judah/Jerusalem [8-16]).

In 28.1-6 the theme of Yahweh's honour/majesty which humbles the debauched, false pride of humans or governments, and which is identified above as a significant theme in chs. 28–33 (30.18; 33.2-24), finds connections within chs. 1–12. Indeed, in 2.6-19 a thesis-like statement is made: The haughty looks of people shall be brought low and the pride of everyone humbled and Yahweh alone will be exalted' (v. 11; cf. v. 9). The vocabulary of the entire piece concerns itself with human arrogance, pride, exaltation, majesty, glory and the humbling thereof by the exalted Lord. The theme recurs in the accusation and threat against the daughters of Zion in 3.16–4.1. Again in 5.15-16 the prideful are brought low and Yahweh is exalted in justice, a passage exhibiting affinities with 30.18 and 33.5, where in both texts the connection between divine exaltation and justice is made. But especially does the pride of the king of Assyria come under attack in 10.12-19, where a long quotation (vv. 13-14) illustrates his 'arrogant boasting and the elevated pride of his eyes' (v. 12), whose presumption of 'glory' (vv. 16, 18) leads to his destruction. Finally, the emphasis on the exaltation of Yahweh in Zion and the ensuing grace and salvation in 33.2-24 has important connections with ch. 12. Both 33.5, 21 and 12.6 envision Yahweh to be in Zion; in both he is exalted (נשׂגב in both 33.5 and 12.4; cf. also 33.3, 10, 21 and the replete vocabulary of majesty, honour etc. in 12.4) and is the bringer of salvation (root ישׁע; cf. 33.22). The thematic and verbal links and the close affinities of both texts with the Psalms make the connection between them exceptionally strong. The connection gains in significance in that both texts conclude major sections.

If there are parallels between the conclusions to the units in chs. 12 and 33, what of the beginnings? In that 28.1-6, the introduction of the unit, reaches back and connects closely with 2.6-22, as noted above, which together with 3.1–4.1 serves as the 'preface' to the next (redactional) unit 5.1–14.27 (thus Clements 1980a), we observe a parallel function of the initial pronouncements of judgment in both units, 28.1-6 and 2.6-22: both serve an introductory function to what follows.

Isa. 28.1-6 contains the first words of salvation in chs. 28–33. Verses

5-6, introduced by the eschatological formula, 'in that day', have, as Duhm noted early on, a very close parallel in 4.2-6, also begun by the same formula. The function of each passage in its respective context is of course different. Isa. 28.5-6 announces a time of salvation for a 'remnant' after the destruction of Ephraim in vv. 1-4, to which vv. 5-6 belong. On the other hand, 4.2-6 is not closely knit to the preceding oracle of doom but rather provides a conclusion to the unit 2.1–4.6 (Duhm, 1892; Fohrer 1966). But the affinities between 28.5-6 and 4.2-6 are not obscure (cf. Duhm 1892; Petersen 1979: 107-108, who both speculate that there is common authorship). In addition to similarities in verse-structure, one notes the verbal linkages made by a shared vocablulary (glory, צבי, and beauty, תפארת; root גאה, 28.1, 3 and 4.2) and reference to a 'remnant' (root שאר, 28.5; 4.3; cf. 10.20-23 with which 4.5 has particular affinities, and Rendtorff 1993a: 159-60 for other examples of the concept in chs. 1–12). Moreover, the phrase רוח משפט occurs in both but functions differently: the spirit of judgment in 4.4 purifies, in 28.6 it empowers judges and warriors. The two similar texts connect chs. 28–33 with chs. 1–12 and suggest by this tie that both sections speak a uniform voice in portraying the impending day of salvation. But further connections to chs. 1–12 are suggested by the 'spirit of justice' that is to rest upon the judges in 28.6, which is within chs. 28–33 linked to 32.1 ('princes will rule in justice') and 32.15 ('spirit is poured out...justice will dwell'). Taken together these texts exhibit a close affinity with 1.26-27, which speaks of restored judges in the purified 'city of justice' (v. 21), for 'Zion shall be redeemed by justice'(v. 27). But 28.6; 32.1, 15 also recall 11.1-9, where the main task of the son of Jesse, equipped with the spirit of Yahweh, is to judge with equity (Wildberger 1982).

The introductory passage in 28.1-6, due to the various connections with chs. 1–12 just explored, brings the reader back to the first section of the book. Immediately a relationship between the two parts is established by the initial woe-cry. But the connection is deepened by the links to the doom announced for Ephraim/Samaria, by Yahweh's rejection of human pride and arrogance, but also by the promise of the spirit of justice and the salvation of a remnant. Finally, the introduction found in 28.1-6 recalls the early 'preface' in 2.6-22; both lead into the series of judgment oracles that follow.

C. The complex interplay of judgment and salvation for Jerusalem within what has been commonly called the 'Zion tradition' in Isaiah is explored widely, although certainly not without debate, within the scholarly literature. Conclusions about the interpretation of the Zion tradition in the book of Isaiah, as is well-known, hinge upon presuppositions concerning literary and redaction-critical approaches and other critical views about development as well as the final shape of texts. Moreover, the interest among tradition critics has been the question of the roots of the tradition in older Canaanite or cultic theology (see the major discussion in Clements 1980b). Without entering into the discussions, for such is not my purpose here, the question to be put is a simpler one: are there significant ties or connections between the two sections of the book, chs. 28–33 and chs. 1–12, which are established by the Zion/Jerusalem theme? Rendtorff (1993a: 155-60), in an essay that especially develops his concern with the 'composition' of the book of Isaiah, offers a brief overview of the Zion/Jerusalem theme, especially as it is found in chs. 1–12 and 40–66. Relative to chs. 1–12, Rendtorff points to the 'link...between the proclamation of judgment and the proclamation of salvation' that emerges within the 'far-ranging group of topics' associated with the Zion/Jerusalem theme, and he finds the whole unit (chs. 1–12) to be encircled by the theme (1.8; 12.6); further, he suggests that the tenor of it all is 'marked by assurances of salvation in 2.2-5; 4.2-6, and chap. 12' (1993a: 156-57). His comparison with the next chapters (13–35) leads him to conclude that there the theme remains undeveloped in any detail and simply appears randomly and somewhat abruptly. But let me explore a few more details of the theme in chs. 28–33 and chs. 1–12. In general it can be said that both sections share the punishment-salvation dialectic. Thus 29.1-8 and 31.1-5 present Jerusalem first as under seige, but then miraculously protected. Such texts immediately refer the reader back to 2.6–4.6, a unit Rendtorff (1993a: 156) says is filled with the 'tension-laden antithesis between indictment and a message of salvation' for Zion. The pattern 'Zion indicted/threatened then rescued' establishes a thematic as well as a structural parallel between chs. 1–12 and 28–33.

In chs. 28–33, various expressions closely associate Yahweh with Zion/Jerusalem: Yahweh *lays* a foundation there (28.16); *fights* against and/or upon Mount Zion; *protects* Jerualem (31.4, 5); his fire *is in* Zion/Jerusalem (31.9); he *fills* Zion with justice/righteousness (33.5); 'there' (in Zion) Yahweh is *'for us'* (33.21). These significant statements about Yahweh's action in or for Zion stretch across the unit and occur at significant intervals in such a way that suggests both continuity and a web of interconnection. Such formulations as we have here, in which the pattern of the expression is 'Yahweh + verb + Zion' occurs only twice in chs. 1–12. In 8.18, Isaiah says, having required the binding and sealing of the testimony, that he waits for 'Yahweh of hosts, who dwells on Mount Zion'. And in 10.12, which serves as an introduction to the long quotation of the king of Assyria (vv. 13-14), a prose summary refers to the future punishment of the king, 'When Yahweh has finished all his work on Mount Zion and Jerusalem'. Such similar expressions in the two units tie them together and signal to the reader that chs. 28–33 take up and reiterate these motifs from chs. 1–12. But it should be noted that the explicit relationship of Yahweh to Zion, as indicated by the six occurrences of the phrases referred to above (28.16; 31.4-5; 31.9; 33.5, 21), represent a further emphasis as well as a development of Yahweh's complex presence in Jerusalem as presented in chs. 1–12.

Yahweh's *saving* presence *in Zion*, however, is the final note sounded in both units in the concluding passages in 33.2-24 and 12.1-6. The connection of salvation with Zion is explicit. After the congregation prays that Yahweh 'be our salvation' (ישׁועתנו) in 12.2, the promise is made that Yahweh will fill Zion with salvation (ישׁעה) in v. 6. And according to 33.20-22, it is in Zion/Jerusalem that Yahweh will 'save us' (יושׁיענו). Zion is mentioned three times and the root ישׁע occurs three times. But the root has an equally important and significant function in 12.1-6 where it is also connected with Zion (12.6). Ackroyd (1987a: 96-97) in particular has pointed out that within chs. 1–12 the root ישׁע occurs only in ch. 12, apart from the previous instances of Isaiah's name, and further, that this language has links to the Psalms. Thus the clear focus on 'salvation' marks an important connection between 33.2-24 and 12.1-6 and this connection is further strengthened by the reference to Zion. But in addition to the verbal linkages between the two texts, it must be emphasized that the similarity of their function as conclusions to the two units is of major significance. Therefore, in that ch. 33 establishes such a parallel to ch. 12, the unit chs. 28–33 is likewise placed parallel to chs. 1–12. But such a conclusion about the close connection between chs. 33 and 12 has implications for Ackroyd's interpretation of ch. 12 within the unit chs. 1–12. He states concerning ch. 12 that 'there is a strong inference that [it] provides an interpretative comment on what precedes, drawing out in a final poetic statement the broadest significance for the prophet's person and message' (1987a: 97-98). In the light of the close relationship of ch. 33 to ch. 12, is it not possible that Ackroyd's understanding of the function of ch. 12 also fits precisely that of ch. 33? And, if we consider the many other linkages between chs. 28–33 and chs. 1–12, is it not possible that Ackroyd's thesis—namely, that chs. 1–12 make a 'presentation of the prophet' (1987a 102)—is not limited to chs. 1–12 (and to chs. 36–39, thus Ackroyd 1987b: 115-16) only? This would mean that chs. 28–33 further, promote and even complete the job of giving Isaiah the status of authority presented in chs. 1–12, as Ackroyd has argued for those chapters (1987a: 103). The main point to be made for the purposes of this essay, therefore, is that chs. 28–33 do not simply present significant ties and connecting threads to the collection of oracles in chs. 1–12, whereby the reader is reminded again and again of similarities, echoes, cross-references and the like. These chapters also participate in the function of enhancing and completing the 'presentation of a prophet' begun in chs. 1–12. It may therefore be suggested that chs. 28–33 are not a supplement but rather a complement to chs. 1–12.

D. But let me explore further, by way of continuing the discussion of the connections between the two units, how chs. 28–33 might 'enhance' and 'complete' chs. 1–12, for such a claim remains too general without further explication.

I took note above of the prophecies of salvation in 29.17-21 and 32.1-5 and their common theme, 'sight to the blind, hearing to the deaf' and of the various interconnections with other texts within chs. 28–33 (esp. 30.20-21; 33.17-20). This theme of course harks back to Isaiah's vision reported in ch. 6 and the words Yahweh commissions him to speak:

'Hear, indeed, but do not understand;
See, indeed, but do not grasp'.
Dull that people's mind,
Stop its ears,
And seal its eyes—
Lest seeing with its eyes
And hearing with its ears,
It also grasp with its mind,
And repent and save [lit. 'heal'] itself. (*Tanakh*, vv. 9-10)

For the reader of chs. 28–33, the link to these words in Isaiah's commission in ch. 6 is impossible to overlook. The 'blind yourself and be blind' of 29.9 echoes the command to 'shut their eyes' in 6.10; the verb in both is שׁעע, the same which occurs in the promise in 32.3: 'the eyes of those who see will not be closed' (reading שׁעע, I, 'to be smeared

over, blinded' [BDB: 1044], instead of שעה [cf. Wildberger 1982]). Isa.
29.18; 30.20-21; and 32.3 as we have seen above, prophesy an impending time of salvation which reverses the spiritual blindness and deafness
of the people of God referred to in 6.9-10 (Clements 1985: 103-104),
while 33.17-20 pick up only the 'seeing' motif to elaborate on the
salvation which is to come. Thus the judgment that 'hardens the
people's hearts' in ch. 6 is pointedly changed to salvation in which they
come to 'understanding'; that is, insight. The inability to 'understand,
discern' (6.9-10; cf. 29.14) is transformed into clear perception (29.18,
23-24; 32.3-4, בין; the root occurs in 6.9-10; 28.9, 19; 29.14, 16, 24;
32.4; 33.19). The ability to see the king and Zion (33.17, 20) in the new
age means the disappearance of confusion due to not 'understanding'
(יבין) a foreign tongue (33.19). Thus the texts in chs. 28–33 exhibit
direct (29.18; 30.20-21; 32.3) or less direct (29.14; 33.17, 19-20) connections to 6.9-10 by virtue of the blind/deaf theme or the related motifs of
'understanding/insight'. These texts thus take the theme and 'enhance'
and supplement it by reinterpreting it in terms of reversal or restoration.

E. A number of other verbal linkages between chs. 28–33 and chs. 1–
12 can be only briefly explored here. (1) The foundation stone in 28.16
might be understood to recall the stone of offence in 8.14-15. (2) The
word-pair 'justice–righteousness' (משפט-צדקה) in 28.17, where it
denotes a measure to be used in the coming judgment and is linked to
Zion in the preceding verse (v. 16), recalls 1.21-28, where 'the words
are already central terms in the divine word about Jerusalem' (Rendtorff
1993b: 186). The word-pair in 28.17 also points back to 5.7: 'he looked
for justice/righteousness'. In 32.1 the king who is to reign in righteous-
ness/justice is reminiscent of the rule of the 'stump of Jesse' in 11.1-9,
whose judgment will be done with righteousness (צדק occurs twice, without משפט), a text with which 33.5-6 has numerous affinities (details in
Beuken 1991: 16-17); compare 33.5-6 with 11.3-5.

(3) In the 'refusal to hear' motif in 28.12 and 30.9, one can discern a
connection with Isaiah's memoir (6.1–8.18), which tells of Ahaz's refusal
to listen to Isaiah's message of hope. As with king, so with people. The
judgment upon those who refuse to listen in 28.12 is that they will
'stumble' (v. 13, כשל) upon a word from Yahweh and be broken. This
punishment in v. 13 is clearly linked to 8.14-15, where Yahweh *himself*
(not his 'word', as in 28.12) becomes a rock of מכשל upon which both
houses of Israel will stumble (כשלו); the connection becomes most direct
in that the words in 28.13bβ correspond precisely to 8.15bβ: 'they shall

fall, be broken, snared, taken'.

(4) The false trust/reliance upon Egypt of which the rulers are accused in 31.1 (cf. 30.1-2, 15-16) consitutes a rejection of the prophetic message which calls for 'return, rest, quietness (בהשקט), and trust' (30.15). These words in 30.15, in the context of a messenger speech from Yahweh God, the Holy One of Israel, are reminiscent of what the prophet was commanded to speak to Ahaz in 7.4: 'Take heed, be quiet (השקט), do not fear...', a connection made especially by the root שקט. The cross-reference made by the similarities of form (messenger speech) and content further tie our two units together.

(5) The significance of the phrase 'Holy One of Israel' (30.15) for Isaiah is well known, and recently Rendtorff has noted especially its function in connecting the three major parts of the book of Isaiah (Rendtorff 1993a: 160-62). The phrase is important within chs. 28–33, where it is found a total of six times (29.19, 23; 30.11, 12, 15; 31.1). In the context of prophecies of salvation, the 'Holy One of Israel' is the object of the people's worship (29.19, 23 [Holy One of *Jacob*//God of Israel]). But it also occurs as a part of prophetic accusations against rulers who say, 'let us hear no more of the Holy One of Israel' (30.11) or who refuse to 'look to the Holy One of Israel' (31.1). Such scoffers indeed will hear more, as 30.12 and 15 make clear, for in these two verses the 'Holy One of Israel' speaks the message of indictment and judgment which the prophet proclaims, and for which the messenger formula '[therefore] thus says the Holy One of Israel' serves as an introduction. These two groups of texts, proclamations of salvation or judgment, stand parallel to the uses of the phrase in chs. 1–12, which according to Rendtorff is connected to themes of rejection (1.4; 5.24) and scorning/mocking (5.19) within prophecies of judgment, or is related to future salvation when the remnant of Israel will 'lean upon Yahweh, the Holy One of Israel' (10.20). But the salvation texts in 29.19 and 29.23 suggest acts of worship in the 'exulting' and 'sanctifying' of the Holy One of Israel. Hence, we find an important, close connection between them and 12.1-6, which throughout has to do with liturgical acts of thanks and praise offered in joy. Thus 29.19, 23 picks up the accents on liturgical action within 12.1-6, and, together with the epithet 'Holy One of Israel' which occurs in 12.6, forges another link between chs. 28–33 and chs. 1–12.

2. *Chapters 28–33 and 13–23*

Are there significant connections between chs. 28–33 and the section known as the 'Oracles Against the Nations' in chs. 13–23? To pose the question a different way, is the reader of chs. 28–33 sent back, as it were, to chs. 13–23 by the occurrence of similar themes or motifs? What, if anything, might tie these two essentially different sections of the book of Isaiah together? Some critics have noted that 28.1-6 would be more at home in chs. 13–23 than in its present location (Fohrer 1966). Wildberger (1982) thinks that 28.1-4 has close affinities with 17.1-6 and was possibly relocated to it present context because of the drunkenness motif (cf. 28.7-13). This itself suggests a link between chs. 28–33 and chs. 13–23 of some significance in that 28.1-6 is the introductory oracle of the section. Further, the series of woe-cries in chs. 28–33, in addition to the series in ch. 5, has a precursor in 18.1. The 'Oracle (משׂא) on the beasts of the Negeb' in 30.6-7, which speaks of Egypt's worthlessness (v. 6), is thought by some critics (e.g. Duhm 1892; Ackroyd 1987a: 92) to have originally belonged to the משׂא oracles in chs. 13–23. In any case, the similarities between 30.6-7 and much of the material in chs. 13ff. suggest another link between chs. 28–33 and chs. 13–23. What other connections might there be?

The arrogance (גאות) and glory (צבי) of a nation and its subsequent destruction, as noted above in 28.1-4 in relation to Ephraim/Samaria, is found in connection with the 'Oracle concerning Babylon' in ch. 13. Indeed, its pride (גאון) will be put to an end and its arrogance (גאות) laid low (13.11; cf. v. 3); Babylon's glory (צבי), splendour (תפארת) and pride (גאון) 'will be like Sodom and Gomorrah' (v. 19), while 14.11 prophesies that 'your pomp (גאונך) will be brought down to Sheol'. In 16.16 Moab's pride and arrogance (root גאה occurs four times; cf. 28.1, 3), insolence and boasting, will end in lamentation, with Moab in a stricken condition (v. 7). Indeed, his 'glory' (כבוד) will be brought into contempt (v. 14). Thus, divine judgment on Yahweh's people for its pride extends also to foreign nations. But in the 'oracle against Damascus' in 17.4, it is also the Northern Kingdom, as in 28.1-6, which will be brought low because of an assumed status of exaltation; that is, the 'glory (כבוד) of Jacob', a corollary of Ephraim's 'garland of honour' in 28.1, 3.

Egypt is the object of Judah's league-making and political hope in 30.1-5 and 31.1-3. The end of the Egyptians is prophesied in 31.3, who as Judah's 'helper' will stumble and perish with Judah. But in the 'oracle concerning Egypt' in ch. 19 (cf. 18.1-2), Egypt's destruction is taken up and expanded greatly in two prophecies: vv. 1-15 and vv. 16-25; civil strife and bad politics (foolish counsel, v. 11) will lead to confusion (vv. 3, 14) and disaster (vv. 5-10). On the other hand, according to vv. 19-20, Egypt will come to worship Yahweh, who will reveal himself to them (v. 21), a theme unknown in chs. 28–33. In ch. 20 Isaiah prophesies the demise of Egypt, which will be led away captive by Assyria. Significantly, v. 6, which closes the passage, speaks of the (false) hope in Egypt, 'to whom we fled for help'. The connection between this verse and 31.1 ('woe to those who go down to Egypt for help') and also with 30.2 ('who set out to go down to Egypt...to take refuge') links chs. 30 and 31 closely with ch. 20. The reader of chs. 28–33 has therefore already heard of the fall of Egypt, so that the passages about the league with Egypt in chs. 30 and 31 are understood in the context of Egypt's demise. The question would thus arise: How can Egypt help Judah if its fate is already sealed?

The close connection between 31.1 and 17.7-8 has been noted by Wildberger (1982), among others. In 31.1 the woe-cry is directed against those who 'do not look (שָׁעוּ) to the Holy One of Israel or consult Yahweh'. But in 17.7, with similar phrasing, a salvation oracle, prefaced by 'in that day', proclaims that 'people will regard (יִשְׁעָה) their maker, and their eyes will look to the Holy One of Israel' (cf. 33.7). The indictment against those who disregard Yahweh's counsel in 31.1 points the reader back to a text which foresees a time when the Holy One of Israel, as creator, will be looked to by faithful people, rather than to the creations of their own hands (v. 8).

The Zion theme surfaces in 14.32, which presents a close parallel to 28.16. In the latter, believers in Yahweh are promised security because of the foundation stone laid (יִסַּד) in Zion. This text recalls the similar words of 14.32, in which the messengers of the nations are told, 'Yahweh has founded (יִסַּד) Zion, and in her the afflicted of his people find refuge.' It further recalls 18.7 ('Mount Zion, the place of the name of Yahweh of hosts'), a promise of comfort which is picked up in 30.19; 31.5; especially 31.9; 33.20-21. These various connections between chs. 28–33 and chs. 13–23, which make no claim to completeness, suggest that these two units, while they contain appreciably different kinds of prophetic material and are separated by the unit chs. 24–27, exhibit significant links that help to establish unity within the book.

3. *Chapters 28–33 and 24–27*

Critical scholarship, in making the customary, strict division between
chs. 24–27 and chs. 28–33 within the book of Isaiah has of course based
this on the many differences of form and content between these two
sections. Wildberger is no doubt representative when he writes that ch.
28 begins a new section of the book of Isaiah: 'der mit 24–27 *eindeutig*
nichts mehr zu tun hat...' (1978: 892; 'which *clearly* has nothing more
to do with 24–27...' [emphasis and trans. mine]). To be sure, Wildberger,
as others, is intent on separating chs. 24–27 from the 'genuine' material;
in this case, in the following chs. 28–31, on the usual historical critical
grounds. But things look differently if we ask about the connections
between sections of the book in terms of a synchronic rather than a
diachronic reading. Ackroyd, whose interests in his article, 'Isaiah 1–12:
Presentation of a Prophet', are diachronic and who focuses on the
composition of the unit, speaks to the issue at hand when he notes that
the division betwen chs. 27 and 28 is 'not entirely satisfactory' and that
'some passages, particularly in 30–33, are again as much like apocalyptic
as are parts of 24–27' (1988a: 92). In the meantime, recent studies have
explored the various connections between the unit chs. 24–27 and other
sections of the book. Seitz (1993: 172-76) has devoted attention to its
relationship to chs. 13–23 and Sweeney (1988b: 39-52) has studied its
redactional connections with other parts of the book of Isaiah, particularly in terms of allusion and citation and their function. But let me now
ask within the context of this essay, What kinds of linkages and interrelationships are to be found between chs. 28–33 and the so-called apocalyptic
section in chs. 24–27 which signal to the reader that the two units ought
to be viewed and interpreted not as separate and distinct units, with
nothing in common, but rather in the light of their connections to each
other.

In that these two sections, chs. 28–33 and chs. 24–27, stand in such
apparent contrast to each other, it is significant that various kinds of
connections can be established. In two prophecies of salvation (29.17-24;
30.18-26), which themselves stand in contrast to their context in chs. 28–
33, we find a close proximity with chs. 24–27. Concerning the first text
(29.17-24), Clements (1980a) writes, 'The affinities are with chs. 24–27,
and this is an expression of post-exilic eschatology, bordering closely on
apocalyptic eschatology.' His assessment of the second text (30.18-26) is
similar. If salvation prophecy in chs. 28–33 can be said to exhibit, in a

somewhat generalized way, close connections with the 'eschatology' of chs. 24–27, what about other kinds of connections?

Sweeney's study points to the close association of 33.1 ('you treacherous one, with whom none has dealt treacherously') with 24.16, concluding that the latter is an 'allusion' to the former (1988b: 44-45). Also, according to Sweeney (1988b: 46), 25.4-5 is a citation of 32.1-2, a passage about shelter from storm provided by king and prince. He thinks 25.4-5, given its wider context, universalizes salvation to include all peoples. But there are other linkages besides such allusions and citations. The emphasis on salvation (root ישע) in 33.2, 5, 22 and its connection to 'waiting' for Yahweh (v. 2) and to Zion (vv. 5, 20) recalls the same constellation of motifs in ch. 26 ('we have a strong city [Zion] and he sets up salvation', v. 1; 'O Yahweh, we wait for thee', v. 8); and similarly in ch. 25, which prophesies what will be said 'on that day' ('This is our God, we have waited for him, that he might save us...and let us rejoice in his salvation', v. 9), we find words particularly reminiscent of 33.2 (cf. also 30.18 [the verb for 'to wait' is קוה in 33.2; 25.9 and 26.8 and the usage is comparable; cf. Wildberger 1982: 1287]). The theme of the exaltation and glory of Yahweh (28.5; 30.18; 33.3, 5, 10, 21) finds its counterpart in 24.14-16, 23; 25.1, where, however, the context is not a prophecy of salvation but rather songs of praise for Yahweh's majesty (cf. 12.1-6), the element of praise being absent in chs. 28–33. Whereas the faithful recognize Yahweh's majesty in 33.20, 21, it is the wicked who do not see that majesty in 26.10, a contrast that suggests a close affinity of these two passages. Yahweh's honour requires that the pride of persons and nations be humbled; the laying low of Moab's pride (גאותו) and its 'high' fortifications (25.11-12) as well as the bringing low of the people and the 'lofty city' (26.5) reflects the same notion we observed earlier in 28.1-4 and 33.3, 10-12. The lament in 33.7-9 contains language that points back to 24.1-13. Wildberger has concluded on the basis of word statistics and theological conception that 33.7-16 and ch. 24 stand in the closest relationship, which he wants to call proto-apocalyptic. The mourning (אבל) and languishing (אמללה) of the land mentioned in 33.9 points back to the vocabulary of mourning and languishing of earth and heaven in 24.4, 7, and the 'broken covenants' of 33.7 links the verse to 24.5, where the same expression occurs (חפר ברית).

Finally, various isolated phrases are found which further suggest interconnections between chs. 28–33 and chs. 24–27. For example, in 32.13

the motivation for the lamentation (v. 12) is that the soil is growing up in 'thorns and briers', an expression that occurs in 27.4 (cf. the Song of the Vineyard, 5.6; also 7.23-25). The destruction decreed not for Judah /Jersalem but for the entire earth in 28.22 echoes the many instances of destruction expected for the earth in chs. 24–27 (e.g. 24.1-13; 26.21). The 'discernment' (בינת) to be hidden from the wise as punishment (29.13) but a blessing of the future age (29.24; 33.19) points back to the indictment and judgment pronounced upon a people without compassion in 27.11: 'This is a people without discernment (בינות), therefore he...will not have compassion on them.'

4. *Chapters 28–33 and 34–39*

A. *Chapters 28–33 and 34–35*
While chs. 34–35 have been thought to exibit many close connections to chs. 24–27, the close affinities with Deutero-Isaiah are also much discussed (Kaiser 1973; Clements 1980a; Seitz 1993). Often these discussions are related to isses of determining date, common authorship and the direction of influence: for example, did the composer of chs. 34–35 also have a hand in writing chs. 40–55 or was he 'influenced' by chs. 40–55? Here I want briefly to explore not matters of date, influence, common redaction or the like, but rather some of the structural, thematic and verbal connnections between chs. 28–33 and chs. 34–35 from the point of view of the reader who reads these chapters as they stand. Granted, the two units are dissimilar in many ways; this has been long established. What are the affinities?

In 28.17-22; 29.1-4; 30.13-14, 17; 31.3; and 32.14, Zion and Judah are the objects of punishments about to befall the land, whether the agent be Yahweh (28.13; 29.1-2, 14 etc.) or a foreign nation(s) (29.5, 7; 30.13-14; 33.1, 19). In 34.8 it is proclaimed that 'Yahweh has a day of vengeance (נקם), a year of recompense (שלומים) for the cause of Zion', which falls upon the nations//peoples (vv. 1-2; cf. 35.4). This vengeance upon nations recalls especially those texts in chs. 28–33 in which the enemy nation, the Assyrians, or unspecified nations, become the object of divine wrath. Isa. 29.5-8 speaks of the 'visitation' (תפקד, which can stand parallel to נקם, Hos. 9.7, and שלם, Jer. 5.9, 29; 9.8; cf. Schottroff 1976: 479-81) of Yahweh upon the 'nations that fight against Ariel'. In 30.27, Yahweh comes to 'sift the nations with a sieve', while in 30.29-33 it is the Assyrians who experience burning divine wrath (cf. 31.8). The imagery of fire and smoke is common to 30.29-33 and 34.8-10; also, both speak of 'brimstone' (גפרית, 30.33; 34; cf. Kaiser 1973). Kissane (1941) has drawn attention to the similarities between 30.27-33 and 34.2, and noted the same structure: divine punishment against the nations is followed by a description of the overthrow of Israel's oppressors in 30.27-33 and 34.1-7. Further, the devastation of Edom and its reduction to a waste of thorn and thistle, inhabited by wild animals in 34.9-15, recalls 32.13-14, which describes the formerly 'joyful city', with its 'soil growing up in thorns and briars', becoming a den for wild asses. The references to the reading and writing of mysterious books suggests another link. The admonition to read the 'book of Yahweh', with its positive context in 34.16, poses a contrast with the command to 'read this (sealed) book' which cannot be read in 29.11-12 (cf. 30.8). Finally, the phrase 'line and plummet' in 34.11, used in connection with chaos and confusion of the nobility of the nations (Edom), recalls the line and plummet of righteousness and justice with which Yahweh measures the rulers in Zion (28.17; cf. Fohrer 1967).

According to 35.1-10 the wilderness will rejoice at the blossoming of the desert and Israel will 'see the glory of Yahweh, the majesty (הדר) of our God' (v. 2) who 'will come and save you' (v. 4). This echoes 33.17-22 and its proclamation that 'your eyes will see the king' who in his 'majesty' (אדיר) will be 'for us' (33.21). In 35.5 at the appearance of God, 'the eyes of the blind shall be opened, and the ears of the deaf unstopped'. These words pick up 29.18; 30.20-21 and 32.3. Despite the well-known, essential differences between chs. 28–33 and chs. 34–35, the two units are nevertheless linked in significant ways by the various interconnections of structure, theme and linguistic usage.

B. *Chapters 28–33 and 36–39*

It was especially Duhm's critical view, voiced more than 100 years ago, that suggested how unintegrated chs. 36–39 are within the book of Isaiah. He supposed that these 'historical additions...derived from various sources were probably collected by the redactor of the books of Kings, and therefore *not for the purpose of being included within the book of Isaiah*' (1892: 14; emphasis and trans. mine). But recent studies of chs. 36–39 show how far we have come since Duhm's assessment, for there is renewed interest precisely in the way chs. 36–39 are redactionally related to, and functionally connected with, other parts of the book of Isaiah (Ackroyd 1987b; Seitz 1991). The question to be put here and addressed with relative brevity is whether the reader of chs. 28–33 and 36–39 is pointed to any meaningful connections between the two sections or units, the first of course a collection of prophetic oracles, the second a narrative framework with poetry inserted at two points (37.22-29; 38.10-20).

In chs. 30 and 31 a prominent theme is that of Judah's reliance on Egypt for military support. The matter is stated succinctly in 31.1: punishment will come upon those who 'go down to Egypt, rely (ישענו) on horses, and trust (יבטחו) in chariots'. The alternative posed by the prophet, which the leaders reject, is to 'look to (שעו) the Holy One of Israel' (v. 1bγ) and to be saved in 'returning, rest, in quietness and trust (בבטחה)' (30.15). In that the Egyptian's are not God, but humans who will perish (31.3), they are not to be relied upon. The rebellion against Yahweh is made politically concrete by a 'league' with Egypt (30.1).

The words of the prophet emphasize the false path taken when Judah and her leaders put their trust in Egypt. In the texts just cited, the key words are שעה and בטח. But in the Rabshakeh's speech to Hezekiah in ch. 36, it is precisely the issue of (false) reliance that he addresses. With rhetorical skill and in a 'disputational style' (Clements 1980a), he relentlessly takes up the matter of reliance/trust in Egypt. He states the theme of his speech at the outset in a sentence that contains the root בטח twice: 'On what do you rest (בטחת) this confidence (הבטחו) of yours?' The root בטח occurs within chs. 36–37 no less than nine times (36.3 [2×], 5, 6 [2×], 7, 9, where the accusative object is Egypt; in v. 15 and 37.10 it is Yahweh) in the hammering, rhetorical questions the Rabshakeh puts to Hezekiah and his men. It is as though he has stolen Isaiah's lines, or rather, that ch. 36 picks up a familiar theme from chs. 30–31 and recasts Isaiah's message concerning Egypt, this time not from Yahweh's but from the Assyrian king's point of view. In any case, the irony, as well as the link between the two sections, is clear: chs. 30 and 31 anticipate or prepare for ch. 36; or, ch. 36 looks backward to chs. 30 and 31. The link is reinforced by the Rabshakeh's words in 36.5 when he speaks of a 'plan' that is forged: 'Do not think that mere words are עצה and power for war', which recalls the prophetic indict-ment in 30.1 against those 'who make a plan (עצה) but not mine'.

The pride (גאות) and glory (צבי) of leaders and their resultant downfall (28.1-6) is also a theme reflected in chs. 36 and 37. The 'blustering arrogance' (Clements 1980a) of the Rabshakeh's speech is attacked in 37.21-29 in the messenger speech Isaiah delivers to Hezekiah concerning

Sennacherib: 'Against whom have you raised your voice, and arrogantly (מרום) lifted your eyes?' (v. 23). The quotation of Sennacherib's words in v. 24 underscore the hybris theme with its common imagery: 'I have gone up the heights (מרום) of the mountains...I have felled its [Lebanon's] tallest cedars' (cf. 10.5-19).

The proclamation that a remnant will survive in 37.31-32, with its elaborate Deuteronomistic style, points back to the simpler promise of salvation in 28.5 which says that 'Yahweh will be a diadem of beauty to the remnant of his people'. A more significant connection could be seen in the prophecies in which the Assyrian threat will come to destruction in 30.29-33 and 31.5, 8, 9 (cf. 29.5-8), to which the prophetic promise in 38.6 is obviously related ('I will deliver you and this city out of the hand of the king of Assyria'). Finally, it must be asked whether the figure of Hezekiah in chs. 36–39 is not anticipated or prepared for in chs. 28–33. Ackroyd (1987c: 175) thinks that the royal oracle in 32.1-8 serves as such a preparation. Seitz (1993), who develops the connection between the righteous and noble king of 32.1-8 and king Hezekiah, thinks that the portrayal of Hezekiah as righteous king par excellence in chs. 36–39 suggests this link; moreover, the pointer to Hezekiah in 9.1-7 offers further evidence, he argues, including the break in the woe pattern in chs. 28–33 with the interjection 'behold' in 32.1, which sets 'Hezekiah apart as the pattern of righteousness and wisdom' (1993: 229). Seitz's interpretation suggests an important connection between chs. 28–33 and chs. 36–39. Seitz also connnects ch. 33 with chs. 36–39, but only with difficulty, in my judgment, can one connect the 'king' of 33.17 with Hezekiah, for the king here is manifestly Yahweh, not a Davidide (cf. Wildberger 1982). Finally, Seitz sees a connnection between the 'obscure speech' of the foreigner in 33.19 and the native tongue of the Rabshakeh referred to in 37.11. It is thus evident that a number of themes found in chs. 36–39 connect the unit with chs. 28–33 in such a way that the reader is prepared for the Rabshakeh's speech about reliance on Egypt, political alliance as 'plan', as well as for the prophet's indictment of Assyria's pride and arrogance, the hope for a remnant and the appearance of a righteous ruler.

5. *Chapters 28–33 and 40–66.*

The fundamental connections between chs. 1–35 and 40–66 have, as is well known, received widespread attention recently by scholars who are

interested in recovering an understanding of the unity of the book of
Isaiah. But the literary and redactional relationships between chs. 28–33
and chs. 40–66 have also been studied. Perhaps Martin Brückner was
one of the first who, in his Leipzig dissertation of 1897, considered the
Berührungspunkte (points of connection) of chs. 28–33 with 'Deutero-
und Trito-Jesaja' (1897: 63-65) in a somewhat systematic way by
compiling a list of analogous texts and commenting on them briefly. His
intention, to be sure, was not first of all to pursue the question of what
ties chs. 28–33 and chs. 40–66 together, but instead to show how
various texts in chs. 28–33 could not be attributed to Isaiah of
Jerusalem. Indeed, Brückner proudly asserted in his conclusion that his
critical examination was successful in destroying 'die widerspruchsvolle
Einheit auch dieser Sammlung [chs. 28–33] des Jesaja-Buches' ('the
unity also of this section [chs. 28–33], required by its various self-
contradictions')and therefore thought that he had done a great service
for 'alttestamentliche Wissenschaft' (1897: 69-70). But here my aim, in
very brief compass, to be sure, is again to ask the same question about
Berührungspunkte, but with the intention of noting connections that
meaningfully link chs. 28–33 and chs. 40–66.

Several larger themes as well as motifs and verbal connections direct
the reader of chs. 28–33 forward to the second (chs. 40–55) and third
(chs. 56–66) major sections of the book. One could begin by expecting
that, for example, especially the salvation prophecies within chs. 28–33
would display some kind of affinity with chs. 40–66, and various kinds
of relationships are mentioned in the scholarly literature. For example,
J.L. McKenzie (1968: xxii) supposes that some kind of connection is
likely when he states that 'Second Isaiah could have known at least
some of the oracles of promise in First Isaiah, in particular those found
in the collection of chapters 28–33 (28.5-6; 29.17-24; 30.19-33; 32.15-
20; 33.17-24).' McKenzie understands these texts to be associated with
'the literary and theologial framework within which Second Isaiah
speaks' (1968: xxii). But let me turn to an overview of several themes
and texts.

The promise of salvation in 29.17-24 has been understood to contain
elements from chs. 40–55 and 56–66 as well as from Deuteronomy
(Vermeylen 1977: 406, noted by Clements 1980a). And of course the
salvation for Zion/Jerusalem proclaimed in 29.5-8; 30.19-33 and 31.5-8
broadly anticipates what has been called 'the Zion-Jerusalem section' in
chs. 49–55 (cf. Rendtorff 1993a: 157). Thus, whereas protection for

Zion against enemy forces is emphasized in 31.5-8 ('Yahweh will protect Jerusalem...spare and rescue it'; cf. 29.5-9; 30.19-33), the focus on Zion in chs. 49–55 shifts some to what Rendtorff calls the unified theme of 'consolation and the assurance of divine help for ruined and depopulated Jerusalem' (Rendtorff 1993a: 158). But the closest affinities are to be found between ch. 33 and chs. 40–66 (cf. Beuken 1991: 13, 18, *passim*; Williamson 1994: 221-39), especially regarding the matter of 'salvation'. The occurrences of the root ישע in 33.2, 6 (nouns) and v. 22 (verb), which connect Yahweh with Zion and his reign as king, clearly point to the motif of salvation in chs. 40–55 (Rendtorff 1993a: 164 n. 57). According to 33.5-6 Yahweh will fill Zion with an 'abundance of salvation', a note which is echoed in 46.13: 'my salvation will not tarry, I will put salvation in Zion...' (cf. 51.3-6, 8, 11, 16; 49.14, 25; also 40.9-10). The formulation in 33.22, 'Yahweh is our king, he will save us', anticipates 52.7, which speaks of the messenger's good tidings of 'salvation, who says to Zion, "Your God reigns"', with the result that all will 'see the salvation of our God' (v. 10). Whereas the inhabitants of Jerusalem will 'see' Zion, secure and saved by Yahweh in 33.20-22 (cf. v. 5), this becomes extended to include the nations, who will see Jerusalem's vindication and salvation (62.1-2, 11-12; cf. 52.10; 63.1, 5, 9). Thus the various Zion passages in chs. 28–33 point forward to the concentration of comforting words for Zion in chs. 40–66. Granted that many sayings about Zion in chs. 1–39 are, as Rendtorff has emphasized, very different and 'find no correspondence' with the second and third section of the book (1993a: 159), the red thread of connection Rendtorff finds drawn from chs. 1 to 12 to 35 and then to chs. 40–66, would still need also to include the significant connections ch. 33 makes with the Zion theme in chs. 40–66.

The blind/deaf theme in 29.18; 30.20-21 and 32.3 (cf. 33.17, 20) has obvious affinities with 42.16, 18-19; 43.8; 44.18, texts which in Clement's view present a 'fundamental theme in chs. 40–55' which consciously alludes back to Isaiah's prophecies (1985: 101). My interest here is not in redactional intention but rather to underscore that, with this example, the reader of chs. 28–33 is prepared for a further explication in chs. 40–55 of an old theme already found in Isaiah's inaugural vision in 6.9-10. The reader learns that the deaf hear and the blind see in the new age of salvation, not first in chs. 40–55, but already within chs. 28–33. Just as especially ch. 33 with its salvation of Zion theme is a link between ch. 12

and chs. 40–66, so also 29.18; 30.20-21 and 32.3 with the blind/deaf theme forge a link between 6.9-10 and chs. 40–55.

Scholars have also identified a variety of verbal links between 28–33 and chs. 40–66. For example, 62.5 speaks of a 'garland of beauty' and a 'royal diadem in the hand of your God', phrases anticipated by 28.5. At the beginning of the second section of the book, 40.2 announces that Jerusalem's iniquity (עֲוֹן) is pardoned, which picks up and reverses 30.13, where Judah's 'iniquity' results in its destruction (cf. 1.4; 5.18; 22.14 and Melugin 1976: 178); but perhaps more significantly, 40.2 is anticipated also by 33.24, which speaks of the forgiveness of iniquity (cf. Rendtorff 1993a: 153). In the promise of salvation in 30.18, Yahweh waits to be gracious and show mercy (רחם), a passage which points forward to a variety of forms in chs. 40–66. Yahweh himself can offer רחם that is yet to come ('with everlasting love I will have compassion on you', 54.8; cf. 60.10) or the heavens can be summoned to praise Yahweh for his mercy (רחם) on the afflicted (49.13) (further, cf. 49.10, 15; 54.10; 55.7). The exaltation or glorification of Yahweh in 28.5; 30.18; 33.3, 5, 10 looks forward to 57.15, which describes Yahweh as the 'high and lofty One' who dwells in the 'high and holy place'. The imagery of beauty that fades like a flower in 28.1, 4 finds a parallel in 40.7. Abraham's redemption in 29.22 anticipates his and Sarah's blessing in 51.2 (cf. 41.8). In 30.12 and 31.1 the motif of false trust and reliance finds a correspondence in 50.10 (Clifford 1984: 162, cited by Williamson 1994: 111). The rebellious (root מרה) people who refuse to hear in 30.9 find their counterpart in 50.4-5 in the figure who now listens, confirming his open ear with the first-person statement, 'I was not rebellious', the only two occurrences of מרה in Isa. 1–55 (cf. Williamson 1994: 109). In the woe passage in 29.15-16, those who hide from Yahweh are accused by means of a rhetorical question: 'Shall the potter be regarded as the clay?' (v. 16). That verse 16 has a close connection with 45.9 is generally recognized (cf. Duhm 1892; also 64.7 [8]), especially in light of the woe-cry as introduction, the motif of creator/creation and the rhetorical question, 'Does the clay say to him who fashions it, "What are you making?"' (cf. Williamson 1994: 58, for an extended discussion of the similarities; his interest, however, is in issues of authenticity and influence). In the prophecy of salvation in 30.19-26, the unit concludes with the promise that Yahweh 'will bind up the hurt of his people and heal (ירפא) the wounds inflicted by his blow' (v. 26; cf. 6.10), a text which is linked to 57.18-19 by the verb to heal:

"I have seen his ways but I will heal him...peace to the far and near, and I will heal him' (cf. Steck 1991: 20, 213 and רפא also in 19.22 and 53.5).

III

Chapters 28–33 present, within the structure of the book of Isaiah, a kind of oddity. It would perhaps not be too much to claim that these chapters, in some scholarly discussions of the book, remain an exegetical step-child. In more recent studies that are interested in the unity of the book of Isaiah, chs. 28–33 have not to my knowledge played a particularly important role. Reasons for this are readily apparent in that it is chs. 1–12 which provide the touchstone for understanding and interpreting the proclamation of Isaiah the prophet as well as the message of the book. Chapters 28–33, on the other hand, while closely related to the first twelve chapters, as I have demonstrated above, are separated from them by two intervening major sections (chs. 13–23; 24–27) and do not seem to fit well into their present literary context. As Becker (1968: 67) has noted, in comparison with the structure of other prophetic books, it would have been more consistent not to have chs. 28–33 follow *after* the oracles against the nations in chs. 13–27 because chs. 28–33 are like a 'functional doublette' to chs. 1–12. Thus not only are chs. 28–33 in some sense out of place, they also, insofar as they are taken as a separate collection or an 'independent block of tradition' (Becker 1968: 66), have not been particularly considered as to their interconnections with the remainder of the book.

While chs. 28–33 are closely related to chs. 1–12, their connection *as a unit* to chs. 13–23 and chs. 24–27 is yet to be satisfactorily clarified. If, for example, chs. 24–27 are understood as the conclusion to the larger section chs. 13–27 (Herbert 1973: 21), then are chs. 28–33 to be read essentially in relation to what follows, or only in connection with chs. 1–12? Or, if chs. 28–33 as a unit are understood as providing the kernel of chs. 24–35 (Fohrer 1966: 4), does this then imply that they are to be interpreted especially in the light of their surrounding context of apocalyptic-like material, without clear connections to chs. 1–12 or 36–39, to say nothing of chs. 40–66? These and similar questions about the place and function of chs. 28–33 take us only part way in an inquiry into the function of chs. 28–33. More recently, a different proposal has been offered which interprets chs. 28–33 as a preparation for the deliverance of Zion and Yahweh's exaltation over the Assyrians which culminates in chs. 36–39 (Seitz 1993: 206, 234-35). While it is clear that more work needs to be done regarding the function and place of chs. 28–33 relative to the book as a whole, these chapters are no longer to be seen merely as a second collection of oracles, many from Isaiah himself, gathered as a 'supplement' to the main block of material in chs. 1–12.

It has been the aim of this essay (parts I and II) to suggest that chs. 28–33 as a major unit within the book present a meaningful composition. As such it exhibits a structure with not only an expanded series of woe passages as the key structural element but also a pattern of regularly alternating doom sayings and promises of salvation. Moreover, chs. 28–33 were found to contain a number of significant themes that recur within the six chapters and knit them together. Various motifs and verbal linkages within the unit further indicate an interconnecting web that helps mold the unit into a unity. But far from being a self-contained, independent piece—a mere collection of materials arranged somewhat artfully— we have seen that chs. 28–33 are significantly connected to every major section of the book. In Janus-like fashion, the section looks in both directions, forward and backward. Some of the major themes, such as the prophecies about Zion or the texts about deafness/blindness, hearing /seeing, point back to texts in preceding units, perhaps expand and in some cases reinterpret them, but at the same time prepare for or anticipate the re-appearance of the same theme in succeeding sections. To be sure, some themes in chs. 28–33 point more backward than forward, such as the exaltation of Yahweh and the humbling of the proud enemy. Or, one hears nothing about false trust in Egypt in chs. 1– 27, but the theme reappears in expanded and narrative form, and with rhetorical flourish, in chs. 36–39. Further, I noted a host of verbal linkages that also connect chs. 28–33 with the other sections of the book. Far from entertaining questions of influence, borrowing, date or redactional intention and arrangement, my focus remained on a synchronic approach, imagining simply how a careful reader could perceive that major threads run throughout the book, connecting it into a larger whole. To be sure, much remains to be clarified, and the title of the essay admittedly claims too much, for chs. 28–33 are indeed a tie, but not *the* tie, that binds the book of Isaiah together. Nevertheless, I hope to have shown that these chapters, occurring toward the end of chs. 1–39, function not as a mere supplement to chs. 1–12, nor are they isolated from their surrounding literary context, but point both forward

and backward and make significant connnections to each of the major
sections of the book and thus help to bind together the immense literary
complexity of the work.

BIBLIOGRAPHY

Ackroyd, P.
1987a   'Isaiah 1–12: Presentation of a Prophet', in *Studies in the Religious
            Tradition of the Old Testament* (London: SCM Press): 79-104.
1987b   'Isaiah 36–39: Structure and Function', in *Studies*: 105-20.
1987c   'The Death of Hezekiah: A Portrait of the Future', in *Studies*: 172-80.
Barth, H.
1977   *Die Jesaja-Worte in der Josiazeit: Israel und Assur als Theme einer
            produktiven Neuinterpretation der Jesajaüberlieferung* (WMANT, 48;
            Neukirchen–Vluyn: Neukirchener Verlag).
Becker, J.
1968   *Isaias—Der Prophet und sein Buch* (Stuttgarter Bibel-Studien; Stuttgart:
            Katholisches Bibelwerk).
Beuken, W.A.M.
1991   'Jesaja 33 als Spiegeltext im Jesajabuch', *ETL* 67: 5-35.
Brückner, M.
1897   'Die Komposition des Buches Jes. c. 28–33' (inaugural dissertation,
            Universität Leipzig).
Clements, R.E.
1978   'Patterns in the Prophetic Canon', in G. Coats and B.O. Long (eds.),
            Canon and Authority: Essays in Old Testament Religion and Theology
            (Philadelphia: Fortress Press): 42-55.
1980a   *Isaiah 1–39* (NCB; Grand Rapids: Eerdmans).
1980b   *Isaiah and the Deliverence of Jerusalem: A Study in the Interpretation
            of Prophecy in the Old Testament* (JSOTSup, 13; Sheffield: JSOT
            Press).
1982   'The Unity of the Book of Isaiah', *Int* 36: 117-29.
1985   'Beyond Tradition-History: Deutero-Isaiah's Development of First
            Isaiah's Themes', *JSOT* 31: 95-113.
Clifford, R.J.
1984   *Fair Spoken and Persuading: An Interpretation of Second Isaiah*
            (New York: Paulist Press).
Conrad, E.W.
1991   *Reading Isaiah* (OBT; Minneapolis: Fortress Press).
Darr, K.P.
1994   *Isaiah's Vision and the Family of God* (Literary Currents in Biblical
            Interpretation; Louisville: Westminster John Knox).
Duhm, B.
1892   *Das Buch Jesaja übersetzt und erklärt* (HKAT, 3.1; Göttingen:
            Vandenhoeck & Ruprecht [cited according to 1968, 5th edn]).

Fohrer, G.
1966   *Das Buch Jesaja*. I. *Kapitel 1–23* (ZBK; Zürich: Zwingli Verlag).
1967   *Das Buch Jesaja*. II. *Kapitel 24–39* (ZBK; Zürich: Zwingli Verlag).
Gray, G.B.
1912   *A Critical and Exegetical Commentary on the Book of Isaiah I–XXVII* (ICC; Edinburgh: T. & T. Clark).
Gunkel, H.
1924   'Jesaja 33, eine prophetische Liturgie', *ZAW* 42: 177-208.
Herbert, A.S.
1973   *The Book of the Prophet Isaiah Chapters 1–39* (CBC; Cambridge: Cambridge University Press).
Kaiser, O.
1973   *Der Prophet Jesaja Kapitel 13–39* (ATD, 18; Göttingen: Vandenhoeck & Ruprecht).
Kissane, E.J.
1941   *The Book of Isaiah*, I (Dublin: Brown and Nolan).
Mauchline, J.
1962   *Isaiah 1–39: Confidence in God* (TB; London: SCM Press).
McKenzie, J.L.
1968   *Second Isaiah: Introduction, Translation, and Notes* (AB; Garden City: Doubleday).
Melugin, R.
1976   *The Formation of Isaiah 40–55* (BZAW, 141; Berlin: de Gruyter).
Mowinckel, S.
1933   'Die Komposition des Jesajabuches Kap. 1–39', *AcOr* 11: 267-92.
Petersen, D.L.
1979   'Isaiah 28: A Redaction Critical Study', *SBL Seminar Papers 2* (ed. P. Achtemeier; Missoula: Scholars Press): 101-22.
Rendtorff, R.
1991   'The Book of Isaiah: A Complex Unity. Synchronic and Diachronic Reading', *SBL Seminar Papers 30* (ed. E.H. Lovering, Jr; Atlanta: Scholars Press): 8-20.
1993a   'The Composition of the Book of Isaiah', in *Canon and Theology: Overtures to an Old Testament Theology* (OBT; trans. and ed. M. Kohl; Minneapolis: Fortress Press): 146-69.
1993b   'Isaiah 56.1 as a Key to the Formation of the Book of Isaiah', in *Canon and Theology*: 181-89.
Schottroff, W.
1976   'פקד', in *THAT*, II: 466-86.
Scott, R.B.Y.
1956   'The Book of Isaiah: Chapters 1–39', in *IB*, V: 151-380.
Seitz, C.
1991   *Zion's Final Destiny: The Development of the Book of Isaiah. A Reassessment of Isaiah 36–39* (Minneapolis: Fortress Press).
1993   *Isaiah 1–39* (Interpretation; Louisville: John Knox).
Stähli, H.-P.
1971   'גאה', in *THAT*, I: 379-82.

Steck, O.H.
  1991   *Studien zu Tritojesaja* (BZAW, 203; Berlin: de Gruyter).
Sweeney, M.A.
  1988a   *Isaiah 1–4 and the Post-Exilic Understanding of the Isaianic Tradition* (BZAW, 177; Berlin: de Gruyter).
  1988b   'Text Citations in Isaiah 24–27: Toward an Understanding of the Redactional Function of Chapters 24–27 in the Book of Isaiah', *SBL* 107: 39-52.
Vermeylen, J.
  1977   *Du prophete Isaie à l'Apocalyptique*, I (Paris: Librairie Lecoffre).
Wildberger, H.
  1978   *Jesaja 12–27* (BKAT, 10.2; Neukirchen–Vluyn: Neukirchener Verlag).
  1982   *Jesaja 28–39* (BKAT, 10.3; Neukirchen–Vluyn: Neukirchener Verlag).
Williamson, H.G.M.
  1994   *The Book Called Isaiah: Deutero-Isaiah's Role in Composition and Redaction* (Oxford: Clarendon Press).

REVERSALS OF FORTUNE IN THE ANCIENT NEAR EAST:
A STUDY OF THE BABYLON ORACLES IN THE BOOK OF ISAIAH*

Chris A. Franke

In my study of the function of the satirical lament against Babylon in Second Isaiah,[1] I discussed the pivotal role that this poem played in the development of Second Isaiah. I showed that the downfall and deposing of Virgin Daughter Babylon was a foil to the elevation and restoration of Virgin Daughter Zion. As Babylon was deposed, was sent from her throne into exile, indeed descended to death, conversely Zion was released from exile, and was restored once again to a position of honour. While one of the main themes of Isaiah 40–46 was the downtrodden Judah, chs. 48–55 emphasized Zion/Jerusalem reborn.

It is generally agreed that chs. 40–48 of Isaiah form a unit by virtue of several common elements—the emphasis on the importance of Cyrus in 40–48, the theme of Jacob/Israel, a concern with the return to Zion—all of which elements disappear, to be replaced in chs. 49–55 by other motifs. Recently, Christopher Seitz has illustrated another feature unifying chs. 40–48: that of the commissioning of one to accept God's call, which call is initiated in 40.1-11 and responded to in 49.1-6.[2] Another feature found in 40–48 but not in 49–55 is the mention of Babylon/Chaldea.

*   The nucleus of this essay was presented at the Seminar on the Formation of the Book of Isaiah at the National Meeting of the Society of Biblical Literature in Washington, DC in November, 1993. I am grateful for the comments of the respondent, John T. Willis, and for the discussion which followed the presentation.
    1.   The Function of the Satiric Lament over Babylon in Second Isaiah (xlvii)', *VT* 41 (1991), pp. 408-18.
    2.   C.R. Seitz, 'The Divine Council: Temporal Transitions and New Prophecy in the Book of Isaiah', *JBL* 109 (1990), pp. 229-47.

References to Babylon/Chaldea in Isaiah

All references to Babylon/Chaldea in the book of Isaiah occur between chs. 13 and 48 of the book.[3] Furthermore, these references are concentrated within three segments of the book, the so-called Oracles Against Nations (hereafter OAN) in 13–23, the Isaiah/Hezekiah narratives in 36–39 and the Jacob/Israel passages in 40–48. None is found in the chapters usually considered to be from Isaiah of Jerusalem. In all, thirteen references to Babylon appear in Isaiah, seven to Chaldea (or Chaldeans): 13.1, 19 (Chaldea also in v. 19); 14.4, 22; 21.9; 23.13 (here, Chaldea); 39.1, 3, 6, 7; 43.14 (also Chaldea); 47.1 (also Chaldea), 5 (here, Chaldea); 48.14, 20 (also Chaldea).

One subsection of chs. 13–23, chs. 13–14, is often referred to as 'the burden of Babylon'.[4] The oracles against Babylon/the Chaldeans in chs. 13–14 speak of the overthrow of Babylon, the downfall of the Babylonian king, and the annihilation of his posterity.[5] Commentators have questioned whether the names Babylon/Chaldea are integral to the oracles, and some suggest that they are redactional additions. Another oracle within chs. 13–23 is ch. 21, the oracle concerning the wilderness of the sea, which refers in 21.9 to the fall of Babylon. A watchman proclaims 'Fallen, fallen is Babylon, and all the images of her gods lie shattered on the ground.' This is reminiscent of Amos 5.2 which speaks of the the fall of Israel: 'Fallen, no more to rise, is maiden Israel.' A problematic reference is in 23.13—*hn ʾrṣ kśdym zh hʿm lʾ hyh ʾšwr.*[6] Some understand this passage to use the fall of Chaldea (Babylon) as an

---

3. See C.T. Begg, 'Babylon in the Book of Isaiah', *The Book of Isaiah/Le livre d'Isaïe* (ed. J. Vermeylen; BETL, 81; Leuven: University Press, 1989), pp. 121-25, for a discussion of references to Babylon in Isaiah.

4. See S. Erlandsson, *The Burden of Babylon: A Study of Isaiah 13.2–14.23* (Lund: Gleerup, 1970), and B. Gosse, *Isaïe 13.1–14.23: Dans la tradition littéraire du livre d'Isaïe et dans la tradition des oracles contre les nations* (OBO, 78; Göttingen: Vandenhoeck & Ruprecht, 1978) for treatments of this section.

5. Although, see R.E. Clements, *Isaiah 1–39* (NCB; Grand Rapids: Eerdmans, 1980), p. 132, who points out that ch. 13 is entitled oracle 'concerning' Babylon, and that the first two utterances are positive toward Babylon, not negative.

6. Translated in NRSV as 'Look at the land of the Chaldeans! This is the people; it was not Assyria'; in JPSV as 'Behold the land of Chaldea—This is the people that has ceased to be. Assyria, which...'; in NAB as 'This people is the land of the Chaldeans, not Assyria.'

example of what happens to a country which defies Assyria.[7] Some read the passage as a gloss.[8] However, the text is difficult, and many others emend and/or eliminate parts of the verse, including the reference to Chaldea. This verse contains the last occurrence of the names Babylon/ Chaldeans within the OAN segment.

The next group of references to Babylon/the Chaldeans appears in the Isaiah/Hezekiah narratives in ch. 39. Babylon is a far-off country; the king of Babylon has sent his envoys to King Hezekiah. This chapter is an ominous warning of days to come when Babylon will carry off all that belongs to the house of David, including some of the king's own descendants. This section of the book presents Babylon as a threat yet to come, as a power which has not yet realized its full potential against God's people.

The references in Second Isaiah in 40–48 return to the theme of the OAN, predictions of the overthrow of Babylon. The Lord promises in 43.13 to break down all the bars of the Babylonians, and to turn the joyful shouting of the Chaldeans to laments.[9] The ironic lament in 47 speaks of the downfall of Virgin Daughter Babylon, Daughter Chaldea. The last references in the book of Isaiah in ch. 48 assert that God will accomplish his purpose on Babylon, and his arm shall be against the Chaldeans (48.14); and urge the exiles to go out of Babylon, and to flee from the Chaldeans (48.20).

The concentration of these references to Babylon within the three sections of the book of Isaiah bears further investigation. The name Babylon first appears at a crucial point in the development of the book, a point at which most scholars agree that First Isaiah has been left behind. Seitz asserts that Isaiah 13–14, the oracle concerning Babylon, 'now works in conjunction with a theology of history embracing the whole book...'[10] The name appears again at another pivotal point in the book, in chapter 39, where it bridges the gap between eighth-century Isaiah, when Babylon was only a distant threat, and the events of the

---

7.   J.D.W. Watts, *Isaiah 1–33* (WBC; Waco: Word Books, 1987), p. 307; see also J.N. Oswalt, *The Book of Isaiah, Chapters 1–39* (NICOT; Grand Rapids: Eerdmans, 1986), pp. 434-35.

8.   For example, Clements, *Isaiah 1–39*, p. 194.

9.   See Watts, *Isaiah 34–66* (WBC; Waco: Word Books, 1987), pp. 127-28, for the various renderings of the verse.

10.   C.R. Seitz, 'Isaiah 1–66: Making Sense of the Whole', in *idem* (ed.), *Reading and Preaching the Book of Isaiah* (Philadelphia: Fortress Press, 1988), p. 112.

sixth century where Babylon prevails. The name eventually disappears after ch. 48, when the fall of Babylon is replaced by the elevation of Zion.

Strategies for Examining Compositional Techniques in Isaiah

This study will examine the poems on King of Babylon (hereafter KOB) in Isaiah 14, and Virgin Daughter Babylon (hereafter VDB) in chapter 47 to determine interdependencies between the poems,[11] and to see how each chapter relates to the larger sections of the book, with the end in mind to understand how the Babylon materials affect the overall structure the book of Isaiah. The following approaches have been taken with other similar sections of the book of Isaiah.

One of the techniques used in studies on the composition of the book of Isaiah to determine relationships between various segments of the book is to identify certain pivotal chapters which seem to show inter-relationships in both directions. For instance, Steck identified ch. 35 as the junction between chs. 1 and 34 and 40–66[12] Seitz's study on Isaiah 36–39 discussed these chapters and their function in the redaction of the whole book.[13]

Another method used in investigating the interdependence between the various parts of the book of Isaiah is the study of parallels between First and Second Isaiah, First and Third Isaiah and so on. An example of this approach to the question can be seen in the recent study of Christopher R. Seitz on parallels between Isaiah 40.1-11 and 6.1-11.[14] Both of these chapters are considered pivotal in the book of Isaiah.

Interdependence has also been discussed by demonstrating the use of

---

11. Gosse, *Isaïe*, pp. 11-12, sees little if any connection between the oracles against Babylon in chs. 13–14 and those in chs. 46–47. The latter are not part of a collection of oracles against nations, and they are more preoccupied with salvation for Israel than with chastisement of Babylon. He also believes that they do not have the violence, the elevated style, the pretensions, that are typical of chs. 13–14, but my study of these chapters illustrates that elevated style and pretensions to power are indeed part of chs. 46–47.

12. O.H. Steck, *Bereitete Heimkehr: Jesaja 35 als redaktionelle Brücke zwischen dem Ersten und dem Zweiten Jesaja* (SBS, 1211; Stuttgart: Katholisches Bibelwerk, 1985).

13. *Zion's Final Destiny: The Development of the Book of Isaiah: A Reassessment of Isaiah 36–39* (Minneapolis: Fortress Press, 1991).

14. 'The Divine Council'.

citations or allusions within the book of Isaiah.[15] Textual citation and allusions in one part of the book can be used 'as a means for understanding the redactional function of these chapters within the book of Isaiah'.[16] Sweeney shows that the author of chs. 24–27 uses other texts from the book of Isaiah to illustrate his own particular hermeneutical perspective.

Isaiah 14 as a Parody of a Lament

The mocking songs or taunts against Babylon in Isaiah 14 and 47 have similarities in language, form and tone. These features of Isaiah 14 will form the basis for the examination of the similarities. The *mashal* against the king of Babylon is considered to be one of the best examples in the Bible of a prophetic parody of a lament.[17] Yee analyzes this parody by first discussing the features of the lament proper. She compares David's lament over Saul and Jonathan with other laments in the Bible, and arrives at six features typical of this form. They are: (1) a rhetorical introduction announcing the death; (2) suppression of the news of the death from enemies; (3) description of the reaction of nature to the person's death; (4) description of the person's life; (5) call to mourners to weep; (6) an expression of the singer's personal grief. In addition, laments are usually written in Qinah meter.

Yee's reading of Isa. 14.4b-21 shows that the poet adhered closely to the features of the lament, but altered these features to achieve the parody by reversing the reader's expectations.[18] She describes these features from ch. 14 in the order in which they appear in the text.

15. M.A. Sweeney, 'Textual Citations in Isaiah 24–27', *JBL* 107 (1988), pp. 39-52.

16. Sweeney, 'Textual Citations', p. 15.

17. G.A. Yee, 'The Anatomy of Biblical Parody: The Dirge Form in 2 Samuel 1 and Isaiah 14', *CBQ* 50 (1988), pp. 565-86. I am indebted to Yee's analysis of this poem, and follow her outline throughout this section of the paper. R.H. O'Connell, 'Isaiah XIV 4B-23: Ironic Reversal through Concentric Structure and Mythic Allusion', *VT* 38 (1988), pp. 407-18, also reads the funerary taunt song in 14.4b-23 as a parody on the fall of the king of Babylon; see especially pp. 414-16. He also suggests that the author of this chapter deliberately inverted themes of the Gilgamesh epic to achieve the parody (p. 415).

18. Yee, 'Anatomy', p. 575.

(1) There is a *rhetorical introduction* announcing the death, opening with the exclamation ʾyk, an expression of astonishment at what has happened. The Qinah meter is also used.[19]

As in (4) above, the person's *life and achievements* are described—in 14.5-6, the staff and scepter are symbolic descriptions of the KOB's oppressive power. Use of participles, apposition and hyperbole further describe and praise the object of a lament. But here in this poem, they are not used to praise the lamented one, but to accuse him of tyranny (14.6).

In 14.13-14, the description of the person's life is not from the mouth of the singer of the lament, but in the KOB's own boastful words, where he describes his pretensions to glory. Heroic laments commonly have the theme of the 'incomparability' of the deceased person to other beings.[20] But the tyrant of ch. 14 is far from incomparable; he is weak, just like the other kings who have died before him (14.10).

(3) True laments show *how nature is affected* by the death of the person. In 14.7-8, the whole earth is at rest at the news of the death, trees rejoice at the news and the underworld itself is aroused by it.

(5) In laments, mourners are *called to weep* or to grieve publicly; in 14.16-17, there is no call to weep. No sympathy is evoked for the deceased. Instead, the crudely exposed corpse of the KOB is an object of scorn to those who pass by and mock it.

(6) True laments contain *expressions of personal grief* over the death of the lamented one. This is often expressed by the use of negatives such as 'never again', or 'no longer'.[21] The sadness is due to the fact that the deceased will no longer be present to those who now mourn. In this parody there is an expression not of grief but of relief, satisfaction, and retribution on the occasion of this death (14.18-21), and the negations (e.g. 'may descendants nevermore be named') 'elicit a sense of relief' that the sufferings are at an end.[22]

---

19. See also these same features in the dirge within the dirge, in 14.12-15, Yee, 'Anatomy', pp. 577-79.

20. Yee, 'Anatomy', p. 571. Saul and Jonathan are described in hyperbolic fashion; in dirges 'historical accuracy' is commonly dispensed with to achieve the effect of superhuman bravery and achievements.

21. See Amos 5.2, 'Fallen, no more to rise…'

22. Yee, 'Anatomy', p. 581.

Comparison of Isaiah 47 with the Lament Features of Isaiah 14

Chapter 47, a poem unique in structure,[23] does have some of the characteristic features of mourning and lament. Its overall form has been
identified as a taunt song,[24] a mocking song,[25] a triumph song,[26] an
oracle against foreign nations.[27] Most see it as a combination of different
formal elements. For instance, Westermann[28] sees evidence of the
diction of the prophetic oracle of doom. Melugin sees it as a 'taunt to a
large extent influenced by the style of the prophetic oracle',[29] but agrees
with Westermann that the chapter is a freely created poem. Whybray[30]
sees two different forms of speech: the mocking- or taunt-song and the
funeral song or dirge over the dead. He shows how the poem has
elements of mocking or taunt, but does not discuss which elements he
believes are related to the funeral song or dirge.

Using the criteria for the lament as outlined in Yee's article, it can be
shown that ch. 47 has several but not all of the elements of a lament
proper. Comparison with Isaiah 14 will illustrate the features of lament
which are present in this poem.

(1) While there is no *rhetorical announcement* of the death of the
individual, the very beginning lines of the poem show the subject of the
poem, VDB, descending from her throne to earth. This descent is not
just to the ground but to the darkness of the underworld (47.5). The
root *yrd* appears only once in Isaiah 47; it is the very first word in the
poem. In Isa.. 14.4b-21 it occurs three times, each time in connection
with the descent to Sheol (14.11, 15, 19). The theme of 'descent' is a
crucial one in both poems.

23. R.F. Melugin, *The Formation of Isaiah 40–55* (BZAW, 141; Berlin: de
Gruyter), p. 155.

24. R. Clifford, *Fair Spoken and Persuading: An Interpretation of Second Isaiah*
(New York: Paulist Press, 1984), p. 135.

25. J. Muilenburg, 'The Book of Isaiah: Chapters 40–66', in *IB* 5, p. 543.

26. B. Duhm, *Das Buch Jesaia* (HKAT, 3.1; Göttingen: Vandenhoeck &
Ruprecht, 4th edn, 1922), p. 354.

27. J. McKenzie, *Second Isaiah* (AB, 20; Garden City: Doubleday, 1967), p. 91;
C. Westermann, *Isaiah 40–66: A Commentary* (trans. D.M.G. Stalker; OTL;
Philadelphia: Westminster Press, 1969), p. 188; R.N. Whybray, *Isaiah 40–66* (NCB;
London: Marshall, Morgan & Scott Publications, Eerdmans, 1981), p. 118.

28. Westermann, *Isaiah 40–66*, p. 189.

29. Melugin, *Formation*, p. 135.

30. Whybray, *Isaiah 40–66*, p. 18.

The descent in 47.1 is 'to the dust...to earth', in 47.5 'to darkness'. In 14.11 KOB descends more specifically 'to Sheol', to the 'pit' (14.15). While most scholars interpret the descent of VDB as the change of her status from ruler to slave, comparison with biblical and non-biblical texts demonstrate that a more radical change is meant here. Tromp[31] shows that the word pair 'earth-dust' is associated with the thought of death. Further, he says that the expression *yrd ʿpr* means 'to go down to the grave/the netherworld'.[32]

In an extended discussion of mourning ritual in Ugaritic literature, Gary A. Anderson[33] points to the prominence of the descent into the underworld in the rituals which mourn the death of Baal. El (in CTA 5.6.1-25) descends from his throne, sits on his footstool, then descends and sits on the ground (*ľrṣ*), and finally states that he will descend to the underworld (*ʾard bʾrṣ*), following Baal. Anat and Shapshu (CTA 6.1.8-9) mourn the death and descent of Baal by themselves descending the underworld.[34] Anderson also cites a line from the funerary liturgy of King Niqmadddu III (KTU 1.161) which is very similar to Isaiah 47.1, which calls for a ritual descent in the cult, following the king to the underworld. Shapshu demands, '...descend to the earth, to the earth descend, lower yourself to the dust' (*ʾrṣ rd, ʾrṣ rd, wšpl ʿpr*).[35]

The thrones of VDB and KOB are prominent features in each poem. VDB sits down on the earth 'unthroned' (47.1). KOB plans to ascend to the heavens, elevate his throne (14.13) and sit on the mount of assembly. Reference is also made to the thrones of the other leaders of the earth (14.9) who are dwelling in Sheol. The funerary liturgy for King Niqmadu III also sheds light on biblical passages dealing with the importance of thrones in mourning rites.[36] Mourning rites are often done to express

31. N.J. Tromp, *Primitive Conceptions of Death and the Netherworld in the Old Testament* (BibOr, 21; Rome: Pontificial Biblical Institute, 1969), p. 23.

32. Tromp, *Primitive Conceptions*, p. 33. See also Jon. 2.7. Ps. 30.10 associates the 'pit' with 'dust', another connection with the underworld.

33. *A Time to Mourn, a Time to Dance* (University Park, PA: Penn State University Press, 1991), pp. 60-82.

34. Anderson, *A Time to Mourn*, p. 64.

35. Anderson, *A Time to Mourn*, p. 65.

36. J.G. Taylor, 'A First and Last Thing to Do in Mourning: KTU 1.161 and Some Parallels', in L. Eslinger and G. Taylor (eds.), *Ascribe to the Lord: Biblical and Other Studies in Memory of Peter Craigie* (JSOTSup, 67; Sheffield: JSOT Press, 1988), pp. 151-77. Taylor, p. 153, and p. 155 n. 9, reads KTU 1.161.20-21 as 'After your [L]ord, *O throne*, after your lord to earth descend...', reading *ksy* for the

identification with the predicament of the dead.[37] The descent of El from the throne at the news of Baal's death is usually interpreted to be merely a preliminary to El's sitting on the ground in mourning. But Taylor suggests it could be an act in which El identifies with Baal's loss of his throne by descending from his (El's) own throne.[38]

Isaiah 47 has elements of a lament over the death of VDB, and these biblical and non-biblical texts support this position. VDB mourns not just because she has to carry out the tasks of a slave. The reference to VDB being 'without a throne' means more than loss of rule; it is written in the language of mourning which relates to death.[39] KOB, like VDB, is also denied his throne. Unlike the other rulers of the earth who have died and reside in Sheol on their thrones, KOB is denied a throne in death—he is to lie on a bed of maggots with worms to cover him (14.11). There is a play on words in v. 9 (*mksᵓwtm*, 'their thrones') and in v. 11 (*mksyk*, 'your covering'). The kings have their thrones, KOB has his covering of worms. Further, as a punishment for his ill treatment of his own people (v. 20), KOB will not be joined with the kings of the nations in death.

There are other features in Ugaritic and Mesopotamian texts and in Isaiah 47 not found in the lament in 2 Samuel, but which support my interpretation of the lament elements in Isaiah 47. Of special note is the ceremonial dishevelment of clothing. El tears off his clothes down to the loin cloth, exhibiting 'stereotypical mourning behavior' in response to the death of Baal.[40] Gilgamesh mourns the death of Enkidu by weeping, pulling his hair and removing his clothes, and by so doing identifies his appearance with those in the underworld.[41] In a ritual for the dead mother of Nabonidus, kings from distant lands gather to mourn by

scribal error *ksh*. He understands the throne as a personification. Shapshu is therefore bidding the throne to descend to the netherworld. In his interpretation of this line, Anderson did not indicate to whom this command of Shapshu was addressed. Taylor, pp. 175-76, reads Isa. 14.9, in which the leaders of the earth rise from their thrones, as an indication that these thrones were provided in a royal funerary ritual.

37. Taylor, 'First and Last', p. 162.
38. Taylor, 'First and Last', pp. 163-64.
39. Taylor, 'First and Last', p. 165: 'In light of the Ugaritic parallel and the dirge style it is highly unlikely that the reference to being without a throne signifies simply the loss of rule.'
40. Anderson, *A Time to Mourn*, pp. 61-63.
41. Anderson, *A Time to Mourn*, pp. 74-75.

stripping themselves of their attire.[42] So also, as VDB prepares to descend silently into the darkness of the underworld, she is to uncover her hair (or remove her veil), strip off her skirt and uncover her leg (47.2). While some interpret these as actions necessary for Babylon to prepare herself for a trip across rivers to a distant land, or to garb herself for the grinding of grain, it is consistent with the motif of lament to see them as part of the preparation for descent to the underworld.

Chapter 47, like 14 and the true laments, is written largely in Qinah meter.

(4) The *life and achievements* of the deceased are mentioned, not in praise, but in condemnation (47.6b). It is not the achievements of the individuals which are highlighted but their faults. The cruelties of KOB in Isaiah 14 include the following: unceasing blows and relentless persecution of nations (14.6), refusing to let prisoners return home (14.17) and destruction of his land and people (14.20). The main condemnation against VDB is her merciless treatment of God's inheritance, God's people. VDB placed a heavy yoke upon the aged (47.6), and in general, failed to show compassion to the exiles.

An additional feature in most of the descriptions of Babylon in the book of Isaiah is VDB's lifelong devotion to magic, astrology and sorcery; from the time of her youth she trafficked with magic (47.10, 12-13). This devotion emphasized VDB's folly, rather than the wisdom she claimed to have. In fact, in the end her life of dedication to sorcery led to her destruction (47.10).

Several times throughout the poem, VDB speaks of herself in a fashion similar to the boastful pretensions of KOB in Isaiah 14. In the true lament, others sing of the incomparability of the deceased. But here, as in Isaiah 14, Babylon vaunts herself as incomparable: 'I am, and there is no other' (vv. 8-10). She exalts herself in an exaggerated fashion as 'mistress forever' (v. 7). But the reader is well aware, from the beginning of the poem to the end, that these are mistaken pretensions of a defeated power. The speaker challenges VDB to depend on her powers, and suggests mockingly, 'perhaps you may succeed, perhaps you will inspire awe' (v. 12). VDB's boasts are empty words; this is a parody of the motif of incomparability, a parody of the hyperbole often included in laments.

As VDB proclaims her incomparability, she also seems to be claiming to be impervious to the powers of death. She believes, mistakenly, that

---

42. Anderson, *A Time to Mourn*, p. 77.

she will never grieve the death of husband or children (vv. 8-9). In fact, these two things will happen to her suddenly, without warning. She will become a widow and she will be bereft of her children.

KOB and his descendants suffer the same fate. Because of his guilt, his descendants will be slaughtered. Because of his evil deeds, they will have no name on earth (14.20b-21).

(5) There is no *call to mourners to weep* in this poem. In fact, no one mourns VDB's fate. VDB and KOB at one time caused nations to tremble and inspired awe (47.12; 14.16). Now, VDB will be exposed to humiliation ('your nakedness will be uncovered, your shame will be seen', v. 3). The implication is that anyone seeing the sorry condition of VDB will rejoice rather than grieve over what has happened. One of the features in the lament of David over Saul and Jonathan is suppression of the news of the death from enemies so they would not be able to gloat (2 Sam. 1.20). VDB's enemies will have occasion to gloat and taunt as VDB is stripped and exposed before all to see. The fate of KOB was that he would be the object of scorn and derision, as people pondered how this once intimidating and powerful ruler could have been brought so low (14.16-17).

(6) No one *expresses grief* at these occurrences. The underlying tone of mocking and taunt throughout express the sense of retribution at what happens to VDB. In true laments, negatives were used to communicate personal grief. In these poems negatives are used for very different reasons. 'No more shall you be called' by grand titles (vv. 1, 5). The tone of mocking comes from the audience's awareness that VDB is deluded in her belief that these titles were hers in perpetuity. As in the parody in Isaiah 14, the negations in 47.14-15 ('no one to deliver, no coal for warming, no one to save') here invoke a sense of satisfaction and retribution as the ignominious end of VDB, her helplessness in the face of what is to come and abandonment by her cohorts, are in sight.

One of the features of the lament not found in Isaiah 47 is the description of the reaction of nature to the person's death. In this paper I do not attempt to prove that chapter 47 is a parody of a lament in the same way that Isaiah 14 is. One of the basic characteristics of the author of chs. 40–55 is the creative use and manipulation of forms which are illustrated in almost every poem. This trait has been most clearly illustrated by Melugin in his form-critical study of Isaiah 40–55, in which he shows the variety of combinations or fusions of forms employed by this author,[43] the creative manipulation of traditional forms[44] and the transformation of genres to such an extent that the structure of a given unit could be considered a new creation of the poet.[45]

Even though the several features of the lament taken up in Isaiah 47 do not constitute a full fledged lament, or a parody of a lament as in Isaiah 14, nonetheless the two poems are similar in many respects, especially since both involve satisfaction at the death of KOB and VDB. The aspect of taunt or mocking song is strong in both. The themes of the downfall of a great and arrogant ruler, and the focus on Babylon are also important features of both poems.

One feature of the lament proper that is exploited in these poems relating to the fall of Babylon is that of the contrast between 'then' and 'now', 'life' and 'death'.[46] The wonder of the past accentuates the agony of loss in the present. A related binary opposition which is played up in the two poems is that of 'up' and 'down'.[47] In the past ('then'), KOB was the mighty ruler who prevailed over nations, 'now' he is powerless, an exposed corpse trodden under foot. VDB in the past was considered to be mistress of kingdoms; she lived in security, relying on her magical powers. Now VDB is dethroned and has no one to rely on.

The up and down movement of the two poems is integral to the development of both.[48] In Isaiah 14 the tyrant's fall is illustrated in a variety of ways.[49] The hewer does not 'come up' to hew trees because he (the tyrant) has been 'laid low'. Sheol wakes up the shades and raises the kings from their throne as the tyrant arrives. Day Star, son of dawn, aspires to ascend to the heavens and to set his throne on high. Instead, he falls from heaven, cut down to the ground, is brought down to Sheol, to the pit. He wants to reach the far recesses of Mount Zaphon, but instead reaches the far recesses of the pit.

The motif of descending and rising is a unifying element in Isaiah 47.

43. Melugin, *Formation*: e.g. pp. 23-26, 40-41.
44. Melugin, *Formation*: e.g. pp. 69, 71, 131.
45. Melugin, *Formation*, p. 175.
46. Yee, 'Anatomy', pp. 572-73.
47. See O'Connell, 'Isaiah XIV 4B-23: Ironic Reversal', p. 409, on the 'upward/downward movement'.
48. See P. Miscall, *Isaiah* (Sheffield: JSOT Press, 1993). This commentary reads the entire book of Isaiah as a vision, and Miscall identifies the theme of high and low as one which pervades the book. See the summary of chs. 1–2 on p. 27, for instance.
49. Yee, 'Anatomy', pp. 576-78.

It begins with the first word, a command to Babylon to 'go down', and continues with the various commands throughout to 'go' into darkness, to 'sit down' in the dust. Not only is VDB's descent described, but also the descent upon her of a variety of evils with which she will be punished (vv. 9, 11, 13). Later on in the poem, VDB is commanded to stand up, to arise and stand for judgment. The poem ends with VDB's cohorts, wandering helplessly, without any direction whatsoever.

Both VDB and KOB presume to attain to the status or near status of divinity. KOB says in his heart (*'mr blbb*) 'I will ascend to the heavens... to the mount of the assembly...I will make myself like the Most High' (14.13-14). VDB says in her heart (*h'mrh blbbh*) 'I am and there is no other' (47.8, 10). This is a claim to divinity. Elsewhere in Isaiah 40–48 similar words are spoken by Yahweh (Isaiah 45.5, 18, 21, 22; 46.9). Both KOB and VDB are brought down, and their claims shown to be without substance.

An obvious connection between the poems is the identity of the addressees. The king of Babylon (*mlk bbl*, 14.4a) is the addressee and subject of 14.4b-21; the mistress of kingdoms, the queen (*gbrt mmlkwt* and *gbrt*), is the addressee and subject of 47. Both poems address and speak of royalty, an imperial power. In the case of ch. 14, the king of Babylon is sometimes identified by scholars with a specific ruler of Babylon (Nebuchadnezzar or Nabonidus have been suggested). VDB in ch. 47 is the personification of the Babylonian empire, or more specifically, the capital city, Babylon. Unlike ch. 14, there is no identification with an actual ruler. In his recent commentary, Peter Miscall interprets several of the references to Babylon as personifications, reading 'Lady Babylon', rather than understanding these as simply references to a city or empire.[50] It is to these other occurrences of Babylon/Chaldea in Isaiah that I now turn.

Isaiah 14 and Isaiah 47 in their Larger Literary Contexts

The *mashal* on KOB occurs within the larger section of 'The Burden of Babylon' in chs. 13–14. There are three references to the Babylonian empire in this section: the first in the title of the oracle (13.1), the second in 13.19, where its overthrow is briefly but graphically described, and the third in 14.22, which speaks of the annihilation of Babylon's offspring. It is worth noting that the book of Isaiah when speaking of

50. For example, Miscall, *Isaiah*, pp. 47, 49, 114.

Babylon usually speaks of the punishments that will come her way but almost never indicates the reason for the punishments.[51] The first time Babylon is mentioned by name in Isaiah the audience is expected to be familiar with the reason for the punishment.

In 13.19-22 Babylon is portrayed as a woman. Miscall translates v. 19 as Babylon, 'jewel of the kingdoms; splendor and pride of the Chaldeans', and asserts that the same terms (ṣby, tpʾrt, gʾwn) are used of Zion in 4.2. 'Zion, a woman, is desolate and will be splendid; Babylon, a woman (vv. 19-22 are feminine singular) is splendid' but will become like Sodom and Gomorrah.[52] In this respect also, Babylon will suffer a similar fate to that of personified Daughter Zion in 1.7-9, who almost became like Sodom and Gomorrah.

In addition to connections with the beginning of the book of Isaiah, there are also allusions to more fully developed themes in ch. 14, and in Second Isaiah. The prophecy in 13.17-22 which predicts the downfall of proud Babylon is echoed in the lament over KOB in ch. 14, as well as in Isaiah 46 and 47.[53] Babylon, once the 'beauty of kingdoms' (ṣby mmlkwt in 13.19) will no longer be called 'mistress of kingdoms' (gbrt mmlkwt in 47.5). Once proud Babylon will see her gods stumble into captivity (46.1-2). The notion that the proud kingdom will become an uninhabited haunt only for wild beasts (13.20-22) is echoed in 14.22-23, as a fitting conclusion to the lament over KOB.[54] Miscall again reads the feminine singular suffixes in 14.22-23 as pointing to a personification of

---

51. Very little historical information about Babylon's activity except in a most general way is found in Isaiah. In the lament over KOB we learn that he ruled with anger and persecution, overthrew cities and nations, would not let prisoners go home, destroyed his land and people. Isaiah's prophecy to Hezekiah in ch. 39 informs the king that all the treasures of the king will be carried to Babylon, and his sons will serve as eunuchs there. The only crime which is alluded to in Isa. 47 is harsh treatment of the elderly. The Babylonian's worship of idols is also mentioned in 21.9 and 46.1-2.

52. Miscall, *Isaiah*, p. 49.

53. Clements, *Isaiah 1–39*, p. 132. Clements also places this prophecy in the period 545–38 BCE, saying, this prophecy 'relates to the same period which is presupposed by the prophecies of chs. 40–55' (p. 137).

54. Yee, for instance, does not include these verses in her analysis of the parody; O'Connell does. Oswalt, *Isaiah*, p. 325, sees them as an indication that the taunt song was meant to be understood as a figure which applied to Babylon as a whole, and not to just one individual.

Lady Babylon, and says of this passage that 'Lady Babylon returns...';[55] she will lose offspring and posterity, she will become a possession of the hedgehog, she will be swept with the broom of destruction. Likewise, VDB in 47.8-9 will become widowed and bereft in one day, and will be met with sudden disaster and ruin (47.11).

The next occurrence of the name of Babylon/Chaldea is in 21.9. The Babylonians must meet a surprise attack, and a watchman observes the events. All that the watchman announces about Babylon is that she has fallen, and that all the images of her gods lie shattered on the ground. As in previous references to Babylon, nothing is said about the offenses of Babylon; only the well-deserved punishment—the fall of the kingdom and destruction of idols—is briefly described.

A concern with idols and idolatry pervades chs. 40–48 of the book of Isaiah.[56] It is a theme present in chs. 46, 47 and 48.[57] The idolatry of the exiles in Babylon threatens to once again cause a rift in the relationship between God and his people. Chapter 46 describes a procession involving Babylonian deities, which are ineffectual and powerless to save their own people (46.1-2). Those among the exiles who worship idols following the model of the Babylonian neighbors are foolish rebels, and need to be reminded that there is only one God (46.6-9). In ch. 47 VDB sets herself up as a rival deity to the God of Israel, but the divine attributes which she applied to herself (47.8, 10) are taken away, and she meets a swift and terrible end. Chapter 48 returns to the theme of the idolatry of God's people (v. 5). God restrains himself from cutting them off because of their idolatry; again the people need a reminder that there is only one God. The idolatry of Babylon which was briefly mentioned in 21.9 is more fully developed in chs. 46, 47 and 48. These chapters explain why it is that the shattering of Babylonian idols was of interest in 21.9. Babylon's idolatry threatened Israel's relationship to God.

The narrative material in ch. 39 deals with the reign of Hezekiah and the visit of Babylonian envoys to Judah. This is the only section in the Book of Isaiah that deals with Babylon as a historic entity. Chs. 36–39 relate the predicted fall of Assyria, over which Virgin Daughter Zion

55. Miscall, *Isaiah*, p. 49.

56. R. Clifford, 'The Function of the Idol Passages in Second Isaiah', *CBQ* 42 (1980), pp. 450-64, has shown that these passages are an integral part of Second Isaiah, and should not be considered secondary.

57. See my *Isaiah 46, 47, and 48: A New Literary-Critical Reading* (Biblical and Judaic Studies, 3; Winona Lake, IN: Eisenbrauns, 1994).

rejoices (37.22), and introduce the Babylonians as an ominous power which will take the place of the oppressive Assyrians. Conrad considers the Lord's military plan to be a governing theme within the book of Isaiah,[58] and he sees this theme connecting 13.1–14.23 and 14.24-27, which announce judgment on Babylon and Assyria, and chs. 36–39 and 40–47 which proclaim fulfillment of this judgment.[59] The fact of the overthrow of Assyria, which God promised earlier and is fulfilled in the time of Hezekiah, should be convincing evidence that God's promise to overthrow Babylon will also be fulfilled. For Conrad, the Hezekiah narrative is a 'pivotal element', relating both to the preceding and following chapters.

Contrasts and Reversals of Fortune

In ch. 47, the figure of VDB functions as a foil to that of Daughter Zion in chs. 40–46 and 48–55.[60] In chs. 40–46, Judah/Israel is downtrodden, oppressed, humiliated, hopeless, living in darkness. By ch. 48 changes are beginning to take place, and in chs. 49–55 Judah/Zion has been transformed. In ch. 48 Zion is urged to go out from Babylon, and to flee Chaldea. In chs. 49–55 Zion will be inhabited with many dwellers, prisoners will come out of darkness, children will be numerous to the surprise of once barren Zion. Kings and queens will now care for the children of the once humiliated Zion, they will bow down to her and lick the dust of her feet. She will be adorned like a bride.

Chapter 47 is the key to the reversal of fortune of Daughter Zion. It functions as a pivot for Second Isaiah in that it is the point in the book where Judah/Israel changes places with the oppressor, Babylon.[61] In ch. 47 Babylon descends into darkness, loses power and status, is clothed like a slave, has no hope for salvation, and now becomes the

58. E.W. Conrad, *Reading Isaiah* (Minneapolis: Fortress Press, 1991); see especially ch. 3, 'The LORD's Military Strategy Concerning All the Earth', pp. 52-82.

59. Conrad, *Reading Isaiah*, p. 79.

60. See my article, 1991, for a full development of this idea.

61. Conrad, *Reading Isaiah*, p. 79, says of ch. 47 that it is 'a fitting climax to the section of the book that began in chapter 13, containing the major theme of the LORD's military plan to conduct warfare against all the nations'. R.H. O'Connell, *Concentricity and Continuity: The Literary Structure of Isaiah* (JSOTSup, 188; Sheffield: Sheffield Academic Press, 1994), p. 152, considers Isa. 47.8-15 the axis in a chiastic arrangement of Isa. 40–55. He divides ch. 47 into a trial against Babylon (vv. 1-7) and a taunt song (vv. 8-15).

oppressed. Everything that Judah once was, Babylon becomes; all that Babylon thought she was is given to Zion.

The KOB in ch. 14 also functions as a foil, but this figure is a foil to the idealized messianic king of Isaiah 11.[62] Clements, for example, sees one of the explanations for the inclusion of the Babylon prophecies of 13.1–14.23 to be related to a preoccupation with the fate of the Davidic kingship, as well as that of the temple.[63] Some examples of identical terminology in Isaiah 11 and 14 will help in demonstrating that relationship between the chapters, and point to the possibility of a third connection, with Isaiah 40–66.[64] A term used to describe the messianic king in Isa. 11.1 is *nṣr*, a 'branch' from the root of Jesse. The same term is used of KOB in 14.19, but the sense is very different. He is referred to as a *nṣr ntʿb*, a 'loathsome branch'. In the first instance (11.1), the coming of the messianic ruler is a sign of the restoration of order and justice.[65] In the case of KOB, he will be known as a loathsome branch in his death, and will be cast out like a rejected carcass. The term *nṣr* appears only three times in the book of Isaiah. The last occurrence is in 60.21, where it is a symbol of God's planting his people once more in the land. The symbol is used first as an image of the ideal Davidic monarch, then of the defeated Babylonian king, and finally of God's people once more planted in the land from which they had been dispossessed.

This messianic king (11.4) will smite (*hkh*) the earth with the rod (*šbṭ*) of his mouth, and will slay the wicked (*ršʿ*). The same terms are used in

62. Ch. 13, which portrays the destruction of the whole earth, and the return of all nature to chaos, has as its opposite the idyllic portrayal of the days of the messianic king, when nature will return to its state of harmony (11.6-9). Isa. 65.25 is a variation on Isa. 11.6-9.

63. R.E. Clements, 'Isaiah 14, 22-27: A Central Passage Reconsidered', in J. Vermeylen (ed.), *The Book of Isaiah/Le livre d'Isaïe* (BETL, 81; Leuven: Leuven University Press, 1989), p. 262.

64. Anderson, *A Time to Mourn*, p. 89, discusses another contrast or reversal, comparing the theme of descent to Sheol in rituals of mourning with the notion of the Temple as the entrance to heaven. He cites R. Clifford, 'Isaiah 55: An Invitation to a Feast', in C. Meyers and M. O'Connor (eds.), *The Word of the Lord Shall Go Forth* (Winona Lake, IN: Eisenbrauns, 1983), p. 31, who interpreted the cultic feast in Isa. 55 as an invitation to experience the very presence of God.

65. P. Ackroyd, 'Isaiah 1–12: Presentation of a Prophet', in *Studies in the Religious Tradition of the Old Testament* (London: SCM Press, 1987), p. 101, sees this as the climax of 9.7-11. He points to the contrast between the overthrow of the exalted trees in 10.33-34 and the establishment of the Davidic shoot.

the description of the reign and defeat of the reign of KOB. The staff of the wicked (*ršʿym*) will be broken by God, as well as the rod (*šbṭ*) of the kings who smote (*mkh*) the nations. The rod or scepter was the sign of the might and power of KOB.

The terms used in ch. 11 to describe the reign of the messianic king are used in ch. 14 to describe God's destruction of KOB. If we interpret these terms in chapter 14 to be allusions to chapter 11, then the role of the messianic king has been taken over by God who will accomplish those things that previously were expectations of a now non-existent Davidic ruler. Furthermore, reading 14.19 and 60.21 as reinterpretations of 11.1, the overall direction of these allusions can show a development from reliance on the righteous Davidic ruler ('branch') in the eighth century (or pre-exilic times) to the destruction of the loathsome Babylonian imperial rule, to the re-establishment of the 'branch' in the form of an entire righteous people.

This essay has not discussed the relationship of chs. 24–27 to the satiric laments against KOB and VDB. But further investigations of the interrelationships between the contrasts of KOB and the messianic ruler, VDB and Daughter Zion, and contrasts in 24–27 may be fruitful. Sweeney has pointed out a number of allusions in Isaiah 24–27 whereby the author of this section has reinterpreted other sections of the book of Isaiah to form striking contrasts.[66] For example, in 26.1-6, the poet develops a contrast between the once lofty fallen city and the strong city. The inhabitants of the lofty city are brought low, down to the earth, down to the dust, much like KOB and VDB. Reading 26.1-6 in the light of 2.6-21, Sweeney sees the day of the Lord to include Yahweh's establishment of Jerusalem as well as the downfall of the lofty city. The fall of VDB in ch. 47 is likewise connected to the flight from Babylon (Isa. 48.20) and the return to Zion.[67]

Sweeney shows a connection between the birth imagery of 26.7-18 and numerous passages in First, Second and Third Isaiah, but especially emphasizes the connections between Isa. 13.8 and 66.17.[68] The imagery and vocabulary of these verses link major themes: 'judgment against Babylon and rebirth for Israel at Zion'. While there is no lexical correspondence between Isaiah 47 and these verses, we are reminded of the

66. Sweeney, 'Textual Citations'.

67. Sweeney, 'Textual Citations', also shows the theme of the restoration of Israel in Zion to be a key theme of Isa. 27.2-13.

68. Sweeney, 'Textual Citations', pp. 48-49.

loss of the children of VDB, and the contrasting theme of the fruitfulness of Daughter Zion in chs. 49–55.[69]

The taunting or mocking aspects of the poems against KOB and VDB may be compared to the taunting of Sennacherib in Isa.. 37.22-29. That there are connections with Second Isaiah Seitz has clearly demonstrated.[70] More specifically, in comparison with Isaiah 47, we note that the taunt song against Sennacherib begins with Virgin Daughter Zion followed by Daughter Jerusalem, as the one doing the mocking. Isaiah 47 begins with VDB, followed by Daughter Chaldea as the object of the taunt. The despised tyrant in 37.24 reveals his plan to ascend to the far recesses of Lebanon, and to hew down the trees, much like KOB in Isaiah 14. A formal analysis of this taunt song may show further interconnections between the three segments of the book of Isaiah which mention Babylon by name.

In his respondent paper,[71] John Willis suggested the possibility that the first and last references to Babylon in Isaiah (chs. 13 and 48) form an inclusio around the material in between, and that the overall structure may be chiastic. My investigation has not been able to determine such an overall structure. However, correspondences between chs. 13–14 and 46–48 do exist, as I have mentioned above.

The prevailing theme about Babylon in all of these chapters has to do with the promises of her destruction. The destruction of Babylon in 13.19-22 corresponds to the salvation of Zion/Israel in 46.13. The glory (*tpʾrt*, v. 19) of Babylon will disappear, but to Israel God promises to 'give my glory' (*tpʾrty*, v. 22). Babylon's time of destruction is close at hand (*qrwb* v. 22), and Zion's salvation will be brought near (*qrbty*) quickly by God.

The threat of loss of offspring for Babylon is found at the beginning of the Babylon section in 13.18; 14.20-22, and at the end of this larger section, in 47.9. Promises of numerous descendants for Zion begin only after the conclusion of the Babylon section in ch. 48. One of the most consistent features to the Babylon material is the personification of Babylon, not only in ch. 47, but in many of the other sections where Babylon is mentioned. Corresponding to this is the personification of Virgin Daughter Zion, both within chs. 13–48, and in chs. 1–12 and 56–66. In a general way, it could be said that the references to Daughter

69. See Isa. 49.20-21; 54.1-4.
70. Seitz, *Zion's Final Destiny*, pp. 84, 200.
71. See n. * above.

Zion form an envelope around the references to Virgin Daughter Babylon which are limited to the centre of the book. In the end, Daughter Zion and her descendants are restored, but Virgin Daughter Babylon has ceased to exist.

LADY ZION'S ALTER EGOS:
ISAIAH 47.1-15 AND 57.6-13 AS STRUCTURAL COUNTERPARTS*

Mark E. Biddle

Conceptual paradigms of the nature and growth of the book of Isaiah have evolved steadily over the course of the last century of scholarly research. Analyses of the divergent historical backgrounds of the materials in the book led first to a distinction between Proto- and Deutero-Isaiah,[1] and, subsequently, between Deutero- and Trito-Isaiah,[2] terms which referred both to prophetic corpora and to the prophetic personalities thought to have produced them. Scholarly attention was devoted to detailing the historical backgrounds of these corpora, to describing the personalities which produced them, and to suggesting mechanisms whereby these two/three smaller books may have been combined into a larger whole.[3] More recently, this paradigm, too, has been challenged by

---

* An earlier version of this essay was read at the annual meeting of the Society of Biblical Literature, Kansas City, MO, November 1991.

1. This view, pre-figured in the observations of Ibn Ezra and B. Spinoza, received its first extensive statement by J.G. Eichhorn (Leipzig: Weid-Mannischen, *Einleitung ins Alte Testament* [1780–1783]) and later by J.C. Döderlein (*Esaias* [Altsofi: 1789, 3rd edn], pp. xii-xv).

2. B. Duhm first proposed the distinction between 40–55 and 56–66 in his commentary, *Das Buch Jesaja* (HKAT; Göttingen, 1892). Various forms of this view (Trito-Isaiah is the product of an individual, of a school, of successive redactions) soon enjoyed widespread acceptance (cf. esp. K. Elliger, *Die Einheit des Tritojesaja (Jesaja 56–66)* [BWANT, 45; Stuttgart: Kohlhammer, 1928]; idem, 'Der Prophet Tritojesaja', *ZAW* 49 [1931], pp. 112-41; idem, *Deuterojesaja in seinem Verhältnis zu Tritojesaja* [BWANT, 63; Stuttgart: Kohlhammer, 1933]; H. Odeberg, *Trito-Isaiah (Isaiah 56–66): A Literary and Linguistic Analysis*, UUÅ, 1; Uppsala: Lundeqvist, 1931]; A. Zillessen, '"Tritojesaja" und Deuterojesaja: Eine literarkritische Untersuchung zu Jes 56–66', *ZAW* 26 [1906], pp. 231-76).

3. See esp. Elliger, *Verhältnis*. See R. Clements's discussion of various scholarly positions regarding the interrelationship of the three corpora in 'Beyond

those who would emphasize the literary interdependence of the various portions of the book as the result of a long process of redactional activity.[4] Purely mechanical explanations for the combination of these materials on one scroll fail to account for similarity of, allusion to, and, often, verbatim citation of materials across the boundaries of the three divisions of the book. Increasingly, the notion of three books anchored in the careers of three prophetic figures has given way to the paradigm of a literary product anchored in the book itself.[5] On yet another front, scholars interested in taking seriously the final product as a whole,[6] and

Tradition-History: Deutero-Isaianic Development of First Isaiah's Themes', *JSOT* 31 (1985), pp. 96-101.

4.　Scholars offer various models of interrelationship. Some envision a separate existence for Deutero-Isaiah at some point in its history, but most agree that Trito-Isaiah was composed as an extension of an Isaiah corpus including Isaiah 1–55 in substantially its present form or to facilitate the unification of 1–39 and 40–55; see D.R. Jones, 'The Traditio of the Oracles of Isaiah of Jerusalem', *ZAW* 67 (1955), pp. 226-46; L.J. Liebreich, 'The Compilation of the Book of Isaiah', *JQR* 46 (1955/56), pp. 276-78; Clements, 'Tradition History', p. 101; O.H. Steck, *Bereitete Heimkehr: Jesaja 35 als redaktionelle Brücke zwischen dem Ersten und dem Zweiten Jesaja* (SBS, 121; Stuttgart: Katholisches Bibelwerk, 1985); *idem*, 'Der Grundtext in Jesaja 60 und sein Aufbau', *ZTK* 83 (1986), pp. 261-296; *idem*, 'Beobachtungen zu Jesaja 56–59', *BZ* 31 (1987), pp. 228-46; *idem* 'Beobachtungen zu den Zion-Texten in Jesaja 51–54: Ein redaktionsgeschichtlicher Versuch', *BN* 46 (1989), pp. 58-90; *idem*, 'Tritojesaja im Jesajabuch', in J. Vermeylen (ed.), *Le livre d'Isaïe: Les oracles et leurs relecteures, unité et complexité de l'ouvrage* (BETL, 81; Leuven: Leuven University Press, 1989); R.P. Merendino, 'Jes 49.14-26: Jahwes Bekenntnis zu Sion und die neue Heilszeit', *RB* 89 (1982), pp. 321-69; S. Sekine, *Die tritojesajanische Sammlung (Jes 55–66) redaktionsgeschichtlich untersucht* (BZAW, 175; New York: de Gruyter, 1989).

5.　As early as 1906, Zillessen ('Tritojesaja', p. 274) called attention to the numerous citations of and allusions to Isa. 40–55 in Isa. 56–66 and concluded that Isa. 56–66 were written 'im beständigen Hinblick auf 40–55...' Recently, this position has been adopted by a number of scholars. Cf. R. Clements, 'Tradition History', p. 101 ('...from the outset, the material in chs. 40–55 was intended to develop and enlarge upon prophetic sayings from Isaiah of Jerusalem'); O.H. Steck (in an extensive series of articles, see note 4); W. Brueggemann, 'Unity and Dynamic in the Isaiah Tradition', *JSOT* 29 (1984), p. 99, and J. Vermeylen, 'L'unité du livre d'Isaïe', in *idem* (ed.), *Le livre d'Isaïe*, pp. 11-53.

6.　Cf. B.S. Childs, *Introduction to the Old Testament as Scripture* (Philadelphia: Fortress Press, 1979), pp. 216-25; J.D.W. Watts, *Isaiah 34–66* (WBC 25; Waco: Word, 1987).

often skeptical of diachronic methodologies,[7] have concentrated upon developing reading strategies which emphasize the thematic unity of the book by discovering various levels and degrees of macro-structure.

This essay will attempt to respect the concerns of both diachronic and synchronic methodologies. Reserving a detailed discussion of methodology per se for another occasion, three fundamental assertions may be made to support the notion that these two concerns need not be and are not mutually exclusive: first, evidence of the growth of the book of Isaiah over time is incontrovertible; second, through this process structures will have arisen which span diachronically divergent sections of the book; and, third, these structures do not so much homogenize various strata of materials as they place them in fruitful tension.

1. *Zion Songs and Personified Cities*

An example of such structuration, and the central focus of this essay, is the extensive body of materials in Isaiah 47–66 which focus upon feminine personifications of cities. These eight extended units, four in the latter half of Isaiah 40–55 (Isa. 47.1-15; 49.14-26; 51.17–52.10; 54.1-17) and four in 56–66 (57.6-13; 60.1-22; 62.1-12; 66.6-13), focus on named (Lady Babylon, Isa. 47; Lady Jerusalem/Zion, Isa. 49; 51; 54; 60; 62; 66) and unnamed (Isa. 57) feminine figures.

Interpreters have long recognized some relationship between these texts, in particular the three Deutero-Isaianic passages which address Zion. The marked shift in emphasis in the latter half of Deutero-Isaiah from Jacob/Israel (40–47) to Jerusalem/Zion (48–55) alone calls attention to the significance of these three Zion poems.[8] The occurrence of a

---

7.   See especially the recent monograph on the interpretation of the book of Isaiah by E. Conrad (*Reading Isaiah* [Overtures to Biblical Theology; Philadelphia: Fortress Press, 1991]). These concerns were pre-figured to a degree in treatments of the constitutive sections of the book of Isaiah. R. Melugin (*The Formation of Isaiah 40–55* [BZAW, 141; New York: de Gruyter, 1976], esp. pp. 81, 89, 175), for example, employed a type of rhetorical criticism of larger units and concluded that 'Isaiah 40–55...is a collection of originally independent units, but the arrangement is kerygmatic' (p. 175).

8.   The predominance of Jacob in Isa. 40–47 and Zion in Isa. 48–55 has not only been noted (most commentators have observed this distinction; see esp. R. Lack, *La symbolique du livre d'Isaïe: Essai sur l'image littéraire comme èlèment de structuration* [AnBib 59; Rome: Pontifical Biblical Institute, 1973], pp. 82, 103-15; H.C. Spykerboer, *The Structure and Composition of Deutero-Isaiah: With Special*

similar grouping of Zion/Jerusalem texts in 56–66 also elicits questions concerning the relationship of these texts to one another and to their counterparts in 40–55.[9]

Reference to the Polemics against Idolatry [Meppel: Krips Repro, 1975], pp. 153-54; Melugin, *Formation*, p. 148) but has been the occasion for literary-critical distinctions. K. Kiesow (*Exodustexte im Jesajabuch: Literarkritische und motifgeschichtliche Analysen* [OBO, 24; Fribourg, 1979], pp. 197-201) has recently argued that Deutero-Isaiah had a *Wegtheologie* and, therefore, that the Zion texts were not authored by Deutero-Isaiah. H.-J. Hermisson ('Einheit und Komplexität Deuterojesajas: Probleme der Redaktionsgeschichte von Jes 40–55', in Vermeylen (ed.), *Le livre d'Isaïe*, pp. 303-305), countering that the notion of life as a pilgrimage is modern and that Israelite exiles leaving Babylon set out for some destination, suggested that the distinction between the two addressees is purely thematic. 'Jacob' represents Israel as the elect underway, like the patriarch, following God's leadership and call; 'Zion', the elect city, mother of all Israelites, represents the destination of the wandering people.

The new addressee in Isa. 49–55 is usually explained in terms of a later phase in the career of the prophet. Isa. 40–48 originated prior to Cyrus's edict; in Isa. 49–55 the prophet turned attention to the opportunity for return to Jerusalem (P.-E. Bonnard, 'Relire Esaïe 40–66', *ETR* 50 [1975], pp. 353-54). An interesting variant of this position was suggested by M. Haran ('The Literary Structure and Chronological Framework of the Prophecies in Is. XL-XLVIII', in G.W. Anderson *et al.* (eds.), *Congress Volume: Bonn 1962* [VTSup, 9; Leiden: Brill, 1963], pp. 150-51), who argued for the unity of 40–66 in part on the grounds that the new historical background which is usually adduced in support of the break between Isa. 55 and 56—namely, a Palestinian orientation—is actually already present between Isa. 48 and 49. One prophet was responsible for the latter half of Isaiah, but his activity had two distinct temporal and local foci.

At the opposite pole, some have found the new addressee to be one indication that Deutero-Isaiah did not author Isa. 49–55. K. Elliger (*Verhältnis*, pp. 106, 128-29, 198-204; cf. 299-301), for example, noted stylistic and thematic similarities and identified Trito-Isaiah as the author of several interpolations in 40–55, including Isa. 47; 49.22-26; and 51.4-5. R. Merendino ('Jes 49.14-26', pp. 368-69) saw the designation 'Zion' as a clue that the texts originated at a time when the elect was no longer comfortable with the name Jerusalem or with appeal to the old institutions of temple, monarchy and priesthood. A number of redaction critics have assigned the Zion materials, or portions of them, to distinct redactional layers (Hermisson, 'Einheit', p. 311; Steck, 'Zur literarischen Schichtung in Jesaja 51', *BN* 44 [1988], pp. 74-86; *idem*, 'Beobachtungen', esp. pp. 61, 66, 79, 81, 83, 90).

9.   Approaches vary: P. Hanson (*The Dawn of Apocalyptic* [Philadelphia: Fortress Press, 1975], p. 61) regards chs. 56–66 as the product of a minority oppressed by the official community, built around the core section, chs. 60–62, an early summary of chs. 40–55. Sekine (*Sammlung*, pp. 182-87) identified a basic

Several scholars have noted parallels in vocabulary and thought between the various Zion texts within the Deutero-Isaiah corpus[10] and across the boundaries of Deutero- and Trito-Isaiah, typically seeing Deutero-Isaiah texts as prototypes of Trito-Isaiah treatments of the Zion theme.[11] A simple yet striking phenomenon, as yet unexplored, is the arrangement of four personified city passages in Deutero-Isaiah and four extended 2fs sections in Trito-Isaiah. The initial passages in each of these sequences, however, do not refer specifically to Jerusalem/Zion and involve a number of source-critical and semantic difficulties. Do they relate to the three subsequent Jerusalem/Zion texts? Do they parallel one another? And, if so, do the two sequences of four poems parallel each other?

layer of materials written by Trito-Isaiah himself (57.1-15b*a*, 16-18b*a*, 19b*b*; 60.1-22; 61.1-11; 62.1-12; 65.16b-23, 25; 66.7-16; 60 and 66 were written between 519 and 515, 61 shortly after 515, and 62; 57 and 65 were written even later), a second block of materials stemming from prior to 538 (63.7-10), between 538 and 515 (59.1-15a; 63.11b–64.3, 9-11; 64.4b-8; 66.1-4), and after 515 (56.1-5a, 5b; 56.9-57.13a; 58.3-14; 63.1-6; 65.2-16a), and a third body of materials which he assigned to the redactor. In a series of studies, Steck (see n. 4 and esp. *Heimkehr*, pp. 65-79) has outlined a detailed redactional history of the final section of the book of Isaiah: the core, Isa. 60–62, an extrapolation of 40–55, was combined, together with 40–55, with Isa. 1–39 in the redactional effort which produced Isa. 35. Isa. 56–59, which deals with the current guilt of the people of God and the possibility of repentance for the whole people, and which was produced at a date when allusion to the prophetic corpus as a whole was possible, was next inserted. The collection was completed by the addition of proto-apocalyptic Isa. 63–66, for which repentance and salvation were possible only for the pious.

Hanson (*Apocalyptic*, p. 61), Sekine (*Sammlung*, pp. 80-83), Steck (*Heimkehr*, pp. 69-71; 'Beobachtungen', pp. 89-90, 245-46), and others (C. Westermann, *Isaiah 40–66: A Commentary* [OTL; Philadelphia: Westminster Press, 1977], pp. 352-53) have all seen chapters 60–62 as the core related to Isa. 40–55 in terms of the delay. They also agree generally, that 56–59 and 63–66 serve as a later parenthetical construction dealing with the increasingly problematic delay of the promised glory and the question of the scope of Israel's involvement (Hanson, *Apocalyptic*, p. 61; Sekine, *Sammlung*, p. 231; Steck, *Heimkehr*, p. 71; 'Beobachtungen', pp. 232-35). Steck and Hanson were particularly interested in specifying the Deutero-Isaiah texts which have provided the authors of Trito-Isaiah texts with conceptual and linguistic components (cf. Zillessen, 'Tritojesaja').

10. See nn. 12-21, 23-25.
11. See nn. 26-33.

2. *Isaiah 47 in Relation to the Zion Songs of 49–55*

Several scholars have noted the unusual form and placement of Isaiah 47. Elliger, who considered it the product of Trito-Isaiah,[12] regarded it as the conclusion of the third major subdivision of 40–55; namely Isaiah 44.24–47.15.[13] Similarly, Melugin grouped Isaiah 47 with 45 and 46, poems dealing with the fall of Babylon and its gods.[14] R. Lack offered a somewhat inconsistent analysis of the structural function of Isaiah 47. It stands alone as the fourth section of his outline, 48.1–49.13, a section treating salvation, and 49.14–55.13, dealing with Zion and her exiles, follows.[15] He went on, however, to relate chapters 47 and 54, maintaining that 'Isaiah 47 is to Babylon as chapter 54 is to Jerusalem. Between the two poems which personify the two antagonistic cities, there are thematic and figurative relationships. Isaiah 47, meanwhile, is much more firmly attached to a motif in the preceding context of Isaiah 40–46.'[16] Lack then discerned a parallel structure in the intervening Zion material, Isaiah 49.14–52.12.[17] Hermisson, who considered the passage to be authentic, recognized a relationship to Isa. 52.1-2, but not to the whole of the Jerusalem corpus. He commented on the 'exchange of roles' which transpires between Lady Babel and Lady Zion. The one must descend the throne, lie in the dust and drink the cup of Yahweh's wrath; the other is relieved of the cup, shakes off the dust, and ascends the throne.[18] Relatedly, Spykerboer called attention to parallels between Isaiah 47 and 51.17–52.2.[19]

12. *Verhältnis*, pp. 106-107.

13. *Verhältnis*, p. 268.

14. *Isaiah 40–55*, p. 136. He called attention to several parallels: 46.1-2//47.1; 46.8-10//47.7; 45.20 and 46.7//47.13.

15. Lack, *Essai*, p. 82.

16. Lack, *Essai*, p. 103; Merendino (*Der Erste und der Letzte: Eine Untersuchung von Jes 40–48* [VTSup, 31; Leiden: Brill, 1981]; see pp. 487, 493, 495) assigned Isa. 47 to an interpolator. In his view, Deutero-Isaiah only addresses Israel's enemies as a prelude to proclaiming salvation for Israel or Jerusalem. Furthermore, he could find no likely cultic setting for this poem. A later redactor expanded the basic poem to tie it to 52.1-2 and 54.1-17 (both 47 and 54.1-17 address female cities and both begin with imperative address forms and a *kî* clause giving a justification), which are also later interpolations/redactions.

17. Lack, *Essai*, p. 111.

18. 'Einheit', p. 305; cf. Steck, 'Beobachtungen', p. 66.

19. 47.9//51.19 (these two things, etc.); 47.9//51.18, 20 (loss of sons); 47.2//52.1

Several phenomena suggest an even more intricate level of interrelationship between Isaiah 47 and subsequent Zion texts in their present state and placement. Lexical, thematic and structural features of each of these four units find parallels in all three of their counterparts, but the manner in which Isaiah 47 functions in partnership with each of the subsequent Zion songs is of particular interest.

Isaiah 49.14-26

Several scholars have pointed out that the language of Isaiah 49.14-26 anticipates Isaiah 51.17–52.10 and 54.1-17, but it also refers extensively to Isaiah 47.[20] Isaiah 49.23 announces that Jerusalem's enemies will lick the dust of her feet, anticipating the reference to Jerusalem shaking off the dust of her humiliation (Isa. 52.2), but also referring back to Babylon's humiliation in the dust (47.1). Zion will be adorned (49.18) as Babylon is stripped of her finery (47.8). The children of widowed Zion will appear to her suddenly and without explanation (Isa. 49.20-21), while Babylon will be widowed and bereft of her children in one day (47.8-9). Yahweh will be the saviour of Zion (49.25, 26) which Babylon will be unable to find (47.13).

In addition to thematic and verbal allusions, 47 and 49 both exhibit a 'praise refrain' celebrating Yahweh as redeemer. Yahweh acts on Zion's behalf so that 'all flesh may know that I am Yahweh, your savior, and your redeemer, the mighty one of Jacob' (Isa. 49.26), a clear reference to the doxology, 'Our redeemer, Yahweh Zebaoth is his name, the holy one of Israel' (47.4).

Finally, the initial consecutive verb of 49.14, 'but she said', also comprises an intriguing allusion to Isaiah 47.7 and 10. Does the conjunction place the following verb in a sequence? Although Merendino and others have noted the possibility that such a verbal construction may stand alone,[21] the best explanation seems to be that it is meant as a

---

(strip off robe//put on garments); 47.1//52.2 (sit in dust//shake off dust); a chiastic structure; Spykerboer, *Structure and Composition*, pp. 153-154; 172-173.

20. Merendino's study ('Jes 49.14-26', pp. 321-69) is the most recent and the most exhaustive devoted to Isa. 49.14-26. He related the *Überlieferungsgeschichte* of 49.14-26 to 50–52 and 54, arguing that it is a late addition intended primarily to anticipate the subsequent Zion materials. He pointed to no overt connections between 49.14-26 and Isa. 47, however (p. 367). Steck ('Beobachtungen', p. 83) saw a possible reference to Isa. 47.8 in 49.20-21 and to Isa. 47 as a whole in 49.24-26.

21. Merendino ('Jes 49.14-26', p. 346) also noted similar constructions in Isa. 47, although he assigned them no structural significance for Isa. 49.14-26, as well as

continuation of the sequence of such constructions in Isaiah 47. It fits poorly in the immediate context (Isa. 49.8-13) which employs 3ms and 3mpl forms in reference to the servant, the people, and the created order. Why does the personified Jerusalem suddenly raise her voice in objection? Yahweh has announced to Babylon that, because of her arrogant and over-zealous prosecution of the commission given her to punish his people, she, too, will be punished. In a pair of objects introduced by the same verb, *wt'mry*, she has haughtily maintained that she 'will be mistress forever' (47.7), supporting her false sense of security with the further claims that 'no one sees me' and that she alone rules the world (47.10). Yahweh rebuts her contentions with renewed assurances of destruction. Who will replace Babylon on the throne? Zion states her fears that she will not be considered. Just as Babylon has failed to 'remember her end' (47.7) and has haughtily acted as if her actions would go unseen, unnoted (47.10), Jerusalem fears that Yahweh has indeed 'forsaken' and 'forgotten' her (49.14). Babylon proudly claims 'in her heart' that she is alone, unrivaled (47.10), but Jerusalem painfully remembers 'in her heart' the loneliness of exile, childlessness, and bereavement (49.21).

In sum, these two passages portray the responses of Lady Babylon and Lady Zion to God's intentions toward them. In Isaiah 47 Lady Babylon arrogantly reacts to Yahweh's plan to unseat her; in Isaiah 49.14-26 Lady Zion humbly anticipates[22] Yahweh's plan to restore her.

Isaiah 51.17–52.10 and 54

The two remaining Zion passages in Isaiah 40–55 mirror different aspects of Yahweh's message to Lady Babylon. In comparison to Isaiah 47, Isaiah 51.17–52.10 contrasts the content of Yahweh's plans for the

---

in Isa. 37.24-29; Jer. 2.31b-32; 45.3-5; Ezek. 28.2, 6-8(9-10); 25.3b-5a. Interestingly, this sort of objection/rebuttal exchange is characteristic of God's discourse with personified cities; cf. M. Biddle, *A Redaction History of Jeremiah 2:1–4:2* (ATANT, 77; Zürich: Theologischer Verlag, 1990), pp. 48-52.

22. How does she know Yahweh's intentions toward her? They are only revealed subsequent to her initial objections of abandonment and are most explicitly stated in the second Zion passage. Merendino ('Jes 49.14-26', p. 367) and others (cf. Steck, 'Beobachtungen', pp. 83-84, although Steck considers the second and third Zion songs to be redactional products standing in a complicated chronological relationship to Isa. 49.14-26) have pointed to this phenomenon as evidence that 49.14-26 was composed with a view to the pre-existent Zion materials of chapters 51–54.

two cities while Isaiah 54 stresses the transience of Babylon's supremacy and Jerusalem's humiliation.

Whereas in Isaiah 47 Yahweh directs Babylon to 'descend', to 'sit in the dust (ʿpr)', and to 'strip off' her robe (47.1-2); in 51–52 he calls upon Jerusalem to 'arise' and 'stand' (51.17), to 'arise' and 'dress' (52.1), and to 'arise' and 'shake off the dust (ʿpr)' (52.2).[23] Babylon shall no longer (lōʾ tôsîpî) be called 'delicate' (47.1) or 'mistress of dominion' (47.5); Jerusalem will no longer (lōʾ tôsîpî) drink the cup of Yahweh's wrath (51.22) or be trodden by the uncircumcised and unclean (52.1, lōʾ yôsîp). Babylon will soon be confronted with the loss of children (47.9) while Jerusalem's bereavement will soon be over (51.18, 20).[24] Babylon will soon be (47.9) and Jerusalem has already been (51.19) overcome by disaster and bereavement ('these two things'). Perhaps the most conspicuous tie between the two passages is the recurrence of the 'praise refrain' in declaration that God redeems (52.9) Jerusalem as the earlier doxology (47.4) has celebrated.

Read in parallel, Isaiah 47 and 54 contrast the limited duration of Babylon's supremacy with Jerusalem's momentary distress. In addition to the fact that Isaiah 54 shares with Isaiah 47 and 51 the imperative followed by kî clauses giving the grounds for the call to action,[25] a number of lexical and thematic parallels center around the transience of the current status of the two cities. 'Shame (ḥrp)' (47.3) and 'widowhood (ʾlmnh)' (47.8) will come upon Babylon in a 'moment (rgʿ)' (47.9), but Jerusalem is to forget her 'shame' and 'widowhood' as a thing of the past (54.4), as a 'momentary' abandonment (rgʿ, 54.7, 8). Indeed, Yahweh delivered Israel into the hands of Babylon because he was 'angry' with them (47.6), but that fleeting anger shall not recur (54.8, 9). Instead, Yahweh's relationship with Zion will continue to be characterized by the constancy (ʿwlm) of his covenant with her (54.8). While Yahweh's covenant with Zion endures, Babylon learns that her claims to eternal (ʿwlm) dominion (47.7) have no basis. She has not considered the

23. On parallels between Isa. 47 and 54, cf. Steck, 'Beobachtungen', pp. 59 n. 6, 61; 'Literarische', p. 77 n. 11; Spykerboer, *Structure and Composition*, pp. 172-173; Merendino, *Erste und Letzte*, p. 493.

24. Cf. Spykerboer, pp. 172-73.

25. Merendino, *Erste und Letzte*, p. 493; Steck, 'Beobachtungen', p. 67; Isa. 54 multiplies kî clauses in comparison with Isa. 47 and 51 and adds a number of citation formulae at the conclusion of sub-sections. The interrelationship between Isa. 51 and 54 is explored in detail by Steck, 'Beobachtungen', pp. 68, 70-76.

consequences of her arrogant violence, she has not 'remembered her end' (47.7). Jerusalem, on the other hand, owing to God's steadfast commitment to her, is encouraged to forget the past consequences of her sin, to remember her disgrace no more (54.4). Jerusalem's pain at Babylon's hands has been a solitary episode; any who threaten her shall fall because of her (54.15) just as Babylon will fall (47.11) because she oppressed Israel with a heavy yoke of bondage (47.6). Finally, the doxological celebration of Yahweh as a God of redemption reappears as a refrain and confirms the sequential interrelationship of Isaiah 47 and the three Zion songs: Yahweh, the holy One of Israel/mighty One of Jacob, redeemer (Isa. 47.4 // 49.26 // 52.9 // 54.5, 8).

In sum, the Babylon portrayed in Isaiah 47 is the polar opposite of the Jerusalem depicted in Isaiah 49; 51–52; and 54 in a number of ways. Her haughtiness contrasts with Zion's humility, her bleak future with Zion's glory, her momentary dominance with Zion's lasting covenant relationship with Yahweh.

3. *Two Cycles of City Songs?*

Do the four poems with feminine addressees in Isaiah 56–66 parallel this structure, as the balanced occurrence of one negative poem followed by three announcements of future glory would seem to suggest? One would expect that the two sequences of four poems could be read as four pairs (57//47; 60//49; 62//51–52; 66//54) and, in fact, a number of linguistic allusions and citations seem to support such a hypothesis. Furthermore, such a parallel structure can help to clarify several exegetical difficulties in Isaiah 56–66.

Isaiah 57.6-13

Among allusions to virtually the entire Isaianic corpus and beyond, including the prophetic corpus as a whole,[26] Isaiah 57.6-13 exhibits definite points of connection with Isaiah 47. For example, Yahweh challenges Lady Babylon to stand firm 'in the many sorceries in which you have labored from your youth (*wbrb kšpyk bʾšr ygʿt mnʿwryk*)' (47.12; cf. v. 9, 'your many sorceries' and v. 15 'those with whom you have labored') and issues a similar challenge to the feminine addressee of 57 ('in your many ways you labored [*brb drkk ygʿt*]', v. 10).[27] Both poems

---

26. Odeberg, *Trito-Isaiah*, pp. 75-77; Steck, 'Beobachtungen', pp. 232-235.
27. Cf. Odeberg, *Trito-Isaiah*, p. 96.

challenge dependence upon sources of assistance other than Yahweh, sources which will ultimately fail (cf. 47.12 and 57.12, $y^c l$),[28] sources which cannot deliver (*nṣl*) themselves (47.14) and cannot deliver (*nṣl*) their cohort (57.13). Isaiah 57.11b (*lōʾ zkrt lōʾ-śʾmt ʿl-lbk*) cites 47.7b in inverted order (*lōʾ śʾmt... ʿl-lbk lōʾ zkrt*) and accentuates the addressee's failure of perception as a failure, not merely to consider the consequences of her behavior, but failure to relate to Yahweh.[29]

Isaiah 60

Ties between Isaiah 60 and 49.14-26 are well-documented[30] and so extensive that Steck can refer to Isaiah 49 as the *Muster* for Isaiah 60. The relationship between 60 and 49 differs radically from that between 47 and 49 in terms of the theme shared between the two texts. Isaiah 60 does not elaborate upon the notion of Zion's humble response to Yahweh's intention but upon the concept of her future glory. Indeed, the Zion of Isaiah 60 offers no response whatsoever to the announcement of her coming glory. Correspondences need only be listed here: 49.14//60.15 (*ʿzb*); 49.18//60.4 (a verbatim quotation); 49.18//60.4, 7 (*qbṣ*); 49.21//60.8 ('who are these?'); 49.22-23//60.4, 9-10 ('sons and daughters', 'kings ministering'); 49.23//60.14 (*wʿpr rglyk//lʾl kpwt rglyk*); 49.23//60.16a (*ynq*); 49.26//60.16b (a near verbatim quotation of the 'doxology' refrain familiar from Isa. 47 and all three of the Zion poems in Deutero-Isaiah); 49.26//60.14 (*mwnyk//mʾnyk*).

Isaiah 62

The second Zion poem in the Trito-Isaiah corpus exhibits fewer direct allusions to its counterpart in the Deutero-Isaiah corpus (62.3//52.1 [*tpʾrt*]; 62.6//52.8 ['sentinels', *šmrym//ṣpyk*]; cf. the interesting homophony, 62.6//52.5 [*kl-hywm wkl hlylh tmyd//yhylylw... wtmyd kl-hywm*]; 62.8-9//51.17, 21-23 ['drinking the cup of wrath'//'drinking wine']). Nevertheless, thematic allusions, especially to the larger context of

---

28. Odeberg, *Trito-Isaiah*, p. 99.

29. Cf. Zillessen, 'Tritojesaja', p. 237; Odeberg, *Trito-Isaiah*, p. 98; W.A.M. Beuken, 'Isaiah 56.9–57.13—An Example of the Isaianic Legacy of Trito-Isaiah', in J. van Henten *et al.* (eds.), *Tradition and Re-interpretation in Jewish and Early Christian Literature* (Festschrift J.C.A. Lebram; SPB, 36; Leiden: Brill, 1986), pp. 55-56.

30. Cf. Zillessen, 'Tritojesaja', pp. 240-42; Odeberg, pp. 236-49; Merendino, *Erste und Letzte*, pp. 236-45; Steck, *Heimkehr*, p. 70; and *idem*, 'Grundtext', pp. 267-68, 273, 277, 282, 284, 292, esp. n. 106.

51.17–52.9, clearly establish a specific relationship between the two poems:[31] both the nations will see Zion's vindication (62.2//52.10), which will result from the demonstration of God's might (62.8//52.10, 'his right hand and his mighty arm'//'his holy arm'); the people need only enter//exit the gates of Zion//Babylon (62.10//52.11).

Isaiah 66.6-13

Isaiah 66, which has become the object of scholarly interest in terms of the ways in which it forms inclusios with passages from Trito-, Deutero- and Proto-Isaiah,[32] reprises up to six elements of Isaiah 54: (1) Zion's joy (66.10//54.1) (2) at the birth of her children (66.7-8//54.1, *yldh* and *ḥlh*)[33] will be realized (3) in a moment (66.8) as brief as the moment of her pain (54.7); (4) this moment will initiate a period of prosperity during which Zion will find it necessary to extend her borders (54.2) due to Yahweh's extension of peace to her like a flowing river (66.12); (5) this new era of divine comfort for Jerusalem (54.11//66.13) will bring (6) destruction upon her enemies, not by flood, but by fire (66.15-16//54.9-10).

4. *Who is the Feminine Addressee of Isaiah 57.6-13?*

If these two series of four poems do, in fact, stand in parallel relationship to one another, the question arises as to the identity of the unnamed feminine addressee of Isaiah 57.6-13 and the function of this passage in the entire sequence. Lady Babylon, negatively portrayed in Isaiah 47, must fall so that Lady Zion may assume her proper status as Yahweh's chosen. Is the reader to understand that the feminine addressee of Isaiah 57 must descend so that Zion may ascend?

A preliminary step toward settling these issues depends upon clarifying the distinction between the 2fs address forms of 57.6-13 and the plurals of the larger unit in which it is situated. Interpreters of the Hebrew Bible have tended to understand any reference to any segment of Israel as a reference to the whole, a circumstance which causes many

---

31. Cf. Hanson, *Apocalyptic*, p. 62; Odeberg, p. 265.

32. Cf. Steck, *Heimkehr*, p. 75; M.A. Sweeney, *Isaiah 1–4 and the Post-Exilic Understanding of the Isaianic Tradition* (BZAW, 171; New York: de Gruyter, 1988), p. 94; Vermeylen, 'L'unité', pp. 43-44; E.C. Webster, 'A Rhetorical Study of Isaiah 66', *JSOT* 34 (1986), pp. 96, 98-99, 103.

33. Cf. Webster, 'Rhetorical Study', p. 98.

interpreters of 56.9–57.13 some difficulty. Sekine, for example, regarded the plurals as references to Israel's leadership, while the singulars, both masculine and feminine, refer to Israel as a whole,[34] and G.A.F. Knight considered the shift to feminine address forms to be 'a device by means of which [the prophet] can include all Israel as one people'.[35] The assumption, however, that biblical writers alternated indiscriminately between feminine and masculine, singular and plural address forms seems to be unwarranted, unhelpful and simplistic. At some level, these variations in address form must reflect some distinction in the identification of addressees. How are references to the sons of this unnamed feminine figure to be understood? Does Israel give birth to itself?

Following J. Lewy,[36] A. Fitzgerald,[37] J. Schmitt[38] and others,[39] I have argued elsewhere with respect to a similar phenomenon in Jeremiah 2, and subsequently with respect to feminine imagery in general, that Old Testament writers consistently employed such 2fs address forms to refer to personified cities in keeping with ANE patterns and in clear

---

34. *Sammlung*, pp. 106-107. With reference to Isa. 54, Beuken has argued, similarly, for an understanding of the figure of Lady Zion, which he did not distinguish referentially from Israel as a whole people, in terms of corporate personality ('Isaiah LIV: The Multiple Identity of the Person Adressed', in J. Barr *et al.* [eds.], *Language and Meaning: Studies in Hebrew Language and Biblical Exegesis* [Leiden: Brill, 1974], p. 63). In his understanding, mother, wife and city represent three successive phases in the history of the people of Israel (p. 70).

35. *The New Israel: A Commentary on the Book of Isaiah 56–66* (ITC; Grand Rapids: Eerdmans, 1985), p. 13.

36. 'The Old West Semitic Sun-god Hammu', *HUCA* 18 (1943–44), pp. 436-43.

37. 'The Mythological Background for the Presentation of Jerusalem as a Queen and False Worship as Adultery in the OT', *CBQ* 34 (1972), pp. 403-16; 'BTWLT and BT as Titles for Capital Cities', *CBQ* 37 (1975), pp. 170-80.

38. 'The Gender of Ancient Israel', *JSOT* 6 (1983), pp. 115-25; see also *idem*, 'The Motherhood of God and Zion as Mother', *RB* 92 (1985), pp. 557-69; *idem*, 'Women in Mark's Gospel', *The Bible Today* (1981), pp. 228-33; *idem*, 'The Wife of God in Hosea 2', *BR* 34 (1989), pp. 5-18; *idem*, 'Psalm 87: Zion, The City of God's Love', in A.V. Joseph *et al.* (eds.), *The Psalms and Other Studies on the Old Testament* (Nashotah, WI: Nashotah House Seminary, 1990), pp. 34-44.

39. See O.H. Steck, 'Zion als Gelände und Gestalt: Überlegungen zur Wahrnehmung Jerusalems als Stadt und Frau im Alten Testament', *ZTK* 86 (1989), pp. 261-81 (with extensive bibliography); cf. Watts, *Isaiah 34–66*, p. 258.

distinction to collective and corporate modes of address.[40] Such shifts in addressee would not necessarily, primarily or automatically have literary-critical implications, although they may inform source analyses. But the conceptual significance of such shifts must not be downplayed or overlooked.[41] The personification of Lady Jerusalem, sometimes virtuous mother, sometimes widow, sometimes harlot, provides the biblical author with an additional character. While in 'objective' terms, she may be a figure representing the people, or elements within it, in terms of the dynamics of biblical poetry, her independence and integrity must be recognized and she must be allowed to play out her role in the drama. She is a dramatic character and not an amorphous reference to the 'people as a whole'.

The setting of Isaiah 57 confirms the hypothesis that the feminine addressee is the personification of a leading city, her sons, its citizens. Again and again in the concluding portions of the book of Isaiah, a personified mother-city is bereft of her children or miraculously reunited with them. In these passages, mother and children may not simply be identified with one another: the people as a group do not return to themselves as a collective.

Who, specifically, is this unnamed feminine figure? She is Zion, herself, in a troubling manifestation. As has been shown, Isaiah 47, the sole condemnatory poem in the first series, depicts Zion's rival Lady Babylon who, because of her haughtiness and cruelty must fall in order to make room for the restoration of Lady Zion to the throne and to permit the return of her children. Does Isaiah 57, the sole condemnatory poem in the second series, depict Lady Zion's alter ego, the 'old Jerusalem', threatening ruin for Yahweh's plans to save?

---

40. *A Redaction History*, pp. 39-82; 'The Figure of Lady Jerusalem: Identification, Deification and Personification of Cities in the Ancient Near East', in B. Batto, W. Hallo and L. Younger (eds.), *The Canon in Comparative Perspective* (Scripture in Context, 4; Lewiston, NY: Mellen Press, 1991), pp. 173-94; Cf. Hosea 2, where the same dynamics pertain.

41. Cf. W. Thiel, *TLZ* 116 (1991), p. 106, and J. Lundbom, *JBL* 110 (1991), p. 516, who misapprehend my treatment of the 2fs materials in Jer. 2 (*A Redaction History*, pp. 39-82) as a mechanical discrimination of sources purely on the basis of shifts in person and number. The importance of these variations lies in the *identity* of those so addressed. Mother Jerusalem and her children are not to be merely identified. Literary distinctions may then be made, not only on the basis of the mere phenomenon of variation in person and number, but owing to radical shifts in the identity of the figures addressed and the accompanying imagery and argumentation.

The author of Isaiah 57 has employed an impressive array of allusions to prior prophetic literature in order to establish an association with this Jerusalem and the Zion condemned by Jeremiah, Ezekiel and other sections of the book of Isaiah for her religio-political infidelity to Yahweh, and not with the Zion of Isaiah 49; 51–52; 54; 60; 62 and 66. Such similarities have even led some scholars to conclude that the passage is a pre-exilic composition included here by redactors.[42] Others have taken it to be a condemnation of the cults of fertility and the dead as they continued to be practiced even into the post-exilic period,[43] ignoring implications of the Zion persona. Instead, the harlotry language of Isaiah 57 seems intended to identify the addressee not only as Jerusalem, but as the old, sinful, unfaithful harlot upon whom Yahweh visited judgement. Steck has noted affinities with Jeremiah 6 and 8, for example,[44] and Watts has called attention to allusions to Jer. 2.20–3.18.[45] Perhaps more telling are the range of parallels and allusions to the 2fs materials distributed throughout the book of Jeremiah: harlotry on the high hills (Isa. 57.7; Jer. 2.20; 13.27); tireless seeking after lovers (Isa. 57.10; Jer. 2.23-24); unwillingness to admit the hopelessness (*nw'š*) of her situation (Isa. 57.10; Jer. 2.25; 20.21); crying out to lovers who will be unable to help (Isa. 57.13; Jer. 2.37; 22.20; 30.13); being driven before the wind (Isa. 57.13; Jer. 13.24; 22.22).[46] In addition, affinities both in vocabulary and tone with disparaging depictions of Zion and other personified foreign capital cities in the book of Ezekiel are palpable (cf. Ezek. 16 and 23; esp. *qibbûṣ* in Isa. 57.13 and Ezek. 16.37; and *wtšry*, which occurs only in Isa. 57.9 and Ezek. 27.25, the indictment of Tyre[47]). Finally, several scholars have noted the way in which Isaiah 57 forms an inclusio with the portrayal of Lady Zion in Isaiah 1.[48] It should be emphasized that all of these passages indict prominent cities, usually Jerusalem,

---

42. Volz, Ewald etc.; for a summary of such positions, cf. Hanson, *Apocalyptic*, p. 186.

43. Cf. S. Ackerman, 'Sacred Sex, Sacrifice and Death: Understanding a Prophetic Poem', *BibRev* 6 (1990), pp. 38-44; C.A. Kennedy, 'Isaiah 57.5-6: Tombs in the Rocks', *BASOR* 275 (1988), pp. 47-52.

44. Steck, 'Beobachtungen', p. 234 n. 34.

45. Watts, *Isaiah 34–66*, p. 255.

46. Cf. also Jer. 4.18, 30; 6.8; See Biddle, *A Redaction History*, pp. 68-82.

47. Cf. Biddle, 'Lady Jerusalem', p. 185.

48. Cf. esp. Isa. 1.21-23 (Steck, 'Beobachtungen', p. 231) and Isa. 1.4 (Vermeylen, 'L'unité', p. 43).

personified as great ladies of the realm, for disloyalty, arrogance and immorality.

5. *Zion Replaced not Restored*

How does this reprise of old charges against Jerusalem, this depiction of her in the old categories, function? The first four poem sequence announces that Lady Babylon will fall making room for her opposite Lady Zion. Haughtiness gives way to humility, temporary glory for the one becomes lasting glory for the other. Babylon will fall, Zion will be restored, her sons returned, her walls rebuilt, her pain banished, her enemies repaid and pacified.

Isaiah 57 problematizes this almost automatic, mechanical sequence of events. The fall of Babylon has not occasioned the immediate restoration. What is the impediment? Babylon has fallen, but so, too, must the Old Jerusalem. Instead of the gloriously restored Zion, the disloyal, immoral, untrustworthy harlot has resurfaced. The Jerusalem whose transgressions motivated Yahweh's displeasure in the days of Isaiah, Jeremiah and Ezekiel, Lady Zion's alter ego, has reappeared. In light of this troubling reality, the restored Jerusalem appears to be little more than a theoretical possibility unless some way can be found to remove the impediment. The second series of four poems turns attention, then, to this problem. Yahweh has not abandoned his intention; he will persevere; 'In its time', he will accomplish it. 'For Zion's Sake I will not keep silent, and for Jerusalem's sake I will not rest' (62.1). Sentinels charged with continually reminding Yahweh of his plans for Jerusalem are posted on Jerusalem's wall (62.6-8). The context of the final poem in the sequence provides the answer (66.22//65.17): Old Jerusalem cannot simply be restored, she has not changed since the days of the first Isaiah nor since the exile; there must be a New Jerusalem. As Babylon fell, so must the harlot Zion. Jerusalem will not be restored, but replaced: a new heaven, a new earth, a new Jerusalem.

'ISAIAH' AS AN EXPONENT OF TORAH: ISAIAH 56.1-8

Roy D. Wells, Jr

Any discussion of Torah in Isaiah 56.1-8 joins the long procession that has formed behind Bernhard Duhm.[1] In this procession, there are few studies of the relation between the traditions in the voice of 'Isaiah' and the traditions in the voice of 'Moses'—with the notable exception of motifs from *Heilsgeschichte*. In his regard for the term 'scribal', Beuken[2] supports new possibilities for reading the text against the background of other texts. His assumption that 'literal correspondences' lead to and back from the other texts is quite a powerful tool for discrimination, as Hillel the Elder taught us long ago. The best case for such an analysis is Isaiah 56.1-8, which clearly deals with issues that Duhm did not associate with proper prophetic activity.

The counterpoint between Isaianic language and traditional legal language is apparent in the opening phrase. The double admonition (imperative plural), and the pairing of משפט and צדקה as virtues associated with God, Zion and kings, expresses connection with the rhetoric of 'Isaiah'.[3] But the vocabulary of the admonition (56.1a),

---

1. Duhm (1892: 391) speaks of a 'Thora über die Zulassung der Fremden und der Verschnittenen zur Gemeinde und zum Kultus'. But the appearance of the term *Werkgerechtigkeit* in the same paragraph mandates a certain wariness. A *Forschungsbericht* would displace the paper, but Silberman (1983) states the matter well.

2. Beuken 1987 concentrates on Isaianic material. Beuken 1989: 36, however, shows a 'kaleidoscope of scriptural material' in Isa. 56–66, and speaks of 56.1-8 as a 'patchwork quilt' (*lappendeken*). See the methodological comments of Lau (1994: 15-17). This work appeared after the body of this paper was completed.

3. See Bonnard 1972: 344 n. 1, Sehmsdorf 1972: 545, and Schmidt 1968: 79-103 (on צדק).

Thus says the LORD:
Maintain justice, and do what is right,[4]

has strong connections with the tradition of legal instruction.[5] Dtr and H ring the changes on the word pair שמר/עשה[6] without offering a precise grammatical parallel, and without using the abstract 'justice' for concrete 'ordinances'.[7]

The basis for the admonition (56.1b),

...for soon my salvation will come,
and my deliverance be revealed,

not only contains thematic Isaianic words,[8] but, as Steck has argued, reflections of specific Isaianic texts.[9] The allusion[10] to the ominous conclusion to a poem announcing the defeat of (the gods of) Babylon (46.12-13),[11]

Listen to me, you stubborn of heart,
you who are far from deliverance (מצדקה).
I bring near my deliverance (קרבתי צדקתי), it is not far off,
and my salvation (תשועתי) will not tarry;
I will put (ונתתי) salvation (תשועה) in Zion,
for Israel my glory.

is fairly simple, bringing forward the context of this reproach as the basis for the general admonition. The allusion to Isaiah 51, addressed to those who pursue (51.1) and know (51.7) righteousness (צדק)(51.4-5),

4. The NRSV is used throughout.

5. See the form critical treatments by Begrich (1964) and Lescow (1970).

6. Sehmsdorf (1972) concentrates on parallels with the 'dtr-chr Bewegung', but this may be a Procrustean bed. The direct pairing of imperfects and waw perfects in admonitions, often with משפטים (4.6; 7.12; 29.8 [ET 9]; —16.12; 26.16; 23.24 [ET 23]), despite the more abstract משפט, is more to the point. See the parallels in the Holiness Code (Lev. 18.4; 19.37; 20.8; 20.22; 22.31; 25.18; 26.3).

7. Fishbane (1985: 128) speaks of 'lay exegesis'.

8. Rendtorff (1993) sees a theological transition at 56.1 marked by the juxtaposition of two meanings of צדקה (1a, 'what is right' and 1b, 'my deliverance').

9. See Steck 1991b and 1991c for a discussion of these references in the context of his theory that this text belongs to the final (Ptolemaic) redaction and reconception of the book of Isaiah. See the summary in Steck 1991a.

10. At this point, Eslinger's (1992) phrase, 'intertextual allusion', is chosen for its generality.

11. See Melugin 1976: 132-34 and Westermann 1991: 45-46, 241.

> Listen to me, my people (עמי),
> and give heed to me, my nation;
> for a teaching will go out from me,
> and my justice (ומשפטי) for a light to the peoples (עמים).
> I will bring near my deliverance (קרוב צדקי) swiftly,
> my salvation (ישעי) has gone out
> and my arms will rule the peoples (עמים ישפטו),[12]

becomes an admonition addressed to those who, in the same context, must be admonished to act in conformity with justice and right. The festal joy of the returning 'ransomed of Zion' (51.11; cf. 51.3),

> So the ransomed of the LORD shall return,
> and come (ובאו) to Zion with singing;
> everlasting joy (שמחת עולם) shall be upon their heads;
> they shall obtain joy and gladness (שמחה),
> and sorrow and sighing shall flee away.

has become (56.7) the rejoicing in the temple by עמים (cf. 51.4) whose sacrifices are offered there—or even foreign cultic functionaries (see below). The reference to the name (for eunuchs—56.6) that is better than sons or daughters may be the counterpoint to the lament of Jerusalem as a woman bereft of the support of children and the corresponding images of the restoration of these children (51.18):

> There is no one to guide her
> among all the children (בנים) she has borne;
> there is no one to take her by the hand (מחזיק בידה)
> among all the children (בנים) she has brought up.

In this context, the phrase יחזיק בה (56.2) is interesting—there has been some discussion of the antecedent of the feminine pronominal suffix. Note also that the general terms for the unsympathetic audience to the lamentation (51.12; cf. 51.7),

> I, I am he who comforts you;
> why then are you afraid of a mere mortal (מאנוש) who must die,
> a human being (ומבן־אדם) who fades like grass?

appear in the beatitude pronounced on those who respond to the opening admonition and its expansion (56.2):

---

12. The appearance of these terms in 51.6 and 51.8 does not add to the argument.

Happy is the mortal (אֱנוֹשׁ) who does this,
the one (בֶּן אָדָם) who holds it fast,[13]

In sum, the references to other Isaianic texts are better described as the work of Steck's authorized transmitter and reinterpreter of a tradition than as 'epigonic allusions'.[14]

The final participial phrase of the benediction forms an *inclusio* with 56.6 that ends the opening (56.2):

> ...who keeps the sabbath, not profaning it,
> and refrains from doing any evil.

The repetition of the verbs שָׁמַר and עָשָׂה[15] from the opening admonition (v. 1a) emphasizes the traditional ethos of the community—especially the Sabbath—in the context of Isaianic words announcing imminent divine manifestation.[16] At the same time, it is a refrain linking the opening admonition and affirmation with the conditional promises to eunuchs (v. 4a) and foreigners (v. 6b). Fishbane has shown that the extraordinary significance of Sabbath observance in this text is expressed in a dialogue with a variety of then current Sabbath *tradita*.[17] The verb 'profane', however, is associated with a particular Sabbath *traditum* (Exod. 31.12-17):[18]

---

13. Or 'who sustains her' (namely, Zion), if this is part of an 'echo' of 51.18, discussed above. See Hollander 1981 for the term. Rhetorically, this also anticipates the unique refrain מַחֲזִים בִּבְרִיתִי (56.4, 6), with a feminine object.

14. Fishbane 1985: 498—see 289; For Lau (1994: 4-5, 18-21, 316-20), these are exegetical citations that indicate the 'canonical' status of an earlier form of the Book of Isaiah.

15. Odeberg's (1931: 18) silence about 'keep your hand from' (NRSV 'refrain from') confirms the independence of the phrasing. Sehmsdorf (1972: 546 n. 146) lists the occurrences of the word pair 'observe/do' and of the phrase 'do evil' in Deut./Dtr.

16. Koenen (1990: 226-27) discusses this connection of 'ethic and eschatology' in his treatment of editorial 'bracketing texts' (including 56.1) that combine words of 'Trito-Isaiah' and connect them to the work of a redactor. The *Mischzitate* (pp. 11-15) in this redactional level also link the redactor's work to a broader textual world.

17. Fishbane 1985: 131-33. Knight (1990: 2) makes a distinction between 'tradition' as 'the materials...that are being handed down' (*traditum*) and as 'the process of transmission' (*traditio*). Fishbane (1985: 14-16) amplifies this distinction.

18. *Pace* Grünwaldt (1992: 170-85), who raises the haunting question of the direction of influence. Ezek. 20 and 44 are treated by Fishbane as variant interpretations of the Exodus text, in whatever form it may have existed.

> The LORD said to Moses: You yourself are to speak to the Israelites: 'You shall keep my sabbaths (את־שבתתי תשמרו), for this is a sign between me and you throughout your generations, given in order that you may know that I, the LORD, sanctify you (מקדשכם). You shall keep the sabbath (ושמרתם את־השבת), because it is holy (קדש) for you; everyone who profanes it shall be put to death (מחלליה מות יומת); whoever does (העשה) any work on it shall be cut off (ונכרתה) from among the people (מקרב עמיה). Six days shall work be done (יעשה), but the seventh day is a sabbath of solemn rest (שבת שבתון), holy (קדש), to the LORD; whoever does (העשה) any work on the sabbath day (השבת) shall be put to death. Therefore the Israelites shall keep (ושמרו) the sabbath (השבת), observing the sabbath (לעשות את־השבת) throughout their generations, as a perpetual covenant (ברית עולם). It is a sign forever (לעלם) between me and the people of Israel that in six days the LORD made (עשה) heaven and earth, and on the seventh day he rested (שבת), and was refreshed.'

A scattering of specific words and phrases in Isa. 56.1-8 seem to allude to, or even echo this Sabbath text. The verb שמר (Exod. 31.12, 16) is quite common in Sabbath laws, but 56.4a (ישמרו את־שבתתי) breaks the pattern of the refrain, and strengthens the impression of influence from this text. The connection of the Sabbath with the structuring of time in creation is common, as is the association of holiness with the Sabbath. Here, the grounding of Sabbath in creation gives it a cosmological status,[19] which mandates death for 'defiling' it and excommunication/ death for labour. In 56.1-8, the emphasis on benefits of 'keeping' the Sabbath (Exod. 31.13, 14, 16/Isa. 56.2, 4, 6) holds the text together. The characterization of the Sabbath as a 'covenant' (Exod. 31.16) may be echoed by the coined refrain 'hold fast my covenant' (4, 6), for which Sabbath observance is the metonym. For the eunuchs, the excommunication formula (Exod. 31.14) is brought into the linguistic realm of blood lines in the assurance that the ('everlasting'—cf. Exod. 31.16-17) name, even without children, would 'not be cut off'.[20] For the aliens, the hallowing of those who observe the Sabbath (Exod. 31.13—cf. vv. 14, 15) may appear in their fitness to be brought to the 'holy mountain' and

19. See Sarna 1991: 201. See especially Fishbane 1985: 131-35, 478-79; 1992: 10-11. His discussion of the Sabbath, and especially his emphasis on the 'axial position' of the Sabbath, may be brought into the discussion of this text and ultimately provide the key to understanding 56.1-8.

20. Note the formula in the plea of the daughters of Zelophehad: 'Why should the name of our father be taken away [יגרע] from his clan because he had no son?' (Num. 27.4).

to participate in the rites of the temple (56.7).[21] If there is a subliminal connection between the observance of the Sabbath by the people and the understanding of exile as an enforced observance of the sabbatical for the land (Lev. 26.34-35—cf. vv. 42-46), another dimension may be given to this text.[22]

Lexical connections with the framework of a number of Sabbath laws (associated with various strata of the Pentateuch) suggest that a developing body of teachings—even texts—takes on a significance even beyond the boundaries of 'schools'. This is especially marked in the phraseology of requirements for foreigners (56.6). In particular, the uncommon phrase 'to love the name of the Lord'[23] may be a telescoping and reconception of words that appear in decalogues (e.g. in Exod. 20.6-7):

> ...but showing steadfast love to...those who love me (אהבי) and keep (ושמרי) my commandments. You shall not make wrongful use of the name of the LORD (שם־י") your God, for the LORD will not acquit anyone who misuses his name (שמו),

as well as in Deut. 5.10-11.[24]

The complaint of the alien (v. 3a) and the complaint of the eunuch (v. 3b) provide the structure for the 'Torah'.[25] Although this chiastic structure links these complaints and their remedy, they will be separated for the sake of discussion. There is a strong tendency to treat the response (v. 6) to the complaint of the alien (56.3a),

21. Cf. Gen. 2.2-3 and Exod. 20.11; 31.17. On v. 7, cf. קדש (Exod. 31.14, 15; 20.8; Deut. 5.12). Note that the Sabbath law in Exod. 31 is spoken from Mount [הר] Sinai. The Sabbath commandment in Lev. 19.3b is followed by 19.5: 'When you offer a sacrifice (תזבחו זבח) of well-being to the LORD, offer it (תזבחהו) in such a way that it is acceptable on your behalf (לרצנכם).' See v. 7.

22. Fishbane 1985: 479. Carroll (1993), offers perceptive comments about our readings of the 'ideological claims' apparent in these texts in the context of a discussion of intertextuality.

23. The occurrences in the Psalms are outside the scope of this study.

24. The phrases 'to be his servants' (Isa. 56.6) and 'better than sons and daughters' (56.5) are more distant from Exod. 20.5: 'You shall not bow down to them or worship them (תעבדם); for I the LORD your God am a jealous God, punishing children (בנים) for the iniquity of parents' (cf. Deut. 5.9), and from Exod. 20.10: 'You shall not do (תעשה) any work—you, your son (ובנך) or your daughter (ובתך), your male (עבדך) or female slave, your livestock, or the alien resident (וגרך) in your towns' (cf. Deut. 5.14).

25. Duhm 1892: 391. See Pauritsch 1971: 43-47.

> Do not let the foreigner joined to the LORD say,
> 'The LORD will surely separate me from his people'...
> And the foreigners who join themselves to the LORD,
> to minister to him, to love the name of the LORD,
> and to be his servants,
> all who keep the sabbath, and do not profane it,
> and hold fast my covenant—

in grandiose terms up to and including 'universalism'. The foil to this grand vision tends to be a dark background of some variety of 'exclusivism', even xenophobia.[26] This presumed attitude toward aliens (בני־נכר/נכרי), despite the Deuteronomistic strictures against Israelites who worship foreign gods (Deut. 31.16-17a),

> The LORD said to Moses, 'Soon you will lie down with your ancestors. Then this people will begin to prostitute themselves to the foreign gods (אלהי־נכר) in their midst, the gods of the land into which they are going; they will forsake me, breaking my covenant that I have made with them. My anger will be kindled against them in that day'

finds little concrete expression in the legal corpus. Deuteronomy excludes the נכרי from idealistic economic benefits (Deut. 15.3; 23.21 [ET 20]) and from the kingship (17.15). At the risk of blandness, it should be noted that the exclusion from the Passover meal (Exod. 12.43) and the provision that the carcass of an animal that dies mysteriously may be sold to a foreigner (Deut. 14.21) are stated without intense rhetoric.[27] In fact, the lengthy discussion in H of 'blemishes' that disqualify an animal for sacrifice, ends by applying these restrictions to animals 'accepted from a foreigner (בן־נכר) as food to your God'. The phrasing does not exclude the possibility that these are offered on behalf of the aliens.[28]

26. Bonnard (1972: 347) speaks of 'un courant de défiance et parfois d'hostilité vis-à-vis des nokrim'. It is common to set this text against the historical background of Ezra and Nehemiah and their policies regarding foreigners.

27. Deut. 14.21: 'For you are a people holy to the LORD your God'. In any case, the positions of Ezek. 44 and Neh. 13 attach far more significance to this distinction.

28. Lev. 22.21, 24, 25. Note the mild description of innocent bystanders (children and aliens) witnessing divine judgment on idolaters (Deut. 29.20-22 [ET 21]): 'The LORD will single out [the servants of the gods of the nations] (הבדילו) from all the tribes of Israel for calamity, in accordance with all the curses of the covenant (הברית) written in this book of the law. The next generation, your children (בניכם) who rise up after you, as well as the foreigner (והנכרי) who comes from a distant country, will see the devastation of that land and the afflictions with which the

In the fear of the alien 'joined to the LORD', the terminology is that of separation/distinction between clean and unclean (succinctly expressed in these terms in Lev. 20.22-26):

> You shall keep (וּשְׁמַרְתֶּם) all my statutes and all my ordinances (מִשְׁפָּטַי), and observe (וַעֲשִׂיתֶם) them, so that the land to which I bring you (מֵבִיא) to settle in may not vomit you out...I am the LORD your God; I have separated you (הִבְדַּלְתִּי) from the peoples (מִן־הָעַמִּים). You shall therefore make a distinction (וְהִבְדַּלְתֶּם) between the clean animal and the unclean... which I have set apart (הִבְדַּלְתִּי) for you to hold unclean. You shall be holy (קְדֹשִׁים) to me; for I the LORD am holy (קָדוֹשׁ), and I have separated you (וָאַבְדִּל) from the other peoples (מִן־הָעַמִּים) to be mine.

Fishbane[29] sees in Isa. 56.1-8 an authoritative prophetic reinterpretation of the terminology of the 'joining' and 'separating' of Levites from the ordinary community for sacerdotal purposes (Num. 18.1-7; Deut. 10.8-12). He has seen in this audacious inversion of language affirming the sanctity of God a concern for the effect of applying this language to categories of humankind. This is amplified by the speaking of aliens who 'minister' to the Lord, and are 'his servants' (Isa. 56.5). The characterization of Israelites collectively as 'servants of God' appears in legal corpora, and the term is a recurrent one in Isaiah 56–66.[30] But in the pairing of עבדים with שׁרת, there is an even more audacious implication of a sacral function for these aliens,[31] which may also carry into the allusion to participation in the offering of the sacrifices alluded to in v. 7. Despite the ambivalence of the text on this point, there is a certain irreverence for this high language that might be termed 'Menippian' if we had an indisputable perception of the underlying social realities or of the social location of the parties in this counterpoint.[32] The

LORD has afflicted it.'

29. Fishbane (1985: 118-20, 138-43, 262-68) sees this interpretation of Num. 18 as an expression of lay opposition to the expansion of priestly prerogatives at some point in the late Achaemenid period.

30. See particularly Beuken 1990.

31. In addition to the above texts, priests are associated with these roots in Num. 3.31; 16.9; 18.6.

32. Hanson (1987) continues to remind us that these questions are worth investigation. Fishbane's (1985: 14-16) discussion of differences of opinion on concrete recurrent issues in the 'postexilic' period is impressive. 'Menippian satire', discussed in the fourth chapter of the revised edition of Bakhtin 1963 (1984: 101-80), has been an influential term. Essentially, it is a play on the language and genre of

offensive language was recognized later by the scribes of Qumran
(1QIs[a]), who omitted לשרתו entirely, reading, 'to be his servants, and to
bless the name of the LORD'.

Except for Sabbath observance, the definition of the obligations is
quite generally stated, and often in unparalleled coinages. An exception
is 'to love [the name of] the LORD' (v. 6), which takes us into the ethos
of Deuteronomy,[33] both in the phrase 'to love the LORD', and also in
the reference to the 'name of the LORD' resident in the sanctuary (v. 7
—see Isa. 18.7 *et passim*).[34]

The sacrificial scene that follows is a climactic removal of the threat of
'separating' aliens from the community. In the light of the liturgical
functions implied in the preceding verse, there is no specific statement
that the sacrifices are carried out by cultic personnel on behalf of the
aliens (56.7):

> ...these I will bring to my holy mountain,
> and make them joyful in my house of prayer;
> their burnt offerings and their sacrifices
> will be accepted on my altar;
> for my house shall be called a house of prayer.
> for all peoples.

If the implied priesthood of aliens is seen as the rhetoric of argumentation, then this scene is entirely consistent with the law concerning
sacrificial animals offered by aliens in the Holiness Code (Lev. 22.18-20,
24-25):

> When anyone of the house of Israel or of the aliens (הגר) residing in
> Israel presents an offering...You shall not offer (תקריב) anything that has
> a blemish, for it will not be acceptable (רצון) in your behalf...Any animal
> that has its testicles bruised or crushed or torn or cut, you shall not offer
> (תקריבו) to the LORD; such you shall not do (תעשו) within your land, nor
> shall you accept any such animals from a foreigner (בן־נכר) to offer
> (תקריבו) as food to your God; since they are mutilated, with a blemish in
> them, they shall not be accepted (ירצו) in your behalf.[35]

the powerful, produced by the less powerful. In any case, it appears that not only
may sacrifices be made on behalf of foreigners (Lev. 22), but the possibility is left
open that the foreigners have the same function as the priests.

33. Sehmsdorf 1972: 549.

34. See Beuken 1989: 30. Lack (1973: 66) associates 18.7 with one expression
of the fundamental *symbolique* of Zion. As mentioned earlier, these words may be
telescoped echoes of Sabbath *tradita*.

35. Note the casual use of technical terms dealing with 'blemishes' and specific

Thi; text also contains phrases associated with sacrifice in Deuteronomy's 'place that the LORD your God will choose as a dwelling for his name', especially as found in Deut. 12.5-7:

You shall go there, bringing there (והבאתם) your burnt offerings and your sacrifices (עלחיכם וזבחיכם)...And you shall eat there in the presence of the LORD your God, you and your households together, rejoicing (ושמחתם) in all the undertakings in which the LORD your God has blessed you.[36]

In various Sabbath *tradita*, sacrificial rules appear in close proximity to the Sabbath mandate,[37] and the decalogue describes the participation of the 'resident alien'.[38] Finally, the worship at the 'holy mountain' has strong connections across the Isaianic tradition.[39]

The complaint of the eunuch[40] is entirely metaphorical, and the response is within the framework of the assumption that a person's 'name' survives in the community through progeny.[41]

sacrifices (Lev. 22.18-24). Rendtorff (1967: 58, 63, and especially 253) sees this as characteristic of pre-exilic groups. It appears that, on the assumption that the technical texts have become available, the popular language persisted.

36. See also 12.11-15; cf. בנך ובתך at 12.18; מזבח at 12.26-27. Within the ethos of the temple, homage from distant foreigners is anticipated, but this is beyond the scope of the paper. 1 Kgs. 8.41-43, 'Likewise when a foreigner (נכרי,) who is not of your people Israel (מעמך ישראל), comes (ובא) from a distant land because of your name (שמך) —for they shall hear of your great name (שמך), your mighty (החזקה) hand, and your outstretched arm—when [a foreigner] comes and prays (ובא והתפלל) toward this house (הבית), then hear in heaven your dwelling place, and do (ועשית) according to all that the foreigner (הנכרי) calls to you, so that all the peoples (עמי) of the earth may know your name (שמך) and fear you, as do your people Israel (כעמך ישראל), and so that they may know that your name (שמך) has been invoked on this house (הבית) that I have built.'

37. Exod. 20.5//25; Lev. 19.3//5; 16.32//24; 23.11//12, 16//18; 38//37. Note the pairing of Sabbath/Sanctuary in Lev. 19.30 = 26.2; Exod. 31.12/9; 34.21/25; 35.2/16.

38. Exod. 20.10; Deut. 5.14. See the Sabbatical law, Lev. 26.5.

39. Steck 1991c: 244-245, 247. See 51.16, for example, and 1991b: 31. Note that Steck (1991c: 247) finds a *Querverbindung* with the contrast between worship and justice in 1.10-17. The present valorization of Sabbath sacrifice and prayer as expressions of justice and righteousness constitutes a 'correction' of an earlier word in a new situation.

40. Steck (1991c: 248) notes the significant textual location of the reference to סריסים of royal blood at Isa. 39.7. The metaphor of withered vegetation in Isaiah might be explored.

41. Cf. Num. 27.4, involving inheritance laws for women, cited earlier in the discussion of 56.2b.

...and do not let the eunuch say,
'I am just a dry tree'.
For thus says the LORD,
'To the eunuchs who keep my sabbaths,
who choose the things that please me
and hold fast my covenant,
I will give, in my house and within my walls,
a monument and a name
better than sons and daughters;
I will give them an everlasting name
that shall not be cut off.'

However the religious history or the physical setting of this gift are conceived, the problem and the solution do not parallel those of the aliens, as Duhm argued long ago.[42] We have here the provision of a 'name' that has the same function as progeny. The commonplace that this has to do with the danger that physical mutilation or deformity poses to the purity of the sanctuary[43] is only an assumption. The text specifically admits only the 'name' into the sanctuary. If lexical connections are important for establishing a relationship between texts, the widely assumed connection with Deut. 23.2-9 (ET 1-8) has little foundation. However critics are fascinated by the 'abrogation'[44] of this primitive rule—banning people with deformed genitalia, bastards and (for example ?) Ammonites and Moabites, from the 'assembly'—Isa. 56.1-8 shows no verbal allusions to this text. If the focus is upon progeny, the coined phrase, 'give a name' seems to echo the conventional phrase, 'give a child/call its name'.[45] This scene is a recurrent one in Isaiah, most immediately expressed in 9.5-6 (ET 6-7):

For a child has been born for us,
a son given (בֵּן נִתַּן) to us;
authority rests upon his shoulders;
and he is named (וַיִּקְרָא שְׁמוֹ)
Wonderful Counselor, Mighty God,
Everlasting Father, Prince of Peace.

42. Duhm (1892: 393) speaks of a 'geistliche Fortleben'. See Whybray 1975: 198.

43. Douglas (1966: 9-28) discusses academic distancing from this concept, ascribed to 'primitive' cultures.

44. Donner (1985) gives a specific term for this assumption. See the detailed critique in Lau 1994: 268-71.

45. Gen. 30.6 for example.

His authority shall grow continually,
and there shall be endless peace
for the throne of David and his kingdom.
He will establish and uphold it
with justice and with righteousness (במשפט ובצדקה)
from this time onward and forevermore (עולם).[46]

The legal codes offer no guidance concerning eunuchs, of whatever social status, but linking this text with Isaianic themes may open new possibilities for the reader.

The hope expressed in the gathering of the dispersed, and possibly of others as well, places this religious instruction in a broader context (56.8):

Thus says the Lord God,
who gathers the outcasts of Israel,
'I will gather others to them
besides those already gathered.'

There are specific verbal links with a common scene in other parts of the Isaiah tradition (11.12):[47]

He will raise a signal for the nations,
and will assemble the outcasts (נדחי) of Israel,
and gather (יקבץ) the dispersed of Judah
from the four corners of the earth.

This text provides the closest prototype for a scene that envisions a less specific diaspora (note that 'my holy mountain' is mentioned near this text: 11.9; cf. 56.7).

Again, the echo of specific Deuteronomic language is quite strong (Deut. 30.1-5):

When all these things have happened (יבאו) to you, the blessings and the curses that I have set before you, if you call them to mind among all the nations where the LORD your God has driven (הדיחך) you, and return to the LORD your God, and you and your children (ובניך) obey him with all your heart and with all your soul, just as I am commanding you today, then the LORD your God will restore your fortunes and have compassion on you, gathering you (וקבצך) again from all the peoples (מעמים) among whom the LORD your God has scattered you (חפיצך). Even if you are exiled (נדחך) to the ends of heaven, from there the LORD your God will gather you (יקבצך), and from there he will bring you back. The LORD

---

46. See particularly 7.10-17; 8.3, and the new name of 62.1-6; 65.13-15.
47. Steck 1991b: 41; 1991c: 248.

your God will bring you (והביאך) into the land that your ancestors possessed, and you will possess it; he will make you more prosperous (והטיבך) and numerous than your ancestors.

In summary, this word represents a response to incompletely specified ethical dilemmas within the community, based on the traditions at the disposal of the community. Despite the echoes of powerful eschatological language, the teaching does not appear to be utopian.[48] The diverse Jewish population,[49] the refugees from neighboring states mentioned in Isaiah and the likelihood in the Achaemenid or Hellenistic period of resident aliens present in the community for economic or administrative reasons, makes it doubtful that 'aliens' were a theoretical eschatological entity in the world expressed in this text. In this closely structured[50] effort to relate a way of life to traditions or traditional texts, prophetic activity appears less adversarial toward law teachers and their constructive concern for general public policy than is generally acknowledged.[51] Here, the 'axial position' of the Sabbath reorders everything.[52] The hallowing power of Sabbath observance breaks down proposed limitations of the worshipping community on mount Zion.

BIBLIOGRAPHY

Bakhtin, M.M.
1984   *Problems of Dostoevsky's Poetics* (ed. and trans. C. Emeyson; repr.; Minneapolis, MN: University of Minnesota Press, 1963).
Begrich, J.
1964   'Das priesterliche Tora', in W. Zimmerli (ed.), *Gesammelte Studien zum Alten Testament* (Theologische Bücherei; repr. München: Kaiser Verlag [1936]): 232-60.
Beuken, W.A.M.
1987   'Trito-Jesaja. Profetie en schriftgeleerdheid', in F.G. Martínez, C.H.J. de Geus and A.F.J. Klijn (eds.), *Profeten en profetische geschriften*

48. Kraus (1966) emphasized the crisis of the delay of eschatological hopes behind these texts.

49. Japhet (1983) offers a *prima facie* reading of available materials.

50. The detailed rhetorical analysis in Polan 1986: 43-90, suggests that the present text is more than a pastiche, although the absence of 'edlen Stil' (Duhm 1892: 393) cannot be gainsaid.

51. See Goshen-Gottstein 1987 and Meyers 1983. Schramm (1995) appeared too late to receive the attention it deserves.

52. Fishbane 1985: 118, 478-79.

(Festschrift A.S. van der Woude; Kampen/Nijkerk: Kok/Callenbach): 71-86.

1989   *Jesaja deel IIIA* [56.1–63.6] (De Prediking van het Oude Testament; Nijkerk: Callenbach).

1990   'The Main Theme of Trito-Isaiah: "The Servants of Yahweh"', *JSOT* 47: 67-87.

Bonnard, P.-E.
1972   *Le Second Isaïe, son disciple et leurs éditeurs: Isaïe 40–66* (EBib; Paris: Gabalda).

Carroll, R.P.
1993   'Jeremiah, Intertextuality and Ideologiekritik' (unpublished paper presented at Consultation on the Composition of the Book of Jeremiah; Washington; DC: Society of Biblical Literature).

Donner, H.
1985   'Jesaja lvi 1-7: Ein Abrogationsfall innerhalb des Kanons— Implikationen und Konsequenzen', in J.A. Emerton (ed.), *Congress Volume: Salamanca 1983* (VTSup, 36; Leiden: Brill): 81-96.

Douglas, M.
1966   *Purity and Danger: An Analysis of the Concepts of Pollution and Taboo* (London: Routledge & Kegan Paul).

Duhm, B.
1892   *Das Buch Jesaia übersetzt und erklärt* (HKAT, 3.1; Göttingen: Vandenhoeck & Ruprecht).

Eslinger, L.M.
1992   'Inner-biblical Exegesis and Inner-biblical Allusion: The Question of Category', *VT* 42: 47-58.

Fishbane, M.
1985   *Biblical Interpretation in Ancient Israel* (Oxford: Clarendon Press).

1992   'Inner-Biblical Exegesis: Types and Strategies of Interpretation in Ancient Israel', in *idem*, *The Garments of Torah: Essays in Biblical Hermeneutics* (Indiana Studies in Biblical Literature; Bloomington, IN: Indiana University Press, 1986): 3-18.

Goshen-Gottstein, M.H.
1987   'Tanakh Theology: The Religion of the Old Testament and the Place of Jewish Biblical Theology', in P.D. Miller, Jr, P.D. Hanson and S.D. McBride (eds.), *Ancient Israelite Religion: Essays in Honor of Frank Moore Cross* (Philadelphia: Fortress Press): 617-44.

Grünwaldt, K.
1992   *Exil und Identität: Beschneidung, Passa und Sabbat in der Priesterschrift* (BBB, 85; Bonn: Peter Hanstein).

Hanson, P.D.
1987   'Israelite Religion in the Early Postexilic Period', in P.D. Miller, Jr, P.D. Hanson and S.D. McBride (eds.), *Ancient Israelite Religion: Essays in Honor of Frank Moore Cross* (Philadelphia: Fortress Press): 485-508.

Hollander, J.
1981   *The Figure of Echo: A Mode of Allusion in Milton and after* (Berkeley: University of California Press).

Japhet, S.
1983   'People and Land in the Restoration Period', in G. Strecker (ed.), *Das Land Israel in biblischer Zeit: Jerusalem-Symposium 1981 der Hebräischen Universität und der Georg-August-Universität* (Göttinger Theologische Arbeiten, 25; Göttingen: Vandenhoeck & Ruprecht): 103-25.

Knight, D.A.
1990   'Introduction: Tradition and Theology', in D.A. Knight (ed.), *Tradition and Theology in the Old Testament* (TBS, 11; Sheffield: JSOT Press, 1977).

Koenen, K.
1990   *Ethik und Eschatologie im Tritojesajabuch: Eine literarkritische und redaktionsgeschichtliche Studie* (WMANT, 62; Neukirchen–Vluyn: Neukirchener Verlag).

Kraus, H.J.
1966   'Die ausgebliebene Endtheophanie: Eine Studie zu Jes 56–66', *ZAW* 78: 317-32.

Lack, R.
1973   *La symbolique du livre d'Isaïe: Essai sur l'image littéraire comme élément de structuration* (AnBib, 59; Rome: Pontifical Biblical Institute).

Lau, W.
1994   *Schriftgelehrte Prophetie in Jesaja 56–66: Eine Untersuchung zu den literarischen Bezügen in den letzten elf Kapiteln des Jesajabuches* (BZAW, 225; Berlin: de Gruyter).

Lescow, T.
1970   'Die dreistufige Tora: Beobachtung zu einer Form', *ZAW* 82: 362-79.

Melugin, R.F.
1976   *The Formation of Isaiah 40–55* (BZAW, 141; Berlin: de Gruyter).

Meyers, E.M.
1983   'The use of tôrâ in Haggai 2.11 and the Role of the Prophet in the Restoration Community', in C.L. Meyers and M. O'Conner (eds.), *The Word of the Lord Shall Go Forth: Essays in Honor of David Noel Freedman in Celebration of his Sixtieth Birthday* (Winona Lake, IN: Eisenbrauns): 69-76.

Odeberg, H.
1931   *Trito Isaiah (Isaiah 56–66): A Literary and Linguistic Analysis* (UUÅ, 1; Uppsala: Lundeqvist).

Pauritsch, K.
1971   *Die neue Gemeinde: Gott sammelt Ausgestossene und Arme (Jesaiah 56–66). Die Botschaft des Tritojesaia-Buches literar-, form-, gattungskritisch und redaktionsgeschichtlich untersucht* (AnBib, 47; Rome: Pontifical Biblical Institute).

Polan, G.J.
1986   *In the Ways of Justice Toward Salvation: A Rhetorical Analysis of Isaiah 56–59* (American University Studies, Series 7: Theology and Religion, 13; New York: Peter Lang).

Rendtorff, R.
1967   Studien zur Geschichte des Opfers im Alten Israel (WMANT, 24; Neukirchen–Vluyn: Neukirchener Verlag).
1993   'Isaiah 56.1 as a Key to the Formation of the Book of Isaiah', in idem, Canon and Theology: Overtures to an Old Testament Theology (trans. M. Kohl; ed. W. Brueggemann; Overtures to Biblical Theology; Minneapolis: Fortress Press, 1989): 181-89.

Sarna, N.M.
1991   Exodus (JPS Torah Commentary; Philadelphia: Jewish Publication Society).

Schmidt, H.H.
1968   Gerechtigkeit als Weltordnung: Hintergrund und Geschichte des alttestamentlichen Gerechtigkeitsbegriffes (BHT, 40; Tübingen: Mohr).

Schramm, B.
1995   The Opponents of Third Isaiah: Reconstructing the Cultic History of the Restoration (JSOTSup, 193; Sheffield: Sheffield Academic Press).

Sehmsdorf, E.
1972   'Studien zur Redaktionsgeschichte von Jesaja 56–66 (I) (Jes. 65.16b-25, 66.1-4, 56.1-8)', ZAW 84: 517-62.

Silberman, L.H.
1983   'Wellhausen and Judaism', in D.A. Knight (ed.), Julius Wellhausen and his Prolegomena to the History of Israel (Semeia, 25; Atlanta: Scholars Press): 75-82.

Steck, O.H.
1991a   'Anschlußprobleme einer redaktionellen Entstehung von Trotojesaja', in idem (ed.), Studien zu Tritojesaja (BZAW, 203; Berlin: de Gruyter): 269-79.
1991b   'Tritojesaja im Jesajabuch', in idem (ed.), Studien zu Tritojesaja (BZAW, 203; Berlin: de Gruyter): 3-48.
1991c   'Zu jüngsten Untersuchungen von Jes 56, 1-8; 63, 7-66, 24', in idem (ed.), Studien zu Tritojesaja (BZAW, 203; Berlin: de Gruyter): 229-68.

Westermann, C.
1991   Prophetic Oracles of Salvation in the Old Testament (trans. K. Crim; Louisville, KY: Westminster/John Knox Press, 1987).

Whybray, R.N.
1975   Isaiah 40–66 (NCB; London: Oliphants).

ALLUSIONS AND ILLUSIONS: THE UNITY OF THE BOOK OF ISAIAH IN LIGHT OF DEUTERO-ISAIAH'S USE OF PROPHETIC TRADITION

Benjamin D. Sommer

Recent decades have witnessed the development of two approaches that focus on intertextual linkages throughout the Hebrew Bible. One of these, canon criticism, stresses elements of unity within and among books; these elements often take the form of lexical and thematic connections between various passages.[1] The other, the study of inner-biblical exegesis and allusion, attends to the use biblical writers made of material from earlier books.[2] These approaches can be mutually enlightening, but they can also come into conflict as they suggest different explanations for a single phenomenon. In this paper I would like to compare the two approaches as they are applied to the book of Isaiah. Specifically, I intend to ask, How does recognizing the role allusion plays in Deutero-Isaiah affect views of this material influenced by canon criticism?

The study of Deutero-Isaiah's use of earlier biblical texts parallels the work of scholars who, following Childs's lead, find elements of unity in Isaiah 1–66.[3] Both approaches note themes, concerns and vocabulary

---

1.   See especially B. Childs, *Introduction to the Old Testament as Scripture* (Philadelphia: Fortress Press, 1979).

2.   See M. Fishbane, *Biblical Interpretation in Ancient Israel* (Oxford: Oxford University Press, 1985). Fishbane terms the phenomenon he studies 'inner-biblical exegesis'. Most of the examples he discusses are cases of what literary critics call allusion, while a smaller number are genuinely exegetical. Consequently, I would prefer the phrase 'inner-biblical allusion and exegesis'. The passages discussed in this essay generally involve allusion, not exegesis. For a discussion of the term 'allusion', see Z. Ben-Porat, 'The Poetics of Literary Allusion', *Poetics and Theory of Literature* 1 (1976), pp. 105-28.

3.   For summaries of the work of this school and bibliographies, see R. Rendtorff, 'The Book of Isaiah: A Complex Unity. Synchronic and Diachronic Reading', in E. Lovering, Jr (ed.), *Society of Biblical Literature: 1991 Seminar*

that extend across the book's major divisions, but the two methods explain the parallels in very different ways. Indeed, I shall argue, the study of inner-biblical allusion in Isaiah 40–66 undermines the claims made by many adherents of the unity school. In order to demonstrate this, it will first be necessary to describe the nature of Deutero-Isaiah's appropriation and revision of earlier material; subsequently, I will compare the two approaches.

Inner-Biblical Allusion in Isaiah 40–66

A great many allusions occur throughout Isaiah 40–66, and they display recurring thematic and stylistic patterns.[4] I would like to sketch out some of these patterns briefly, first as they appear in Deutero-Isaiah's allusions to material from the first part of the book of Isaiah, and then as they appear in his allusions to Jeremiah.[5]

Words and images that earlier prophets used to rebuke the people or

Papers (Atlanta: Scholars Press, 1991), pp. 8-20; and C. Seitz, *Zion's Final Destiny: The Development of the Book of Isaiah; A Reassessment of Isaiah 36–39* (Minneapolis: Fortress Press, 1991), pp. 26-35. M. Sweeney, in a paper read at the 1990 meeting of the Society of Biblical Literature ('The Unity of the Book of Isaiah in the History of Modern Critical Research') discussed the forerunners of this approach prior to the rise of the canonical approaches to Isaiah associated with Childs and Rendtorff. For Childs's own suggestions, see his *Introduction*, pp. 325-38.

4.   These patterns occur with equal frequency in Isaiah chs. 35, 40–55 and 56–66. Others have long noticed the consistent literary style of these chapters (see, for example, C. Torrey, *The Second Isaiah: A New Interpretation* [New York: Charles Scribner's Sons, 1928], pp. 183-204; Y. Kaufmann, *The Babylonian Captivity and Deutero-Isaiah* [trans. C.W. Efroymson; New York: Union of American Hebrew Congregations, 1970], pp. 68-87). Whether or not these elements point to common authorship, they justify treating the whole second part of the book of Isaiah as a unified literary corpus. I shall refer to the author or authors of that corpus as 'Deutero-Isaiah'. For a strong defense of the authorial unity of 40–66 (along with 34–35), see also M. Haran, *Between RI'SHONÔT (Former Prophecies) and ḤADASHÔT (New Prophecies): A Literary-Historical Study of Prophecies in Isaiah XL–XLVII* (Jerusalem: Magnes Press, 1963), pp. 79-92, 101-102 [Heb.].

5.   What follows is by no means a comprehensive review of Deutero-Isaiah's use of earlier biblical, or even prophetic, material. For such a review, including a discussion of the methods used to distinguish between genuine cases of allusion and similarities that result from coincidence or the independent use of stock biblical language, see for now my dissertation, '*Leshon Limmudim*: The Poetics of Allusion in Isaiah 40–66' (University of Chicago, 1994).

to predict their doom often reappear when Deutero-Isaiah comforts the exiled Judeans or announces their restoration. Thus Deutero-Isaiah consoles the people with language resembling that with which Isaiah or Jeremiah castigated them. Allusions of this sort belong to a category I term *reversal*.

A case of reversal that depends on writing attributed to Isaiah ben Amoṣ[6] occurs at the outset of Deutero-Isaiah's prophecies. Isaiah had reproached the inhabitants of Samaria, the capital of the northern kingdom, predicting their downfall with these words:

> Woe, haughty crown of Ephraim's drunkards! His magnificent (צבי) honor is a flower that fades (וציץ נבל). Those above the fertile valley (גיא)[7] are smashed with wine. Behold a strong and powerful one is the Lord's (הנה חזק ואמץ לאדני), who like a stream of hail...will throw [the drunkard of Ephraim] down to earth with a hand (ביד). The magnificent (צבי) honor of the city above the fertile valley (גיא) will be a flower that fades (ציצת נבל)... On that day, YHWH of hosts (צבאות) will become a magnificent (צבי) crown and an honorable diadem for those of his people (עמו) who remain. (Isa. 28.1-5)

Many of Isaiah's phrases appear in the opening words of Deutero-Isaiah's preaching to the Babylonian exiles:

> Comfort, comfort my people (עמי), your God is saying. Speak tenderly to Jerusalem and proclaim to her that her term of service (צבאה) is complete, that her punishment has been fulfilled, that she has taken double from the hand (מיד) of YHWH for all her sins. A voice calls: 'Set up the way for YHWH!... Every valley (גיא) will be exalted and every mountain and hill will be lowered...' A voice proclaims, '...All flesh is grass, and all its loyalty like the flower in the field (כציץ השדה). The grass withers, the flower fades (ציץ נבל) when the wind from YHWH blows on it... The grass withers, the flower fades (ציץ נבל), but the word of our God stands

---

6. We cannot be sure that it was in fact the historical Isaiah who composed each utterance in 1–33. What is important for my argument is that these passages simply precede Deutero-Isaiah. In certain cases, I shall need to argue for a pre-exilic dating against some contemporary scholarship. For convenience, I refer to the authors of these passages as 'Isaiah', even though it is possible that some of them were added to the Isaiah traditions by a later pre-exilic hand.

7. The text here is difficult. I take the phrase, אשר על־ראש גיא־שׁמנים, to refer to the inhabitants of the city of Samaria, which was located on a hill above a valley. In any event, my point regarding the parallel between these verses and Deutero-Isaiah is not affected by the philological issue.

forever... ' Behold! the Lord YHWH is coming as a strong one (הנה אדני ה' בחזק יבוא).[8] (Isa. 40.1-10)

The two passages share vocabulary and themes (e.g., the constancy of God and the frailty of the people), some of which scholars from the unity school have noted.[9] Both these themes and the words עם (people) and יד (hand) occur quite often in the Hebrew Bible. Consequently, they cannot by themselves demonstrate that Deutero-Isaiah knew and alluded to the earlier passage; it remains possible that two authors coincidentally used common vocabulary. Similarly, the words ציץ (flower) and נבל (fades) appear together in a figure of human frailty several times in the Hebrew Bible, and they seem to stem from a stock vocabulary cluster that both Isaiah and Deutero-Isaiah knew. But the connection between the passages goes deeper than the use of these frequent terms, since both passages utilize an additional phrase that is unique to them, the phrase consisting of the words הנה (behold), חזק (strong), and אדוני (Lord). In light of this additional correspondence, the similarity between these passages may result from Deutero-Isaiah's deliberate reference to the older text. This possibility is strengthened by the presence of two stylistic patterns that typify Deutero-Isaiah's allusions. The exilic prophet often splits up a phrase from his source, so that words that had appeared next to each other in the source are separated by an intervening word or phrase in the alluding text. This technique, which I term the *split-up pattern*, occurs here. In Isaiah, הנה appeared immediately before חזק, but in Deutero-Isaiah they are separated by another word which appeared later in Isaiah: הנה חזק becomes הנה אדני ה' בחזק. Further, Deutero-Isaiah often alludes to a word from his source not by repeating it by using a similar-sounding word—that is, he borrows the consonants and the sound of his predecessor's word, but not the word itself. I call this

8. Because MT has an adjective (חָזָק) rather than a noun (חֹזֶק or חֵזֶק), the *bêt* must be seen as a *bêt essentiae*. LXX, like 1QIsa[a] (which has בחזוק), seems to have read the word as a noun, however; it translates ἰδοὺ κύριος μετὰ ἰσχύος ἔρχεται: 'Behold, the Lord is coming in strength.' Nonetheless, in view of the dependence on Isa. 28, MT is to be preferred: Deutero-Isaiah's point may be that in the past God utilized a strong person to punish Israel, but now God himself is the strong one who will redeem Israel. On the other hand, even if one prefers 1QIsa[a] and LXX to MT, the link between the phrases in chs. 28 and 40 remains clear.

9. See C. Seitz, 'The Divine Council: Temporal Transition and New Prophecy in the Book of Isaiah', *JBL* 109 (1990), p. 242, who points out some of the common themes and the words ציץ and נבל.

technique sound play,[10] and it appears here as well. The word צבאה (term of service) in Isa. 40.2 hints back at the similar sounding word צבי (magnificence) in Isa. 28.1 and 28.5.[11] Not only the repetition of vocabulary and of themes but these stylistic features—the split-up pattern and sound play, which are typical of Deutero-Isaianic allusion—mark the relationship between these passages as a borrowing.

Figures that served to rebuke and to predict doom in 28.1-5 reappear in 40.1-10 as harbingers of hope. In Isaiah, the powerful one whom אדוני sends will punish Israel, but in Deutero-Isaiah אדוני himself comes as the powerful one to redeem his people. The thematic reversal Deutero-Isaiah performs here also involves a change of reference. The passage from Isaiah predicts the punishment of Ephraim brought by the Assyrians. Deutero-Isaiah, however, is no longer concerned with the Assyrians or with the northern kingdom. As he borrows, he shifts the referent of Isaiah's vocabulary to the issue of his own day: the return of Judean exiles from Babylonia. Thus he implicitly contrasts the victory of the Assyrians over Israel with the downfall of the Babylonians, the latter-day counterparts of the Assyrians. This passage, then, provides an example of *historical recontextualization*, another category that typifies Deutero-Isaiah's re-use of earlier prophetic material.

Other cases of reversal and historical recontextualization occur in Deutero-Isaiah's allusions to Isaiah ben Amoṣ,[12] but I would like to

---

10. Sound play characterizes Deutero-Isaiah's writing even outside his allusions to earlier material. He loves to place similar sounding words near each other: for example, נמסו...נמקו (34.4); כנחל שטף...כנחל שלום (54.8); פאר תחת אפר (61.3); מעטה...מעטה (61.3); למני...ומניתי (65.11-12); ירעו...ירעו (65.25). Elsewhere, he repeats certain sounds over and over: for example, sibilants and the letter *ḥēṭ* in 40.6b-8. (For further examples, see Torrey, *Second Isaiah*, pp. 195-196, and Kaufmann, *Babylonian Captivity*, pp. 80-87.) Thus the feature of Deutero-Isaiah's poetics of allusion which I note here reflects a characteristic of his style generally.

11. Further, I have translated גיא in Isa. 28.1 and 28.4 as 'valley', which is what גיא means in Isa. 40.4. However, if Ibn Ezra is correct that the word in Isa. 28.1 means 'haughty', then this parallel represents a case of another Deutero-Isaianic tendency, which I call *word play*. This technique is based on the existence of homonyms: Deutero-Isaiah repeats a word from the source, but he uses it in another sense (here, 'valley' instead of 'haughty'). On the other hand, if we read גיא (which clearly would mean 'haughty') in Isa. 28.1 with 1QIsaᵃ, the parallel remains strong as a case of sound play.

12. For example, Isaiah's proclamation of doom in 6.10-12 is reversed in 49.19-20 and perhaps also in 62.4. The statement in 40.28-31 may reverse the negative trope of 5.27. Cases of historical recontextualization occur elsewhere as well. To cite

move on to another category of Deutero-Isaianic re-use of older material. This category involves the confirmation of older prophecies: Deutero-Isaiah alludes to specific predictions of his predecessors in order to assert that they have been fulfilled. For example, in the following passage the earlier prophet proclaimed judgment on the people for their rebellion:

> It is a rebellious people (עם מרי הוא); they are deceptive children, children who would not consent to listen to the teaching of YHWH (לא־אבו שמוע תוע תורת ה'), who said to the seers (לראים), 'Do not see (לא תראו)!... Depart from the path (דרך), turn aside from what is right!...' Therefore, this punishment will come upon you like a broken wall which falls...whose breach happens all of a sudden... Even a shard (חרש) to snatch up a firebrand from kindled wood or to scoop up water from a cistern will not be found among the ruins [of the wall]. (Isa. 30.9-14)

Isaiah describes the people as refusing to listen to what the prophets tell them—worse, they demand that the prophets alter their statements to reflect what the people want to hear. Put differently, they have eyes and ears but they make themselves blind and deaf. As a result, God will bring destruction on them. Deutero-Isaiah agrees that the people are morally deaf and blind, and he describes their current plight as matching Isaiah's prediction of an utter, apparently irremediable disaster.

> O deaf ones (החרשים), hear (שמעו), and blind ones, look carefully (לראות)!... You saw (ראות) much but did not pay attention; with open ears, you would not hear (ישמע)... And it is a people (והוא עם) that has been plundered and spoiled... They have been plundered and there is none to save them... Who among you will give ear to this, will pay attention and hear (וישמע) concerning the future? Who gave Jacob over to plunder and Israel to those who take spoils? Was it not the one against whom we sinned, by not consenting (ולא־אבו) to follow his paths (בדרכיו), by not listening (שמעו) to his teaching (בתורתו)? He poured down his furious anger on them... Flames engulfed them all around and they did not understand; [the flames] burned them, but they did not pay attention. (Isa. 42.18-25)

Some of the shared vocabulary (שמע, hear; דרך, path; אבה, consent) appears in other biblical passages that treat the theme of obedience. The

one example: in Isa. 29.9-10 the prophet announces that the Assyrians are the tool that YHWH will use to chastise the people. Deutero-Isaiah reuses language from that passage in Isa. 51.17-22, but he says that YHWH appointed the Babylonians to bring Israel's punishment. Thus, in this passage the later prophet recontextualizes elements that referred to Assyria in the older text so that they now refer to Babylonia.

confluence of other elements is unique to these two texts, however: the passages share fire imagery, the root ה״אר (to see) and a short sentence including the words עם (people) and הוא (it). Consequently, one begins to suspect that the parallel does result from more than the common use of formulaic vocabulary. Furthermore, the passage contains the typical stylistic features that mark Deutero-Isaiah's use of borrowed material: the split-up pattern and sound play. The clause from Isaiah, שמוע לא־אבו תורת ה׳, is split into two clauses in Deutero-Isaiah: ולא־אבו בדרכיו הלוך and ולא שמעו בתורתו. The word החרשים ('the deaf ones') in Deutero-Isaiah points back to חרש ('shard') in Isaiah, a completely different word built from similar consonants. Deutero-Isaiah's choice of word also recalls Isaiah's theme of the people who refused to listen, who made themselves deaf, in the source. This word, then, alludes doubly. The presence of the stylistic techniques, along with the parallel vocabulary and imagery, makes clear that the similarity between the passages constitutes a genuine case of allusion.[13]

As Deutero-Isaiah incorporates vocabulary and themes from the older passage, he describes as fact what his predecessor had announced as prediction. By confirming the accuracy of the oracle, the exilic prophet avows that YHWH and his messengers are reliable. The disaster that struck the nation does not indicate that YHWH is weak; on the contrary, it demonstrates that he knew in advance what was to occur and that he is powerful enough to carry out his will. Just as the nation saw YHWH's

---

13. Recognizing the allusion in 42.18-25 may help solve an exegetical crux. The tone of the passage is surprisingly bleak and angry in comparison with most of this section of Deutero-Isaiah, and it appears to indict the exilic audience for sins against YHWH. Such an accusation hardly matches an attempt to comfort them (as J. Skinner points out in *The Book of the Prophet Isaiah: Chapters XL–LXVI* [CBC; Cambridge: Cambridge University Press, rev. edn; 1917]; all references to commentaries in this paper are to the section concerning the verse under discussion). It may be, however, that here as in other passages Deutero-Isaiah is referring to the sins of the past, those described by his predecessors, in order to explain to the people why they are in their current state. They need not despair of YHWH's attention or power to save; the nation's plight is fully understandable and justifiable. At the same time, just as the negative prophecies of the past were fulfilled, so too the people can have confidence that the new, positive ones will come true. Thus this apparently bleak pericope functions in an optimistic way in its exilic context. On this theme in Deutero-Isaiah generally, see Haran, *RPSHONÔT*, p. 85.

power working against them, they can be confident that it will work for them when appropriate.[14]

But not all the older predictions came true, and consequently Deutero-Isaiah often repeats predictions that have yet to be fulfilled.[15] *Repredic-tion*, then, forms another category of Deutero-Isaianic appropriation of older material. For example, Deutero-Isaiah alludes to Isaiah's famous depiction of a peaceful world in the future and Jerusalem's place in it. Isaiah had predicted,

> In future days, the mountain of the House of YHWH will be ensconced as the greatest of mountains and raised (ונשא) above the hills. All nations will flow towards it (ונהרו אליו כל־הגוים), and many peoples will come (והלכו עמים) and will say, 'Come! Let us go up (ונעלה) to the mountain of YHWH, to the House (בית) of the God of Jacob, so that he will teach us some of his ways...for out of Zion comes teaching (כי מציון תצא תורה), and the word of YHWH from Jerusalem. And he will judge (ושפט) among the nations...and they will beat their swords (חרבותם) into plow-shares and their weapons into pruning forks; nation will not lift up sword (חרב) against nation, and they will learn war no more.' (Isa. 2.2-4)[16]

14. Confirmation of Isaianic prophecies also occurs in 51.17-22, which notes the fulfillment of the warning in 29.9-10 (Deutero-Isaiah replaces the Assyrian conqueror predicted by Isaiah with a Babylonian one); and in 59.11, where the people repeat God's statement of disappointment from 5.7, implicitly acknowledging that the punishment which resulted from that disappointment has come to pass.

15. Fishbane already notes the existence of this category among the prophets generally and its prominence in Deutero-Isaiah's work (*Biblical Interpretation*, pp. 497-498).

16. Some commentators date this passage to the post-exilic era, which would mean that Deutero-Isaiah could not have known it. Thus R.E. Clements asserts that the passage 'expresses a picture of the future exaltation of Jerusalem and Mount Zion, not one that was currently thought to exist... Quite certainly, therefore, we must ascribe the prophecy to a time after the destruction of Jerusalem in 587' (*Isaiah 1–39* [NCB; Grand Rapids: Eerdmans, 1980]). But Clements's claim that the Jerusalem described does not currently exist finds no textual support. The passage refers neither to the rebuilding of the city nor the reconstruction of the 'House of YHWH', so that there is no reason to believe either was destroyed.

Hermann Barth (*Die Jesaja Worte in der Josiazeit* [WMANT, 48; Neukirchen–Vluyn: Neukirchener Verlag, 1977], pp. 291-92) argues that the positive view of the nations in this passage as well as in 19.18-25 can only have been possible at a time of relative calm in Judah and warfare among the nations; namely, the beginning of the fourth century. In fact, we should ask, Why is it implausible that an eighth-century thinker would have hoped for peace in Israel and among the nations? Even if such an idea were surprising, this would not make it impossible. Isaiah conceived of

A similar prophecy appears with similar language in Deutero-Isaiah:

> For YHWH has comforted Zion (צִיּוֹן), comforted all her ruins
> (כָּל־חָרְבֹתֶיהָ); he has made Zion's wasteland as Eden, her desert as a
> garden of YHWH... 'Listen to me, my nation (עַמִּי), and my folk, give
> ear! For teaching goes forth from me (כִּי תוֹרָה מֵאִתִּי תֵצֵא), and I will give
> my judgment (וּמִשְׁפָּטִי) as a light of the nations (לְאוֹר עַמִּים)...and my
> arms will judge nations (עַמִּים יִשְׁפֹּטוּ). Islands will look eagerly to me, and
> in my arms they will have hope.' (Isa. 51.3-5)

The parallels are not limited to the vocabulary noted in parentheses. The
idea of peoples gathering appears in both passages, and both predict that
YHWH will teach the nations as well as judge them at his mountain. In

notions which were unexpected, even bizarre. Therein lies the genius of any original
thinker. To deny that an idea could have been thought of in a given age, as Barth and
so many biblicists do, is to deny the possibility of intellectual creativity. In addition,
we should note that the absence of Late Biblical Hebrew in these two passages
speaks against Barth's extremely late dating; and it is easier to see the reference to
Assyria in 19.23-25 as a reference to Assyria rather than (what Barth would suggest)
a reference to Persia.

Marvin Sweeney (*Isaiah 1–4 and the Post-Exilic Understanding of the Isaianic
Tradition* [BZAW, 171; Berlin: de Gruyter, 1988], pp. 165-74) notes the similarity
of the passage to 51.4-6 and claims that 2.2-4 must be the later passage. He suggests
two reasons for this. First, Deutero-Isaiah depicts YHWH as returning to Jerusalem,
while in 2.2-4 he is 'already' there. In fact, 2.2-4 more likely presents YHWH as
never having left, since no reference to his exit or return occurs. Second, Sweeney
notes that visions in which nations come to Jerusalem occur in other post-exilic texts
such as Trito-Isaiah and Zechariah. But this hardly means that any such vision must
stem from the same era. Sweeney dates the passage to the final years of Cyrus's
reign, arguing that its bright outlook and vision of universal peace fit that era of
universal peace well. Could not such a vision be dated just as easily to a time of
turbulence, when a writer longed for the universal peace that was lacking? Or, if the
thinker was original enough, to any other time?

It is difficult to date this passage with precision. Its appearance in the collection of
another eighth-century prophet (Mic. 4.1-4) may bolster an eighth-century dating. It
has several characteristic features of Isaiah's utterances: a focus on Zion's centrality,
concern for peaceful and just relations among international powers, and the anticipation of a generally unrealistic state of affairs. On the integral place of the vision in
Isaiah's thought, see further Y. Kaufmann, *Toledot ha-ʾEmunah ha-Yisraelit* (4
vols.; Tel Aviv: Mosad Bialik and Devir, 1937–56), III, pp. 99-200 (where he also
criticizes the view that the universalism of the passage would be impossible for an
eighth-century thinker) and III, pp. 221-22. While it is impossible to prove that the
passage stems from Isaiah himself, there is no reason to view it as post-exilic or to
doubt that Deutero-Isaiah could have known it.

both passages agricultural images (plowshares and pruning hooks in the source, gardens in the allusion) take the place of figures of destruction expressed with the root חר״ב (swords, חַרְבוֹתָם) in the source and ruins (חָרְבֹתֶיהָ) in the allusion; the correspondence constitutes a fine case of sound play. The consistent use of several themes in both passages suggests that these parallels are no coincidence. The presence of a typical stylistic feature of Deutero-Isaianic allusion shows that the parallel results from borrowing.

Deutero-Isaiah repeats the older prediction, affirming that an era of peace and equity is imminent. But he alters it slightly. His message initially concentrates not on the nations but on what is relevant for the Judeans themselves; his perspective is more national than universal. Further, while Deutero-Isaiah shares Isaiah's focus on Zion, he clarifies that the source of YHWH's teaching is not merely geographic ('for from me [rather than Zion] does teaching go forth'). This change may be more than coincidental. Deutero-Isaiah's exilic audience has reason to doubt the power of Zion's God over Babylon or its conqueror. The prophet reminds them that YHWH's might is not constrained by location. Moreover, they may suspect a person claiming to be a prophet of Zion's God when that person does not speak on or even near the holy mountain. Deutero-Isaiah avers that YHWH's words come from YHWH himself and can be revealed anywhere in the world he created.

In many other passages Deutero-Isaiah utilizes the writings ascribed to Isaiah ben Amos,[17] but these few suffice to show some typical features of Deutero-Isaianic allusion. The same features appear in Deutero-Isaiah's allusions to Jeremiah.[18]

Just as Deutero-Isaiah reversed grim statements from Isaiah, so too he turns negative passages from Jeremiah on their heads. For example,

17. Additional cases of reprediction occur; to cite only a few: 66.12-24 restates the prediction in 30.27-33; 35.1-8 (a Deutero-Isaianic passage) is based on 32.1-6. Another allusion to Isa. 2.1-4 occurs in 60.1-7. Isa. 53.1-12 contains a complete reworking of 11.1-10

18. Many, although by no means all, of Deutero-Isaiah's allusions to Jeremiah have been catalogued in two earlier studies: U. Cassuto, 'On the Formal and Stylistic Relationships between Deutero-Isaiah and Other Biblical Writers', in *idem, Oriental and Other Studies* (trans. I. Abrahams; Jerusalem: Magnes Press, 1973), I, pp. 143-60 (he also notes parallels between Deutero-Isaiah and other prophets, pp. 160-77); and S. Paul, 'Literary and Ideological Echoes of Jeremiah in Deutero-Isaiah', in P. Peli (ed.), *Proceedings of the Fifth World Congress of Jewish Studies* (Jerusalem: World Union of Jewish Studies, 1969), I, pp. 109-21.

Jeremiah laments the inevitable catastrophe coming upon Israel:

> [God said:] 'Pack your bags to leave the land, O you sitting (יושבת) under
> siege! For thus says YHWH: I am about to cast out the inhabitants of the
> land (יושבי הארץ)...' [The people lament:] 'Woe is me because of my
> injury! My wound is terrible (נחלה)!... My tent (אהלי) has been destroyed;
> all my tent-strings (מיתרי) have been cut; my children (בני) have gone
> away from me and are no more. Nobody is left to stretch out my tent (נטה
> עוד אהלי אין) or to raise up its flaps (ומקים יריעותי)...' Listen! A voice, a
> report is coming! 'Great noise from the north—to make the cities of
> Judah a desolation (שממה)'. [The prophet prays on behalf of the doomed
> nation:] '...O YHWH, chastise me—indeed, [this] is just; but not in
> anger, lest you make me naught. Pour out your anger on the nations (גוים)
> who do not know you...for...they have desolated (השמו) Jacob's dwelling
> places.' (Jer. 10.17-25)[19]

The vocabulary found in this passages occurs also in the following song
in Deutero-Isaiah:

> Sing, barren one who has not given birth; break forth into joy and shout,
> you who have not gone into labor (חלה)! For the children (בני) from the
> time of desolation (שממה) outnumber those of the married years, says
> YHWH. Widen the space of your tent (מקום אהלך), extend the sides
> (יריעות...יטו) of your dwelling! Don't be stingy—lengthen the strings
> (מיתריך) and strengthen the pegs! For you will spread out to the south and
> the north and dispossess nations (גוים); [your children] will settle the
> desolate cities (נשמות יושיבו)... And your redeemer will be called the Holy
> One of Israel, the God of all the earth (הארץ). (Isa. 54.1-3, 5)

Most of the parallels consist of a word that appears in both texts. One,
however, is based on an aural similarity and constitutes a case of sound
play. The word מקום (place) in Isa. 54.2 recalls ומקים (raise up). The
connection between these words is strengthened by their appearance in
both texts next to the words אהל (tent), יריעות (side) and נט"ה (extend).
The split-up pattern occurs here as well. The words ומקים יריעותי in
Jeremiah constituted a single phrase, but in Deutero-Isaiah מקום is
separated from ויריעות by the intervening noun, אהלך. The shared terms
and the presence of typical stylistic features of Deutero-Isaianic allusion
confirm the suggestion that Deutero-Isaiah borrowed from the older
passage.

---

19. On the attribution of lines in the passage to various speakers, see the sensitive
reading of W. Holladay, in *Jeremiah 1: A Commentary on the Book of the Prophet
Jeremiah Chapters 1–25* (Hermeneia; Minneapolis: Fortress Press, 1986).

In Jeremiah the people lamented the loss of their children, but Deutero-Isaiah tells Zion that she will have children again, and more than before. In Jeremiah the people mourned, 'My tent (אהלי) is destroyed'. Because the children were killed, rebuilding was not feasible: 'nobody is left to stretch out (נטה) my tent, no one to set up the sides (מקים יריעותי)'. Deutero-Isaiah, on the other hand, assures Zion that not only will she have a tent, she will need to enlarge it to accommodate the abundance of her family. Thus the prophet directs her to do precisely what the people were unable to do in Jeremiah. The earlier prophet reported that people spread out because invading nations scattered them, but in Isa. 54.3 the people spread out because they are reclaiming land from the foreigners. The invaders had made the cities of Judah into desolation, but now the Israelites repopulate them. Words, images and metaphors that signified negatively for Israel in the older prophet herald restoration in Deutero-Isaiah.

Reversals occur with great frequency in Deutero-Isaiah's allusions to Jeremiah,[20] but I would like to move on to examples of other categories. Deutero-Isaiah confirms the fulfillment of Jeremiah's oracles in several cases. For example, God announced in Jeremiah that he would punish the people by treating them like metal which is being smelted:

> Thus says YHWH of Hosts: I am about to smelt them and refine them (הנני צורפם ובחנתים), for what can I do (כי איך אעשה) because of my people?[21] (Jer. 9.6)

Deutero-Isaiah uses the same vocabulary as he describes the chastisement the people experience in exile:

20. To cite a few: Isa. 49.14-18 reverses Jer. 2.32; Isa. 62.12 depends on Jer. 30.17; Isa. 52.13–53.12 and 54.1-5 both borrow vocabulary from Jer. 10.18-25. Isa. 65.18-23 reverses Jer. 29.4-6.

21. The second half of the verse is difficult. The MT reads כי איך אעשה מפני בת עמי. For other cases of מפני meaning 'due to, because of', see BDB, p. 818b. Alternatively, read מפני רעת בת עמי מפני, following LXX and Targum. Holladay's suggestion (*Jeremiah 1, ad. loc.*) that we read איד instead of איך would undermine the argument I am making here, since איך is one of the borrowed items demonstrating Deutero-Isaiah's reliance on Jeremiah. But his reconstruction of the verse is somewhat too involved to be fully convincing. Further, the question introduced by the word איך in the MT of Jer. 9.6 corresponds with the similar question found in Jer. 9.8.

Behold, I have smelted you, but not for silver ([22]הנה צרפתיך ולא בכסף), I have tested you ([23]בחרתיך) in the furnace of affliction. For my sake, for my sake I acted (אעשה), for how could [my name] be defiled ([24]איך יחל כי)? And I shall not give my glory to another. (Isa. 48.10-11)

One might doubt that these passages are related as source and allusion, because the image of the people being assayed appears elsewhere (see Isa. 1.25; Jer. 6.27-29; Zech. 13.9; Mal. 3.2-3). Isa. 48.10-11, however, shares additional vocabulary with Jer. 9.6 not found in the other texts where the smelting theme appears: כי איך, אעשה. Further, Jeremiah's phrase הנני צורפם ובחנתים re-appears in Deutero-Isaiah, but there the words are divided into two parts: first we read הנה צרפתיך, and several words later we read בחרתיך. The presence of the split-up pattern increases the likelihood that this passage refers back to Jeremiah. Finally, a rhetorical question comes at the end of both verses, creating additional similarity between the passages. As a result, Deutero-Isaiah's dependence on the passage in Jeremiah becomes clear.

Thematically, the allusion works at several levels. Deutero-Isaiah not only asserts that Jeremiah's prediction has come to pass, but he alters the reason God gives for the punishment. Jeremiah stressed the people's deceptiveness and sinfulness, which gave God no alternative but to

22. This is a difficult phrase. To read, 'I have refined you, but not as silver (בכסף)', yields no clear sense, because the people *have* in fact been refined as silver is refined: through their suffering, they have become better material. C. North (*The Second Isaiah* [Oxford: Oxford University Press, 1964]) argues that the *bēt* can mean 'for the sake of', yielding the sense, 'I have assayed you, but not for the sake of silver accrued through the process.' Although North does not note this, LXX supports his suggestion, as it reads, οὐχ ἕνεκεν ἀργυρίου.

23. Some commentators read בחנתיך with 1QIsaa, while others understand the MT as an Aramaism which means 'refine, smelt' (as I have translated). Either way, the parallel with Jeremiah remains strong. Indeed, even if one reads בחרתיך and understands it to mean 'I chose you', the word would still allude to Jeremiah through word play.

24. It is clear from 48.9 and the second half of this verse that God's name or glory is the implied subject of this verb; LXX adds τὸ ἐμὸν ὄνομα, probably for clarity, but perhaps because its Hebrew text in fact included the word שמי. Alternatively, read a first person niphal from the root חל"ל with 1QIsaa (איחל = 'how can I be dishonored?'; see Goshen-Gottstein's comment cited in E.Y. Kutscher, *The Language and Linguistic Background of the Isaiah Scroll* [STDJ, 6; Leiden: Brill, 1974], p. 242). The Qumran reading may confirm the suggestion of H.D. Chajes (cited in Cassuto, 'Deutero-Isaiah', p. 166 n. 93) that the text originally read אחל but was changed to the third person due to a *tiqqûn sôf*ᵉ*rîm*.

punish them (see 9.7-8). Deutero-Isaiah, however, shifts the focus from the people to God and his honor. He uses Jeremiah's vocabulary to express a new reason for the assaying: '*For my sake, for my sake* I do *this*, for how can *my name be dishonored*?' By stressing God's honor, Deutero-Isaiah shifts attention away from the nation's guilt and implicitly assures them that redemption will come. Just as his honor required action against the nation, so too it will lead God to act on his people's behalf. Lest the people worry that they have lost any claim to a part in that honor, the prophet continues, 'But I will not give my glory to another'.

Just as cases of confirmation appear in Deutero-Isaiah's allusions to Jeremiah,[25] so do repredictions. The prophecies of comfort in Jeremiah 30–31 and 33 provided the richest mine for Deutero-Isaiah as he repeats positive prophecies from Jeremiah.[26] A fine example appears already in Isaiah 35, which most critics agree belongs to the Deutero-Isaianic collection. Jeremiah had stated,

---

25. Deutero-Isaiah alludes to fulfilled prophecies of Jeremiah in several other passages as well. A clear example occurs in Isa. 51.19, which combines vocabulary from Jer. 4.20 and 15.2, 5. The specific disasters which Jeremiah foresaw (שׁד, שׁבר, חרב, and the absence of anyone to comfort the afflicted) are described as realities in Deutero-Isaiah (cf. Paul, 'Echoes', pp. 116-17). Isa. 58.12 and 61.4 may represent a confirmation of Jer. 25.9 and 49.13.

26. The abundant parallels between Jer. 30–31 and Isa. 40–66 have been noted before, and some scholars suggest that the chapters from Jeremiah have in fact been influenced by Deutero-Isaiah. However, the presence of material in those chapters which refers to the northern kingdom shows that at least that section's kernel derives from early in the career of Jeremiah. There is no reason to doubt that additional material in these chapters stems from the same prophet's pronouncements. Jeremiah's mission was both to warn and encourage, to break down and to build up; the concentration of the positive part of his message in these chapters does not indicate separate authorship. Further, the same thematic and stylistic characteristics which appear in Deutero-Isaiah's use of material from earlier sections of Jeremiah also appear in his use of 30–31. This makes clear that the similarities between 30–31 and 40–66 result from Deutero-Isaiah's reliance on the Jeremiah collection, not the other way around. For a convincing defense of Jeremiah's authorship of chs. 30–31, see Holladay, *Jeremiah 2*, pp. 155-66; and, more briefly, O. Eissfeldt, *The Old Testament: An Introduction* (trans. P. Ackroyd; New York: Harper and Row, 1965), pp. 361-62 (who regards most of the material as coming from Jeremiah but the redaction as exilic); and J. Bright, *Jeremiah* (AB, 21; Garden City, NY: Doubleday, 1965), pp. 284-87.

Thus says YHWH: Sing (רנו) to Jacob joyously (שמחה), and shout to the chief (ראש) of nations... Make it known! Give praise! And say (ואמרו):... I am about to bring (הנני מביא) them from a northern land, and I will gather them from the ends of the earth; the blind and the lame ([27]עור ופסח בם) will be among them, together with those who are pregnant and giving birth. A great multitude will return here (ישובו הנה). With weeping they will come (יבאו) and because of supplications[28] I will bring them in (אובילם). I will lead them (אוליכם) to streams of water (נחלי מים) on a straight path (דרך); they will not falter on it. (Jer. 31.7-9)

The passage refers to return of the northern kingdom's exiles, as the continuation of v. 9 indicates: 'For I have been to Israel as a father, and Ephraim is my eldest son.' Deutero-Isaiah uses the same images when he describes the returnees of his day:

Say (אמרו) to the anxious, Be strong! Do not fear. Behold your God will come with requital (הנה...יבוא)... Then the eyes of the blind (עור) will open and the ears of the deaf will be unsealed. Then the lame (פסח) will jump like gazelles, and the tongue of the mute will sing (ירן). For water (מים) gushes in the desert, and streams (נחלים) in the desolate places. The dry land will become a pool, and a parched wilderness—founts of water (מים)... And there will be a way and a path (דרך), and it will be called the path (דרך) of the Holy One... Those who go on this path, even fools (ואוילים), will not err. No lion will be there... The redeemed will go (והלכו). Those ransomed by YHWH will return (ישבון), and they will come to Zion in song (ובאו ציון ברנה), with eternal happiness (שמחת עולם) on their heads (ראשם); they will achieve joy and happiness (שמחה), and sorrow and sighing will flee. (Isa. 35.4-10)

The large amount of shared vocabulary already suggests that the correspondence between these two passages is more than a coincidence. Moreover, vocabulary from the earlier passage is subject to the split-up pattern and sound play. Jeremiah refers to the blind and lame in a single phrase: עור ופסח. These words appear in Deutero-Isaiah as well, but they

---

27. LXX seems to be based on a *Vorlage* reading במועד פסח. But the subsequent words make clear that Jeremiah is describing not the timing of the event but rather the range of participants, which includes those who normally would have difficulty on such a journey. Thus the reading reflected in LXX may be a simple *Schreibfehler* (במ עור ופסח < במועד פסח).

28. Heb. ובתחנונים. LXX reads ἐν παρακλήσει, which seems to assume a Hebrew text reading ובתנחומים. Further, LXX seems to have read יצאו rather than יבאו earlier in the verse. This seems initially to make more sense: 'They went out weeping and will come back comforted.' But MT is probably to be preferred, for reasons discussed below.

are split apart there, occurring in two separate clauses: first Deutero-Isaiah says אז תפקחנה עיני עורים; then, after mentioning the deaf, he says אז ידלג כאיל פסח. Sound play affects the word אובילם. The later writer does not repeat that word, but he hints at it with the similar sounding word אוילים.[29] In light of both of these patterns, it is clear that Deutero-Isaiah utilized Jer. 31.7-9 specifically. Further, some markers are insistently repeated, as if to make sure one can't miss them: דרך appears three times, מים twice.

Jeremiah directed this message to northern exiles, but Deutero-Isaiah shifts the reference of the prediction to his own contemporaries from the south. This is precisely the same historical recontextualization that occurred in Isa. 40.1-10, which alludes to Isa. 28.1-5. Other adjustments occur as well. Jeremiah's tone is oddly forlorn considering his positive message: the exiles will return with weeping and by means of supplications. Jeremiah may have stressed the need for repentance to avoid the disaster (which had already taken place in the north and which Jeremiah came to regard as inevitable for the south) but to bring the punishment to its end.[30] But Deutero-Isaiah is not as interested in recalling sorrow and proposing repentance; he focuses more exclusively on comfort. As if he speaks to an audience who have Jeremiah's slightly less joyful prediction in mind, he says to the 'anxious', 'Do not fear'. Alluding to Jeremiah's 'With weeping they will come', he states, 'In song they will come'. His assurance that 'sorrow and sighing will flee' (35.10) may also respond to the tone of the earlier prediction.

Additional examples of Deutero-Isaiah's re-use of Jeremiah could be given,[31] but these three cases suffice to show that Deutero-Isaiah utilized

29. We do not know how Deutero-Isaiah pronounced Hebrew—perhaps these words were spoken as (ōbīlēm) and (awīlīm)—but the similarity remains regardless. In both words the glottal stop is followed by a labial, then *lāmed*, and then *mem*.

30. It is for this reason that the MT text (ובתחנונים) is preferred over the LXX (which is based on ובתנחומים). At the same time, it is interesting to note that the LXX, by shifting תחנונים to תנחומים, effects the same revision of tone which Deutero-Isaiah did.

31. Many other cases of reprediction occur. Deutero-Isaiah alludes to Jer. 31.7-9 again in 43.5-9; 49.12 and 55.12. In 40.9-10 Deutero-Isaiah repeats Jer. 31.16, and in 42.5-9 he revises the prophecy from Jer. 31.31-36. Not all cases of reprediction of Jeremiah's prophecies are taken from Jer. 30–33. Isa. 55.6-12 is based on Jer. 29.10-14, and Jer. 3.12-22 provides the building blocks for Isa. 57.16-19. Isa. 60.7-13 utilizes word play as it repeats the prediction from Jer. 3.16-18.

Other examples of historical recontextualization occur as well. The linkage of the pronouncements of Jeremiah in precisely the ways that he reworked the oracles of Isaiah ben Amoṣ: he reversed, confirmed, repredicted, and recontextualized; he employed sound play and the split-up pattern.[32] Having noted how Deutero-Isaiah reworked older prophetic texts, we can turn to the question, what does the study of Deutero-Isaiah's inner-biblical allusions tell us about the relation between the two major segments of the book of Isaiah?

Redactional Unity: Illusion Resulting from Allusion?

Many recent scholars influenced by canon criticism note elements of unity linking the sections of the book of Isaiah that modern scholarship rent asunder. How does the study of Deutero-Isaiah's allusivity affect these claims that Isaiah is a unified whole?

Assertions regarding the unity of the book of Isaiah made in the past few decades fall into two categories.[33] On the one hand, the thematic coherence of Isaiah 1–66 on a synchronic level can be stressed. Such a reading does not involve any historical claims, and it does not so much contradict conventional ideas about the separate origins of First, Second and Third Isaiah as it moves beyond them. On the other hand, more historical claims regarding the authorship or redaction of the book of Isaiah can be—and have been—made. Scholars who make these more historical claims call into question the extent to which the three sections

Assyria and Babylonia occurs in Isa. 40.9-10's allusion to Jer. 31.16. Isa. 45.12-13, by borrowing vocabulary from Jer. 27.5-6, links Nebuchadnezzar and Cyrus as kings charged to bring about YHWH's will regarding Israel (see Paul, 'Echoes', p. 111).

32. The same tendencies also occur in Deutero-Isaiah's allusions to other prophets. Isa. 40.2-8 and Isa. 49.26 both contain vocabulary that reverses the doom pronouncement in Ezek. 21.2-12; the allusion in Isa. 40 contains the split-up pattern. Isa. 52.1-8 contains a repredicting of Nah. 2.1 that involves historical recontextualization and contains several cases of the split-up pattern. Zeph. 2.13-15 forms the basis for Isa. 47.5-11, which repredicts the older text while changing its historical referent; the borrowing utilizes sound play. Isa. 58.1-11 at once repeats the complaint found in Micah 3.6-12 and reverses its prophecy of doom; sound play occurs in this borrowing as well.

33. Most scholars working in this area have failed to keep them distinct. R.E. Clements is an exception, however; see his remarks in 'Beyond Tradition History: Deutero-Isaianic Development of First Isaiah's Themes', *JSOT* 31 (1985), p. 97. See also the comments of D. Carr, 'Reaching for Unity in Isaiah', *JSOT* 57 (1993), pp. 62-64.

of the book ever worked as distinct units. They assert that chs. 40–66 were written as a supplement to earlier Isaianic oracles and did not circulate independently of them. Further, these scholars surmise that sections of Isaiah 1–39 that resemble Deutero-Isaiah in language and theme were influenced, edited or even written by the schools responsible for Isaiah 40–66; indeed, some go so far as to suggest that the traditions we know from 1–39 were collected and shaped by the same hands that penned 40–66, and that to speak of a First Isaianic collection that was distinct from 40–66 is impossible.

My study of Deutero-Isaiah's allusions has no methodological ramifications for the purely synchronic approach to the unity of Isaiah, although it supplies additional examples of parallel material in the two halves of the book. However, my study has a more complicated relationship with the redactional or historical approaches to the unity of Isaiah. I agree with these scholars (especially Clements and Seitz[34]) that Deutero-Isaiah was based on First Isaiah; that Deutero-Isaiah was written as a reaction to or, in some sense, a continuation of, First Isaiah; and that Deutero-Isaiah utilized written oracles attributed to First Isaiah to compose his own prophecies. I disagree in two ways. First, the study of Deutero-Isaiah's inner-biblical allusions shows that the same point can be made regarding Deutero-Isaiah's relationship to Jeremiah: Deutero-Isaiah is based on, reacts to, continues and utilizes written oracles of Jeremiah—in precisely the same manner. Second (and following from the first), I believe that Isaiah 40–66 were not written to be a part of the book of Isaiah or to be included in the Isaiah traditions but were added to it secondarily; consequently, Deutero-Isaiah was (or claimed to be) a prophet in his own right, rather than a disciple, annotator or pseudepigrapher.[35] Let me flesh out these two points.

We saw above that Deutero-Isaiah's allusions to and revisions of Isaiah and Jeremiah fall into the same thematic categories: Deutero-Isaiah confirms that the dire prophecies of Isaiah and Jeremiah have achieved fulfillment; he reverses their tropes of condemnation to ones of comfort; he repredicts their unfulfilled prophecies; he links individuals or nations in his text with others in the older texts (some of the same linkages

34. See Clements, 'Beyond Tradition History', p. 101; Seitz, *Zion's Final Destiny*, p. 35.

35. My point here affects conclusions regarding the history of prophecy one might reach based on Seitz's speculation in *Zion's Final Destiny*, p. 34, and in 'Temporal Transition', pp. 246-47.

occur in allusions to both Jeremiah and Isaiah; e.g., Assyria is replaced by Babylonia). These categories occur with similar frequency in Deutero-Isaiah's allusions to each source. Cases of confirmation are relatively rare in both. Reversals are common, as are cases of historical recontextualization. Repredictions are the most frequent; examples of this category involving both sources can be divided into comparable sub-categories. Deutero-Isaiah restates prophecies of restoration or triumph most often, but in a small number of cases he repeats accusations or predictions of disaster from Jeremiah and Isaiah.[36] Further, Deutero-Isaiah repeats a particular prophecy from each source several times and revises that prophecy by leaving out some salient element. He recalls Isaiah 11[37] in numerous passages (42.1-9; 49.22; 60.17–61.1; 62.10; and

36. Thus, negative predictions from Jer. 12.7-13 and Isa. 30.9-14 are restated (not reversed) in Isa. 56.10–57.6

37. Because many scholars date all or parts of Isa. 11 to the post-exilic (or, at the earliest, the exilic) period, I need to pause to defend my assertion that this chapter indeed predates Deutero-Isaiah.

Clements (*Isaiah 1–39* [NCB; Grand Rapids: Eerdmans, 1980]) argues that vv. 1-9 of this chapter must have been written after 587 because the term גזע ישי ('stump of Jesse') indicates that the Davidic dynasty has lost its throne (i.e., the 'tree' of the Davidides has been cut down and only a stump remains). However, the semantic range of גזע is not limited to 'stump'. As J. Hayes and S. Irvine point out (*Isaiah, the Eighth-Century Prophet* [Nashville: Abingdon, 1987], p. 212), in Isa 40.24 this word refers to the part of a live tree which comes out of the ground. Thus the term's semantic range includes 'trunk' as well as 'stump'. (This sense of the word continues in later Hebrew; note *m. B. Bat.* 4.5, where context requires 'trunk'). Thus Clements fails to demonstrate that vv. 1-9 must have been written after 587. Barth (*Jesaja Worte*, pp. 59-62) admits the Isaianic authorship of 11.1-5 but judges vv. 6-9 to be later. However, vv. 6-9 continue the description of the peaceful future described in vv. 1-5 and contain no disjunction suggesting a late interpolation (contra, e.g., Odil Steck, '"ein kleiner Knabe kann sie leiten"—Beobachtungen zum Tierfrieden in Jesaja 11,6-8 und 65,25', in J. Hausmann and H.J. Zobel [eds.], *Alttestamentlicher Glaube und Biblische Theologie: Festschrift für Horst Dietrich Preuß* [Stuttgart: Kohlhammer, 1992], esp. pp. 105-108; Steck's view that 11.1-16 contains four sources depends on a discovery of multiple disjunctions in a text that coheres quite well).

The arguments for the lateness of vv. 10-16 initially appear to be more serious. Barth holds that the formula והיה ביום ההוא indicates an interpolation (p. 58), but, as Hayes and Irvine point out (p. 216), the phrase can also introduce a new section within a composition by a single author. Skinner (Isaiah), Clements and Barth (pp. 58-59) see the references to the return of exiles as necessarily dating after 587; further, for these critics, the description of exiles in Egypt, Pathros, Cush and other

65.25), but he consistently omits reference to Isaiah's vision there of an enduring Davidic line.[38] Similarly, he alludes to Jer. 31.31-36 again and again (e.g. 42.5-9; 54.10-13; and 59.21) but always passes over Jeremiah's description of a new covenant impervious to infraction.[39] Not

lands (11.11) must be dated well into the post-exilic era. But northerners had already been exiled in Isaiah's day; and even before 722 the Assyrian policy of deportation was well known and feared throughout the ancient Near East. It is for this reason that, even before the fall of Samaria, eighth-century prophets anticipated that Israelites would become refugees in Egypt and Assyria (see Amos 9.3; 11.5; Hos. 8.13). Thus the reference to exiles in and around Egypt is not surprising in an eighth-century document. Indeed, the list of locations in 11.11b corresponds in content and order to an eighth-century topographical list of Esarhaddon and is likely to stem from that time (see M. Weinfeld, *Deuteronomy* [AB, 5; New York: Doubleday, 1991], p. 48). The description of exiles in 'four corners of the earth' (11.12) is hardly surprising in an era when peoples feared the Assyrians, who notoriously labeled themselves the rulers of *arbaʾi kibrāti erṣēti*.

In short, there are no good reasons to see any parts of ch. 11 as exilic or post-exilic. Many elements of the chapter, especially in vv. 10-16, reflect typical eighth-century concerns. Moreover, vv. 11-16 emphasize the return of victims of Assyrian deportation but contain no explicit reference to Babylonian exiles (see A. Laato, *The Servant of YHWH and Cyrus: A Reinterpretation of the Exilic Messianic Programme in Isaiah 40–55* [ConBOT, 35; Stockholm: Almqvist and Wiksell, 1992], pp. 116-17). This points strongly to a dating before 597. Finally, the phrase ואסף נדחי ישראל in verse 12 is unlikely in the late post-exilic period, when כנס replaced אסף (see M. Rooker, *Biblical Hebrew in Transition: The Language of the Book of Ezekiel* [JSOTSup, 90; Sheffield: JSOT Press, 1990], p. 166).

38. This omission is especially clear because he so often repredicts ch. 11 without adopting its stress on the Davidic family. The promises regarding the monarch are not simply dropped, however. Deutero-Isaiah implies that the promises which Isaiah vouchsafed to the Davidic line now apply to the people as a whole. The transfer of royal promises to the whole nation occurs in other passages from Deutero-Isaiah and has been noticed before (see J. Begrich, *Studien zur Deuterojesaja* [TBü, 20; Munich: Chr. Kaiser Verlag, 2nd edn, 1969], p. 105, and the lengthier discussion in Kaufmann, *Deutero-Isaiah*, p. 189). The theme becomes especially clear in the allusions to ch. 11.

39. Jeremiah claimed in 31.31-36 that God had renounced his covenant with Israel, as the destruction of the temple and the Davidic monarchy indicated. But the prophet averred that a new covenant would be made at the time of the restoration to replace the old one. Unlike the old covenant, which the people had to learn, the new covenant would be internalized by the people so that they would never break it. Deutero-Isaiah repeats Jeremiah's prophecy but shies away from its more surprising aspects. Like Jeremiah, he predicts that the people will have a covenant with YHWH. However, his allusions to Jer. 31.31 leave open the question of whether Deutero-

only does Deutero-Isaiah relate to these older texts in the same thematic ways; he recasts wording from both prophets with identical stylistic techniques: the split-up pattern, sound-play and (less often for both) the repetition of borrowed vocabulary in the source's order.[40]

The resemblance between Deutero-Isaiah's allusions to Isaiah and his borrowings from Jeremiah indicates that neither of these pre-exilic prophets played a unique role in Deutero-Isaiah's work. Both are important influences. Deutero-Isaiah does not function merely as a disciple in an Isaianic school or a devotee in a Jeremianic circle; he participates in a wider prophetic tradition, using the same techniques to recast the work of more than one predecessor.

Deutero-Isaiah depends on Isaiah and Jeremiah in similar ways—but not to the same extent. His affinity to Jeremiah is stronger. This becomes evident in two ways. First, he displays a greater familiarity with the Jeremiah traditions. There are twenty-seven discrete statements[41] of Jeremiah to which Deutero-Isaiah clearly alludes, and twelve additional statements from Jeremiah to which he may allude.[42] There are only

---

Isaiah is referring to an already existing covenant (which seems more likely) or a new one. In any event, he avoids describing the covenant as 'new'.

40. For example, 40.9-10, which is based on Jer. 31.16 (this example also includes sound play and the split-up pattern); 42.1-9, which is based on Isa. 11; 60.5-7, which borrows from Isa. 2.1-4; 60.7-13, which alludes to Jer. 3.16-18.

41. By 'statement', I mean a verse or set of verses used by Deutero-Isaiah in at least one particular allusion. Thus, I am counting Isa. 1.12-15 separately from Isa. 1.28-29, since he alludes to each statement separately and because they are discrete sub-units of a single longer composition; similarly, I count Jer. 31.1-9 and 31.31-36 separately, since the allusions to each occur in different passages and because they are discrete sub-units. Long units which Deutero-Isaiah utilizes repeatedly as units (such as Isa. 6 or Jer. 3) I count as a single case. One might define 'statement' differently, but this does not affect my argument, since I am interested in a ratio, not an absolute number; what matters is that I have used the same criteria for defining statements from each source.

42. The complete list is as follows (I put the doubtful cases in parentheses): Jer. 1.9-10 // Isa. 51.16. Jer. 2.6-8 // Isa. 63.11-12. Jer. 2.23-25 // Isa. 57.10. Jer. 2.32 // Isa. 49.14-18. (Jer. 3.1 // Isa. 50.1). Jer. 3.12-14, 21-22 // Isa. 57.16. Jer. 3.16-18 // Isa. 60.7-13. (Jer. 4.13 // Isa. 66.15). Jer. 4.20 // Isa. 51.19. Jer. 4.22-25 // Isa. 41.23-29; (Isa. 60.18-22). (Jer. 6.7 // Isa. 60.18; 65.3). Jer. 6.13-14 // Isa. 57.17-21. Jer. 6.20, 22 // Isa. 60.6-9. (Jer. 7.13 // Isa. 65.12). Jer. 9.6 // Isa. 48.10-11. (Jer. 9.8 // Isa. 57.6). (Jer. 10.1-16 // Isa. 40.19-22; 41.6-7; 44.9-14). Jer. 10.17-25 // Isa. 54.1-5; 52.13–53.12. Jer. 11.18-21 // Isa. 51.12-14; 53.3-18. Jer. 12.7-13 // Isa. 56.9–57.5. Jer. 14.2-9, 12 // Isa. 42.10-16; 59.9-19. Jer. 15.2, 5 // Isa. 51.19. (Jer. 15.13 // Isa.

sixteen statements of Isaiah's to which Deutero-Isaiah certainly alludes, and another seven to which he may allude.[43] Second, passages that contain allusions to Jeremiah are slightly more frequent than passages containing allusions to Isaiah.[44] Thirty-three passages contain allusions to Jeremiah; of these, six allude to more than one passage in Jeremiah. An additional nineteen passages may contain allusions to Jeremiah. Thirty-two passages contain allusions to Isaiah; of these, eight contain allusions to more than one passage in Isaiah. An additional four cases may contain allusions to Isaiah.

These figures indicate that Deutero-Isaiah's connection to his more immediate predecessor is slightly stronger than his connection with his eighth-century forerunner. As a result, whatever claims one makes regarding Deutero-Isaiah as a continuation of Isaiah's prophecy apply even more strongly to Jeremiah. Similarly, if it is true that Deutero-Isaiah was a 'disciple' of Isaiah or a 'member' of an 'Isaianic school', it is equally true that he was a 'disciple' of Jeremiah or part of an

65.13). Jer. 16.16-18 // Isa. 40.2; 61.7; 65.6-7. Jer. 20.7-13 // Isa. 50.4, 9. (Jer. 25.9 [49.13]) // Isa. 34.2; 58.12; 61.14). Jer. 27.5-6 // Isa. 45.12-13. Jer. 29.4-6 // Isa. 65.18-23. Jer. 29.10-14 // Isa. 55.6-12. (Jer. 30.10-11 [1.8] // Isa. 41.8-15; 43.1-7; 44.1-3). Jer. 30.17 // Isa. 62.12. (Jer. 30.24 // Isa. 55.11). Jer. 31.1-9 // Isa. 35.4-10; 41.14-16; 43.5-9; 55.12. Jer. 31.16 // Isa. 40.9-10. Jer. 31.31-36 // Isa. 42.5-9; 51.15; 54.10; 59.21. Jer. 33.3 // Isa. 48.6. Jer. 33.7-9 // Isa. 61.1-4. (Jer. 48.3 // Isa. 51.19; 59.7; 60.18). (Jer. 49.23 // Isa. 57.20).

43. The complete list is as follows (I put the doubtful cases in parentheses): (1.5-6 // 53.4-5). (1.12, 15 // 65.1-3, 24). 1.28-29 // 65.12-13; 66.17, 24. 2.1-4 // 51.3-5; 60.5-7. 2.5-21 // 57.5-20. 5.7 // 59.11. (5.11 // 56.12). 5.26 // 49.22; 62.10. (5.27 // 40.28-31). 5.30 // 50.10-11; 60.1-5. 6 // (40.1-8); (40.21-28); 44.9-14; 49.19-20; 52.13–53.12; (54.1-3, 14); 57.5-20; (62.4); (63.17). 8.22-9.1 // 50.10-11; 60.1-5. (9.3 // 60.17). (10.22 // 66.12, 14). 11.1-10 // 42.1-9; (53.1-12); 60.17–61.1; (65.1-2); 65.25. 11.10–12.3 // 49.22; 62.10. (12.6 // 60.14). 14.24-25 // 46.9-13. (22.13-14 // 56.12). 28.1-2 // 40.6-10. 29.9-10 // 51.17-22. 29.16 // 45.9-10. 30.9-12 // 42.23-24; 56.10-57.6. 30.28-33 // 66.12, 24. 32.2-6 // 35.1-8.

44. By 'passage' I mean a set of verses over which vocabulary pointing back to the source is spread. These can be short (e.g., 40.2, which alludes to Jer. 16.16-18; or 45.9-10, which alludes to Isa. 29.16) or long (e.g., 42.10-16, which alludes to Jer. 14.1-20; or 42.1-9, which alludes to Isa. 11). If a passage alludes to more than one passage in the source, I am counting it as a single case (e.g., 57.5-20, which alludes to Isa. 2.5-21 and Isa. 6; and 51.12-16, which alludes to Jer. 1.9-10, 11.19 and 31.35). Again, one could define 'passage' differently or count cases of allusion in some other way, but I am interested in the relative frequency rather than absolute numbers, so that what matters is a consistent method of counting.

'Jeremianic school', and he seems to have studied Jeremiah somewhat more intensively.

The existence of a close relationship between Deutero-Isaiah and Jeremiah undermines the assertion that Isaiah 40–66 was originally intended to be a part of the Isaiah traditions. That assertion is based on the similarities between 40–66 and the first part of the book. However, given that the same sort of similarities link Deutero-Isaiah and Jeremiah, it is clear that the relationship between the two halves of Isaiah is not unique, and that no special redactional or authorial bond existed between those two corpora. It is possible to put this point differently: on the basis of the type of evidence that is supposed to demonstrate the unity of Isaiah, we could equally well argue that Isaiah 40–66 was written to be a continuation of Jeremiah. But 40–66 was certainly not written to be a part of two different books. Rather, these chapters were composed as an independent corpus, and they were added to the Isaiah traditions at some later time. It is quite possible that the similarities between these chapters led some scribes to place the Isaiah traditions and the writings of the exilic prophet on the same scroll,[45] and to this extent the two halves did attain unity. However, that unity is historically secondary; and it would have been equally or even more logical for scribes to associate these chapters with Jeremiah.[46]

Inclusio or Allusion?

One argument of the unity school deserves additional attention. Isaiah 1 and Isaiah 65–66 display affinities to each other which lead some scholars to suggest that chs. 65–66 were written specifically to form an inclusio with ch. 1.[47] If chs. 65–66 were written by Deutero-Isaiah (which I think is overwhelmingly likely),[48] this may imply that Deutero-

---

45. Clements recognizes this possibility but rejects it ('Beyond', pp. 100-101).

46. In fact, the Chronicler may have done so. As G.B. Gray notes (*A Critical and Exegetical Commentary on the Book of Isaiah* [ICC; New York: Charles Scribner's Sons, 1912], pp. xxxvii-xxxix), in Ezra 1.1-5 and 2 Chron. 36.22-23 the Chronicler seems to attribute Isa. 44.28 to Jeremiah, when he states that Jeremiah prophesied that Cyrus would return the exiles to Judah and allow the rebuilding of Jerusalem.

47. See Sweeney, *Isaiah 1–4*, p. 24; A. Tomasino, 'Isaiah 1.1-24 and 63–66 and the Composition of the Isaianic Corpus', *JSOT* 57 (1993), pp. 93-96. For a sympathetic but critical evaluation of these theories, see Carr, 'Unity', pp. 71-75.

48. The chapters abound with examples of Deutero-Isaiah's poetic style, such as the sound play in 65.11-12 and 65.25 (cf. Torrey, *Second Isaiah*, pp. 193-94, and

Isaiah intended to append his work to an already existing collection of Isaiah which began with ch. 1. Before one arrives at this conclusion, however, several questions need to be answered. How impressive are the similarities between chs. 1 and 65–66? Are the connections between them really unique enough to assert that they form an inclusio, or do similar resemblances link these chapters with other passages in the book of Isaiah? If in fact the similarities between the chapters are significant, must they result from the attempt of the author of 65–66 to form an inclusio, or do other explanations for those similarities exist?

Scholars have long noted that these chapters share many vocabulary items[49] and themes,[50] which need not be listed yet again here. Most of these parallels consist simply of individual words that fail to display patterns of re-use or transformation. Further, much of this vocabulary results from the shared themes of sacrifice, sin and punishment, which are hardly uncommon in the Hebrew Bible and necessarily suggest certain words. These parallels are of little significance, and they cannot by themselves demonstrate that one text is based on the other or that they were composed in tandem.[51]

On the other hand, a few of the parallels do involve interesting

Kaufmann, *Babylonian Captivity*, pp. 80-81). Further, they contain allusions to Jeremiah and other chapters of Isaiah which also are typical of Deutero-Isaiah's project of allusion and include cases of sound play, word play and the split-up pattern. Several lines and themes reflect Deutero-Isaiah's concerns elsewhere. Thus, cf. 50.2 with 65.12 and 66.4, and the *rishonot* passages with 65.17. Similarly, in 65.1, YHWH tells his people, הנני. As Rabbi Yehiel Poupko pointed out to me, only in the last part of the book of Isaiah does YHWH call, הנני, to his people (also in 52.6; 58.9); elsewhere in conversations between God and humans, only the humans use the term as they respond to YHWH's call (e.g. Gen. 22.1, 11; Exod. 3.4).

49. See the lists in L. Liebreich, 'The Composition of the Book of Isaiah', *JQR* 46 (1955–56), pp. 276-77 and *JQR* 47 (1956–57), p. 127; R. Margalioth, *The Indivisible Isaiah* (Jerusalem: Sura Institute and New York: Yeshiva University, 1964), esp. pp. 216-18.

50. See the discussion in Sweeney, *Isaiah 1–4*, pp. 21-24 and references there.

51. Tomasino remarks ('Composition', p. 82 n. 4), 'While Liebreich's list is impressive...it is not entirely persuasive as a case for literary dependence. A study of the distribution of the vocabulary in ch. 1 in the book of Isaiah shows that nearly the same amount of overlap can be shown for other chapters of Isaiah as well (e.g., chs. 43-44, 49, and even ch. 53).' In other words, for all the attention scholars have lavished on the relation between chs. 1 and 65–66, the relationship is hardly unique, and therefore it is not clear that the similarities between the chapters can form the basis of far-reaching conclusions.

thematic patterns. Several of Isaiah's negative statements are reversed by Deutero-Isaiah. In Isaiah, YHWH announces that he will ignore the people's prayers:

> When you come to appear in my presence (פני), who asked (בקש) that you should trample my courtyards?... When you spread your arms (כפיכם ובפרשכם) [in petition], I shall hide my eyes from you; even if you pray a great deal, I shall not listen (אינני שמע). (Isa. 1.12, 15)

In Deutero-Isaiah YHWH states something quite different. Not only will he accept their petitions; he will respond before they even call to him:

> I responded without them calling; I was present without them asking for me (בקשני). I declared, 'Here I am, here I am', to a nation not called by my name. I constantly spread my hands (פרשתי ידי) [in welcome] to a rebellious people... who made me angry in my own presence (על-פני) [i.e. blatantly]... Before they call, I answer; while they are yet speaking, I listen (ואני אשמע). (Isa. 65.1-3, 24)[52]

Further, some of Deutero-Isaiah's oracles in 65–66 seem to be restatements of oracles from Isaiah 1. This is particularly evident in the last verses of ch. 1:[53]

---

52. The parallel vocabulary suggests that Deutero-Isaiah depended on Isa. 1, and the type of utilization of the source (a reversal) is typical of Deutero-Isaiah's project of allusion. Nonetheless, one cannot assert the presence of a borrowing with assurance, because the issue at hand—whether YHWH will listen to the people or not—is common in the prophets and the psalms. In fact there are significant points of contact between these verses and Jer. 7.17; 11.11-14 (which share זעק and שמע), and 14.11-13. Thus, Deutero-Isaiah may depend on Isaiah or Jeremiah, or on both of them, or on a widespread motif rather than these specific passages.

53. Many critics view the last verses of the chapter as an exilic or post-exilic addition. For Sweeney, 'the focus' of vv. 27-28 'on the redemption of Zion is an indication of their post-exilic origin since this presupposes that the city had been cast away by YHWH and that the redemption was a viable expectation' (*Isaiah 1–4*, p. 131). However, redemption would be an important issue not only for a writer who had seen the events of 587 but also for one, such as Isaiah, who predicted and witnessed dire threats to Zion. If the word שביה means 'returnees', the verse refers to the post-exilic situation, but the term could simply mean 'those who repent'. In that case, the word continues the theme found in 1.16-17, 19, setting up a contrast between the sinners and those who do repent in 1.28. Sweeney is correct to sense that the concerns of 1.29-31 differ from those in the rest of the chapter, but this hardly demonstrates that the verses are exilic or post-exilic. According to Clements (*Isaiah*), vv. 27-28 'evidently presuppose that Jerusalem has suffered severe setbacks, and that the way forward could be pursued only by a deep act of repentance...';

The downfall of the sinners and wrongdoers [will take place] at once (יחדו), and those who forsake YHWH will perish. You will be shamed (תבשו)[54] by the terebinths you coveted; you will be embarrassed by the gardens (מהגנות) you chose (בחרתם)... The strong one will be like tow, and his work like a spark; both will burn together (יחדו), with none to quench the fire (ואין מכבה). (Isa. 1.28-29, 30)

Deutero-Isaiah issues a similar prophecy, again specifying that the evil-doers will receive the punishment:

I have singled you out for the sword...because you chose (בחרתם) what I did not desire. Therefore, thus says YHWH:...behold, my servants will rejoice, and you will be ashamed (תבשו)... Those who sanctify themselves and purify themselves in the gardens (אל־הגנות)...[and] those who eat the flesh of swine and rodents and mice will come to an end together (יחדו): a statement of YHWH... The worm that eats the bodies of those who sin against me will not die, and their fire will not be quenched (לא תכבה)... (Isa. 65.12, 13; 66.17, 24)

These more ramified parallels suggest that the passages are likely to be related. Because the parallels display reversal and reprediction, it is possible that they result from Deutero-Isaiah's borrowing from ch. 1. The question remains, then: if Deutero-Isaiah alluded to the first chapter of Isaiah in the last chapters of his own work, must the allusion indicate an attempt on his part to form an inclusio, thus demonstrating that Deutero-Isaiah intended to append his work to already existing Isaiah traditions?

In fact, other explanations are possible. When we limit the links between ch. 1 and chs. 65–66 to those that are unique to these two chapters, it becomes clear that the inclusio is somewhat insubstantial. It consists of some typical Deutero-Isaianic allusions, which are no more present here than in many other passages. Deutero-Isaiah utilized whole

---

consequently, he says, the verses are exilic. Again, the verses may anticipate rather than presuppose a severe setback; moreover, even if it has already occurred, many events before 587 match that description. On the other hand, Liebreich ('Composition' [1956–57], p. 129) demonstrates that an inclusio marks off 1.2-28 as a unit, leaving a strong possibility that vv. 29-31 are an addition. When that addition was made cannot be ascertained, but there is no reason to see it as post-exilic.

54. Reading thus, with Targ. Jonathan (and some MT MSS; see Moshe Goshen-Gottstein, *The Book of Isaiah* [The Hebrew University Bible Project; Jerusalem: Magnes Press, 1975]), instead of MT's יבשו. MT's third person for this verb seems to result from attraction to the third person in the previous verses.

passages in extended allusions elsewhere.[55] This case is more noticeable only because it creates the appearance of an inclusio, which may be no more than a coincidence. Even if the inclusio is deliberate, it does not necessarily result from Deutero-Isaiah's own work. Kaufmann suggests that chs. 34–35 were originally the last chapters of Deutero-Isaiah's collection and that they were displaced 'erroneously' to their present place at the end of the work of Isaiah ben Amoṣ.[56] I think, however, that the displacement may have been deliberate. The redactor who combined the scroll of Isaiah ben Amoṣ with that of Deutero-Isaiah may have moved the last chapters of Deutero-Isaiah (i.e., what we know as chs. 34–35) to their present place because he noticed correspondences between the section preceding those chapters (i.e., what we know as chs. 65–66) and the beginning of Isaiah ben Amoṣ's work. By making this change, the redactor created an inclusio linking the hitherto separate works, and thus formed the canonical book of Isaiah that we know today.[57]

In the absence of strong arguments that Deutero-Isaiah appended his work to Isaiah's, it is unlikely that the alleged inclusio is the work of Deutero-Isaiah himself. Rather, it probably results from the activity of a

55. Examples of these long allusions include ch. 6//52.13–53.12; 11.1-24//42.1-9; ch. 2//ch. 57.

56. See Kaufmann, *Babylonian Captivity*, pp. 184-185, where he notes that these chapters are typical of the later stage of Deutero-Isaiah's preaching (i.e., those found in the third section of Deutero-Isaiah's corpus, chs. 58–66), and that these chapters summarize and complete the exilic prophet's work.

57. A final possibility remains, which does not depend on Kaufmann's suggestion that chs. 34–35 were originally the end of Deutero-Isaiah's work. Fohrer has argued that Isa. 1 consists largely of genuine but originally separate utterances of Isaiah (see 'Jesaja 1 als Zusammenfassung der Verkündigung Jesajas', in *Studien zur Alttestamentlichen Prophetie* [BZAW, 99; Berlin: Töpelmann, 1967], pp. 148-166; the essay appeared earlier in ZAW 74 [1962], pp. 251-68). He suggests that these utterances were edited into their current form after the time of Isaiah in order to serve as an introduction to, and digest of, the prophecies of Isaiah. If this occurred after (or at the same time that) Deutero-Isaiah's collection was appended to that of Isaiah, it is possible that material from Isaiah was selected not only to form a digest but also to contain terminology from the last section of Deutero-Isaiah (i.e. 65–66). In that case, Isa. 1 was created to form an inclusio with the last chapter of what we know now as the canonical book of Isaiah. The parallels involving these verses, then, would not represent cases of Deutero-Isaianic allusion. It is worth noting that the prevalence of negative reprediction in Deutero-Isaiah's putative use of these verses is somewhat atypical.

later redactor. Canon critics and others are correct to note that the book of Isaiah displays this element of unity. They err only in the historical conclusions they reach on the basis of that synchronic parallel.

The Work of the Unity School: Final Reflections

I have explained the parallels between Deutero-Isaiah and Isaiah as representing a part—but only a part—of the exilic prophet's re-use of older prophetic material. This explanation undermines the attempt to use these parallels as evidence for an original redactional or authorial unity in the book of Isaiah. My reasoning, I think, helps to highlight three fallacies that appear in work of historically oriented adherents of the unity school.[58]

(1) Scholars support their conclusions regarding the book of Isaiah's unity by citing elements common to both halves of the book. However, most of these elements (which include words, phrases and themes) are shared with other biblical books as well. As a result, they no more prove that the two halves of Isaiah have a common origin than they prove that either half originally belonged together with some other book. For example, Rendtorff, Childs and Albertz are correct to note that Isaiah 40 resembles Isaiah 6;[59] but it resembles Jeremiah 1, Ezekiel 1–3 and Zechariah 1 in similar ways. Thus it is difficult to argue that 40 utilizes 6 specifically, that 6 and 40 were composed in tandem or that 40 must be read as a continuation or renewal of 6.[60] Such conclusions would follow only if the relationship between these chapters were shown to be closer than their relation to other related texts. Similarly, a number of scholars have suggested that when Deutero-Isaiah speaks of 'former things'

58. I do not intend to present here a comprehensive critique of the approach, but only to point out some assumptions common to the unity school which are relevant to the discussion that follows. For some reflections on shortcomings in the unity theory, see Carr, 'Unity', esp. pp. 77-80.

59. See Rendtorff, 'Jesaja 6 im Rahmen der Komposition des Jesajabuches', in J. Vermeylen (ed.), *The Book of Isaiah* (BETL, 81; Leuven: Leuven University Press, 1981), pp. 79-81; Seitz, 'Temporal Transition', *passim*; R. Albertz, 'Das Deuterojesaja-Buch als Fortschreibung der Jesaja-Prophetie', in E. Blum, C. Macholz and E. Stegemann (eds.), *Die Hebräische Bibel und ihre zweifache Nachgeschichte: Festschrift für Rolf Rendtorff* (Neukirchen–Vluyn: Neukirchener Verlag, 1990), pp. 244-48.

60. See Seitz, 'Temporal Transition', and Albertz, 'Deuterojesaja-Buch', for intriguing, but unjustified, attempts to read ch. 40 as a sequel or supplement to ch. 6.

(ראשונות), he means the fulfilled prophecies of Isaiah.[61] While Deutero-Isaiah does sometimes use the term 'former things' to refer to older prophecies that have come to pass,[62] there is no indication that he specifically means the prophecies of Isaiah ben Amos, rather than oracles of other prophets whom he utilizes. These passages express Deutero-Isaiah's concern for attesting to the fulfillment of older prophecies in general, not those of Isaiah in particular.[63] Thus they cannot serve as evidence that Deutero-Isaiah was composed as a continuation of Isaiah by tradents who shaped the Isaiah traditions.[64]

(2) Nevertheless, many elements do link Deutero-Isaiah specifically to Isaiah, as examples in the first part of this essay help to demonstrate. Thus, scholars of the unity school are correct to argue that Deutero-Isaiah's message complements that of Isaiah and continues it. On the basis of this premise, some scholars conclude that Deutero-Isaiah's work is not self-contained, and that his writing must have been part of the complex of Isaiah traditions from the outset.[65] This conclusion by no

61. D. Jones, 'The Traditio of the Oracles of Isaiah of Jerusalem', *ZAW* 67 (1955), pp. 245-46; Childs, *Introduction*, p. 329; C. Seitz, 'Isaiah 1–66: Making Sense of the Whole', in *idem* (ed.), *Reading and Preaching the Book of Isaiah* (Philadelphia: Fortress Press, 1988), p. 110.

62. See Haran, *RPSHONÔT*, pp. 23-28; this is the case in 41.22; 42.9; 43.9, 12, 18; 44.6-7; 48.3. The term ראשונות does not always signify older prophecies, however. For example, Deutero-Isaiah uses it to refer to YHWH's cosmogonic or redemptive acts in the past; see, for example, 43.18.

63. In other passages, Deutero-Isaiah does in fact point towards the fulfillment of earlier prophecies. We saw above that 42.18-25 refers back to 30.9-14, while 48.10-11 confirms Jer. 9.6; similarly, Isa. 54.1-14 includes an allusion to Hos. 1.2-6 and 2.1-25 that confirms the accuracy of Hosea's dire prediction. In these cases, the linkage between the text containing the prediction and the one noting its confirmation is marked by borrowed vocabulary. The *rishonot* passages, on the other hand, are quite general, and there is no reason to assume that they refer specifically to prophecies of Isaiah. Incidentally, allusions in which Deutero-Isaiah confirms the fulfillment of Jeremiah's prophecies are far more frequent than ones in which he notes that Isaiah's have come to pass.

64. The articles of Rolf Rendtorff on the unity of Isaiah are especially affected by this fallacy; he cites numerous themes and vocabulary items that occur throughout the book, but he does not explain why these elements (most of which are quite common throughout the Bible) have the significance he attributes to them. See especially 'Zur Komposition des Buches Jesajas', *VT* 34 (1984), pp. 295-320.

65. See, for example, Clements, 'The Unity of the Book of Isaiah', *Int* 36 (1982), p. 127.

means follows from the premise. A later work can complement an earlier one while remaining distinct. Noting the dependence of one work on another does not mean that it is impossible to read either work on its own.

(3) Several scholars maintain that passages in Isaiah 1–39 that prophesy good fortune were included there in order to prepare the way for chs. 40–66, or that they were added to the book of Isaiah under the influence of Deutero-Isaiah, after his work was already part of the book.[66] Such a view presumes that Isaiah was a prophet of doom who would not utter anything other than condemnation. But the same thinker who predicted disaster could also foresee its end; two ideas do not indicate the existence of two authors. Indeed one of Isaiah's most characteristic notions, that of the remnant that will return,[67] itself combines his positive and negative viewpoints: yes, there will be survivors of the coming disaster, but only a few. To attribute anything positive in First Isaiah to Deutero-Isaiah or his influence is to suggest a bizarre dichotomy in which the older author or authors could think no happy thoughts.

How did assumptions such as these become the bedrock of those who argue that the book of Isaiah is a redactional unity? The last assumption exemplifies a sort of historicism gone awry; it reflects the notion (unfortunately common in biblical studies) that certain ideas could not have been uttered at given times or by particular individuals. The first two assumptions reflect sensible concerns of a critic looking for elements of synchronic unity in an already existing text. Features shared by the two halves of Isaiah do indicate a degree of coherence within the canonical book, even if those features appear in other texts as well. Only when canon critics began to arrive at conclusions concerning the redaction of the book did this sort of evidence create problems. When making diachronic claims, they needed not only to note these features within the book but to attend to evidence from other books as well; however, they failed to do so. Similarly, scholars are justified to note the extent to which Isaiah 40–66 complements Isaiah 1–39. Some canon critics, having noted this element of unity in the book as it now exists, mistakenly assumed that it results from the intent of the author(s) of chs. 40–66 to

66. See Clements, 'Beyond', p. 121; Seitz 'Making Sense', pp. 112-14; and cf. Sweeney, *Isaiah 1–4*, pp. 192-97.

67. See, for example, Isa. 7.33; 10.20-22. Kaufmann shows that the signs based on the names Emanuel and Shear-Yashuv both attach a cloud to the silver lining in a typically Isaianic rhetorical move; see *Toledot*, III, pp. 212-13.

append those chapters to the earlier material, when in fact many other explanations should have been considered. Thus unjustified claims result from confusion about two different sorts of unity; these scholars argue for diachronic unity on the basis of synchronic unity.

A comparison of two perspectives on the book of Isaiah clarifies how two types of biblical scholarship differ. An approach oriented towards inner-biblical allusion helps scholars to form conclusions about the development of the book and hence about the history of ideas in ancient Israel. A canonical or unity-oriented method attends to elements in the existing book, aiding readers who desire to note certain features in the crystallized text sacred to post-biblical religions. But when unity-oriented criticism attempts to encompass conclusions involving the history of the texts in their ancient setting, it sows mingled seed based on reasoning of diverse kind, and hence it inevitably produces results that cannot stand.[68]

68. I would like to thank Professors Michael Fishbane, Marc Brettler and John Collins for their helpful remarks on earlier drafts of this material.

Part II

IS MEANING LOCATED IN THE READER?

READING ISAIAH FROM BEGINNING (ISAIAH 1) TO END (ISAIAH 65–66): MULTIPLE MODERN POSSIBILITIES

David M. Carr

Reading biblical texts like Isaiah in their final form is obviously not new.[1] Reading biblical texts as cohesive 'literary unities', however, is relatively new, and this practice has opened up new possibilities for interpreting them. It is as if the book of Isaiah were an inkblot, and ancient and modern readers use different rules to make sense of this inkblot.[2] This article focuses on some of the differences these rules make. In particular, I will use Isaiah 1 and 65–66 as focus texts for exploring some differences between ancient construals of the Isaiah tradition and potential modern ways to read Isaiah as a 'book'. After a brief review of modern scholarship on the relations between the Isaiah tradition and these chapters, I will give an initial sketch of some differences between such modern reading of the Isaiah tradition and ancient reception of it. This then will serve as a context for my exploration of how Isa. 1.2-31 and Isaiah 65–66 are examples of divergent ancient construals of the Isaiah tradition. In the final section I will look at how the presence of both of

1.   A shorter version of this paper was read July 28, 1993 in the Isaiah section of the Society of Biblical Literature Meeting in Münster, Germany. I thank the participants of that section for their helpful responses to the paper. In addition, I thank Professors R. Melugin, E. Blum and R. Rendtorff for their reading and discussion of various drafts of the paper with me. It is stronger thanks to their careful work. I also wish to acknowledge with thanks two forms of support I received during the latter half of my work on this article during a sabbatical in Germany during 1993–1994: fellowships from the Alexander von Humboldt Foundation of Germany and the Association of Theological Schools and the generous hospitality of Professor Bernd Janowski and the Wissenschaftlich-Theologisches Seminar, Heidelberg Universität, Heidelberg, Germany.
2.   This image of a text as 'inkblot' is drawn from an illustration given by J.L. Mays in his contribution to the session on 'Amos: Where Do We Go From Here?', at the 1992 Society of Biblical Literature Meeting in San Francisco.

these construals in the book of Isaiah opens up multiple interpretive possibilities to modern readers attempting to read the whole.

Previous Scholarship on Isaiah 1 and 65–66 in Relation to Isaiah as a Whole

I begin with a brief look at a variety of modern readings of Isaiah 1 and 65–66 in relation to the book as a whole. Sustained study of this topic began with a pair of articles by Liebreich in the late 1950s. The first article included observations of terminological parallels between Isaiah 1 and 66, and the second article added terminological parallels between Isaiah 1 and 65. As a result of both of these sets of parallels, Liebreich concluded that Isaiah 1 and 65–66 form an *inclusio* surrounding and uniting the overall Isaiah tradition.[3]

Then, in a monograph published in 1973, Lack consolidated Liebreich's terminological observations and added observations of some important larger thematic parallels and differences between the chapters. Both Isaiah 1 and 65–66 focus on cultic abuses which have led to a break between Yahweh and Yahweh's people, more specifically practices involving a sacred garden (1.29-31; 66.17). In both sections, normalization of relations between God and the people is to be achieved through separation of the righteous from the wrongdoers. The wrongdoers will be 'put to shame' (1.29; 66.5) and burned with an unquenchable fire (1.31 and 66.24).[4] In contrast, by the end of the book the righteous receive a new name (65.15), just as Jerusalem will in 1.26. Yet, Lack points out that there are also some elements in 65–66 which are *not* found in ch. 1, themes such as the cosmic, nonviolent order centred on the holy mountain (65.25), the incredible fertility of the people (66.7-9), and the worldwide revelation of God's glory (66.23). Thus, despite numerous connections between Isaiah 1 and 65–66, there are also some important differences to be recognized.[5]

In recent years, as interest in reading the Isaiah tradition as a whole has grown, Liebreich's and Lack's proposals have been appropriated

---

3. L.J. Liebreich, 'The Compilation of the Book of Isaiah', *JQR* 46 (1955–56), pp. 276-77; 47 (1956–57), pp. 126-27.

4. Cf. Liebreich, 'The Compilation of the Book of Isaiah', part 1, p. 277.

5. R. Lack, *La symbolique du livre d'Isaïe: Essai sur l'image littéraire comme élément de structuration* (AnBib, 59; Rome: Biblical Institute Press, 1973), pp. 139-41.

and developed in a variety of ways. Thus, for example, in the process of arguing for the 'redactional unity' of the book of Isaiah, Sweeney briefly summarizes Liebreich's and Lack's studies, expands some of their observations to include 1.29-31, and coordinates these observations regarding Isaiah 1 and 65–66 with Fohrer's and Becker's observations regarding the introductory character of Isaiah 1.[6] As he points out, all of these studies agree on the important macrostructural role of Isaiah 1. Another important study building on Liebreich and Lack, is Beuken's paper for the Leuven IOSOT conference, initially presented in 1988 and published in 1992.[7] In this paper, Beuken builds on his previous study of Isaiah 40–66 to argue that Isaiah 65–66 is made up of a series of gradated conclusions to the book: Isa. 65.1–66.14 serving as a conclusion to Trito-Isaiah; Isa. 66.15-20a [20b-21] as the conclusion to a section encompassing both Deutero- and Trito-Isaiah and 66.22-23 [24] as the conclusion to the book as a whole.

In contrast to Beuken, Steck's 1987 article on Isaiah 65–66 exhaustively develops the argument that this section is made up not of three units, but two—a pair of responses to the preceding supplication[8] (63.7–64.11 [Eng. 63.7–64.12]). The first is Isa. 65.1–66.4 and is addressed to the apostates of Israel, while the second, Isa. 66.5-24, is addressed to the pious.[9] Moreover, Steck persuasively argues that this pair of addresses is

6. M. Sweeney, *Isaiah 1–4 and the Post-Exilic Understanding of the Isaiah Tradition* (BZAW, 171; Berlin: de Gruyter, 1988), pp. 21-24. Cf. G. Fohrer, 'Jesaja 1 als Zusammenfassung der Verkündigung Jesajas', *ZAW* 74 (1962), pp. 251-68; J. Becker, *Isaias - der Prophet und sein Buch* (SBS, 30; Stuttgart: Katholisches Bibelwerk, 1968), pp. 45-47.

7. W.A.M. Beuken, 'Isaiah Chapters LXV–LXVI: Trito-Isaiah and the Closure of the Book of Isaiah', in J.A. Emerton (ed.), *The Congress Volume: Leuven 1989* (VTSup, 43; Leiden: Brill, 1991), pp. 204-21.

8. Here I follow W. Beyerlin, *Die Rettung der Bedrängten in den Feindpsalmen der Einzelnen auf institutionelle Zusammenhänge untersucht* (FRLANT, 99; Göttingen: Vandenhoeck & Ruprecht, 1970), pp. 152-55, in terming such a text a 'supplication' rather than using the more usual term 'lament'. Isa. 63.7–64.11, like many other 'laments', is essentially built around a petition for help, not a mourning for death or other kinds of irreversible suffering.

9. O.H. Steck, 'Beobachtungen zur Anlage von Jes 65–66', *BN* 38/39 (1987), pp. 103-16; revised version in *idem, Studien zu Tritojesaja* (BZAW, 203; Berlin: de Gruyter, 1991), pp. 217-28. Sweeney likewise treats Isaiah 65–66 as an answer to the preceding supplication, see his *Isaiah 1–4*, p. 91. Sweeney also refers to earlier treatments which suggest that Isa. 65 or 65–66 is an answer to the preceding lament, including C.C. Torrey, *The Second Isaiah: A New Interpretation* (New York:

explicitly focused on rejecting the all-Israelite concept upon which the preceding communal supplication (63.7–64.11) is based. Whereas the supplication calls on God to restore the people as a whole from foreign destroyers, the paired set of replies attributes the present devastation to *Israelite* wrongdoers and explicitly divides the world between the pious who will be rewarded—whether Israelite or foreign—and the impious who will be destroyed. This concept of the form and function of these chapters leads Steck in a later review of literature on Isaiah 65–66 (1991) to reject the bulk of Beuken's theory of gradated conclusions to the book.[10] Instead, Steck attempts to add precision to previous proposals that Isaiah 65–66 and even 63.7–64.11 form an *inclusio* with the beginning of the book. Thus, for example, Steck notes that there are parallels between the communal supplication which 65–66 is answering (Isa. 63.7–64.11), and the situation and lament found in Isa. 1.5-9. Moreover, just as parts of Isa. 1.2-9 are parallel with 63.7–64.11, Isaiah 65-66 has been composed as a careful counterpoint to 1.10-31. Thus Steck observes several thematic and conceptual parallels between the two units, such as those between 1.19 and 65.9b-10 and between 1.20 and 65.11-12. In addition, 66.5-24, although now addressed to the pious (66.5aß) rather than the faithless (1.10), confirms the themes of 1.10-31 and begins identically to it (שמעו דבר־יהוה; 66.5aα//1.10aα1-2). Indeed, Steck proposes that 1.29-31 and other parts of 1.10-31 may have been inserted by the author of 65–66 in order to further sharpen these connections across the Isaiah tradition.

Conrad's 1991 synchronic reading of Isaiah has some interesting similarities and contrasts with Steck's diachronic approach. Like Steck,

Charles Scribner's Sons, 1928), pp. 466-67 and D.R. Jones, *Isaiah 56–66 and Joel: Introduction and Commentary* (TB; London: SCM Press, 1964), pp. 104-105.

I have also made somewhat similar observations along these lines in 'Reaching for Unity in Isaiah', *JSOT* 57 (1993), pp. 73-74. Unfortunately in this earlier piece, I mistakenly overlooked Professor Steck's earlier observations regarding Isa. 65–66, and did not acknowledge his previous work in this area. As is evident in the discussion below, Steck's proposals have been helpful in strengthening my treatment of Isa. 65–66.

10. O.H. Steck, 'Zu jüngsten Untersuchungen von Jes 56,1-8; 63,7–66,24', in *idem*, *Studien*, pp. 263-65. Steck does agree with Beuken that there may be special connections to Trito-Isaianic themes in 66.7-14 (as well as Deutero-Isaianic themes), but observes that otherwise Beuken's theory of gradated conclusions appears a bit more systematic than the evidence warrants, particularly in failing to recognize connections to the entire Isaiah tradition throughout 65–66.

Conrad observes connections between the lament in 1.9 and the communal supplication in 63.7–64.11.[11] Like Steck, Conrad observes an exact correspondence between the call to hear the word of the LORD in 1.10 and the call to hear the word of the LORD in 66.5.[12] Yet Conrad interprets these and other indicators differently. Whereas Steck is particularly interested in making precise and historically grounded observations about the final redactional formation of the book, Conrad is particularly interested in how these and other Isaiah texts develop an 'implied audience' for the Isaiah tradition read as a literary unity. Thus, not only does 1.9 record this audience's lament, but Conrad reads 1.10 as this audience's call to their opponents to 'hear the word of the LORD', just as they themselves, 'who tremble at God's word' (66.2) are later told by God to 'hear the word of the LORD' (66.5). Furthermore, Conrad argues that the beginning and end of the book provide important details on both this implied audience and their opponents. According to him, the implied audience is described in both 1.9-10 and 66.18-21 as a community of 'survivors', a community who has begun to experience the same catastrophic 'Sodom and Gommorah' judgment against their community that was once predicted would hit Babylon (Isa. 1.9; cf. 13.19). Their opponents are described at both the beginning and end of the book as eventually being burned with fire (1.30-31; 66.24) for carrying out sacrifices abhorrent to God (1.10-14; 66.3-4), committing violent acts against others (1.15; 66.3), and engaging in various idolatrous acts in gardens (1.29; 65.3; 66.17).[13]

In the midst of this textual drama, the implied audience itself comes to speech many times throughout the book, including 25.9; 26.1b-21; 42.24; 59.9-15; and, at most length, in 63.7–64.11, the supplication to which Isaiah 65–66 is the divine answer. Like Steck, Conrad observes important differences between this supplication's picture of wrongdoers and the portrayal of wrongdoers in the reply to the supplication. Whereas in the following reply to the supplication the opponents' destruction is predicted, the supplication itself in 63.7–64.11 positively depicts a third-person group whom God has saved despite their sin (63.8-9). This distinctive all-Israel solidarity of the prayer leads Steck to assign 63.7–64.11

---

11. E. W. Conrad, *Reading Isaiah* (OBT; Minneapolis: Fortress, 1991), pp. 102, 106, 116.

12. Conrad, *Reading Isaiah*, p. 98.

13. Conrad, *Reading Isaiah*, pp. 88-98.

to a different (albeit closely related) literary layer from Isaiah 65–66.[14] In contrast, Conrad attempts to reconcile the relatively positive perspective on the outside group—the 'them'—in 63.8-9 with the picture of their destruction in the following texts (e.g. 66.24). He states that 'the salvation of the "they" [in 63.8-9] does not mean that the guilty will escape judgment'.[15]

Overall, Steck and Conrad's brilliant, yet divergent investigations well illustrate the continuing methodological pluralism so characteristic of contemporary biblical studies. To be sure, there are important areas of convergence. Both scholars are interested in relations of texts across the full stretch of the Isaiah tradition. Moreover, both scholars often observe similar data. But the two are diametrically opposed in how to interpret this data. On the one hand, Conrad explicitly claims to go beyond previous, ever-varying historical-critical speculations regarding the transmission history of the book of Isaiah.[16] On the other hand, Steck promotes his approach as securely based in just such a historical perspective, rather than in 'the uncertainties of an ahistorical synchronic reading of the Isaiah tradition'.[17]

An Initial Contrast of Ancient and Modern Reading Methods

My main point at this juncture is that despite their differences, these modern readings of Isaiah 1 and 65–66 share a number of things not found in the ancient reading situation. All of these modern studies focus on the written text, usually read silently in the scholar's study, and moreover worked with in codex/book form (that is, with pages). Moreover, such studies are often informed by intense work with other written resources, such as concordances, which facilitate detailed comparison of texts within the book. These modern studies share a conspicuous interest in understanding Isaiah as *a discrete book*, standing at least temporarily apart from the rest of the biblical tradition. Finally, and perhaps most important, these studies lack multiple and explicit connections between

---

14. O.H. Steck, 'Tritojesaja im Jesajabuch', in J. Vermeylen (ed.), *Le livre d'Isaïe: Les oracles et leurs relectures unité et complexité de l'ouvrage* (BETL, 81; Leuven: Leuven University Press, 1989), pp. 396-400 (reprinted in *idem, Studien*, pp. 37-40); *idem*, 'Jes 56,1-8; 63,7–66,24', pp. 242-43.

15. Conrad, *Reading Isaiah*, p. 108.

16. Conrad, *Reading Isaiah*, pp. 3-33.

17. My translation of Steck's comment in his 'Jes 56,1-8; 63,7–66,24', p. 265.

details of their interpretation of the text and a believing community for which the text is normative.

In contrast, ancient readings although intensely interested in the text, usually have a broader theological/legal horizon in the forefront. This means that ancient readings are less interested in the individual book of Isaiah than they are in using Isaiah as part of Scripture to discern and articulate Truth. Moreover, very few early receivers of Isaiah would have read a text of Isaiah silently and alone.[18] Recent studies of literacy in the ancient world indicate that reception of ancient texts like the Bible was predominantly oral. Only a minority could read, and even then, their ability to read a book like Isaiah—as opposed to seals or graffiti—is still an important question.[19] Thus most people would have heard the

18. For a helpful survey of literature and data regarding ancient silent reading see F.D. Gilliard, 'More Silent Reading in Antiquity: *Non Omne Verbum Sonabat*', *JBL* 112 (1993), pp. 689-96, who concludes that though silent reading was not so unheard of as is often supposed, reading was still predominantly oral (p. 696).

19. Here I am thinking particularly of W. Harris, *Ancient Literacy* (Cambridge: Harvard University Press, 1989). Although some biblical scholars continue to assert mass literacy in Israel approaching that of ancient Greece, Harris has argued persuasively that ancient Greek literacy even at its height did not exceed levels of ten to fifteen percent. J.H. Humphrey (ed.), *Literacy in the Roman World* (Journal of Roman Archaeology Supplementary Series, 3; Ann Arbor, MI: Journal of Roman Archaeology, 1991), contains a helpful set of reviews of Harris's work. Overall, several of the reviewers discuss certain brief public notices which presuppose that much of the population can read. In addition, a few raise questions about the extent to which Harris adequately evaluated the skewed nature of surviving evidence for ancient literacy. Nevertheless, most of the reviewers do not question Harris's main thesis regarding ancient literacy: that ancient societies had less need of mass literacy than modern societies, and less resources to educate people. The burden of proof lies not on those who would deny mass literacy in an ancient society like Israel, but on those who would affirm it. Also, Harris's study suggests that there are significantly different levels of literacy (and numeracy). As a result the presence of abecedaria and brief notices in a few finds do not suffice to prove the capability to read a complex work like Isaiah. Thus, in order to ascertain the level of literacy in Ancient Israel, it is no longer enough to list and quantify various inscriptional materials. Instead, one must also use these materials to critically analyze the societal structure of ancient Israel and determine who would have needed to read, how much and where they were given the skills to do so.

For some recent reflections on Israelite literacy along similar lines to these see P.R. Davies, *In Search of 'Ancient Israel'* (JSOTSup, 148; Sheffield: JSOT Press, 1992), pp. 106-107. Cf. E. Dhorme, 'L'ancien Hébreu dans la vie courante', *RB* 39 (1930), pp. 62-73; J. Naveh, 'A Palaeographic Note on the Distribution of the

book of Isaiah read aloud, not read it themselves, and would have heard only parts of a large book like Isaiah at a time.[20] Moreover, insofar as Isaiah functioned as a public tradition fairly early in its history, even the scribes who worked with and revised Isaiah would have been doing so with an eye toward the book's oral reception.[21] Finally, they worked with scrolls, a medium less amenable to systematic textual comparison and redaction than the codex form.

This is certainly not to deny that ancient readers had a detailed knowledge of Isaiah. But here I emphasize that ancient readers' detailed knowledge was primarily directed toward Isaiah as a sub-part of a larger authoritative tradition. Moreover, this knowledge was used not to construct a picture of the textual-literary unity of the individual book, but instead to develop a *biblically-based* unity standing outside the text, whether that be a theological or legal unity. Take, for example, early Jewish rabbinic scriptural discourse, a case fairly distant from the Bible, but often mentioned as an example of early encyclopaedic knowledge of biblical detail. Such readings selectively appropriate and recombine biblical texts to articulate a biblically-based legal-conceptual unity standing outside the text. There is nothing approaching the modern interest in the syntagmatic unity of Isaiah as a discrete book.

Hebrew Script', *HTR* 61 (1968), pp. 68-74; A. Millard, 'An Assessment of the Evidence for Writing in Ancient Israel', in J. Amitai (ed.), *Biblical Archaeology Today: Proceedings of the International Congress on Biblical Archaeology, Jerusalem, April 1984* (Jerusalem: Israel Exploration Society, 1985), pp. 301-10 (see also the contributions by A. Demsky and J. Naveh in the 'Respondents' section on pp. 349-53 of the same volume, and the discussion on pp. 367-70); A. Demsky, 'Writing in Ancient Israel and Early Judaism', in M.J. Mulder (ed.), *Mikra: Text, Translation, Reading and Interpretation of the Hebrew Bible in Ancient Judaism and Early Christianity* (CRINT, 2.1; Assen: Van Gorcum, 1988), pp. 10-16. Also, in note 23 on p. 309 of Millard's 'Assessment' article, Millard briefly refers to cautions raised by Harris in an article length piece prior to the appearance of his monograph.

20. For some preliminary observations of the importance of such oral considerations in ancient readings of Isaiah see Conrad, *Reading Isaiah*, pp. 84-87.

21. This is not to rule out the cases of other texts—such as some apocalypses, divinatory catalogues and so on—which were clearly written by scribes for other scribes to read. The point here is simply that revisions to Isaiah as early as the seventh century seem to indicate that already by that point the Isaiah scroll was becoming a public tradition. On these revisions see in particular H. Barth's influential study, *Die Jesaja-Worte in der Josiazeit: Israel und Assur als Thema einer produktiven Neuinterpretation der Jesajaüberlieferung* (WMANT, 48; Neukirchen–Vluyn: Neukirchener Verlag, 1977), pp. 109-17.

In sum, what I am briefly outlining here is a contrast between modern scholarly *reading* of Isaiah as a discrete book on the one hand, and ancient reception of Scripture (including Isaiah) on the other, a reception which was community-based and largely oral. These differences can be summed up in the following comparison:

Modern Text Reception (particularly of a biblical Text as a Whole)	*Ancient Text Reception*
Oriented toward written text, read silently.	Oriented primarily toward the text as heard.
Work with text is in 'codex' form (with pages), and using concordances and other resources.	The written text is in scroll form, and reference aided primarily by human memory.
Often specific interest in the overall coherence of the 'book'.	Lack of such clear interest in systematic coherence. Instead, primary interest in coherence of the community's world. Detailed knowledge of the text is used to discern and articulate a unity standing outside the text.
Lack of multiple and explicit connections between details of the interpretation of the text and a community for which the text is normative.	Integral and often explicit connection between interpretation of the text and a community for which it is normative.

Such distinctions need not imply that ancient author-redactors had no interest whatsoever in some kind of syntagmatic unity of their material. There are many examples of comprehensively shaped works—Ruth, the Wisdom of Solomon, Luke–Acts to name only a few—that suggest the contrary. The point is that we modern readers may well have more of an interest in such a textually focused unity and a different concept of such 'unity' than many ancient authors and audiences did, and that existence of any such unity 'in' an ancient text like Isaiah must not be presupposed, but shown case by case.

But enough of initial broad suggestions. Let us focus now on a specific case, looking at Isaiah 1 and 65–66 as keys to how the Isaiah tradition as a whole may have been received in ancient contexts. However, in order to understand the construal of the Isaiah tradition at the beginning of the book, we must first examine the limits of the first major unit, its structure and rhetorical stance.

Isaiah 1.2-31

Limits, Structure and Rhetorical Stance of the First Major Unit
Definition of the limits of this first major unit of the book is important since studies have diverged as to whether the first major unit of the book is defined as Isa. 1.2-20; 1.2-31; 1.2–2.5 or some other set of verses.[22] The clearest basis for discussion of this issue would seem to be the establishment of explicit indicators of structure in Isaiah, most particularly superscriptions such as those present in 1.1 and 2.1. Such labels serve as separate meta-textual keys to the reader/hearer of the parameters of various macrostructural units.[23] They are *meta*-textual because they help to mark major units of a text and guide the reader/hearer in understanding them. In this case, the superscription in 1.1 seems to introduce the book as a whole,[24] while the superscription in 2.1 introduces a major

22. For a broad survey of various proposals see J. Willis, 'The First Pericope in the Book of Isaiah', *VT* 34 (1984), pp. 64-68.

23. On this, the text-linguistic discussions of metalanguage indicators of Gühlich and Raible continue to be helpful. See, for example, W. Raible, *Satz und Text: Untersuchungen zu vier romanischen Sprachen* (Beihefte zur Zeitschrift für die romansiche Philologie, 132; Tübingen: Niemeyer, 1972), pp. 33-241, especially pp. 230-7; E. Gühlich and W. Raible, 'Textorten-Probleme', in H. Moser (ed.), *Linguistische Probleme der Textanalyse* (Jahrbuch des Instituts für deutsche Sprache, 35; Dusseldorf: Pädagogischer Verlag Schwamm, 1975), pp. 151-60; *idem, Linguistische Textmodelle: Grundlagen und Möglichkeiten* (Unitaschenbücher, 130; München: Wilhelm Fink, 1977), pp. 21-59; *idem*, 'Überlegungen zu einer makrostrukturellen Textanalyse: J. Thurber, The Lover and his Lass', in T. van Dijk and J. Petöfi (eds.), *Grammars and Description: Studies in Text Theory and Text Analysis* (Research in Text Theory/Untersuchungen zur Texttheorie, 1; Berlin: de Gruyter, 1977), pp. 133-50. For more recent literature and discussion of issues in application of text-linguistics to Hebrew biblical literature see the excellent discussion in C. Hardmeier, *Prophetie im Streit vor dem Untergang Judas: Erzählkommunikative Studien zur Entstehungssituation der Jesaja- und Jeremiaerzählungen in II Reg 18–20 und Jer 37–40* (BZAW, 187; Berlin: de Gruyter, 1990), pp. 63-71.

24. This has been the natural reading for centuries of readers of Isaiah, and such a reading is plausible given the lack of any subsequent superscription that attributes any following material in the book to either someone other than Isaiah or to a time other than that between the reigns of Uzziah and Hezekiah.

macrostructural unit of the book. In between these two major macro-structural indicators, 1.1 and 2.1, stands a body of material, which, whatever the lower-level, structural divisions within it, is marked off by these macrostructural markers; that is, the superscriptions, from the rest of the Isaiah tradition.[25] This body of material, 1.2-31, will be my focus for the rest of this section.

Although there have been some attempts to find one or two major speeches in this section,[26] most previous treatments of this material have used form-critical criteria to isolate six units in the chapter, most of which were originally independent: an accusation speech in 1.2-3; a woe oracle in 1.4-9; a prophetic announcement of Yahweh's appeal to begin a legal proceeding (1.18-20); a prophetic inverted lament (1.21-26); and an announcement of judgment (1.29-31).[27] In addition, most analyses identify redactional material in 1.27-28 and other locations in the above mentioned units. From Fohrer onward, several have suggested that this chapter was shaped by this redactional material to encourage its audience to repent.[28]

The approach taken here agrees with the latter overall thesis. More specifically, my thesis regarding 1.2-31 is that whatever the originally independent origins of the material, it has been molded into a whole now focused on encouraging a persistently faithless audience to cease their faithlessness and repent. This is indicated first of all by the movement from a pair of oracles accusing the whole people of faithlessness in 1.2-3 and 1.4-9 to a description of two groups in this people in 1.27-31: those in Zion who repent and will be redeemed (v. 27), and those who persist in evil and will be burned up (vv. 28-31). The key move in defining the split in the people occurs in the prophetic Torah of 1.10-17, a Torah where the audience is called on to repent. Having received this summons,

---

25. For a similar position see also Sweeney, *Isaiah 1–4*, pp. 27-32; and S. Deck, *Die Gerichtsbotschaft Jesajas: Charakter und Begründung* (FB, 67; Würzburg: Echter Verlag, 1991), p. 93.

26. Willis, 'The First Pericope', pp. 68-72; S. Niditch, 'The Composition of Isaiah 1', *Bib* 61 (1980), pp. 511-29; Y. Gitay, 'Reflections on the Study of the Prophetic Discourse: The Question of Isaiah I 2-20', *VT* 33 (1983), p. 216.

27. See Sweeney, *Isaiah 1–4*, pp. 101-23, for a helpful survey of literature on genres in Isa. 1.

28. See, for example, Fohrer, 'Jesaja 1', pp. 267-8; Sweeney, *Isaiah 1–4*, pp. 131-33; T.L. Steinberg, 'Isaiah the Poet', in V.L. Tollers and J. Maier (eds.), *Mappings of the Biblical Terrain: The Bible as Text* (London and Toronto: Associated University Presses, 1990), pp. 301-306.

the audience is offered in 1.18-20 the same two options with which the chapter concludes: repent and eat the good of the land (v. 18), or refuse and be eaten by the sword (vv. 19-20). In sum, there is an overall movement in 1.2-31 from accusation of the whole people in 1.2-9 to a call to repent, 1.10-17, to a rationale for this call through outlining the consequences of a choice for or against it (vv. 18-31). Within this context, the description of purging judgment in Jerusalem in 1.21-26—whatever its original function—now serves to describe the process by which those who persist in evil will be purged from Zion, while those who repent will be able to enjoy a purified city. The following outline summarizes my observations so far:

Exhortation to Repentance	1.2-31
I. Divine Description of the Problem: Persistent Evil of Israel.	1.2-9
II. Divine Prescription of Solution: Call to Repentance.	1.10-17
III. Divine Argument for Participating in Solution: Outline of Consequences of Different Responses to II.	1.18-31

Notably, this outline diverges from several recent studies in placing 1.18-20 with what follows (1.21-29), rather than in a larger unit with what precedes, such as 1.2-20. These studies have tended to place 1.18-20 with what precedes for two major reasons: 1) 1.18-20 corresponds in several specific ways to what precedes—the shared legal language, the cleansing of sin in 1.16 and 1.18, פי] כי יהוה דבר in 2aα and 20bß[29]—and 2) the following section, 1.21-26, seems to represent a new beginning in its focus on Zion.[30] Yet even though 1.18-20 draws on themes and wording of 1.2-17, it draws on them in the process of shifting the focus of the chapter from a direct call for certain behavior, 1.10-17, to a justification of that call. In addition (as will be argued in greater detail below), even though the oracle in Isa. 1.21-26 introduces a new extended focus on Zion, it does so in the context of the two descriptions of consequences of response to that call; 1.18-20 on the one hand and 1.27-31 on the other. In sum, once one shifts attention from shared themes in themselves

---

29. Gitay, 'Reflections', p. 216 (also, *idem, Isaiah and his Audience: The Structure and Meaning of Isaiah 1–12* [SSN, 30; Assen: Van Gorcum, 1991], pp. 15-17); Willis, 'The First Pericope', pp. 68-72; J. Vermeylen, *Du prophète Isaïe à l'apocalyptique: Isaïe, I—XXV, miroir d'un demi-millénaire d'expérience religieuse en Israël* (EBib; Paris: Gabalda, 1977), I, pp. 42-49; Sweeney, *Isaiah 1–4*, pp. 120-23.

30. This latter point is particularly stressed by Gitay, 'Reflections', p. 216 and *idem, Isaiah and his Audience*, pp. 17 and 36.

to an examination of how such themes *are functioning* differently in different parts of Isa. 1.2-31, the structural focus of the chapter on repentance becomes clear. Everything in 1.2-31 revolves around the call to repentance in 1.10-17, whether preparing for it with accusation (1.2-9) or motivating a response to it through prediction (1.18-31).

Within this overall focus of the literary context on repentance, the smaller functional units in this exhortation to repentance turn out to be somewhat different from the units defined by the purported original genre. For example, it could be argued that 1.2-3, 4-9 may be distinguished in terms of original genre. Nevertheless, now that these verses exist in a context focused on repentance, the most important break in 1.2-9 is between the accusation in 1.2-4 and the rhetorical question about lack of repentance in 1.5a and following. In 1.2-3 the text describes the unnatural failure of Israel to recognize its master, and 1.4 adds detail to this initial description of failure.[31] In 1.5a the audience is addressed with the question of why they have persisted in their faithlessness, and this question is then directly supported and expanded through description of the consequences they have already endured as a result of their failure (1.5b-9). In sum, 1.5-9 as a whole now serves as a rhetorical question *involving the audience* in reflection on their pattern of persistent and unnatural faithlessness, a pattern initially described in 1.2-4.

The second major unit of 1.2-31, as already discussed, is the call to repentance in 1.10-17, a unit previously identified by more traditional form-critical studies. The third major macrostructural unit (1.18-31), however, has not been as widely recognized. It contains several different types of material. Nevertheless, all of this material is united by a common purpose. Everything in 1.18-31, from the initial description of the consequences of repenting or not repenting in 1.18-20 to the concluding description of contrasting fates of the repentant and non-repentant in 1.27-31, *all* now functions to justify the initial call to repent in 10-17. Even 1.21-26 now begins an elaboration of the brief description of options in 1.18-20, an elaboration focusing particularly on the negative consequences of failure to repent. Whereas this judgment oracle probably once stood alone and proclaimed certain judgment on the wicked, its

---

31. R. Alter similarly treats Isa. 1.2-4 as a unit distinguished from 1.5-6 in his synchronic study of 1.2-9, *The Art of Biblical Poetry* (New York: Basic Books, 1985), pp. 143-45. In addition, Willis, 'The First Pericope', p. 69, makes some observations which could provide further support for reading 1.4 in close relation to 1.2-3, whether or not 1.4 is understood as originally beginning a separate unit.

context—following on the call to repentance in 1.10-17 and standing between 1.18-20, 27-28—makes this oracle function now in a different way: pointing to the certain judgment that will meet those who do not heed the call to repentance.

Through explicitly mentioning 'Zion's repenters' in 1.27, the concluding description of options in 1.27-31 builds directly on the oracle of 1.21-26, describing the contrast in fates between repenters and sinners which will result from the purging of Jerusalem which is described in 1.21-26. Moreover, just as in 1.21-26, the description of consequences of behavior in 1.27-31 focuses much more on the negative consequences of non-repentance (1.28-31) than on the benefits of repentance (1.27). Indeed, after an initial description of the fate of those who fail to repent (1.28), the text actually concludes with an oracle directed specifically at them (1.29-31). I will return at the end of this article to the problems this oracle raises. But for now it suffices to observe that 1.21-31 taken as a whole elaborates the initial description of consequences in 1.18-20, with an emphasis on the negative consequences of failure to repent.

In sum, a closer look at the present functions of the various parts of material in 1.2-31 indicates the intense focus throughout this text on repentance, more specifically encouraging its audience to cease their persistence in evil and repent, thus avoiding the dire fate of those who fail to heed this call. The following outline summarizes my observations thus far:

Exhortation to Repentance		1.2-31
I.	Divine Description of the Problem: Persistent Evil of Israel.	1.2-9
	A. Accusation: The Unnatural Failure of Israel to Recognize its Master.	1.2-4
	B. Resulting Rhetorical Question: Query Regarding the Persistence of Judah in Failure.	1.4-9
II.	Divine Prescription of Solution: Call to Repentance.	1.10-17
III.	Divine Argument for Participating in Solution: Outline of Consequences of Different Responses to II.	1.18-31
	A. Initial Description of Consequences of Repentance and Non-Repentance.	1.18-20
	B. Elaboration of Description in III.A with Emphasis on the Negative Consequences of Non-Repentance.	1.21-31
1.	Description of Zion-Purging Process.	1.21-26
2.	Description of Resulting Contrast in Fates.	1.27-31
	a. Initial Description.	1.27-28
	b. Anticipatory Address to Those to be Punished.	1.29-31

Construal of the Isaiah Tradition in Isaiah 1.2-31

This overview of the shape and rhetorical focus of Isa. 1.2-31 can now illuminate an examination of its use of certain themes and/or topics which occur across the full range of the following Isaiah tradition, termed here 'trans-Isaiah themes'. First and foremost among these is the focus of the book as a whole on Zion. The conceptual context of Isa. 1.2-31's treatment of Zion is the text's emphasis on the audience's persistent sin (1.2-9). This has left them sick and wounded (1.5-6), a metaphor which is soon explicated through description of the people's desolate land in which only Zion is left (1.8). Given this background, it is appropriate that the description of the consequences of not repenting would include an explicit description of Zion's fate (1.21-26). More specifically, the oracle regarding the purging of Zion in 1.21-26 now functions within a broader context to assert that *even Zion* will not continue to be a refuge for those in this audience who persist in their crimes. Instead, Zion, the 'whore', will be purged, and the criminals shall be destroyed (1.24-25, 28-31), while those in Zion who repent will be redeemed by righteousness (1.27). In sum, this text, particularly 1.8 along with 1.21-28, seems to address an audience of survivors *in Zion* (whether fictive or not; cf. 1.8-9) and argues that Zion will not long remain a refuge for those of them who persist in unfaithfulness.[32]

Such a picture of Zion is somewhat different in emphasis from the discussions of Zion elsewhere in the book of Isaiah. To be sure, like the rest of the Isaiah tradition, Isaiah 1.2-31 includes a significant focus on Zion, which is presented as God's special city and the ultimate locus of redemption: 2.2-5; 4.2-6; 8.18b; 10.24-27; 11.9; 12.6; 14.32; 24.23; 25.6-8, 10a; 26.1-4; 27.13; 30.19, 29; 31.4-5, 9; 33.5; 35.10; 40.1-2, 9-11; 49.14-26; 51.3; 54.11-17; 56.7; 59.20; 60–62.[33] Unlike much of that tradition, however, the emphasis in 1.2-31 *taken as a whole* seems to be less on exalting Zion's (future) status than on preventing the audience from relying on Zion's status to persist in their faithlessness. Thus, even as Isa. 1.2-31 introduces a major theme of the Isaiah tradition, its particular treatment of that theme is distinctive.[34]

Similarly, Isaiah 1 differs from other parts of the book in its treatment

32. See also Conrad, *Reading Isaiah*, pp. 87-91, on this audience of 'survivors'.

33. J.H. Eaton, 'The Origin of the Book of Isaiah', *VT* 9 (1959), p. 154 n. 3; J.J.M. Roberts, 'Isaiah in Old Testament Theology', *Int* 36 (1982), pp. 136-42.

34. The closest any other text in the Isaiah tradition comes to such a position is the proclamation of God's destruction of sinners in Zion in Isa. 33.10-14.

of the trans-Isaiah theme of God as Israel's father. God's people are imaged in 1.2-3 as God's children, as in several passages later in the book (43.6; 45.10-11; 63.16; 64.7 [64.8]).[35] These latter passages in Isaiah use the image of God's fatherhood (45.10-11; 63.16; 64.7) or parenthood (43.6) to stress God's investment in saving God's people. In contrast, Isa. 1.2-3 uses this same image to stress the severity of the faithlessness from which the people need to repent: the people of Israel have failed to recognize their own parent.

Thus, Isa. 1.2-31 adds a similar 'spin' to both of the trans-Isaiah themes discussed so far: Zion and parent imagery for God. In both cases, an image which is traditionally used to reassure the people is used in Isa.1.2-31 to shock the people and remove barriers to repentance. 'Zion' will not long remain a refuge for those who persist in crimes against God. God's 'children' have committed the unnatural sin of not recognizing their parent-master, the very parent they might turn to for forgiveness (1.2-3).

Indeed, Isaiah 1 as a whole can be seen as a repentance-focused presentation of many central themes of the Isaiah tradition, from the initial description of the people as God's children to the final invective against those who sacrifice in gardens. Thus, for example, the accusation of the people in 1.2-9 uses the distinctive epithet of God as the 'holy one of Israel' (1.4)[36] and refers to the characteristic Isaianic theme of Israel's persistent 'sin' and 'bloodguilt' (1.4).[37] In this case, these characteristically Isaianic expressions are part of a sub-unit in the chapter which establishes the audience's need to repent. In other cases, certain trans-Isaiah themes, such as the issue of 'the nations', are conspicuously absent from this chapter, most likely because of their lack of direct relevance to the chapter's focus on Israel's repentance.[38]

35. Eaton, 'Origin', p. 153 n. 6.

36. Roberts, 'Isaiah', pp. 131-33; R. Rendtorff, 'Zur Komposition des Buches Jesaja', *VT* 34 (1984), pp. 310-12.

37. R. Melugin, *The Formation of Isaiah 40–55* (BZAW, 141; Berlin: de Gruyter, 1976), p. 177; Rendtorff, 'Komposition', pp. 302-305.

38. To be sure, some have been tempted to add the nations text in 2.2-5 to the unit beginning in 1.2 so that the whole might be a better 'introduction' to the Isaiah tradition, a tradition which includes a significant focus on the role and fate of non-Israelites. Nevertheless, such a move not only ignores the explicit signal of the beginning of a new major unit in 2.1, but it also misses the distinctive focus of the composition in 1.2-31. This composition focuses not on God's Zion-centered plan for the cosmos (so 2.2-5 and other Isaiah texts), but on the urgent need for its *Judean* audience to

In sum, Isaiah 1 is not just an initial presentation of major themes in the Isaiah tradition. It stands now as a strategic reconceptualization of that tradition. This first chapter of the book selectively presents and recasts relevant strands of the Isaiah tradition, forming a new theological whole out of them, and thus prepares the audience to hear subsequent Isaiah texts in a new way.

Isaiah 65–66

Isaiah 65–66 is a strategic conceptualization of the Isaiah tradition along somewhat different lines. Whereas Isa. 1.2-31 encourages a faithless audience to repent, Isaiah 65–66 rejects the possibility of repentance for such evildoers. Instead, Isaiah 65–66 reassures the *already* righteous. Moreover, just as various Isaiah themes were drawn upon in 1.2-31 to encourage repentance, many of these same themes are drawn upon in 65–66 to describe a situation where repentance is no longer a possibility. But before I explore these contrasts in more detail, I begin by examining the structure and rhetorical aim of the end of the book.

Isaiah 63–64 as the Setting for 65–66
The beginning point for understanding Isaiah 65–66 in context, is recognition of its integral structural relation to the preceding communal supplication, Isa. 63.7–64.11.[39] To be sure, as many have pointed out, there are important conceptual and theological differences between this supplication and the following divine reply to it. Thus, for example, Whybray says regarding Isaiah 65:

> Although at first sight verse 1 might suggest that this chapter contains Yahweh's answer to the preceding lamentation [Isa. 63.7–64.11] there is no connexion between the two passages. The most prominent feature of

cease their persistent faithlessness and repent (Becker, *Isaias*, p. 47).

39. Here I am not making any specific claims regarding the transmission history of Isa. 63.7–64.11. I only presuppose that the author of Isa. 65–66 was aware of this text. For further discussion of transmission, historical issues and references to literature, see Steck, '56,1-8; 63,7–66,24', pp. 233-42 (for Isa. 63.7–64.11), and 248-62 (for Isa. 65–66) and a persuasive presentation of the more traditional exilic dating of this text in R. Albertz, *Religionsgeschichte Israels in alttestamentlicher Zeit. II. Vom Exil bis zu den Makkabäern* (ATD Supplement, 8.2; Göttingen: Vandenhoeck & Ruprecht, 1992), pp. 385, 387 (including qualifications in note 9), 415.

this chapter [65.1-25], the fact that it is addressed to a religiously divided community, is entirely absent from the preceding chapters.[40]

Nevertheless, as Steck has most recently and forcefully emphasized, the contrast between 65–66 and the preceding can be misleading. For although Isaiah 65–66 are not the reply anticipated in 63.7–64.11, these final two chapters do specifically answer that supplication by correcting its perspective.[41]

In order to get a clearer picture of this correction of the supplication in Isaiah 65–66, we must first examine the structure and apparent function of the supplication itself. Previous studies have been almost unanimous in distinguishing the historical retrospective in 63.7-14 from the following petition for salvation in 63.15–64.11. This shift is clearly signalled by the shift from narrative (and the statement of intent to narrate in 63.7) in 63.7-14 to a section introduced by an imperative in 63.15a and focused on arguing for this and other imperatives throughout the rest of the petition, 63.15b–64.11.[42] As in many such communal

40. R.N. Whybray, *Isaiah 40–66* (NCB; London: Oliphants, 1975), p. 266. See also P.D. Hanson, *The Dawn of Apocalyptic: The Historical and Sociological Roots of Jewish Apocalyptic Eschatology* (Philadelphia: Fortress, rev. edn, 1979), pp. 80-81 and C. Westermann, who does not appear to consider a potential link between these chapters, see his *Das Buch Jesaia: Kapitel 40–66* (ATD, 19; Göttingen: Vandenhoeck & Ruprecht, 1966), pp. 242, 317, 319 (English: *Isaiah 40–66* [trans. D.M.G. Stalker; OTL; Philadelphia: Westminster, 1969], pp. 303, 399-400 and 402). Even Bonnard, who does recognize several important points of contact between the lament and Isa. 65, ends up arguing like Whybray that the relationship between the units is confined primarily to the beginning of Isa. 65 (*Le second Isaïe: son disciple et leurs éditeurs* [EBib; Paris: Gabalda, 1972], p. 462). Webster, 'The Rhetoric of Isaiah 63–65', *JSOT* 47 (1990), pp. 96-101, sees a larger relationship between Isa. 65 and the preceding supplication, but limits the relationship to this chapter.

41. Steck, 'Anlage', pp. 107-13 (in *idem*, *Studien*, pp. 221-5); *idem*, '56,1-8; 63, 7-66, 24', pp. 248-49. See also, C.C. Torrey, *The Second Isaiah: A New Interpretation* (New York: Charles Scribner's Sons, 1928), pp. 466-67; J. Muilenburg, 'Isaiah 40–66', in *IB*, V, pp. 744-45; Jones, *Isaiah 56–66 and Joel*, p. 104; and Sweeney, *Isaiah 1–4*, p. 91.

42. This emphasis on a fundamental break between 63.7-14 and 63.15–64.11 most closely matches studies such as J. Muilenburg, 'Isaiah 40–66', p. 729; Westermann, 'Das Buch Jesaia', pp. 306-16 (English, pp. 385-98); and R.J. Clifford, 'Isaiah 40–66', in J.L. Mays (ed.), *The Harper's Bible Commentary* (San Francisco: Harper & Row, 1988), pp. 592-93. Nevertheless, many other studies have recognized a major break here, including Bonnard, *Le Second Isaïe*, p. 444; Whybray, *Isaiah 40–66*, p. 255; and E. Webster, 'The Rhetoric of Isaiah 63–65', pp. 90-92. Cf. the

supplications, the hymnic remembrance of God's past salvation in 63.7-14 helps to ground the request for further salvation in 63.15–64.11. Yet as Williamson has particularly stressed, there are also some important differences between Isa. 63.7–64.11 and other communal supplications. Whereas most such supplications include a protestation of innocence, Isa. 63.7–64.11 has an unusually strong emphasis on the community's misdeeds. Indeed, this emphasis occurs in both major parts of Isaiah 63.7–64.11. The historical remembrance in 63.7-14 is of God's past salvation *despite* past misbehavior (63.10a; cf. 63.8a), and then the following supplication asks for God's salvation *despite* the community's recent misbehavior (64.4b-6).

The crucial petition section in 63.15–64.11 (63.15–64.12) is made up of three major parts: a call to God to cease withholding help and to repel foreign occupiers (63.15–64.4a [63.15–64.5a]), a confession of the whole people's sin (64.4b-6 [64.5b-7]), and a final plea for God to cease God's withholding of help because of that sin (64.7-11 [64.8-12]). This final plea has been widely recognized as a unit, and is clearly marked off from the preceding by the conjunction ועתה.[43] All of the verses following this conjunction share a focus on God's ending of a withdrawal from the people because of their misdeeds. The preceding unit, the confession of the misdeeds in 64.4b-6, is less widely recognized.[44] Nevertheless, the shift in perspective is once again marked by a clear syntactic marker, הן־אתה, and the unit is unified by its focus on the community's misdeeds and God's reaction to them. Finally, each of these units stand over against the initial plea for help in 63.15–64.4a. Although there are various kinds of speech in this plea and some more minor breaks in it, this section functions as a piece in relation to the following confession (64.4b-6) and plea (64.7-11). It gives the initial arguments for God's intervention without yet discussing at length the community's misdeeds that have caused God's withdrawal up to this point. The closest anticipation of the latter theme is in 63.17a, but even in this verse the accusation is against God, not the community: 'Why, oh

quite different division in H.G.M. Williamson, 'Laments at the Destroyed Temple: Excavating the Biblical Text Reveals Ancient Jewish Prayers', *BibRev* 6 (1990), p. 17. The latter scholar, however, is focusing not so much on the individual structure of Isa. 63.7–64.11 as on its parallels with other texts.

43. Muilenburg, 'Isaiah 40–66', p. 729; Bonnard, *Le Second Isaïe*, p. 444; Whybray, *Isaiah 40–66*, p. 255.

44. But see Muilenburg, 'Isaiah 40–66', p. 729; Whybray, *Isaiah 40–66*, p. 255.

Yahweh, have you caused us to wander from your ways and hardened our hearts from fear of you?' In contrast to all of this initial unit (63.15–64.4a), the confession of sin in 64.4b-6 marks a major break, certainly more major than any that exist within 63.15–64.4a. And this confession in turn sets up a modified plea for divine help in 64.7-11. The latter plea repeats specific terminology from the first call for help in 63.15–64.4a, but now explicitly asks if God, the community's 'father', will be angry forever over the sin confessed in 64.4b-6 (cf. 63.15-16//64.7, 11). My observations thus far can be outlined as follows:[45]

I.   Hymnic Remembrance: God's Past Salvation Despite Past
     Misbehavior.   63.7-14
II. Resulting Petition: For Present Salvation Despite Recent
     Misbehavior.   63.15–64.11
     A. Initial Plea: For Cessation of Divine Withholding of Aid.   63.15–64.4a
     B. Confession of the Community's Sin: Acknowledgment of
         God's Reason for Withholding.   64.4b-6
     C. Concluding Plea: For Cessation of Divine Withholding of
         Aid Despite Community's Sin.   64.7-14

Overall, this text appears to be a communal supplication for divine rescue from foreign occupiers despite the community's misdeeds.

The Structure and Rhetorical Stance of Isaiah 65–66 in Relation to 63.7–64.14

Isaiah 65–66 replies to the supplication in 63.7–64.14 first of all by rejecting its premise, that God might rescue the entire community despite its misdeeds. Instead, according to Isaiah 65–66, the community has now been divided by the unforgivable sin of some of its members. This division, however, is only gradually sprung on the audience of this pair of chapters.

Rather than beginning with the contrast in fates of the righteous and unrighteous, ch. 65 begins in 65.1-7 with a specific pronouncement of judgment on a group of evildoers who is spoken of in the third person:[46]

45. The resulting division of 63.15–64.11 into three parts most closely matches the overviews of Muilenburg, 'Isaiah 40–66', p. 729; and Whybray, *Isaiah 40–66*, p. 255.

46. The MT diverges here from the Septuagint and Peshitta in having second-person suffixes in Isa. 65.7a. This is not the context for a detailed discussion of the text-critical issues. Nevertheless, the MT version of this text appears to be a harmonization of 65.7 with the second-person language that follows. In the earliest version of the tradition, here represented by the Septuagint and Peshitta, the second-

I continually reached out
    to a rebellious people,
To ones walking in a way that was not good,
    after their own thoughts
The people provoking me
    to my face all the time... (65.2-3a)

This type of behavior prompts a precise reply to the supplication. Whereas the supplication concluded by asking if God would be 'inactive' forever before the devastation of God's temple by foreigners (64.11 [64.12]), the reply asserts that God's own people are idolaters (65.1-5a) and that God will not be 'inactive' before *their* rebellion (65.5b-6). Because of that rebellion, God will not forgive as asked in the supplication, but will repay their sin in full (65.6-7). Nevertheless, up to this point the divine reply to the supplication, however stark, is still not directly addressed to the evildoers. Instead, 65.1-7 is distinguished from what follows by a separate messenger formula (65.7; cf. 65.8) and its use of third-person language to describe the doomed evildoers. Such traits have lead many to plausibly suggest that 65.1-7 may have once been an originally independent pronouncement of judgment. But its probable independent origins are not as important to our purposes as its present function in the wider literary context. And that function appears to be to entrap the audience of unrighteous into initially hearing what up until now sounds like a distant pronouncement of judgment, a pronouncement still framed in the third person rather than directly addressed to them. In sum, the whole of 65.1-7 is an elegant indirect, although specific, judgment of the unrighteous.

This initial indirect judgment then paves the way for an address explicitly directed to the unrighteous in 65.8–66.4. Isa. 65.8-10 uses a proverb about wine left in a grape cluster to introduce a group of righteous servants who will not receive the destruction promised in 65.1-7. Then, using an emphatic second person pronoun in front-extra position, 65.11-12 explicitly shifts to an address to the unrighteous audience, renewing the pronouncement of judgment in 65.1-7:

But as for those of you who abandoned Yahweh...
I shall consign you to the sword,

person language would have first appeared only in 65.8 and following. Notably, this shift in the MT seems to be part of a broader drift in the development in the text of Isa. 65–66 toward early anticipation of shifts of address. On this see Steck, 'Anlage', in *idem*, *Studien*, p. 218 (no equivalent in the earlier *BN* version).

and all of you shall bow down to the slaughter,
because I called and you did not answer,
  I spoke and you did not listen.
You have done what I consider evil,
  and what displeases me is what you chose.

This pronouncement of judgment echoes many of the charges initially raised in 65.1-5a, but with a decisive difference. Whereas the charges in 65.1-7 were initially leveled against a third-person group 'out there', now they are directly addressed to the audience of the oracle. In sum, 65.8-12 introduces the contrast in fates which was not previously explicit in 65.1-7, between the evildoers whose sin will be repaid in full (65.11-12), and the righteous servants who will be spared the punishment and enjoy a renewed Zion (65.8-10).

The next major unit, the divine speech in 65.13-25, develops the contrast in fates introduced in 65.8-12. It begins with a speech introduction that clearly indicates the focus of the speech on developing the implications of the preceding unit: 'Therefore thus says the LORD Yahweh'. The first unit of the following speech, 65.13-15, is an explicit point-by-point juxtaposition of the immediate future of God's servants on the one hand, and the unrighteous audience of the speech on the other: reward for the servants and impending destruction for the unrighteous. Isa. 65.16-25 then follows up on 65.13-15 through describing the longer range future, a future where only the righteous survive to enjoy God's restoration of Zion, and indeed, creation as a whole.[47]

Isaiah 66.1-4 is the last speech addressing the unrighteous, and it returns to topics from the supplication and from the initial oracle in 65.1-7. First, whereas the supplication concluded with a plea for God to restore the temple (64.10-11), 66.1-2a, 3 condemn the temple and its cult. Secondly, in the process of condemning the cult, 66.2b commends the individual who 'is humble, of broken spirit, who trembles at my word'. Thirdly, 66.4 concludes the address to the unrighteous by proclaiming a judgment on them, a judgment justified in almost identical

---

47. For a detailed survey of syntactic signals of the structure of Isa. 65.13-25 and an intriguing observation of parallel signals in 66.5-24, see Steck, 'Anlage', pp. 103-107 (in *idem, Studien*, pp. 217-20). As Steck points out, the conspicuous call to rejoice over the glorious future of the righteous in 65.18 does not clearly fit with the idea that 65.8-25 is addressed to the righteous. Nevertheless, it may be part of the wider phenomenon of early anticipation of shifts in address that is seen in Isa. 66.4 and the MT of 65.7.

terms to those used in a direct address to them in 65.12:

65.12 (NJB)	66.4 (NJB)
You I shall destine to the sword	I too take delight in making fools of them,
and all of you will stoop to be slaughtered,	I shall bring what they most fear down on them,
because I called and you would not answer,	because I called and no one would answer,
I spoke and you would not listen;	I spoke and no one listened.
you have done what I consider evil, you chose to do what displeases me.	They have chosen what I regard as evil, have chosen what displeases me.

Clearly, although a clear shift in addressee has not yet occurred, this final address to the unrighteous is distinguished from its parallel in 65.12 by its use of third-person language to describe the unrighteous. In this way, 66.1-4 shifts back to the third-person stance present at the outset of the address to the unrighteous, 65.1-7. More importantly, through shifting to the third person for the unrighteous, 66.4 begins to anticipate the constant use of third-person language throughout 66.5-24 to describe this group.[48]

Isa. 66.5a is an explicit signal that a shift in addressee has occurred: 'hear the word of Yahweh those who tremble at God's word'. This call explicitly redirects the address away from the unrighteous and to the righteous who were described in third-person terms in 66.2b; that is, to those who 'tremble at my [God's] word' (66.2bß//5aß). The following unit, 66.5b-24, can be roughly divided into two major parts: a promise to the servants of vindication over their enemies in 66.5b-6 and a promise of restoration of Jerusalem in 66.7-24.[49] As Steck has observed, the address in 66.5-24 is parallel in many ways to Isaiah 65, in particular there are parallels between the syntactic conjunctions used in 65.17-25

---

48. Steck, 'Anlage', p. 218 (no equivalent in the earlier *BN* version).

49. On the basis of the presence of the syntactic particle, כי, in 66.8b, Steck posits a major division there rather than in 66.7 ('Anlage', pp. 217-20). Yet a look at the contents of 66.5b-24 indicates that the break marked by the כי in 66.8b is not as functionally significant as the break between the proclamation of reversal of fortunes of the enemies in 66.5b-6 and the promise of the restoration of Jerusalem in 66.7-24. To be sure, syntactic signals can add a certain methodological control to structural discussions. Nevertheless, this is a case where such syntactic observations must be balanced by consideration of the semantic fields covered by the various units.

and 66.12-24.[50] Nevertheless, even as these two chapters explore many of the same themes, there are important differences. Not only does 66.5-24 shift to an explicit address to the righteous, but it adds a new focus on the fate of the nations. Isa. 65.1–66.4 has already rejected the implication of the supplication (63.7–64.11) that God's primary task is to rescue God's whole people from foreigners. Now, 66.5-24 follows up on that by discussing a place for foreigners in God's plan to restore Jerusalem (66.18-21).

In sum, Isaiah 65–66 is dominated by an overall shift between explicit address to the unrighteous in 65.11-25 and to the righteous in 66.5-24. The addressee in other parts of Isaiah 65–66 is less clear. Indeed, the material itself, especially as transmitted in various manuscript traditions, betrays a lack of a fixed concept of where these boundaries lie. The MT of 65.7 already anticipates an address to the unrighteous, and 66.4 anticipates the address to the righteous beginning in 66.5. Even the call to the unrighteous to rejoice in 66.18 may already anticipate this shift. Be that as it may, 65.1-7 and 66.1-4 now seem to function as part of a proclamation to the unrighteous extending from 65.1 to 66.4. As argued before, 65.1-7 is only an apparent proclamation of judgment on the whole people, before the judgment is specified and explicitly directed to the unrighteous in 65.8–66.4. Taking this approach, my results regarding Isaiah 63.7–66.24 can be outlined as follows:

I.	Communal Supplication for Divine Rescue from Foreign Occupiers Despite the Community's Misdeeds.			63.7–64.11
II.	Divine Response: Divided Fates of Ungodly and Righteous.			65.1–66.24
	A.	Address to the Unrighteous.		65.1–66.4
		1.	Divine Speech Report: Indirect Pronouncement of Judgment on the Unrighteous.	65.1-7
		2.	Divine Speech Sequence: Explicit Address to the Unrighteous.	65.8–66.4
			a. Divine Speech Report: Introduction of a Contrast of Fates between the Leadership and Servants.	65.8-12
			b. Divine Speech Report: Development of the Contrast in Fates.	65.13-25
			(1) Immediate Fate of Both Groups, Culminating in Destruction of the Unrighteous.	65.13-15
			(2) Longer Range Fate of Both Groups:	

50. Steck, 'Anlage', pp. 217-20.

The above observations should make clear in a preliminary way how the very structure of Isaiah 65–66 reflects a radical reconceptualization of the God–people relationship when compared with the supplication which these chapters answer. Whereas the supplication calls for a restoration despite the people's misdeeds, the responding oracle predicates such restoration on separation of the righteous from the unrighteous. Sin and judgment recognized in the supplication have now been applied to only one group in Israel, the unrighteous. The requested divine intervention has been promised, but only for God's servants. Finally, whereas the supplication drew its main dividing line between God's people and their foreign occupiers, the reply to this supplication draws its main dividing line between the unrighteous and righteous. Now many of God's people are included in the impending judgment, and righteous foreigners are among those who participate in God's restoration.

As has often been pointed out before, such a focus on community definition and reconceptualization of community boundaries seems to be directed at an outsider group of Israelites, a group apparently standing outside of and in opposition to the temple leadership of the post-exilic Palestinian establishment. Through an initial address to that insider leadership in 65.1–66.4 and then an address to the marginalized 'servants' in 66.5-25, the whole of Isaiah 65–66 reassures the outsider 'servants' of their insider status with God and encourages them to persevere in their faithfulness and even include a place for righteous foreigners in their vision of the restored Zion which they will enjoy as their reward. Whereas in Isaiah 1.2-31 a division in God's people is merely predicted in the process of encouraging repentance, now in Isaiah 65–66 that division has already taken place. Not only that, but the division has been extended into the world beyond the community, so that the evildoers within the community are given the same fate as the evil nations surrounding Judah, while righteous foreigners participate in the restoration of Zion following the destruction of God's enemies. This decisive shift in stance has an important impact on how a whole range of Isaiah traditions are treated, and so now I turn to an examination of how various trans-Isaiah themes are drawn upon in Isaiah 65–66, particularly themes which also occur in Isaiah 1.2-31.

Construal of the Isaiah Tradition in Isaiah 65–66

One important place where the above discussed shift in rhetorical stance from Isaiah 1 to Isaiah 65–66 makes a difference is in the treatment of Zion. Certainly, the holy city is important in both Isa. 1.2-31 and 65–66, as it is throughout much of the book of Isaiah. Moreover, in both Isaiah 1 and 65–66 one of the primary rewards of the righteous is being able to live in a Zion purified of wrongdoers (1.26-27; 65.19-25; 66.10-24). Nevertheless, there are also some crucial differences in the treatment of the Zion image. Thus Isa. 1.2-31 begins its first extended discussion of Zion by talking about what a 'whore' she has become (1.21; cf. 1.8). In contrast, the corresponding use of feminine imagery in Isaiah 65–66 focuses exclusively on the mother image for Zion, assuring the righteous servants that Zion will soon bear her children, and they will nurse at Zion's breasts (66.7-14). Whereas in Isa. 1.2-31 the emphasis is on tearing away the rebels' false complacency about their security in Zion, in Isaiah 65–66 the focus is on stressing the benefits of a restored Zion to an embattled, but already righteous group (see esp. 65.18b-25).

The distinctive rhetorical stance of Isaiah 65–66 also governs how other trans-Isaiah themes are treated in the final part of the book. For example, I have already briefly discussed how 1.2-31 introduces the themes of Israel's 'sin' and 'bloodguilt', and God's parent relationship to this rebellious Israel. In Isa. 1.2-31 these themes are introduced in such a way as to stress the serious and unnatural quality of Israel's sin, and the consequent importance of repentance. Now in the supplication the community confesses its 'sin' and 'bloodguilt' (64.4b-6), and asks God their 'father' (63.16; 64.7; cf. 45.10-11) to redeem them despite their sin. Yet Isaiah 65–66 rejects this plea (65.1-7), and does not use the image of God as father at all. Instead, it reassures the righteous through describing God's comfort of them like a *mother* comforting her children (66.13). This radical shift in use of imagery in Isaiah 65–66 corresponds to the overall aim of Isaiah 65–66: to reassure and comfort a specific group within larger Israel, while rejecting the possibility of divine forgiveness for the sinners in the community, a group who has false confidence in the mercy of God, their 'father'.

Similar points could be made about the move from God as the 'holy one of Israel' in Isa. 1.4b to an exclusive focus on God's 'holy mountain' in 65–66 (65.11; 66.20; cf. 63.15, 18; 64.9-10), the narrowing of the cultic indictment of Isa. 1.10-17 to focus on a specific group of God's people in Isa. 66.3-4, or the new emphasis on the fate of the nations in Isa. 66.5-24 when compared with Isa. 1.2-31. Nevertheless, by now the point should be clear. Like Isaiah 1, Isaiah 65–66 is a strategic, selective presentation of central themes from the Isaiah tradition. Moreover, this presentation is placed at the end of the book, so that it now can function as the final word on the Isaiah tradition, emphasizing and recasting certain strands as part of a *reassurance-focused* framework.

Reading Isaiah as a 'Whole'

Certainly the contrasting, indeed irreconcilably different, rhetorical stances of Isa. 1.2-31 and 65.1–66.24 do not mean that these two units cannot be read in conjunction with one another, particularly since Isa. 1.2-31 occurs before Isaiah 65–66. Although ancient readers rarely read a large book like Isaiah from beginning to end, *we* can read it as a drama opening with a call to repentance and closing with paired proclamations to those who answered the call and those who did not. Alternatively, we modern readers can 'read' the entire Isaiah tradition through the lens of Isa. 1.2-31 or Isaiah 65–66. As M. Sweeney's book has shown, not just Isa. 1.2-31, but the whole of Isaiah, can be read as a call to repentance to a stubbornly corrupt community.[51] Now, the description of alternative fates in Isaiah 65–66 stands as an anticipation of the address God will give the community at a future time when the division between righteous and sinner has been made. Alternatively, the Isaiah tradition can be read through the lens of Isaiah 65–66 as a reassurance to an already righteous group. E. Conrad's reading of Isaiah as a whole comes closest to this position, a position which works not just for Isaiah 65–66, but for much of the rest of the book as well.[52] Now the call to repentance in 1.2-31 can function as a look back at the opportunity for righteousness which the righteous chose and their opponents rejected. And these are only two ways that the Isaiah tradition encompassing Isaiah 1 and 65–66

51. Sweeney, *Isaiah 1–4*, pp. 27-99.
52. Conrad, *Reading Isaiah*, pp. 34-168.

can be read as a whole. The presence of such multiple and often para-doxical connections between texts like Isaiah 1 and 65–66 means that there is a particularly rich mine of semiotic potential in the book, a potential which can be drawn on for various readings of the whole, whether focused through particular texts in it, or not.

In any case, these modern approaches to reading Isaiah as a 'book' probably do not reflect the way ancient editors approached the diversity of the tradition. We have evidence for this in the redactional insertion of 1.29-31 into Isaiah 1. Although 1.29-31 has been linked with the pre-ceding by the conjunction כי and the modification of its initial verb to third person to match the preceding,[53] it stands apart from what precedes by its primary use of the second person, the new focus on the problem of cultic apostasy (cf. 1.10-17, 21-23), and by its new perspective vis-à-vis the possibility of the audience's repentance.[54] Whereas the rest of Isaiah 1 encourages its audience to repent through *predicting* judgment on those in the community who persist in their evil, this brief fragment *proclaims already certain judgment* on a group for their past idolatry. All of these elements link 1.29-31 with Isaiah 65–66, particularly with the direct proclamation to the evildoers of irreversible judgment (Isa. 65.1–66.4). Whether 1.29-31 was actually written by the author of Isaiah 65–66 or by a later editor, the point that interests us is the following: here a redactor has taken the very part of the conceptual world of Isaiah 65–66 which is most diametrically opposed to a call to repentance—the proclamation of *irreversible* judgment to evildoers—and inserted it into the call to repentance in Isaiah 1. Yet, the chapter as a whole is not con-formed to this perspective. The result is that Isaiah 1 is not 'cohesive' in a modern literary sense. The tensions in the tradition are confronted here,

53. From a likely תבשו to יבשו. See Sweeney, *Isaiah 1–4*, p. 130. Here I am working with the reading in the MT and 1QIsaᵃ, a reading which moves from an initial third-person form, יבשו, to second-person forms beginning with חמדתם. Most textual traditions and a fair number of modern scholars have dealt with this difficult reading by either conforming all of 29–31 to the second-person forms which follow (Targum and some Masoretic manuscripts), or to the third-person forms which precede in 1.28 (Septuagint, Peshitta and Vulgate). For persuasive arguments that the MT and 1QIsaᵃ preserve our earliest reconstructable reading, see D. Barthélemy, *Critique textuelle de l'Ancien Testament* (OBO, 50.2; Göttingen: Vandenhoeck & Ruprecht, 1986), pp. 10-11.

54. For discussion of the redactional character of Isa. 1.29-31 and references, see Sweeney, *Isaiah 1–4*, pp. 117-18, 130.

but not resolved in the kind of comprehensive way that a modern author or editor might employ.

But let us return for a moment to the sketch of ancient text reception. The kind of sharp, but partial, modification of a text that we see in Isaiah 1.29-31 may not match how we would deal with the book of Isaiah's diversity, but it does make sense in the ancient context. In that context, cohesiveness is nowhere near as obvious an issue. When the book is read in scroll form and received orally, syntagmatic cohesiveness of a book is considerably less important. Instead, ancient readers were more interested in the cohesiveness of their world, particularly embattled communities of the sort to which texts like Isaiah 65–66, and the insertion in 1.29-31, seem to have been addressed. In this case an assertion appears to have been added at the end of Isaiah 1, perhaps in a margin, the bottom of a column, or some other means. In any case, the Isaiah scroll as a whole is not modified. Instead, Isaiah 1.29-31 is pegged to the end of the call to repentance, perhaps standing as a sign of the competing rhetorical perspective at the other end of the book.

In sum, although ancient readers seem to have been conscious of major themes stretching across the Isaiah tradition, they do not seem to have had the same preoccupation with literary 'coherence' that modern readers often have, particularly literary coherence across large blocks of material like the sixty-six chapters of the Isaiah book scroll. Such a conclusion is only a problem for the increasingly small proportion of approaches to Isaiah which attempt to recover a single structure and/or conceptual perspective of the book in its final form.[55] I have used the

---

55. Here I am thinking of the gradual influx into biblical studies of a broader range of methods rather than the unity-focused 'new' literary-critical approach popular in the 1950's and 60's. This having been said, such an interest in larger wholes and on cohesiveness in them remains remarkably dominant in some present biblical literary studies, even as it has been mixed with elements of other approaches. In particular, in the last few years this focus on the unity of biblical texts has often been combined with a very text-oriented reader-response criticism, often drawing liberally on M. Sternberg's influential *Poetics of Biblical Narrative* (Indiana Studies in Biblical Literature; Bloomington, IN: Indiana University Press, 1987). For an excellent discussion of this drift toward coherence in biblical studies see S. Moore's, 'Are the Gospels Unified Narratives?', in K.H. Richards (ed.), *SBLSP* 26 (Atlanta: Scholars Press, 1987), pp. 443-58. For a broader bibliography and survey of various types of literary theory in biblical criticism see M.A. Powell, *The Bible and Modern Literary Criticism: A Critical Assessment and Annotated Bibliography* (Bibliographies and Indexes in Religious Studies, 22; New York: Greenwood, 1992).

example of Isaiah 1 and 65–66 to argue that a construal of these two texts as parts of an overarching literary whole does not represent any reconstructable intent of the editors. Part or all of Isaiah 65–66 was probably written in relation to parts of Isa. 1.2-31 (among other Isaiah texts). Certain parts of Isa. 1.2-31, particularly Isa. 1.29-31, seem to have been written in relation to Isaiah 65–66. But there is no evidence that the author/editors who produced these connections also fully incorporated the divergent rhetorical perspectives of these two texts into a cohesive, literary whole.

On the other hand, I am also arguing that this does not mean that modern readers cannot choose to read the tradition in this way. Indeed, the complex web of connections between texts like Isaiah 1 and 65–66 open up a wide range of interpretive possibilities for modern readings of the Isaiah tradition as a whole. In sum, the semiotic potential of the book can be drawn on to develop and support these various readings, but there is no evidence of an indigenous coherence to serve as a *textual* basis for adjudication between them.

In the final analysis, much progress has been made and will continue to be made in the observation of inter-textual connections across Isaiah, and the same may be said for the analysis of the structure of smaller units of material. But particularly as the scope of such studies extends over larger and more complex blocks such as the book of Isaiah as a whole, the evidence that such blocks were ever meant to be read as a whole diminishes. This means that although a scholar's given perspective is an indispensable ingredient in their study of a text at any level—and this includes my analyses of Isaiah 1 and 65–66 above—this perspective plays an ever more pivotal role the more the scholar attempts to creatively read as literary unities blocks of material such as Isaiah which do not seem to have been shaped to be read this way.

The more the modern reader moves into the territory of specifically modern readings the more the natural context for evaluation of such irresolvably diverse proposals becomes not the biblical scholarly guild, but the broader religious context of those who read and revere these texts. To be sure, because perspective plays such an important role at every stage of textual reception and analysis, no sharp lines can be drawn here between proposals more dependent on their relevance to a specific interpretive community and observations that are inherently relevant to a broader scope of readers. Nevertheless, I am arguing that some kind of methodological continuum exists here, such that one can make a meaningful distinction in the level of dependence on a particular perspective between, say, 1) the observations of striking similarities between Isaiah 1 and 65–66 on the one hand, and 2) a construal of these two quite different texts as part of a literary whole on the other.

Both types of work can be useful, but the differences in the range of relevant criteria for evaluation of such work should be recognized. As one works toward a creative modern construal of a large and complex ancient text like Isaiah, the criteria for such a construal must be less exclusively the text itself, and more explicitly the extent to which the given reading speaks in an effective way to a given community's issues.[56] In other words, such a creative construal must not only dig deep into the text's semiotic potential, but it must be ethically and/or theologically reflected, contextually conscious and ideologically self-critical. Observations of connections between texts like Isaiah 1 and 65–66 can provide helpful raw material for such broad readings of the whole, but they cannot provide the basis for adjudication between the best of these modern synthetic proposals. Rather, as parts of biblical scholarship pursue the possibilities introduced by modern literary interpretive modes, the resulting readings may well depend *as much* on their elegance, poetry, relevance and depth as on their intricate interaction with the textual data at hand.

56. I have made some preliminary observations along these lines in my 'Synergy Toward Life: A Paradigm for Liberative Christian Work with the Bible', *Quarterly Review* 10 (1990), pp. 40-55.

No Strength to Deliver: A Contextual Analysis of Hezekiah's Proverb in Isaiah 37.3b[*]

Katheryn Pfisterer Darr

Introduction

The focus of this essay is a proverb about childbirth complications purportedly uttered by an esteemed king, Hezekiah, at a critical moment in Judah's history (Isa. 37.3b).[1] My goals are fourfold: first, on the basis of both biblical and extrabiblical evidence, I shall discern what I can about the proverb's possible meanings within Israel's ancient Near Eastern culture; secondly, I shall determine its function within the narrative world of Isaiah 36–37; thirdly, I shall assess the proverb's significance for the reader's assessment of Hezekiah in Isaiah; fourthly, I shall identify two additional Isaianic texts in which childbirth imagery functions to evoke trust in God's strength and readiness to deliver.

Hezekiah's Proverb

A City Imperiled

Moving from Isa. 35.10 to 36.1, sequential readers of Isaiah's vision experience yet another sudden shift in tone.[2] A poetic description of

---

*   This essay is both an abridged (at some points) and an expanded (at other points) version of Chapter 6 in my *Isaiah's Vision and The Family of God* (Darr 1994) entitled 'No Strength to Deliver: Bringing to Birth in the Book of Isaiah'.

1.   Isaiah 36–39 also appears, with some variation, in 2 Kgs 18.13–20.19. The majority view about the original locus of these materials, expressed already by Gesenius (1821: 22, 932), holds that Isa. 36–39 was copied from Kings. This judgment has been challenged, however, by Smelik (1986: 70-76; 1992) and Seitz (1991).

2.   I set out a reader-oriented method for interpreting Isaiah and explain the importance of identifying the critic's reader in Chapter 1 of *Isaiah's Vision and the*

Yahweh's redeemed joyfully marching upon a sacred thoroughfare gives way to a prose account of Sennacherib's ferocious march against the fortified cities of Judah.[3]

According to Isa. 36.2, Sennacherib sent his Rabshakeh to Jerusalem with a large force to quell the city. In the hearing of Jerusalem's inhabitants, the Rabshakeh shouted demoralizing messages at Hezekiah's representatives. His words ridiculed Hezekiah's ostensible *trust* in Egyptian assistance, and ultimately in Yahweh, and stressed God's *inability* to save the city (Isa. 36.4-20).

Learning of the Rabshakeh's message, Hezekiah tore his clothes, donned sackcloth and went to the temple. But he also sent a small group of influential government and religious leaders to Isaiah with a message. The communication began with a straightforward assessment of the disastrous circumstances: 'Thus says Hezekiah', his envoys told the prophet, '"This day is a day of distress, of chastisement, and of contempt"' (37.3a). But this literal statement was followed by a traditional saying, or proverb: 'Babes are positioned for birth, but there is no strength to deliver' (v. 3b; author's trans.). 'Perhaps', Hezekiah's message continued,

---

Family of God (Darr 1994), 'Reading Isaian Metaphors'. My method describes textual meaning as the result of the interaction between text, reader and the extra-textual repertoire the sequential reader brings to the reading process. For the purposes of this essay, my reader is part of post-exilic Israel's cognoscenti, a scribe or religious leader and educator enjoying such legal rights and social standing as were possible under Persian rule at the beginning of the fourth century BCE (I place my reader at 400 BCE for at least two reasons: first, this is a likely, although not universally-accepted, date by which to posit Isaiah's existence in its final form. Second, it enables us to avoid wrestling with Hellenism's considerable influence upon Israel's long-lived conventional ideas regarding women and children. See Frymer-Kensky 1992: 203-12). Culturally literate and fully at home within his society, he knows—or at least thinks he knows—basic facts (historical, political, geographical, religious, ethnic) and conventions (social, cultural, literary etc.) extant to Israel and its broader environs. Although this is his first reading of Isaiah, he knows other of Israel's religious texts, including the Torah of Moses, certain prophetic collections, psalms and so on. He also knows the literary 'classics' of his larger culture. For the vast majority of his contemporaries, of course, access to Isaiah consists essentially of hearing brief excerpts read aloud in contexts of worship; such a scenario appears in Lk. 4.16-20. But our reader, a minority in his society, enjoys the opportunity, access, expertise and time to read and interpret the unfolding Isaiah scroll on other than just a pericope by pericope basis.

3. Sennacherib's reasons for attacking the cities of Judah are not mentioned in the abrupt opening verses of this Isaianic prose account.

'the Lord your God will take note of the words of the Rabshakeh, whom his master the king of Assyria has sent to blaspheme the living God, and will mete out judgment for the words that the Lord your God has heard—if you will offer up prayer for the surviving remnant' (v. 4; *Tanakh*). Here, at the very end of his message, Hezekiah has finally revealed its purpose. He wishes the prophet to offer an intercessory prayer to Yahweh on behalf of Jerusalem and its populace, the 'surviving remnant' among the Judean cities attacked by Assyria's army.

Yahweh's response through the prophet was immediate, the words comforting and predictive of future deliverance (Isa. 37.5-7):

> Isaiah said to them, 'Say to your master, "Thus says the Lord: 'Do not be afraid because of the words that you have heard, with which the servants of the king of Assyria have reviled me. I myself will put a spirit in him, so that he shall hear a rumor, and return to his own land; I will cause him to fall by the sword in his own land.'"'

Identifying Hezekiah's Proverb

Hezekiah's words in v. 3b are not explicitly identified as a *māšāl*.[4] They are not introduced by a formula such as 'and therefore they say'.[5] Nevertheless, O. Eissfeldt included Isa. 37.3b among passages outside Israel's wisdom literature that 'sound like proverbs' (1913: 43), and many commentators agree that v. 3b is a folk saying.[6] This classification is suggested by the phrase's brevity (just seven words in Hebrew) and by its nicely-crafted binary structure.[7] The first colon, introduced by *kî*, sets out an event drawn from everyday human experience:

---

4. Compare 1 Sam. 10.12; Ezek. 12.22. The noun *māšāl* refers to proverbs, but also to parables, similitudes and various types of poems.

5. Compare Gen. 10.9 and 1 Sam. 24.13 (ET 14).

6. When I use the word 'folk', I intend that it be construed according to Dundes's definition (1977: 22):

> The term 'folk' can refer to *any group of people whatsoever* who share at least one common factor. It does not matter what the linking factor is—it could be a common occupation, language, or religion—but what is important is that a group formed for whatever reason will have some traditions which it calls its own... A member of the group may not know all other members, but he will probably know the common core of traditions belonging to the group, traditions which help the group have a sense of group identity. With this flexible definition of folk, a group could be as large as a nation or as small as a family.

7. Of course, not all short utterances are proverbs, and not all proverbs are terse. By the same token, many proverbs exhibit formal features of everyday prose.

kî	*bāʾû*	*bānîm*	*ʿad mašbēr*
(because)	have come	babes	to the birthing
		(lit.	position (lit.
		'sons')	'breaking')

But a second colon supplies additional, alarming information about this situation:

wᵉkōaḥ	*ʿayin*	*lᵉlēdâ*
but strength	there is not	to deliver

Combined, these two halves become the briefest of narratives, producing the proverb's message.[8]

Crucial for recognizing Hezekiah's proverb *qua* proverb, however, is its out-of-context subject matter. In some other literary context, v. 3b could be construed literally as the aggrieved king's dramatic and somewhat stylized report of childbirth complications in the royal harem. Given the situation identified in preceding verses, however, the audience (both Isaiah and our reader) will almost certainly recognize that a literal interpretation of the statement is highly improbable, if not impossible, and identify it as a metaphorical proverb.[9]

The Social Function of Proverbs

Determining how proverbs functioned in ancient Israelite society is no easy task. The majority of biblical sayings appear grouped in collections, and collections of proverbs tell us nothing about how a given saying could be employed in an actual social exchange. Such collections, many of which are decidedly didactic in character, likely were used to teach Israel's youth how to master life. However, educational situations, whatever their forms in ancient Israel, were already secondary settings for proverbs.

Proverbs lodged in narrative accounts of social interactions can shed light on Israel's proverb usage, but again, problems abound. Direct observation of ancient proverb performances is impossible, of course; we have recourse only to the relevant texts of Israel and its neighbors. We cannot

---

8. 'Narrativity', writes Williams, 'is the telling of a process of acts, events, or experiences. It would obviously not be present except in very compact form in proverbs, which make up a genre lying to the contrary extreme of narrative forms. But the use of tightly controlled narrative phrases empowers many of the proverbs' (1987: 273-74).

9. Although the proverb is metaphorical in its application to the situation, it contains no internal metaphors.

be certain that biblical narratives depict proverb performances accurately, although C. Fontaine (1982: 67) rightly concludes that literary portrayals must have borne some resemblance to actual proverb usage since otherwise, original audiences could not have understood the texts. Even if we assume that the events related in Isaiah 36–37 actually transpired, and that Hezekiah spoke precisely those words recorded in Isa. 37.3b, we cannot know whether he (or the author) was quoting a well-known saying, or creating one on the spot.[10] Clearly, however, he expected Isaiah (and the author expected the reader) to understand the proverb and its relationship to the crisis at hand (assisted, perhaps, by the more straightforward sentence in v. 3a and the immediately preceding *kî*).[11] Finally, written documents inevitably omit information accessible to modern anthropologists doing field work. We cannot recover vocal inflection or any facial expressions and gestures that accompanied Hezekiah's words. Neither do we know whether the strategic use of proverbs was regarded as a skill instilled in Israel and Judah's future monarchs as part of their necessary equipment for ruling. Was the ability to employ proverbs to define situations and commend behaviors prized in Israel's kings?[12]

Despite these obstacles, our narrative provides enough contextual information to permit analysis of the proverb performance in Isaiah 37, tentative though our conclusions must be. In 'Proverbs: A Social Use of Metaphor' (1969: 143-61), P. Seitel sets out a model for 'viewing proverbs as the strategic social use of metaphor; that is to say, the manifestation in traditional, artistic and relatively short form of metaphorical

10. In what follows, I am interpreting Hezekiah's proverb within its narrative world and canonical context. I cannot know whether events recorded in Isa. 36–37 actually occurred. Smelik (1986: 1992) argues that Isa. 36–37 has virtually no relationship to the actual historical events of 701 BCE.

11. If we do not ascribe the actual proverb performance to the historical Hezekiah, then we can at least say that the author expected his audience to understand the proverb's relationship to events within the narrative world of Isa. 36–37.

12. The book of Proverbs is attributed to King Solomon (1.1), the Israelite king who was as renowned for his wisdom as he was for his harem. Prov. 25.1 speaks of 'the men of King Hezekiah of Judah' who copied Solomon's proverbs. The root underlying *māšāl, mšl*, appears in two Hebrew verbs—'to be like' and 'to rule'. Might an ancient audience have construed David's proverb performance during his confrontation with Saul (1 Sam. 24.13) as one demonstration of his own worthiness for kingship?

reasoning used in an interactional context to serve certain purposes'.[13] Seitel's heuristic model helps us to discover toward what end this metaphorical proverb appears in Hezekiah's message to Isaiah.

A Model for Proverb Analysis
When a proverb is uttered, Seitel explains, three separate situations or domains are involved: the one present in the proverb itself when it is understood *literally*; the domain to which the proverb is applied; and the one in which the proverb is actually spoken. The following diagram illustrates these three domains:[14]

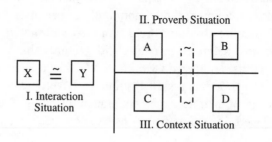

According to this model, a proverb speaker (X) asserts to the intended hearer (Y) in an *interaction situation* that the relationship obtaining between persons or entities (A and B) in the *proverb situation* is analogous to the relationship between persons or entities (C and D) in the *context situation* (1977: 77). The broken lines connecting the proverb and context situations signify the analogous relationship claimed by the speaker to exist between these two domains.

Hezekiah's proverb situation, understood literally, sketches the following scenario: labour has progressed to the point that the time for birth is at hand, but the mothers-to-be, utterly exhausted by painful and protracted travail, lack the strength to push out their babies. These women are not explicitly mentioned in Hezekiah's proverb, of course, but they are implicitly present. (Perhaps the proverb describes the

13. See also Seitel 1972; 1977. Only after reading his work and discerning its usefulness for analyzing Isa. 37.3b did I discover that Fontaine also has adopted his model for analyzing proverb performances.
14. This diagram appears in a version of Seitel's 1969 article as reprinted in *Folklore Genres* (129).

dilemma of a sole woman carrying two or more babies.)[15]

The context situation for Hezekiah's proverb is the already-identified Assyrian threat against Jerusalem. Its interaction situation, however, is more difficult to detail. In our text, Hezekiah (X) utters the proverb and the prophet Isaiah is its intended hearer (Y).[16] The symbol linking X and Y represents the relationship between speaker and hearer including gender, age and social status (Seitel 1969: 147-48). Although Isaiah's precise age in 701 is unknown, he was certainly the elder of the two males.[17] One would suppose that as king of Judah, Hezekiah's status and concomitant authority were second to none among his subjects, be they younger or older. But the book of Isaiah testifies to the prophet's willingness to chastise Judah's monarchs, give them unpopular advice and even condemn their actions (see, for example, his confrontation with King Ahaz in Isa. 7). Over against the status and authority of the crown, therefore, readers must weigh the status and authority of the prophet claiming to speak for God.

Having described these three domains, we next attend to what Seitel calls 'correlation'; that is, the way in which the speaker 'correlates a term in the proverb situation with an entity in the context situation and also (possibly) with a person in the interaction situation' (1977: 78). Seitel borrows grammatical categories, speaking of *first*, *second* and *third person* correlation:

> In a proverb in which only one term in the proverb situation can be correlated with a person in the context situation (henceforth, a 'single correlation proverb'), these possibilities exist: the person who is correlated with a term in the proverb situation may be the speaker, or the hearer, or someone else—who may be absent or present but not the addressee. If the

15. Note also the plurals in the well-known proverb shared by Jeremiah (31.29) and Ezekiel (18.2), 'parents have eaten sour grapes and children's teeth are blunted'.

16. The message is actually delivered by envoys: Eliakim, who oversees the palace; Shebna, the scribe (perhaps the same Shebna who earlier received a solid rebuke from Isaiah [22.15-19]); and an unspecified number of senior priests. Their use of the messenger formula, 'Thus says Hezekiah', however, purportedly insures that Hezekiah's words are repeated accurately. Note that the messenger formula is employed by Isaiah to convey Yahweh's response in v. 6.

17. According to 2 Kgs 18.2, Hezekiah was twenty-five years old when he came to the throne *ca.* 715 BCE. He was, therefore, approximately thirty-nine years of age when the Assyrian forces marched against Jerusalem. According to Isa. 6.1, however, Isaiah's temple vision occurred already in 742, approximately two years before Hezekiah's birth in 740 BCE.

speaker correlates himself with the term in the proverb situation, I call this a 'first person correlation'. If the *addressee* is correlated with a term in the proverb situation, I call this a 'second person correlation'. If *someone other* than the speaker or the addressee is correlated with a term in the proverb situation, I call this 'third person correlation' (1977: 78; Seitel's italics).

The Function of Hezekiah's Proverb Performance in Isaiah 36–37

How does Hezekiah correlate entities in the proverb and context situations? The answer to this question is important, for, as Seitel demonstrates, the same proverb, correlated in different ways, can have various meanings and perform quite diverse social functions. What might be the meaning and purpose of v. 3b, for example, if Hezekiah were making a third-person correlation in which Yahweh and members of the divine council (see Isa. 6.1-7) were identified with helpless females? In light of the Rabshakeh's accusation that Judah's deity is powerless to save Jerusalem, Hezekiah's proverb could be construed as a lamentable admission that Yahweh is indeed unable to rescue the city's inhabitants. Or imagine that Hezekiah employed the proverb in a joyous communication to Isaiah about Judah's victory over a Moabite city. In such a situation, Hezekiah might intend a third-person correlation between Moabite deities and powerless women; and his strategy of proverb usage would be to mock and belittle foreign gods. In its present context, however, neither of these hypothetical third-person correlations pertains. Hezekiah is concerned with Jerusalem's plight, not with some other nation's troubles. Moreover, the king does not believe Yahweh incapable of delivering Jerusalem, as his request that Isaiah pray to God demonstrates.

One could be content simply to say that the correlation is as follows: just as in the proverb situation there is no strength to give birth, so in the context situation there is no strength to repel Assyria.[18] This reading is accurate in the sense that Hezekiah's proverb invites Isaiah (and the reader) to perceive the military crisis through the 'lens' of childbirth imagery. We should not let matters rest there, however, for questions immediately arise: Why did the king (or at least the author of this narrative) select a proverb about parturition complications when numerous

18. So Fontaine (1982: 252). In terms of Seitel's model, the relationship would be as follows: in the proverb situation, A = babes positioned for birth, while B = no strength to deliver. Analogously, in the context situation C = the need to repel Assyria, while D = lack of strength to do so.

other options surely existed? What was it about endangered women and their unbirthed babies that best captured Jerusalem's plight? And if lack of strength is strategic, then whose powerlessness did Hezekiah emphasize?

It is also possible, however, that instead of correlating crisis to crisis, Hezekiah's proverb correlates entities *within* the respective crisis situations. Imagine, for example, that this is a single correlation saying in which only one entity in the proverb situation is identified with an entity in the context situation; and the king is making a first-person plural correlation. In that case, two options emerge. On the one hand, Hezekiah could be correlating himself and his subjects with the *women* who are incapable of delivering their infants.[19] So correlated, his proverb could be understood to emphasize the inability of Jerusalem's inhabitants to rescue themselves from a desperate situation.[20] On the other hand, he could be identifying himself and his subjects with the unborn *babes* ('we are trapped and in danger of death').[21]

If Hezekiah's saying is a dual correlation proverb in which *two* entities in the proverb situation are being identified with entities in the context situation (see Seitel 1969: 150), however, then he might be understood to correlate Jerusalem's inhabitants with the endangered babies (a third-person plural correlation) and himself, along with his advisors, with the helpless women (a first-person plural correlation).[22]

---

19. True, the city's inhabitants are not actually present in the interaction situation. According to Seitel's definition, their identification with an entity in the proverb situation would be an example of third-person correlation. But because Hezekiah is king, he can speak not only for himself, but also for his subjects.

20. Although Isaiah also is among the city's inhabitants, Hezekiah both logistically (he *sends* messengers to Isaiah, rather than summoning the prophet to join him) and rhetorically distances Isaiah from himself through the proverb performance itself and the words following it: 'Perhaps the Lord your God will take note of the words of the Rabshakeh...and will mete out judgment for the words that the Lord *your God* has heard—if you will offer up prayer for the *surviving remnant*' (37.4; emphasis mine). Roberts has noted a similarly strategic use of pronouns in Isaiah's exchange with Ahaz in Isa. 7 (1985: 197).

21. Of course, a proverb cannot be paraphrased without loss of content and impact. My attempts to paraphrase the meaning of Hezekiah's proverb in its various correlations are strictly for purposes of clarification.

22. Note that when Isaiah criticizes Judah's participation in the rebellion, he does not single out Hezekiah; rather, he rebukes Jerusalem's leaders as a group. See, for example, Isa. 30.1 ('Oh, disloyal sons!') and 31.1 ('Ha! Those who go down to Egypt for help...').

The question of correlation cannot be resolved until we have first delved more deeply into the proverb and interaction situations as they would have been understood *within Hezekiah's culture*. This saying is not, after all, a product of our own social and temporal context; and we dare not blithely assume that the biblical Israelites would have perceived, for example, the proverb situation, as we do or that it would have triggered for them the same intellectual, imaginative and emotive responses.[23]

The Proverb Situation: Ancient Near Eastern References to an Inability to Bring to Birth

Archaeologists have recovered ancient Near Eastern texts referring, like Hezekiah's proverb, to an inability to bring to birth. A Hittite myth, for example, describes the ruinous results of the god Telepinus's angry abandonment of the land: 'So grain (and) spelt thrive no longer. So cattle, sheep and man no longer (15) breed. And even those with young cannot bring them forth' (Goetze 1969: 126). Here appears the same scenario encapsulated in Isa. 37.3b, although Hezekiah's saying is a metaphorical proverb, while the Hittite myth purports to be a literal depiction of barrenness, famine and its consequent weakness, and parturition difficulties following Telepinus's departure.

Even more interesting for our purposes is a Middle Assyrian medical text perhaps dating from the time of Tiglath-pileser I (*ca.* 1100 BCE; Lambert 1976: 28-39). This text combines four medical prescriptions for the treatment of colic in pregnant women (lines 1-31) with two incantations on behalf of females experiencing difficulty in childbirth (lines 33-50, 51-62). The second incantation was probably recited as women in labour were anointed with oil and sprinkled with amniotic fluid in hopes of insuring imminent, normal deliveries (line 62). The first incantation reads as follows:

> (33) The woman in childbirth has pangs at delivery,
> (34) At delivery she has pangs, the babe is stuck fast,
> (35) The babe is stuck fast. The bolt is secure—to bring life to an end,
> (36) The door is made fast—against the suckling kid...

---

23. Naturally, we cannot suppose that everyone in any culture, ancient or modern, would respond to the proverb in exactly the same way. A woman who had been through the experience described or a person who had witnessed (or heard) a close relative in such a situation would likely react differently than someone lacking experience in such matters.

(37) The mother is enveloped in the dust of death.

(38) Like a chariot she is enveloped in the dust of battle,

(39) Like a plough she is enveloped in the dust of the woods,

(40) Like a warrior in the fray, she is cast down in her blood.

(41) Her eyes are diminished, she cannot see; her lips are covered,

(42) She cannot open (them)* the destiny of death and destinies* her eyes are dim,[24]

(43)...ever fears; her ears cannot hear.

(44) Her breast is not... her locks are scattered,

(45) She wears no veil and has no shame.

(46) Be present and... merciful Marduk.

(47) 'Now is the battle on, I am surrounded! Reach me!'

(48) Bring forth that sealed-up one, a creation of the gods,

(49) A creation of man. Let him come out to see the light.

(50) Enenuru, an incantation for a woman in childbirth (cited in Lambert 1976: 32).

In discussing this text, Lambert identifies traditional literary motifs and phrases found not only here, but also in other Sumerian and Akkadian texts of the same or related types. This first incantation, he argues, has largely been cobbled together from pre-existing blocks of literary material, although certain of its features—for example, the metaphorical references to 'bolt' and 'door'—are not otherwise attested in this partic-ular sequence (but see Lambert 1976: 35). In his view, lines 37-40 have no inherent connection to labour and delivery. Lines 41-43 also lack a specific link with birth pangs and do not appear in other extant birth incantations. Lines 44-45 are even less related to their present context; they apparently describe a 'shameless woman...breasts bare (?), hair loose and no veil' (1976: 36). The corrupt line 46, an appeal to a deity for help, is a common element in such incantations. Line 47 has a coun-terpart in another Akkadian inscription; in this context, Lambert surmises, it quotes the unborn babe's cry for help. Finally, a variation of lines 48-49 appears in the same Akkadian inscription also containing line 47.

Comparative analysis, Lambert concludes, illustrates 'the way in which incantations were being built up from literary elements and motifs in the period 1500–500 BC' (1976: 37). He undoubtedly is correct; yet more should be said about this text in its final form, whatever the prehistory of its parts. Lines 37-40 could, it is true, describe a woman whose situa-tion was other than the inability to achieve parturition. In its present

---

24. Lambert marks with an asterisk those portions of the text where he cannot discern the flow of meaning.

context, however, it is certainly a moving description of the travailing woman's plight. Moreover, that she should be likened to a fallen warrior is an ironic reversal of numerous extrabiblical and biblical texts in which warriors are described pejoratively either as becoming women (e.g. Jer. 50.37; Nah. 3.13) or as acting like women, including women in travail (e.g. Jer. 49.22; see Hillers 1964: 66-68).

References to a woman's diminished senses, disheveled appearance and lack of shame despite the absence of proper attire, are not inappropriate to a description of prolonged and difficult childbirth, although they could make sense within other literary contexts as well. Particularly poignant, however, is the baby's cry: 'Now is the battle on, I am surrounded! Reach me!' Lambert finds the military imagery distasteful. The line, he remarks, 'seems to be intended as the cry for help from the babe yet in the womb, whose immaturity ill agrees with the military metaphor' (1976: 36). But the infant's cry is not just an example of military imagery. It is siege imagery ('I am surrounded! Reach me!'); and the image of an army or city hemmed in and unable to escape is both powerful and apt for a baby trapped in the birth canal of the nurturing body that suddenly threatens 'to bring life to an end'. Finally, the climactic lines 48-49 are a stirring challenge—to the deity, of course, but also to the exhausted woman—to 'bring forth that sealed-up one'.

This investigation of references to childbirth complications in Israel's ancient Near Eastern world has illumined our understanding of Isa. 37.3b. Should problems render a mother incapable of expelling her baby, both were in danger of dying. The Telepinus myth linked the inability to bring to birth with the weakness consequent upon famine and brought on by divine anger and abandonment. Hittite and Akkadian midwives sought, through rituals and prayers describing their patients' suffering, to move the deities to pity and intervention on behalf of mother and child. Clearly, the inability to achieve parturition was a religious, as well as a physical crisis within the ancient Near Eastern world.

Having recovered, at least in part, ancient Near Eastern associations with the inability to achieve parturition, I take up the question of the strategy motivating Hezekiah's proverb performance.

Hezekiah's Strategic Proverb Performance
Earlier in this essay, we identified four possible correlations for Hezekiah's proverb. First, his saying could be understood to suggest that lacking strength to give birth is analogous to lacking strength to repel

Assyria. Such an analogy is better understood in light of my analyses of both literal and figurative references to childbirth, for we have gained a better sense of how a proverb about parturition complications might seem especially appropriate to the military crisis of an impending siege.

Alternatively, Hezekiah's proverb could be understood to correlate entities *within* the respective crisis situations. In that case, the following options seem possible: On one hand, his saying could be viewed as a single correlation proverb in which Hezekiah identified himself and his subjects either with the helpless women (as in the Telepinus myth; i.e., 'we are powerless to change our desperate situation') or with their unborn babes (as in the Middle Assyrian medical text; i.e., 'we are trapped and in danger of death'). On the other hand, it could be construed as a dual correlation proverb in which Hezekiah identified Jerusalem's inhabitants with trapped infants and identified himself, along with his advisors, with helpless women (i.e., 'our babes are stuck fast and we are unable to deliver them').

If one chooses to view Isa. 37.3b as a single correlation proverb, its import is not greatly altered regardless of which correlation option is chosen. Because the lives of both mother and child were threatened by the inability to bring to birth, the proverb's point in either case would be that both Hezekiah and his subjects face imminent death and cannot save themselves.[25]

But what of the possibility that Hezekiah's saying is a dual correlation proverb wherein the king identifies Jerusalem's inhabitants with endangered infants ('we are trapped and in danger of death'), and himself, along with his advisors, with helpless women ('our babes are stuck fast and we are unable to deliver them')? Is this option a more compelling way for readers to understand Hezekiah's proverb *within its larger Isaianic context*? Answering this question first requires that the proverb's significance for our reader's assessment of Hezekiah, based upon a sequential reading up to and including Isa. 37.3b, be ascertained.

---

25. One might argue on the basis of a text like Gen. 35.17 (in which the dying Rachel is consoled by her midwife with the words, 'Have no fear, for it is another boy for you') that a correlation with the unborn infants would have the greatest rhetorical effect, since the prospect of losing sons would be regarded as the greater tragedy. If we choose to view the saying as a single correlation proverb, however, we must finally concede that either correlation is possible.

The Significance of Hezekiah's Proverb for the Reader's Assessment
of Hezekiah in The Book of Isaiah

The Interaction Situation of Hezekiah's Proverb
Thus far, I have focussed upon understanding Hezekiah's *proverb situa-*
tion within ancient Israel's broader cultural context, and have described
the *context situation* of Hezekiah's proverb as depicted within the
narrative world of Isaiah 36–37. In order finally to discern the correlation
and function of Isa. 37.3b, however, the proverb's *interaction situation*
must also be explored—in particular, the relationship between speaker
and intended hearer—as construed by competent, sequential readers of
Isaiah's vision to that point. What, on the basis of material read thus far,
will they surmise about the nature of Hezekiah's and Isaiah's
relationship prior to the king's communiqué in Isa. 37.3-4? Will they
perceive in Hezekiah's message an attempt to alter that relationship in
some way? Indeed, beyond the issue of relations between these two
men, does Hezekiah's proverb performance seek to alter his relationship
with the deity he refers to twice in a single half-verse as 'Yahweh, *your*
God' (37.4a)?

These questions lead us into highly-contested terrain. Much has been
written about the relationship between Hezekiah and the prophet Isaiah,
and about the former's depiction within the book of Isaiah (not to
mention his assessment by the Deuteronomistic Historians in 2 Kings).
Scholars undertaking such investigations emerge with a variety of (often
contradictory) answers.[26] To my knowledge, however, such studies have
neglected Hezekiah's proverb and so have overlooked its import both
for the immediate scenario recounted in chs. 36–37(38), and for our
reader's broader assessment of Hezekiah's portrayal in the book of
Isaiah.[27]

For my purposes, two questions are relevant: (1) do sequentially prior
Isaianic texts assist readers who, arriving at Isa. 37.3-4, seek to ascertain

26. For a survey of major hypotheses advanced since Gesenius, see Seitz 1991:
47-118.

27. In his recent, extensive study of Isa. 36–37, for example, Seitz refers only
briefly to Hezekiah's message to Isaiah in Isa. 37.3-4. Of the proverb's content he
says nothing at all. Seitz is at pains to determine how Hezekiah is presented in the
book of Isaiah, yet so great is his interest in Hezekiah's prayer (37.16-20) that he
hurries past the king's initial communiqué (1991: 47-118). We shall return to the
significance of this omission below.

the status of the relationship between Hezekiah and Isaiah in the midst of Sennacherib's threat against Jerusalem?;[28] and (2) how will readers of Isaiah 36–37 interpret the Rabshakeh's initial message (Isa. 36.4-10), given what they have learned from preceding texts in the book of Isaiah, from the rhetorical strategies evident in the message itself, and in light of the reference in Isa. 37.9 to King Tirhakah's possible appearance on the scene?

Hezekiah's Rebellion?

For many scholars, certain Isaianic texts not in proximity to our passage preserve Isaiah's (and, *mutatis mutandis*, God's) negative response to Hezekiah's decision to join with other Assyrian vassals in rebellion against their overlord—a decision contrary to the prophet's counsel. J. Bright claimed, for example, that, 'In spite of the earnest warnings of Isaiah, who branded the whole thing folly and rebellion against YHWH, Hezekiah joined in and sent envoys to Egypt to negotiate a treaty (cf. Isa. 30.1-7; 31.1-3). In fact, he became a ringleader in the revolt' (1981: 285). R. Clements concurs: 'concerning Isaiah's attitude to Hezekiah's joining the coalition which rebelled against Assyria in 705, the answer is clear and definitive. Isaiah condemned it firmly and decisively, and foretold that it would lead to ruination' (1980a: 29). For F. Gonçalves (1986: 264), Hezekiah's policy showed him to be no better than Ahaz, his predecessor: 'In the same way that Ahaz relied on Assyria to remove the Syro-Ephraimite danger, Hezekiah relied on Egypt' (translated by Seitz 1991: 7).

These and similar observations rest upon two assumptions. The first is that the tools of modern critical biblical scholarship enable us to date various texts within chs. 1–35 to the time of Hezekiah and, more precisely, to periods preceding, during and immediately after the Assyrian threat against Jerusalem in 701 BCE, even when such texts are not explicitly linked to those periods. This assumption may, in a number of cases, be borne out to the satisfaction of many scholars. We should remember, however, that interpreting a text like Isa. 31.1-3 against a specific historical background (the formation of international alliances as a means of escaping Assyrian hegemony) and with a specific question in

---

28. Whatever one's conclusions regarding the relationship between Isa. 36–39 and 2 Kgs 18.13–20.19, or between Sennacherib's Annals and 2 Kgs 18.14(13)-16, the Isaiah narratives can legitimately be read and interpreted in their canonical form within their Isaianic context.

mind (what can this text tell us about Isaiah's attitude toward Hezekiah's decision to join the rebellions of 705–701 BCE?) is a very specialized enterprise requiring the critic's import of information not present in the texts themselves. Given that Hezekiah's name first appears in the scroll's superscription (Isa. 1.1), but does not reappear until the announcement of Sennacherib's attack against the cities of Judah 'in the fourteenth year of King Hezekiah' (Isa. 36.1), it is by no means certain that our reader would have understood the words of Isa. 31.1-3, for example, as an address to Judah's political leadership in the specific context of the late eighth-century crisis depicted in Isaiah 36–37.

Indeed, it is not even certain that modern *critics* would interpret Isa. 30.1-7 and 31.1-3 against the background of 'Hezekiah's rebellion' were it not for their second assumption; namely, that Isaiah 36–37 must be interpreted in conjunction with information supplied by other biblical and also extrabiblical texts. The narrative abruptly begun in Isa. 36.1 contains no accounts of foreign alliances, rebellion against Assyria or the paying of tribute. It likewise contains no explicit notice of rebuke on Isaiah's part. It simply informs us of Sennacherib's destructive campaign against Judah's cities. Outside Isaiah, however, we read in 2 Kgs 18.7b that Hezekiah 'rebelled against the king of Assyria and would not serve him'. We learn further that Hezekiah was forced to pay tribute to Sennacherib (18.14-16). The essential historical accuracy of this account is confirmed, many scholars believe, by a portion of Sennacherib's annals:

> As to Hezekiah, the Jew... I laid siege to 46 of his strong cities, walled forts and to the countless small villages in their vicinity... Himself I made a prisoner in Jerusalem, his royal residence, like a bird in a cage... Hezekiah himself...did send me, later, to Nineveh, my lordly city, together with 30 talents of gold, 800 talents of silver, precious stones, antimony, large cuts of red stone, couches (inlaid) with ivory, *nîmedu*-chairs (inlaid) with ivory, elephant-hides, ebony-wood, boxwood (and) all kinds of valuable treasures, his (own) daughters, concubines, male and female musicians...(Oppenheim 1969: 288).

These two texts, although different in significant details, nonetheless agree that Hezekiah was forced to pay tribute to his Assyrian adversary. Neither refers to a Judean alliance with Egypt. But if specialists supply that piece of information from the aforementioned oracles appearing earlier in Proto-Isaiah (e.g. 1.4-8; 22.1-4; 29.1-4; 31.1-3) and add a bit of reconstructed ancient Near Eastern history, the following scenario becomes the background for interpreting Isaiah 36–37: when Assyria's King Sargon II (721–705) died, the king of Babylon, Marduk-apal-iddina, incited Assyria's vassals to revolt; and despite the prophet Isaiah's vehement protests, Hezekiah decided to join his neighbors' rebellion. Assyria's new ruler, Sennacherib, responded with a punitive campaign, subduing centers of revolt in Phoenicia, Philistia and a number of Judean cities. Jerusalem escaped destruction, but only after Hezekiah paid significant tribute.

Efforts to reconstruct the events of 705–701 BCE are certainly worthwhile, as are attempts to identify those processes by which 2 Kgs 18.13–19.37 and Isaiah 36–37 attained their final forms. Also important, however, is the question of how our sequential reader of Isaiah's vision construed chs. 36–37(38) in their *Isaianic* context, without recourse to parallel narratives in other bodies of literature. Are the words and actions of Hezekiah in Isaiah 36–37, including his proverb performance, better (or at least differently) understood if they are read in light of prior Isaianic material, including Sennacherib's first message to Hezekiah via his Rabshakeh?

These questions are raised afresh by C. Seitz in his provocative study, *Zion's Final Destiny* (1991). They are relevant to his larger arguments about the original locus of the Hezekiah-Isaiah narratives (for Seitz, their Isaiah setting is primary) and about the role of those narratives in the ongoing growth of the Isaiah scroll.[29] Seitz's judgments concerning the pertinence of sequentially prior texts for assessing Hezekiah in Isaiah 36–39 are germane to our topic, as is his understanding of the meaning and function of the Rabshakeh's initial speech. Is Seitz correct when he concludes, 1) that the depiction of Hezekiah in Isaiah 36–37 is thoroughly positive, and 2) that this positive presentation of Hezekiah is congruent with preceding portions of the scroll? Because readers arrive at Isa. 36.1 already knowing the contents of chs. 1–35, the second question must be addressed first.

Hezekiah and the Prophecies of Isaiah

Seitz refuses to interpret Isaiah 36–37 in light of a critically-reconstructed Judean rebellion bolstered by Egyptian promises of military assistance. True, Isaiah consistently condemns foreign alliances (Isa. 10.20; 18.1-7;

---

29. For Seitz, the complex and ambiguous nature of Zion theology in pre-exilic Isaianic poetry and prose (including Isa. 36–38) played a key part in Isaiah's extensive growth during the years following Jerusalem's destruction in 587 BCE.

22.3; 28.11-13; 30.1-7, 16; 31.1) as indicators of inadequate faith in Yahweh (Isa. 1.4; 7.9; 22.11; 30.8-14; 31.1-3); and 'the notion of reliance on Egypt is fairly prevalent in Isaiah's oracles' (Seitz 1991: 73). Nevertheless, Hezekiah himself is nowhere explicitly charged with forging foreign alliances in Isaiah 1–35. In chs. 28–33, for example, various leaders are accused of political intrigues; but the noun *melek* appears only in Isaiah 32.1, a text describing the reign of a righteous king.[30]

Like Seitz, I urge caution in assessing the pertinence of passages within Isaiah 1–35 for our reader's evaluation of Hezekiah, and of his relationship with Isaiah at the time of his proverb performance. With the exception of Isa. 1.1, Hezekiah is not named explicitly until 36.1; and although deprecatory oracles are hurled at various groups in 28–33, the king is not singled out directly for criticism. Against Seitz, however, I argue that neither a refusal to read Isaiah 36–37 through the lens of a reconstructed rebellion by Hezekiah, nor the absence of *explicit* references to him from 1.2 until 36.1, rules out the possibility that certain oracles in chs. 1–35 could influence the reader's understanding of his proverb's *interaction situation*. The relevance of sequentially prior oracles for determining how Hezekiah is assessed in chs. 36–37 does not turn on the presence of an explicit, critical word about the king in Isaiah 1–35, but rather on whether the reader comes to believe that *Hezekiah has participated, whether directly or indirectly, in acts consistently condemned by the prophet in sequentially prior texts*. Isaiah 1.4-8; 22.1-4; 29.1-4; and 30.1-3 may not be addressed specifically to Hezekiah. Readers may not even associate them with precisely those events

---

30. Seitz identifes Hezekiah with the king who rules in righteousness (1991: 80). Clements follows Barth in identifying 32.1ff. as part of a Josianic redaction of Isaiah, and the king of 32.1 as an idealized portrayal of Josiah (1980b: 259-60). In his assessment of chs. 28–33, Seitz emphasizes the culpability of various officials criticized there, all the while maintaining that Hezekiah receives no such rebuke. But Isa. 32 may contain an implicit criticism of kings who allow their officials to behave unjustly, for it begins with the affirmation that a righteous king's rule goes hand-in-hand with a just governance by his administrators. Sweeney suggests in a private communication that we should not be surprised that explicit condemnations of the king are hard to come by in the book of Isaiah (with the exception of Isa. 7, a narrative which may, Sweeney suggests, have been composed on the basis of chs. 36–37). Since Isaiah served in proximity to the royal court (and presumably at the pleasure of the king), his ability explicitly to criticize the monarch himself may well have been limited.

surrounding the crisis in 701 BCE. But their message is clear: they speak, in Seitz's own words (1991: 78), of 'misplaced trust and its consequences', of the folly of looking to any save Yahweh for security in the midst of calamity.

Isa. 36.1 says nothing about the formation of foreign alliances or rebellion against Assyria. But if the narrative introduction is silent on such issues, the Rabshakeh is not. We must ask, therefore, how readers arriving at the Rabshakeh's first speech understand his claim that Hezekiah is '...relying on Egypt, that splintered rod of a staff, which enters and punctures the palm of anyone who leans on it' (36.6; *Tanakh*).

The Rabshakeh's Speech

Will readers believe the Rabshakeh's charge that Hezekiah has resorted to Egyptian aid and judge him negatively on the basis of condemnations expressed in texts like Isaiah 20, 30.1-3, and 31.1-3? For Seitz, whose larger argument requires that no significant tension exist between the thoroughly positive assessment of Hezekiah that he finds in chs. 36–37(38) on the one hand, and the contents of Isaiah 1–35 on the other, the answer to this question is 'no'.[31] Within the narrative world of Isaiah 36–37, Seitz claims, the Rabshakeh's speech is a strategic, but failed attempt to 'drive a wedge' between Hezekiah and his subjects. True, the officer begins (36.4-6) by leveling his charge of reliance on Egypt directly at the king (via his envoys). But in the very next verse, he addresses the delegation, disparaging Hezekiah's destruction of Yahweh's shrines and altars, mocking Judah's military machine, and averring that Sennacherib has attacked Judah on Yahweh's orders.

How do readers understand the Rabshakeh's charge of Judean reliance on Egypt, Seitz asks, given his manipulative rhetorical strategies?

> Is this absolute fact, or an accusation that functions to anticipate the rumor regarding Tirhakah (19.9)?[32] Moreover, what is one to make of the factual nature of Rabshakeh's address when he concludes his remarks on a note that is surely to be construed as bombast and manipulation? 'Is it without YHWH that I have come up against this place to destroy it? YHWH

---

31. Tension between material in Isa. 1–35 on the one hand, and chs. 36–37(38) on the other, would mitigate against Seitz's theory that the Hezekiah narratives were part of a pre-exilic redaction of the Isaianic tradition undertaken near the time of Hezekiah's death for the purpose of instructing his son and heir, Manasseh.

32. In discussing the Rabshakeh's speech, Seitz works from the text as it appears in 2 Kings.

said to me, Go up against this land and destroy it' (18.25). Whether or not this item can be classified as historical, it clearly functions in the narrative to indict the Rabshakeh as a blasphemer. Given this, it is difficult to accept the Rabshakeh's charge of reliance on Egypt as objective proof of Hezekiah's foreign policy...the notion of Egyptian reliance is in and of itself not fantastic, not even in the mouth of a crafty Assyrian official. But whether the same official is to be trusted when he charges Hezekiah with such a policy, given both the circumstances of siege and the logic of the narrative that reports it, is far less likely (1991: 73).

This judgment is confirmed, Seitz believes (1991: 73), by the Rabshakeh's second speech. In 36.13-20 Sennacherib's envoy 'gets to the heart of the matter', abandoning the charge that Hezekiah has entered into a foreign alliance and ridiculing him, instead, for urging the people to rely on Yahweh (36.15). This second charge against Hezekiah, Seitz writes, must be taken as seriously as the initial one, for

> ...it is not possible to use the Rabshakeh's charge of foreign alliances with Egypt as objective proof of Hezekiah's policy (one that would be at odds with the prophet Isaiah) without similarly accepting his characterization of Hezekiah as the one man (not Isaiah) whose counsel to trust in YHWH threatens to mislead the people (1991: 74).

Seitz's assessment of how readers interpret the Rabshakeh's charge of Judean reliance upon Egyptian aid is problematic at several points. First, his assertion that 36.5-6 'functions to anticipate the rumor regarding Tirhakah' (37.9) ignores the sequential and cumulative nature of reading.[33] Lacking introductory information to explain Sennacherib's sudden destruction of Judean cities and threat to Jerusalem (36.1), readers are forced to interpret events, including the Rabshakeh's charge of international intrigue, and to make judgments on the basis of relevant *prior* information—including the prophet Isaiah's claims that Judean leaders travel to Egypt seeking assistance (e.g. 30.1-3; 31.1-3) and his condemnations of such a ploy (e.g. Isa. 20.3-6). And they are more likely to understand the rumor of Tirhakah's possible assistance later in the narrative (37.9) as confirmation of the Rabshakeh's claim that Judah and Egypt are in cahoots, than to interpret it as an unanticipated, tempting, but ultimately rejected opportunity to escape destruction (contra Seitz 1991: 74).

33. Readers interpret the appearance of Tirhakah in light of sequentially prior materials, including the Rabshakeh's earlier claim; they do not construe the Rabshakeh's charge on the basis of an as yet unread reference to Tirhakah's possible appearance in 37.9.

Secondly, it is by no means clear that readers of Isaiah would dismiss out of hand the Rabshakeh's claim that Yahweh lies behind Assyria's military aggression, for prior texts like Isa. 8.7-8; 9.8-21; and 10.5-6, while concluding with pronouncements of future judgment against the Assyrian king, nevertheless warn of God's intention first to use Assyria as a weapon against Judah. Yet even if the Rabshakeh's statement in 36.10 were flatly rejected as 'bombast and manipulation' (Seitz 1991: 73), this does not necessarily mean that immediately preceding claims will also be dismissed out of hand. Seitz's comments presuppose that a rejection of the claim in 37.10 necessarily carries with it a rejection of the prior charge that Judah is relying on Egypt. But it is as likely—if not more so—that the Rabshakeh, in his 'wily' way, strategically moves from irrefutable statement ('You are relying on Egypt'), to half- (i.e. distorted) truth ('But if you say to me, "We rely on Yahweh our God", is it not he whose high places and altars Hezekiah has removed...'; 36.7),[34] to an unverifiable assertion ('Yahweh said to me, "Go up against this land, and destroy it"'; 36.10b) that is buttressed, nonetheless, by its proximity to preceding, more verifiable claims. Such a line of argument —from the realized and irrefutable to the unrealized yet emphatically asserted—is far from rare. It is at work, for example, in the book of Isaiah's argument for the inevitability of 'new things' on the basis of the prior fulfillment of 'former things'.

Seitz claims that, 'it is not possible to use the Rabshakeh's charge of foreign alliances with Egypt as objective proof of Hezekiah's policy... without similarly accepting his characterization of Hezekiah as the one man (not Isaiah) whose counsel to trust in YHWH threatens to mislead the people' (1991: 74). But his argument requires careful examination. On the one hand, we must distinguish between the possibility of Hezekiah urging the people to trust in Yahweh, and the Rabshakeh's characterization of such urging as misleading. On the other hand, Seitz seems to presuppose that readers will reject the possibility that Hezekiah could *both* urge his subjects to have faith in their God's ability to save them during periods of national crisis *and* engage in international intrigue to better the odds of survival. Readers might agree with the prophet Isaiah that the two strategies—reliance on foreign nations and reliance

34. The Rabshakeh's implication, of course, is that Yahweh disapproves of the removal of these shrines and altars—an interpretation of Hezekiah's reforms that may well have had some credence among the country folk and their local cultic leaders, but would be decidedly at odds with the biblical historiographer's views.

on Yahweh—are incompatible. Who can say? But that does not mean that they could not conceive of Judah's monarchs engaging in both sorts of activity at the same time. Surely they would not presume that Hezekiah, having sanctioned an Egyptian alliance, would order cultic officials to desist from offering prayers and sacrifices to Yahweh on the grounds that his political strategy ruled out any possibility of assistance from the divine sphere! No, regardless of how readers *judge* the pairing of political intrigue and reliance on Yahweh, they are unlikely to conclude, on the basis of the Rabshakeh's words, that Hezekiah cannot possibly be involved in both activities. What they will recognize is the distortion introduced by the Rabshakeh's claim that Hezekiah's urgings to trust in Yahweh *mislead* his subjects.

Finally, by arguing that readers will reject, from the outset, both the veracity of the Rabshakeh's initial charges of Egyptian reliance,[35] and claims that Yahweh supports Sennacherib's campaign, Seitz collapses to a considerable degree the story's suspense. This is a surprising move since elsewhere he agrees with Smelik that Isaiah 36–37 is a unified literary account characterized by suspense-creating repetitions, ambiguity and retarded action (1991: 66-72).

Against Seitz, I argue that readers who suddenly encounter Sennacherib's (unexplained) destruction of Judah's cities and the Rabshakeh's speech in 36.1-10 will interpret the charge of reliance on Egypt against the background of sequentially prior condemnations of just such practices among Judah's leadership.[36] Hezekiah is not singled out specifically in those prior texts. But because they are not explicitly tied to specific events, oracles like 30.1-3 and 31.1-3 can be understood to pertain to *any* recourse to Egypt under *any* circumstances by *any* of Judah's leaders.[37] This interpretation of the Rabshakeh's accusation is confirmed, in retrospect, by the later reference to Tirhakah's possible military intervention in 37.9. Subsequent charges by the Rabshakeh—

35. In which case, the Tirhakah rumor functions as no more than a turn of events, albeit one foreshadowed already in 36.6.

36. Note that no authoritative voice—indeed, no voice at all—contradicts the Rabshakeh's claim that Hezekiah has relied on Egyptian assistance. The judgment oracle against Egypt contained in Isa. 20.1-6 also functions to present reliance upon Egypt as utterly foolhearty.

37. Moreover, one cannot assume that Hezekiah would be relieved of responsibility for foreign policy decisions pressed by his advisors. Both the prophetic literature and the Deuteronomistic History make it clear at numerous points that kings were accountable for the actions of the realm.

consisting of half-truths and unverifiable assertions—do nothing to blunt the force of his initial accusation. Indeed, the first charge serves to buttress subsequent claims.[38]

If this interpretation is correct, then Seitz's claim that Hezekiah is cast as an idealized role model whose behavior is the antithesis of that of his predecessor, Ahaz, must be modified at a strategic point. The Hezekiah of 37.8 and following indeed behaves in faithful and appropriate ways that secure the city's deliverance (37.21). But at the beginning of Isaiah 36, he stands accused of reliance on Egypt, in violation of Isaiah's (and Yahweh's) repeated condemnations of such policy. The question, then, is this: What happens to heal the damage that recourse to Egypt has dealt Hezekiah's relationship with Isaiah and 'Yahweh *your* God' (37.4)? One would think that because Seitz perceives no tension between a thoroughly idealized presentation of Hezekiah in chs. 36–37(38) on the one hand, and Isaiah 1–35 on the other, and views the Rabshakeh's speech as thoroughly discredited from the outset, Seitz would offer no help. Yet his statement concerning 2 Kings 19, already quoted in part, signals where we should begin to look for the answer to this question:

> The Rabshakeh may be correctly depicted as wily, and he may even inadvertently tell the truth. But his second charge against Hezekiah has as much claim to objectivity as his first, read within the constraints of the narrative that contains them both. In fact, given the manner in which Hezekiah responds, first in penitence (19.1-4) and then in prayerful appeal (19.14-19)—when finally the Rabshakeh gets back to the task at hand and addresses him directly—it is difficult to avoid the impression that the second charge was the correct one (1991: 74).

Here is Seitz's first and only reference to Hezekiah's first communiqué to Isaiah. The brevity of his remarks about 2 Kgs 19.1-4 (= Isa. 37.1-4) is striking, since readers would expect a king's *initial* words to Yahweh's *prophet* in the midst of *extreme national calamity* to be especially significant. Yet Seitz nowhere analyzes the contents of Hezekiah's message or even refers to the proverb in 37.3b. He does, however, characterize that message as 'penitence'. The same word appears a bit

---

38. The Rabshakeh's second speech (36.13-20) intensifies the attempt to divide monarch and audience. There, however, trust in Yahweh receives even greater emphasis. The Rabshakeh's explicit claim that faith in the Lord's ability to save Jerusalem is folly reveals this second speech to be more blasphemous than the first. As readers of Isa. 1–35 already have learned, trust in Yahweh must be maintained, even if God brings nations against Israel and Judah (e.g. Isa. 8.7-8; 9.8-21; 10.5-27).

later in his summary of chs. 36–37: 'The function of the narrative is to hold up Hezekiah as the model of obedient kingship, as the king who through penitence and prayer averts a merited sentence of judgment' (1991: 114).

These two statements, cursory though they may be, immediately raise questions: What is the misdeed or sin for which a penitent Hezekiah must express remorse; and why is the 'sentence of judgment' averted by his penitence 'merited'? One begins to suspect that Seitz's near-neglect of Isa. 37.1-7 is no accident, for words like 'penitence' and 'merited... judgment' suggest that some offense has indeed been committed and must be set right. That setting right occurs, I believe, as a result of Hezekiah's first words to Isaiah, and ultimately to God, in vv. 3-4. When these verses receive the attention they deserve, it becomes clear that Hezekiah's message, including his strategic proverb performance, marks a turning point in his relationship to Isaiah and to Isaiah's God.

The Strategic Confession of a Powerless Monarch

Read in isolation from their Isaianic context, Isaiah 36–37(38) have much to say about Hezekiah that is positive. But readers of 36.1–37.4 face a host of questions: Why is Sennacherib destroying Judean cities, and what of his charges and threats? Why must Hezekiah send Isaiah a penitent message culminating in a request for intercessory prayer on behalf of Jerusalem and its inhabitants?

When these chapters are read within their broader Isaianic context, however, readers are able to resolve such questions: the Rabshakeh's initial charge that Hezekiah is relying on Egyptian assistance is construed to mean that Judah's king has violated the prophet Isaiah's frequently voiced opposition to such a policy, while his claim that Yahweh has ordered Sennacherib to attack Judah's cities must at least be considered in light of sequentially prior assertions that Assyria is the weapon of God's wrath against a sinful nation. Will the reprobate actions of Hezekiah and his advisors lead to Jerusalem's demise? The Rabshakeh's second speech sharpens the issue lying at the heart of these chapters: *Whom do you trust? Will you rely on Yahweh, or place your fate in the hands of another?* Readers of Isaiah 1–35 already know what the answer *should* be. But what will be Hezekiah's response?

> When King Hezekiah heard it, he tore his clothes, covered himself with sackcloth, and went into the house of the Lord. And he sent Eliakim, who was in charge of the palace, and Shebna the secretary, and the senior

priests, covered with sackcloth, to the prophet Isaiah son of Amoz. They said to him, 'Thus says Hezekiah, "This day is a day of distress,[39] of chastisement,[40] and of contempt.[41] Babes are positioned for birth, but there is no strength to deliver"' (Isa. 37.1-3).[42]

Understood within its Isaianic context, Hezekiah's saying functions as the confession of a now powerless monarch who, in violation of the expressed policy of Yahweh's prophet, has willfully chosen to rely on his own strength and that of his allies. Note the proverb's emphasis upon lack of strength ($w^e k \bar{o} a h$ $^c a y i n$ $l^e l \bar{e} d \hat{a}$). It is not, of course, the babies' lack of strength that is bemoaned. Unlike Hosea (Hos. 13.13), Hezekiah does not expect infants to assist in their own deliveries. Neither does he believe that Yahweh lacks the strength to rescue. Rather, the mothers' strength is required to push out babies. And it is Hezekiah, along with his advisors, who bears responsibility for his city and its inhabitants—a responsibility that at this desperate hour he is utterly unable to honour.[43]

But his proverb performance also marks a turning point for Hezekiah, albeit a strategic one intended to maximize the chances that Isaiah, and ultimately Yahweh, will respond favorably despite his past disobedience. At this most crucial moment, Hezekiah—unlike his predecessor, Ahaz—

39. The noun is $\bar{s} \bar{a} r \hat{a}$; NRSV translates 'distress'. In Jer. 49.24 (see also Jer. 4.31), this word appears in a simile about birth pangs. BDB suggests (II, $\bar{s} r r$) that a hiphil form of the root $\bar{s} r r$ referred specifically to the pain accompanying labour (Jer. 4.31; 49.24; see also Jer. 48.41; 49.22). The noun $\bar{s} \bar{a} r \hat{a}$ is particularly appropriate in this context, therefore, since it presages Hezekiah's proverb situation and, I shall argue, his own plight depicted figuratively.

40. *Tôkēḥâ*; this verb is suggestive of what God is doing to Hezekiah and his nation; i.e., chastizing them for relying on Egyptian aid. NRSV renders it 'rebuke'.

41. Both NRSV and *Tanakh* translate 'disgrace', but this feminine noun, from the root $n^3 \bar{s}$ (to spurn, contemn), probably means 'contempt'. It is a *hapax legomenon*, and may be suggestive of the king of Assyria's attitude toward both Judah and its God (as revealed by the words of the Rabshakeh).

42. Again, this translation of Hezekiah's proverb is my own.

43. Booth notes that 'the deliberate use of a recognizable metaphor (a special case of the deliberate use of any abnormality, any figuring) inevitably invites judgments of the speaker's character' (1979: 174). His observation is interesting in light of Hezekiah's ambivalent character at the beginning and end of Isa. 36–39. Sweeney observed in a private communication that Hezekiah is like his proverb: almost the ideal king, his actions nevertheless bring the Assyrians to Jerusalem's door and raise the spectre of Babylonian exile (to which he offers a rather cavalier response in Isa. 39.8). Hezekiah can bring to the point of birth, but he cannot quite pull off the delivery.

chooses *to repent and trust in Yahweh*. Here is our paradigmatic Hezekiah: he is exemplary not because he never acts contrary to God's will, but because he does what was called for already in Isa. 1.27. He repents. Once the rupture in his relationship with Isaiah and with 'Yahweh your God' is repaired through a humble confession of weakness and other acts of contrition (torn clothes, sackcloth, a trek to the temple, Isa. 37.1) and he receives Isaiah's positive oracular response (37.5-7), Hezekiah can approach God directly in prayer, without Isaiah's further intercession (37.15-21).

Assuming that the correlations in Hezekiah's proverb are between endangered babes and Jerusalem's inhabitants on the one hand, and the powerless women and Jerusalem's leadership on the other, what can we conclude about Hezekiah's reason for including the saying in his message to Isaiah? This strategic, rhetorical use of a metaphorical proverb functions both as penitent confession and as an invitation to perceive the crisis in a way most likely to move the prophet himself, and ultimately Yahweh (via Isaiah's intercessory prayer), to pity and action on Jerusalem's behalf. 'See', Hezekiah is saying, 'this city's inhabitants are precious sons—helpless, surrounded and in deadly peril. Its leaders are powerless women, utterly incapable of rescuing either their infants or themselves.'[44] Hezekiah, the once rebellious monarch whose international politics stood at odds with Isaiah's prophetic word, now depicts both self and subjects trapped in the most fragile and dangerous of situations. Surely Isaiah and Yahweh will take pity.[45] Surely, in Queen Puduhepa's words, 'to a woman in travail the god yields her wish'.[46]

---

44. In light of the pejorative connotations associated with likening men to women in biblical and extra-biblical sources, it is possible that Hezekiah intends not only to depict himself and his advisors as powerless, but also to suggest self-debasement. See Hillers 1964: 66-68; Holladay 1966: 237.

45. In the following verse, Hezekiah further buttresses his appeal for help by referring to the hubris and blasphemy of Sennacherib who, through the words of his Rabshakeh, has asserted Yahweh's inability to save Jerusalem and ridiculed Hezekiah for trusting in God.

46. In the thirteenth-century Hittite prayer of Queen Puduhepa to the Sun-goddess of Arinna (Fontaine 1987: 98), the royal supplicant first quotes a proverb ('Among men there is a saying: "To a woman in travail the god yields her wish"'), and then applies it to herself ('[Since] I, Pudu-hepa, am a woman in travail [and since] I have devoted myself to thy son, yield to me, Sun-goddess of Arinna, my lady'). From the context, it seems highly unlikely that Puduhepa was actually pregnant and in labour. Rather, she voices the cultural belief that deities are particularly

Summary

How do readers of Isaiah understand Isaiah 36–37, including its presentation of King Hezekiah? So long as scholars have analyzed the narrative apart from its broader Isaianic context, primarily in its (supposedly original) setting in the Deuteronomistic History, and/or in light of a reconstructed historical scenario informed by both biblical and extra-biblical materials, this question has been neglected. In recent years, however, scholars have begun reading and interpreting the Hezekiah-Isaiah narratives within their immediate and broader Isaianic literary context. P. Ackroyd (1982: 3-21) has shown how Isaiah 36–39 plays a transitional role within the larger scroll, since Isaiah's announcement of a future Babylonian exile in Isa. 39.5-7 contextualizes the following prophecies of Second Isaiah. Scholars like Conrad and Seitz have urged us, albeit in very different ways, to reconsider majority opinions and put fresh questions to these texts. (For Conrad, the Hezekiah narrative, in particular, is 'strategically located in the book because it provides the persuasive basis on which the implied audience can look forward to salvation from the Babylonians' [1991: 49-50].) Seitz also recognizes the pivotal role of these chapters, although he is particularly concerned with diachronic questions about the placement of the Hezekiah-Isaiah narratives at the conclusion of the Proto-Isaiah tradition, and with the impetus their presence created for the subsequent, extensive supplementation of that tradition in chs. 40–66 (1991: 127).[47]

Different though these scholars' studies may be, Ackroyd, Conrad and Seitz share 1) the conclusion that the depiction of Hezekiah in Isaiah 36–37(38) is positive, and 2) a neglect of Hezekiah's proverb in 37.3b. But our investigation of the king's initial communiqué to Isaiah, read in light of the prophet's condemnation of international alliances and the Rabshakeh's charge of reliance on Egypt, has led us to modify that view at a crucial point. True, Hezekiah behaves in exemplary ways throughout the bulk of the narratives. At the outset of the Jerusalem crisis, however, his relationship with both Isaiah and his God is imperiled. In the midst of

attentive to the petitions of labouring women, and correlates herself with the proverbial woman in travail in an attempt to secure a prompt and positive response to her request (108-12).

47. For Seitz (1991), tension between the deliverance of Jerusalem in 701 BCE and its destruction in 587 BCE led to the subsequent expansion of then-existing Isaianic traditions.

that religious/military crisis, Hezekiah is guilty of resorting to Egypt. But
he responds appropriately, with a humble confession of human frailty
and a request for intercessory prayer on behalf of his subjects.
Throughout much of Isaiah 36–38, Hezekiah is a role model for kings;
but in 37.1-4 he is also a role model for 'those in Zion who repent' (Isa.
1.27).

The story told in Isaiah 36–37(38) plays a strategic role in the book of
Isaiah as a whole. Significant for its function as a bridge between chs. 1–
39 and 40–66, it undoubtedly drew readers' attention by virtue of the
miraculous denouement of its plot. My analysis has focused primarily on
the early stages of Jerusalem's crisis—on the Rabshakeh's initial speeches
and Hezekiah's response to them. But the story goes on to describe
Jerusalem's extraordinary rescue. Why and how was the city saved?
According to Sennacherib's own annals, Hezekiah bought Jerusalem's
survival at a high price; 2 Kgs 18.13-16 states that Hezekiah saved his
city by contritely paying the king of Assyria an enormous quantity of
silver and gold taken from the temple and palace treasuries.[48] But for
readers of Isaiah, the crisis ends without the payment of any tribute.
Rather, one-hundred-eighty-five thousand Assyrian soldiers are struck
down in a single night by the 'angel of the Lord'; and the once-proud
Sennacherib is forced to return home—a stunning rebuke of the
Rabshakeh's claim that trust in Yahweh is folly.

Bringing to Birth in the Book of Isaiah

Two additional texts about trust in God's strength and readiness to
deliver echo in striking ways the childbirth imagery of Hezekiah's
proverb situation in Isa. 37.3b: Isa. 26.18 and 66.7-9. Together, these
three texts constitute a recurring, unfolding motif contributing to the
reader's construal of Isaiah as a coherent literary work.

Isaiah 26.18

Isaiah 26.18 forms part of a lament within Isaiah 24–27, the so-called
'Isaianic Apocalypse'. The chapter begins with an eschatological salvation
song celebrating God's final victory on behalf of Israel and its 'mighty
city', Jerusalem. 'The use of the liturgical form of a hymn is carefully
planned', Clements writes, 'and serves to bridge the gap between the
fears and tensions of the present, in which the final triumph appears

---

48. 2 Kgs 18.13-16 has no parallel in the book of Isaiah.

remote and improbable, and the certainty of ultimate victory and joy.
The use of the hymnic form...[draws] the reader more directly into the
confidence of this ultimate victory by drawing forth his own confession
of its certainty' (1980b: 211):

> Trust in the Lord for ever and ever,
> For in Yah the Lord you have an everlasting Rock
> For He has brought low those who dwelt high up,
> Has humbled the secure city,
> Humbled it to the ground,
> Leveled it with the dust—
> To be trampled underfoot,
> By the feet of the needy,
> By the soles of the poor (Isa. 26.4-6; *Tanakh*).

Following verses give way to lament, since suffering threatens to obviate
hope. The lament begins with a confession of trust borne of God's way
in the world. But if the righteous are rewarded, so also must the wicked
be punished. Should their offenses go unchecked, not only would they
continue doing evil, but also God's justice and majesty would appear to
be undermined (v. 10). In v. 11, the lamenters appeal directly to God to
destroy their enemies. Verses 12-15 contain assurances that Yahweh,
who is righteous, will intercede on behalf of the oppressed while slaying
the wicked.

Verse 16, the beginning of a poetic description of the lamenters'
distress, has challenged many a translator.[49] *Tanakh* renders the verse:

> O Lord! In their distress, they sought You;
> Your chastisement reduced them
> To anguished[50] whispered prayer.

Among the difficulties with this translation, however, is the rendering of
laḥaš ('incantation, charm') as 'prayer',[51] a meaning attested nowhere
else.

Since emendations of *laḥaš* lack textual support, critics investigate its
meanings elsewhere in the Hebrew Bible. In Jer. 8.17 and Eccl. 10.11,
laḥaš bears explicit associations with snake charming:

---

49. The LXX reads, 'Lord, in affliction (*en thlipsei*) I remembered thee; thy
chastening was to us with small affliction'.

50. Reading *ṣāqûn* as a noun.

51. So also the NRSV; its translation of *ṣāqûn*, 'they poured out [a prayer]',
identifies the form as a qal pf. 3 c. p. of *ṣûq*, 'to pour out, melt' (see also Job 28.2),
but such an identification remains uncertain.

> Lo, I will send serpents (*n^eḥāšîm*) against you,
> Adders (*ṣip^cōnîm*) that cannot be charmed (*^ʾên lāhem lāḥaš*),
> And they shall bite you—declares the Lord (Jer. 8.17; *Tanakh*).

> If the snake (*hannāḥāš*) bites because no spell was uttered (*b^elo^ʾ lāḥaš*),
> no advantage is gained by the trained charmer (Eccl. 10.11).

Skilled charmers (*n^ebôn lāḥaš*) were among those leaders threatened in Isa. 3.3. In v. 20 of the same chapter, *hall^eḥāšîm* ('amulets') appeared among the objects Yahweh will strip from the bodies of Jerusalem's upperclass women. The juxtaposition of snakes (symbols of fertility in Israel's ancient Near Eastern world [McCullough 1962: 289-91]), women (in Isa. 3.20) and childbirth imagery (in Isa. 26.16-18) intrigues: does the text voice its anguished plea for assistance in terms evocative of incantations associated with women's pain in childbirth and rituals attending parturition? Given our lack of information concerning fertility objects and childbirth practices in ancient Israel, we cannot answer this question with certainty. The presence of *laḥaš* in v. 16 suggests, nonetheless, that its link with childbirth imagery may be stronger than contemporary translators have recognized.

Verses 17-18, employing discontinuous terms drawn from travail, continue the description of the lamenting community's anguish:

> Like a pregnant woman (*hārâ*) approaching childbirth (*taqrîb lāledet*),
> Who writhes (*tāḥîl*) and cries out in her pangs (*baḥ^abālêhā*),
> So were we before you, O Lord!
> We conceived (*hārînû*); we writhed (*ḥalnû*);
> We gave birth to nothingness (*yāladnû rûaḥ*).
> We accomplished no salvation on earth;
> No inhabitants of the world are born (*Tanakh*).[52]

Within Israel's ancient Near Eastern world, travailing woman similes stereotypically describe the psychological anguish and physiological reactions of persons facing impending doom (see Darr 1987a; 1994: 101-105). We are not surprised, therefore, that a labouring woman simile (v. 17) functions to illumine the speakers' anguish and dismay. But this text differs from most other examples of travailing woman similes. While such tropes normally do not encourage readers to contemplate the birth (either literal or metaphorical) of anyone (or anything), in this instance

---

52. The phrase is difficult. Kaiser (1974: 209; see also NRSV) points to the noun *nēpel*, meaning 'untimely birth, abortion' (Ps. 58.9) to support his translation, 'and no inhabitants of the world are born'.

the poem moves from a vivid description of maternal pain to the delivery's outcome—or in this case, to the lack thereof. By describing itself as a woman in labour, the lamenting community—like the Hittite Queen Puduhepa—undoubtedly intends to present itself as pitiful, incapacitated and in desperate need of divine help. But by its admission in v. 18a, 'we gave birth to nothingness' (*rûaḥ*, commonly translated 'breath', 'wind' or 'spirit'), it also acknowledges its utter inability to bring about sorely-needed salvation. These righteous sufferers have 'conceived' and their 'labour' is anguished indeed. But they cannot birth 'a new thing on earth' (Jer. 31.22b). Such an accomplishment lies beyond human resources; only God can perform that task.

In its canonical form, v. 18 is followed by a reference to resurrection. Commentators disagree concerning whether this refers to the resurrection of individuals (Kaiser 1974: 215-20) or of the faithful community whose lament it follows. In any case, the chapter concludes with instructions and encouragement from an unidentified voice:

> Go, my people, enter your chambers,
> And lock your doors behind you.
> Hide but a little moment,
> Until the indignation passes (v. 20; *Tanakh*).

Your suffering is not quite over, the voice explains, but in just a 'little moment', God will instigate a final judgment upon the earth. In the midst of anguish and an overwhelming sense of futility, then, the lamenting community is urged to sing of its trust in Yahweh, to affirm God's dealings with the world, to anticipate the destruction of the wicked and to suffer patiently in expectation of divine recompense.

Isaiah 66.1-16

Isaiah 66.1-16, part of the scroll's concluding chapter, is striking both for its divine warrior imagery (and the ultimate undoing of God's enemies) and for its climatic, joyous conclusion to personified Zion's story.[53] The initial oracle begins with the messenger formula, 'Thus says the Lord' (v. 1)—the poet's claim that the following words are Yahweh's, not his own—and continues with God's scornful dismissal of an earthly temple.

Because our reader knows that the post-exilic Jewish community

---

53. I trace Zion's unfolding story for sequential readers of Isaiah in Chapters 3 and 4 of my book, *Isaiah's Vision and the Family of God* (Darr 1994).

erected a new temple in Jerusalem between 520–515 BCE (certainly an auspicious event in the post-exilic community's life), the oracle in Isa. 66.1-16 can be linked to that period.[54] Apparently, however, the author of these verses regards the temple builders of his own day as obstacles to, rather than instruments of, the divine will.

The following lines convey a different tone because, in contrast to the condemnation in vv. 1-2a, they affirm the behaviour of another group. Immediately, however, the tenor shifts again. Verses 3-4 collect images from what are ostensibly the most horrid of pagan rituals,[55] and then equate such rituals with the religious rites of foes. In v. 5, the poet again addresses the faithful described in v. 2b. Here, we learn that the author's enemies are Jews, not foreigners. Their mockery of those who 'tremble' at God's word suggests that to this point, the oppressed folk's hopes for divine intervention have been frustrated.

A prophetic word of assurance at the end of v. 5 ('But theirs shall be the shame') is followed in v. 6 by a theophanic vision. The description of this vision is interrupted, in a sense, by the quite different tone of vv. 7-14. The poet returns to it in vv. 15-16, however, further detailing the divine warrior's approach. These verses contain phrases that elsewhere in Isaiah appear in oracles about God's judgment upon foreign nations. For that reason, some comentators have insisted that vv. 15-16 also were originally concerned only with the fate of foreigners, despite the reference to 'your kinsmen who hate you' in v. 2b.[56] Identical phrases can be used in diverse contexts and toward various ends, however, so the appearance of certain words and phrases within Isaianic oracles concerning foreign nations does not preclude their being used elsewhere in utterances against others. It is possible, of course, that Isa. 66.1-16 includes non-Jewish, as well as Jewish, foes among the victims of

54. This statement presupposes, of course, that the reader will construe the contiguous lines of these verses in relation to one another. Historical critics have traditionally denied their unity, claiming that originally discrete units were only secondarily stitched together by redactors whose efforts account for the sudden shifts between words of judgment (vv. 1, 3-4, 6) and words of salvation (vv. 2, 5, 7-14). Hanson has argued convincingly, however, that post-exilic prophetic oracles increasingly detailed both the punishment awaiting the wicked and Yahweh's salvation on behalf of the faithful (1975: 161-86). The reader is able, therefore, to make sense of such shifts in the course of moving through the text.

55. So Hanson (1975: 179-80) and, cautiously, Westermann (1969: 413-14).

56. So Westermann (1969: 421), who insists that vv. 15-16 did not originally address the fate of Jewish foes.

Yahweh's imminent attack. Clearly, however, the traditional division between Israel and the nations has, in the strife of the post-exilic period, become a new division between the wicked and the righteous; and Jews can count members of their own community among Yahweh's enemies.[57]

Now just as the theophany begun in v. 6 and resumed in vv. 15-16 describes Yahweh's imminent, ultimate victory over the Lord's foes, so vv. 7-14 depict the other side of the coin; that is, the deliverance awaiting those faithful persons who presently endure their oppressors' derision. Employing childbirth imagery to describe the future salvation of Jerusalem and her inhabitants, the poet celebrates an event that is the precise opposite of Hezekiah's proverb situation in Isa. 37.3b:

> Before she writhed (*tāḥîl*), she gave birth (*yālādâ*);
> Before her pangs came upon her, she bore (*himlîṭâ*)[58] a son (*zākār*).
> Who has heard the like?
> Who has seen such things?
> Can a land pass through travail (*yûḥal*)
> In a single day?
> Or is a nation delivered (*yiwwālēd*)
> All at once?
> Yet Zion travailed (*ḥālâ*)
> And at once bore (*yālᵉdâ*) her sons (*bānêhā*)!
> Shall I position for birth (*ʾašbîr*) but not bring forth?
> —says the Lord.
> Shall I who cause birth (*hammôlîd*) shut [the womb]?
> —says your God (66.7-9; author's trans.).

Here, Jerusalem—not its inhabitants, but the city itself—appears as a pregnant woman miraculously spared a prolonged, painful and exhausting labour. Indeed, her children (literally 'sons') are born before the onset of labour pains. The announcement of this astonishing, never-before-witnessed event is followed by two rhetorical questions placed in God's mouth: 'Shall I position for birth (*ʾašbîr*) but not bring forth? Shall I who cause birth shut the womb?' These questions seek to reassure those whose own prolonged suffering at the hands of their foes has forced them to question whether Yahweh is able and can be trusted to act on

57. In addition to Hanson, see Rofé (1985). Although critical of Hanson's ideological bias toward the so-called 'visionary group', Rofé agrees that these texts bespeak intracommunal strife within the post-exilic community.

58. This hiphil perfect 3 f.s. form of the verb *mlṭ* ('to slip away') depicts the infant effortlessly slipping from the womb.

their behalf. But v. 9a also evokes memory of Hezekiah's proverb, for the verb *ʾašbîr* ('[Shall] I position for birth?') recalls the reference to *mašbēr* (the birth canal) in Isa. 37.3b. Through 'textual echoes', readers are reminded of a crucial moment in the past when the Lord miraculously rescued Jerusalem; and they are emboldened to believe that at any moment, Yahweh again will act on their city's behalf, bringing salvation to its righteous inhabitants and destruction to their enemies.

Mother Zion escapes the birth pangs that, according to Gen. 3.16, have been everywoman's lot since the time of Eve, the first progenitrix. Indeed, there are hints that Isa. 66.1-14 intends to stir thoughts of that first woman's punishment for rebellion against God. When vv. 12-14 depict a new paradisiacal realm in which streams of prosperity and wealth flow to Jerusalem, we recall the river that flowed from Eden and divided to water the entire earth.[59] Moreover, the image of a mother comforting her son—called *ʾîš* ('man') in v. 13—recalls Eve's remark at the birth of Cain: 'I have gained a male child (*ʾîš*) with the help of the Lord' (Gen. 4.1). The noun *ʾîš* appears hundreds of times in the Hebrew Bible, of course. Its use to refer to an infant or small boy is unusual, however; and so its presence in conjunction with a mother and child in Isa. 66.13 further links this text with Eve's story in the minds of readers steeped in their religious traditions.

Note the difference in strategy motivating the rhetorical use of natal imagery in Hezekiah's proverb performance on the one hand and Isa. 66.1-16 on the other. In the former, the proverb functions as an invitation to perceive the plight of king, capital and subjects in a way most likely to move Isaiah, and ultimately Yahweh, to pity and action. In the latter, the metaphor functions to convince the reader that God is able and ready to intervene on behalf of the faithful, not only as the avenging warrior who utterly destroys enemies, but also as a divine midwife who oversees the painless, speedy births of Zion's sons. So confident is the poet of Yahweh's imminent intervention that he speaks as if the deliverance were already accomplished.

Did the author of the childbirth imagery in Isa. 66.1-16 compose with Isa. 37.3b in mind? Did he intentionally reverse Hezekiah's proverb, so that a metaphorical description of a city's desperate situation was transformed into a metaphorical account of its imminent salvation? The

59. Within the Hebrew Bible, we find the recurring motif of a sacred stream flowing from Zion (e.g. Isa. 33.20-24; Zech. 14.8; Ezek. 47.1-12; and Joel 4.18 [ET 3.18]). See Levenson 1976: 7-36; Clifford 1972; and Darr 1987b: 272-79.

answer to this question can never be known with certainty, of course. But our reader brings both Isaiah 26 and 36–37 to his reading of Isa. 66.7-9; he knows the story of Jerusalem's miraculous rescue and the destruction of Sennacherib's troops by the Lord's messenger. And lexical correspondence suggests that he will discern within the latter tradition a poetic vehicle by which to convey the tenor of Zion's glorious future.[60]

These observations suggest, moreover, that the reader of this poetic description of Zion's painless delivery in Isaiah 66 who looks back to Isa. 37.3b will construe the relationship between entities in *Hezekiah's* proverb and context situations in a way that differs from the four correlation options identified and discussed earlier in this essay. Steeped in the woman Zion imagery that abounds throughout Isaiah, he may correlate Jerusalem 'herself' with the woman lacking strength to bring forth her sons (Isa. 37.3b). If so, then Isa. 66.7-9 describes a diferent understanding of YHWH's reversal of Jerusalem's proverbial plight. She may lack strength to deliver, but Israel's God does not.

Conclusion

In this essay, I have both scrutinized a childbirth proverb spoken by an important king to a major prophet at a crucial moment on the eve of God's miraculous rescue of Jerusalem and investigated two additional Isaianic texts containing (in)ability-to-bring-to-birth imagery. Isaiah 26.17-18 begins with a hymnic celebration of Zion's strength, enjoining the righteous to trust in Yahweh. But singing gives way to a communal lament in which the supplicants employ childbirth imagery to describe their present pain, despair and helplessness. In the climactic Isaiah 66.7-9, Jerusalem's redemption is described using imagery that is the opposite of the proverb situation in Isa. 37.3b. (Indeed, because the metaphors in 37.3b and 66.7-9 are two sides of the same coin, their relationship may be considered as close, if not closer, than that between Isaiah 66 and other Isaianic texts depicting Zion as both woman and mother.)

---

60. We have already pointed to the presence of *ʾašbîr* in Isa. 66.9 and of *mašbēr* in Isa. 37.3b. Both forms of the root *šbr* are rare; the verb appears in the hiphil only at Isa. 66.9, while the noun appears only in Hezekiah's proverb and in Hos. 13.13. Note, as well, that while Isa. 66.7b announces the birth of a single male child (*zākār*), v. 8b proclaims the multiple births of Zion's sons, *bānêhā*, employing the same (admittedly common) plural noun appearing in Isa. 37.3b.

How, then, does the inability/ability to give birth motif function for competent sequential readers of the Isaiah tradition? It appears first in a description of desperate, helpless human beings who care deeply about Jerusalem and who struggle to maintain trust in Yahweh in the face of anguish and their own failure to bring about salvation. Their lament is not immediately answered and their suffering continues. They are, however, assured of deliverance, urged to trust God and encouraged to be patient. The motif reappears in a pivotal text about a specific, crucial and memorable crisis wherein the inability-to-bring-to-birth metaphor, expressed proverbially, elicits from Isaiah an intercessory prayer leading to Jerusalem's miraculous deliverance—clear proof of Yahweh's power and trustworthiness and a stunning refutation of the Rabshakeh's blasphemous words. Finally, it appears in an announced demonstration of Yahweh's presence with Zion, bringing forth her sons so quickly and painlessly that the world is astonished. Once a widow bereaved of her children, Zion will raise her offspring in a new paradisiacal age—a fitting fate for the beloved bride of Isaiah 62.

BIBLIOGRAPHY

Ackroyd, P.R.
1982   'Isaiah 36–39: Structure and Function', in W.C. Delsman *et al.* (eds.), *Von Kanaan bis Kerala* (AOAT, 211; Neukirchen–Vluyn: Neukirchener Verlag): 3-21.
Booth, W.
1979   'Afterthoughts on Metaphor', in S. Sacks (ed.), *On Metaphor* (Chicago: University of Chicago Press): 173-74.
Bright, J.
1991   *A History of Israel* (Philadelphia: Westminster Press, 3rd edn).
Clements, R.E.
1980a   *Isaiah and the Deliverance of Jerusalem: A Study of the Interpretation of Prophecy in the Old Testament* (JSOTSup, 13; Sheffield: JSOT Press).
1980b   *Isaiah 1–39* (NCB; Grand Rapids: Eerdmans).
Clifford, R.
1972   *The Cosmic Mountain in Canaan and the Old Testament* (HSM, 4; Cambridge, MA: Harvard University Press).
Conrad, E.
1991   *Reading Isaiah* (Minneapolis: Fortress Press).
Darr, K.P.
1987a   'Like Warrior, Like Woman: Destruction and Deliverance in Isaiah 42:10-17', *CBQ* 49: 560-71.

1987b   'The Wall Around Paradise: Ezekelian Ideas about the Future', *VT* 37: 272-79.

1994   *Isaiah's Vision and the Family of God* (Literary Currents in Biblical Tradition; Louisville: Westminster/John Knox).

Dundes, A.
1977   'Who are the Folk?', in W.R. Bascom (ed.), *Frontiers of Folklore* (American Association for the Advancement of Science Selected Symposium, 5; Boulder, CO: Westview Press): 17-35.

Eissfeldt, O.
1913   *Der Maschal im Alten Testament* (Giessen: Töpelmann).

Fontaine, C.R.
1982   *Traditional Sayings in the Old Testament: A Contextual Study* (Bible and Literature Series, 5; Sheffield: Almond Press).

1987   'Queeny Proverb Performance: The Prayer of Puduhepa (DUB XXI, 27)', in D.G. Hoglund *et al.* (eds.), *The Listening Heart: Essays in Wisdom and Psalms in Honor of Roland E. Murphy, O. Carm.* (JSOTSup, 58; Sheffield: JSOT Press): 95-126.

Frymer-Kensky, T.
1992   *In the Wake of the Goddesses: Women, Culture, and the Biblical Transformation of Pagan Myth* (New York: The Free Press).

Gesenius, F.H.W.
1821   *Philologisch-dritischer und historischer Commentar über den Jesaja* (Leipzig: F.C.W. Vogel).

Goetze, A. (trans.)
1969   'The Telepinus Myth', in *ANET*: 126-28.

Gonçalves, F.J.
1986   *L'expédition de Sennachérib en Palestine dans la littérature hébraïque ancienne* (Paris: Gabalda).

Hanson, P.
1975   *The Dawn of Apocalyptic* (Philadelphia: Fortress Press).

Hillers, D.R.
1964   *Treaty-Curses and the Old Testament Prophets* (BibOr, 16; Rome: Pontifical Biblical Institute Press).

Holladay, W.L.
1966   'Jer. xxxi 22B Reconsidered: "The Woman Encompasses the Man"', *VT* 16: 236-39.

Kaiser, O.
1972   *Isaiah 1–12* (trans. R.A. Wilson; London: SCM Press).
1974   *Isaiah 13–39* (trans. R.A. Wilson; Philadelphia: Westminster Press).

Kort, A. and S. Moschauser (eds.)
1985   *Biblical and Related Studies Presented to Samuel Iwry* (Winona Lake, IN: Eisenbrauns).

Lambert, W.G.
1976   'A Middle Assyrian Medical Text', *Iraq* 31: 28-39.

Levenson, J.D.
1976   *Theology of the Program of Restoration of Ezekiel 40–48* (Missoula, MT: Scholars Press).

McCullough, W.S.
1962   'Serpent', *IDB*, IV: 289-91.
Oppenheim, A.L.
1969   'Babylonian and Assyrian Historical Texts', in *ANET*: 265-317.
Roberts, J.J.M.
1985   'Isaiah and his Children', in Kort and Moschauser (eds.) 1985: 193-203.
Rofé, A.
1985   'Isaiah 66:1-4: Judean Sects of the Persian Period', in Kort and Moschauser (eds.) 1985: 205-17.
Seitel, P.
1969   'Proverbs: A Social Use of Metaphor', *Genre* 2: 143-61; reprinted in D. Ben-Amos (ed.), *Folklore Genres* (Austin: University of Texas, 1972): 125-43.
1977   'Saying Haya Sayings: Two Categories of Proverb Use', in J.D. Sapir and J.C. Crocker (eds.), *The Social Use of Metaphor: Essays on the Anthropology of Rhetoric* (Philadelphia: University of Philadelphia): 75-99.
Seitz, C.R.
1991   *Zion's Final Destiny: The Development of the Book of Isaiah: A Reassessment of Isaiah 36–39* (Minneapolis: Fortress Press).
Smelik, K.A.D.
1986   'Distortion of Old Testament Prophecy: The Purpose of Isaiah xxxvi and xxxvii', in J. de Moor *et al.*, (eds.), *Crises and Perspectives* (Leiden: Brill): 70-93.
1992   *Converting the Past: Studies in Ancient Israelite and Moabite Historiography* (Leiden: Brill).
Westermann, C.
1969   *Isaiah 40–66* (trans. D.G.M. Stalker; OTL; Philadelphia: Westminster).
Williams, J.G.
1987   'Proverbs and Ecclesiastes', in R. Alter and F. Kermode (eds.), *The Literary Guide to the Bible* (Cambridge, MA: Belknap): 263-82.

THE 'SCOPE' OF ISAIAH AS A BOOK OF JEWISH
AND CHRISTIAN SCRIPTURES

Gerald T. Sheppard

Today we seem to have far more, and often radically conflicting, 'visions' of the book of Isaiah than in the century before. This proliferation of possibilities and newer methodologies perhaps marks the end of the modern age and a period of epistemological disequilibrium. In order to seek a fresh way to evaluate and to assess critically this current 'pluralism' of 'visions' of the book of Isaiah, I want to draw a distinction between two moments of scholarly disagreement:

1) When scholars opt for approximately the same vision of 'the book of Isaiah' but have different perspectives in their description of it, and 2) when scholars use the same jargon, 'the book of Isaiah', but, in fact, interpret entirely different 'texts'. When scholars do not even share the same 'text', they may unconsciously talk past each other as though they are competing to illuminate the same thing. Just as Michel Foucault tries to describe a 'history of resemblances' across epochs dominated by radically different 'forms of knowing', I think we need a criticism of criticisms to know whether the same 'text' or 'texts' are envisioned at the focal point of our scholarly debates.[1] Of course, radically different 'texts' of Isaiah may be relevant in different ways to the illumination of any one particular envisioned text or successive texts of the book. However, we need to be aware of these differences in our visions of the book of Isaiah in order to adjudicate that possibility, to argue compellingly with each other and to evaluate each other's capacity to 'see'

---

1. M. Foucault, *The Order of Things: An Archaeology of the Human Sciences* (ed. R.D. Laing; New York: Vintage Books, 1973 [1966]), pp. xxii-xxiii. For a careful argument that at minimum, 'we are living within a borderline region between modernity and a new, as yet inadequately theorized social situation' (p. 261), see S. Best and Douglas Kellner, *Postmodern Theory: Critical Interrogations* (New York: Guilford Press, 1991).

and/or to 'hear' the same text. Even the tradition of Isaiah itself suggests that 'seeing' and 'hearing' its true import entails more than an everyday 'reading' of this prophetic book (cf. 'On that day', Isa. 29.18).

After some general hermeneutical comments, I will first consider the second distinction about different envisioned 'texts' concealed behind the same labels and illustrate its significance in the work of several recent scholarly efforts to interpret Isaiah. In the second part, I will concentrate on what I would call the book of Isaiah as part of Jewish and Christian scripture, in line with Childs, Rendtorff and, to a great degree, Seitz. Here I will push beyond my own earlier efforts to consider specifically questions of the cental message of the book and the relation of the book to the Torah. Throughout this essay, I will be drawing on parts of two earlier papers published in the Annual Papers of the Society of Biblical Literature. More detailed exposition on certain points can be found there.[2]

1. *Differing Visions of a 'Text': Some Hermeneutical Considerations*

Most of us who are trained in biblical studies do not find our primary orientation in hermeneutical theory of a philosophical sort, but that fact probably makes us all the more easily seduced by the philosophical climate of opinion in which we work and breathe. Since the 1970s in the United States, various structuralist approaches (not necessarily 'structuralism') and views of language as 'representing reality' have gained ascendancy over older modern phenomenological (genetic, referential or neo-Kantian) accounts of how we encounter reality through texts.[3] The

2.   G.T. Sheppard, 'The Book of Isaiah: Competing Structures according to a Late Modern Description of Its Shape and Scope', in E.H. Lovering, Jr (ed.), *Society of Biblical Literature: 1992 Seminar Papers* (Atlanta: Scholars Press, 1992), pp. 549-82; and his 'The Book of Isaiah as a Human Witness to Revelation within the Religions of Judaism and Christianity', in E.H. Lovering, Jr. (ed.), *Society of Biblical Literature: 1993 Seminar Papers* (Atlanta: Scholars Press, 1993), pp. 274-80.

3.   For an excellent overview of the phenomenological arguments of New Critics and their successors, in conflict with the newer structuralists, see F. Lentricchia, *After the New Criticism* (Chicago: University of Chicago Press, 1980). On the critique of structuralism since 1980, see Best and Kellner, *Postmodern Theory*. For a defense of a conventional literary theory and canon against these latest postmodern critics, see C. Altieri, *Canons and Consequences: Reflections on the Ethical Force of Imaginative Ideals* (Evanston: Northwestern University Press, 1990). Worth noting is, also, M.H. Abrams's criticism of deconstructionists, in his collected essays, *Doing*

phenomenological approaches, in oversimplified terms, stand in tension with the structuralist, so that structuralist strategies try to avoid problems associated with older modern historical approaches invested in phenomenological assumptions. Many efforts in recent biblical studies have similarly sought to avoid the subjectivism so blatant in the phenomenological presuppositions of standard historical criticism by giving greater priority to 'the literary structure' of a biblical text or a pre-biblical tradition. Any such approach in pursuit of a more objective strategy, as though one can view a text with an innocent eye and a pristine desire, confronts Jacques Derrida's most telling criticism. For each effort at such a structuralist description, Derrida relentlessly exposes the various moments of '*aporia*' or 'gaps' that require decisions between two equally valid possibilities. A reader overcomes these gaps in a structure by invoking some conception of a 'center' which, in turn, depends on some 'subjective' phenomenological conception of presence, intention, intrinsic bond between reality and language, historical reference, symbolic system or whatever. Christopher Norris states the dilemma well:

> Subjectivism is not the only trap philosophy has to avoid. Structuralism has its own special dangers, the nature of which Husserl was quicker to grasp than most of its modern day practitioners. The concept of structure (as we have already seen) can easily be immobilized by assuming it to possess some kind of 'objective' or self-validating status. In this sense it is possible to argue, like Derrida, that 'a certain structuralism has always been philosophy's most spontaneous gesture'.[4]

We ought to expect that the 'most spontaneous' moves are, of course, the easiest to attribute to one's objectivity. For example, some newer applications of 'literary' theory have lately drawn remarkably assured historical conclusions simply from evidence of 'coherency', 'chiasm', 'unity' or a structured order to a larger composition. So, J.A. Moyter offers only meager literary evidence when he dismisses a citation from H.H. Rowley regarding 'a different tenor of the message' in Isaiah 40–66 from 1–39 with the confident statement, 'But it is simply not so, either broadly or in detail.'[5] Partially in debt to Y. Kaufmann, John H.

Things with Texts: Essays in Criticism and Critical Theory (ed. M. Fischer; New York: W.W. Norton & Co, 1991), pp. 237-63.

4.   C. Norris, *Deconstruction: Theory and Practice* (New York: Methuen, 1982), p. 50.

5.   J.A. Motyer, *The Prophecy of Isaiah* (Leicester: Inter-Varsity Press, 1993), p. 29.

Hayes and Stuart Irvine assert that Isaiah was 'a rhetorician' so that literary differences found in Isaiah 1–33 simply correspond to 'the nature of the rhetorical situation' which can be correlated to historical events in the life of the prophet.[6] In my view, one cannot so easily establish *historical* conclusions on such structuralist, predominantly synchronic 'literary' or 'rhetorical' arguments about the book.

Also, we should not be surprised that quite different structures can be 'found' and rationalized for the same text. None exists as the product of a purely objective encounter with 'the text', and, just as importantly, there is no transcendental logic of pure reason, expressed in terms of literary competence, that can decide absolutely the validity of one appeal to structure over another. A critical understanding of different 'visions' of the book of Isaiah invites a deconstruction of each one of them so that all false promises of innocence and neutrality are betrayed. Nonetheless, if all of our structural descriptions lack an entirely neutral objectivity, the alternative is neither to avoid structural appeals nor to assume they result from an entirely arbitrary subjectivity. Even Derrida, besides affirming the 'freeplay' of interpretation, states emphatically in his seminal presentation on 'Structure, Sign, and Play in the Discourses of the Human Sciences',

> I didn't say that there was no center, that we could get along without the center. I believe that the center is a function, not a being—a reality, but a function. And this function is absolutely indispensable. I don't destroy the subject, I situate it... It is a question of knowing where it comes from and how it functions.[7]

6.　　J.H. Hayes and S.A. Irvine, *Isaiah the Eighth-Century Prophet: His Times and his Preaching* (Nashville: Abingdon Press, 1987), pp. 60-61. Another example of such a 'literary' analysis of the 'present text' of Isaiah is B. Wiklander's *Prophecy as Literature: A Text-Linguistic and Rhetorical Approach to Isaiah 2–4* (Malmö: Gleerup, 1984). He discovers 'a remarkable semantic coherence and continuation' in Isa. 2–4, proving that these chapters must have been composed by a single author and used as oration to persuade, perhaps in 734–622 BCE (pp. 244-45). Based on the 'fundamental criterion of coherence', Wiklander argues, 'the analysis revealed such an inner completeness in Isa. 2–4 that relating it to Isa. 1 and 5 would dissolve this unity' (p. 244).

7.　　R. Macksey and E. Donato (eds.), *The Structuralist Controversy: The Languages of Criticism and the Sciences of Man* (Baltimore: John Hopkins University Press, 1972), p. 271. For a further discussion of Derrida on this point, see Frank Lentricchia, *After the New Criticism* (Chicago: University of Chicago Press, 1980), pp. 174-77.

Consequently, although Derrida allows for an infinite number of centered structures one might 'find' in a text, Derrida questions the innocence of each discovery without doubting the necessity of finding and using centered structures. Deconstruction is, therefore, not destructive in its aim but exposes the hidden moments of phenomenological decision that accompany and partly determine any appeal to a structure, including its context and syntax. The reader must face squarely some degree of circularity, which comes close to an admission of what the older hermeneutical discussion identified as a self-consciousness of some preunderstanding in interpretation. The preunderstanding partly explains why a particular structure may function as something more than another opportunity for freeplay. Whatever might justify one particular preunderstanding over another will depend on other philosophical, spiritual, historical, or pragmatic motivations and concerns. Within a given preunderstanding, there are certain rules that will distinguish competent and incompetent reading so that the subjectivity of a given interpretation is given bounds, aim, self-critical restriction, limited potential and can, by argument, hope to persuade and gain social consensus. An affirmation of the value of freeplay does not in itself negate the value of certain pragmatic preunderstandings a reader might have regarding the purpose of envisioning a particular text, for whatever reasons. Since a reader never lives in isolation from some community of discourse, either actual or remembered, then the social location of the reader calls the bluff on all claims of either absolute objectivity or an entirely serendipitous subjectivity.

If 'structural' descriptions, based on a historical and literary preunderstanding, betray the tyranny and temporality of their readers' own choices, then they are best done with a full awareness of these limitations. The reward is a relative rather than absolute objectivity, an objectivity peculiar to this particular relationship between reader and text, and the prospect of new discoveries within the possibilities intrinsic to this pragmatically limited hermeneutical system. The consequences are real; a reader's choice may be a matter of life or death. When confronted with a household fire, it may be crucial to read the instructions on the extinguisher in a shallow, telegraphic fashion rather than to take the time to explore all the semiotic structures of such notices on emergency equipment.

Just as I have argued against the absolutizing of 'the text' and its 'structure', I would argue strongly against the absolutizing of the reader as found in some types of reader-response criticism. I would be suspicious of any universal conception of a 'competent' reader since substantially different visions of a text require very different competencies. Without questioning many common dimensions to the human activity of reading texts, including the possibility of Noam Chomsky's 'universal grammar', I would not accept what has become a commonplace axiom of the modern period, that scriptural books ought to be read 'like any other book'.[8] Similarly, I would question Schleiermacher's distinction between a 'general hermeneutic' for all literature with a 'special hermeneutic' subsumed under it, to account for features peculiar to Scripture itself. The question of what is an ideal general hermeneutic cannot, in my view, be resolved on such an empirical basis.[9]

With these hermeneutical concerns in mind, I want now to describe different implicit visions of 'the text' of the book of Isaiah underlying several recent monographs on Isaiah. I will argue that these scholars do not simply have different perspectives on the same text, but actually read entirely different envisioned texts of Isaiah.

1. Marvin Sweeney's monograph, *Isaiah 1–4 and the Post-Exilic Understanding of the Isaianic Tradition* (1988), initially offers a brilliant and concise discussion of four key elements in the unity of the entire book.[10] However, his actual treatment of 'the text' in the later chapters concentrates on describing 'the structure' of various 'blocks of material' and the relationship between 'sub-units' within those blocks. Block after block is discussed, followed by his conclusion, 'the structure is...' (e.g. pp. 46, 48, 49). This 'structure', displayed in the form of an outline, is heavily invested in signs of thematization. At many places, after examining the end of one 'unit' and the beginning of another, Sweeney concludes that there is 'no syntactical connection' or that the units are 'syntactically unconnected' (e.g. pp. 36, 38, 39, 67). What Sweeney

8. Against this older modern view, see C.M. Wood, 'Hermeneutics and the Authority of Scripture', in G. Green (ed.), *Scriptural Authority and Narrative Interpretation* (Philadelphia: Fortress Press, 1987), pp. 3-20. Conversely, for a structuralist proposal of a general hermeneutic, that employs Chomsky's distinction between 'competence' and 'performance', see J. Culler, *Structuralist Poetics: Structuralism, Linguistics, and the Study of Literature* (Ithaca: Cornell University Press, 1975), p. 9.

9. G.T. Sheppard, 'Biblical Interpretation after Gadamer', *Pneuma* 16.1 (1994), pp. 121-41.

10. M.A. Sweeney, *Isaiah 1–4 and the Post-Exilic Understanding of the Isaianic Tradition* (BZAW, 171; Berlin: de Gruyter, 1988), pp. 1-25.

signifies is that he can find no connective particle; for example, the preposition *kî*. In my estimate, Sweeney sees 'the text' as primarily a temporal series of changing structures of new texts that build upon earlier textual compositions, each with its own 'reinterpretation' of prior stages, structures and units of tradition. Sweeney interprets these different 'stages' and 'structures' by trying to describe a similar or different hermeneutic that each employs.

2. Edgar Conrad, in his *Reading Isaiah* (1991), contrasts his own position with that of biblical scholar Georg Fohrer by stating that Fohrer 'has shaped it [the Book of Isaiah] in such a way as to enable him to carry out his interpretive goal of discovering the intentions of the prophet Isaiah'.[11] Fohrer's detection of key-word connections between smaller units of tradition (for example, in Isaiah 1) 'is shaping the text to accomplish his other goal of discovering the background of each of the oracles of Isaiah' (p. 10). My problem with this description of Fohrer is that it seems to imply that Fohrer merely distorts the text for his own self-interest. I would prefer to say that Fohrer envisions the text consistent with the strengths and limitations of his methodology, invested as it may be in a particular modern historical set of questions.

After this criticism of Fohrer and others, Conrad lays out his own approach (pp. 27-33) by stating bluntly, 'Every reading is of necessity a reading *into*, or eisegesis' (p. 29). But, just as quickly, Conrad claims his approach 'will reflect primarily objective theories or interpretation in combination with pragmatic ones' (pp. 28-29). This 'strategy' is 'structuralist' in nature and allegedly aims 'to do what historical criticism started out to do: to treat the biblical text as other texts are treated rather than to give it special treatment as a special kind of text' (p. 29). Conrad distinguishes his own conception of structure from that of redaction criticism. The latter is concerned with the text as 'historically developed' while Conrad is concerned with its 'aesthetic momentum' (p. 29). His criteria for discerning the structure of the text are: 'repetition in vocabulary, motif, theme, narrative sequence, and rhetorical questions, pronominal shifts, and forms of address' (p. 30). He will also employ the concepts of 'the implied reader and the implied audience'(p. 31). Consequently, he can treat '*the* structure' of this text as something 'in' the text rather than something he reads into it. For example, he seeks to describe 'essential elements in the text's structure' (p. 80); 'the text's

11. E.W. Conrad, *Reading Isaiah* (Overtures in Biblical Theology; Minneapolis: Fortress Press, 1991), p. 10.

structure (p. 111)'; 'An essential feature of the book's structure' (p. 118); 'the larger structure of the book' (pp. 119, 138); and 'the structure of the book' (pp. 130, 141).

This objectivist 'literary', 'structuralist' and text-oriented description stands in tension with his occasional use of standard form criticism. Relying on his earlier form-critical study of the 'fear not' formula as originally part of 'war oracles', Conrad selectively finds evidence of an important historical retention in this otherwise predominantly synchronic literary description. Whenever the text suggests a 'plan' of God, Conrad notes that other historical critics 'have not stressed the military connotations of this plan, as I do in this chapter' (p. 53). In my view, his justification for this consistent emphasis derives from his form-critical conclusions rather than from the 'literary' analysis he advocates. This one instance of form-critical background is often retained in his interpretation even when the word-clues are common and the context might not require it. So, he states after considering the occurrence of words with military connotations in the narratives about Ahaz and Hezekiah that 'The words ʿṣh and yʿṣ and associated words elsewhere in the book have military connotations as well' (p. 54). Consequently, military motifs related to the war oracle 'represent essential elements in the structure of the book' (p. 80). Yet, the appeal to form-critical retentions in support of subtle 'connotations' and essential 'motifs' negotiates a very different vision of the text as units of oral tradition, distinguished from his otherwise more synchronic, literary approach.

Conrad presupposes that his literary approach will 'treat the biblical text as other texts are treated rather than to give it special treatment as a special kind of text' (p. 29). This universal theory of 'all texts' is impressively applied, but envisions the book of Isaiah in only one possible aesthetic manner. This vision of the book of Isaiah underplays the complexity of its prehistory and shows little interest in a vision of the book as part of two distinct scriptural intertexts, Jewish and Christian. Nothing is wrong with his approach except that we may not accept its claim to find an 'objectivist' position. Even Conrad shows hesitancy on that score, when he states that 'The Bible is a myriad of presences in the contemporary world. All its readers should be heard' (p. 168). What remains unclear is whether every reading ought to be of equal status to every interpreter. Depending on how one envisions the text of the book of Isaiah, some readings will surely prove much more illuminating than others.

3. H.G.M. Williamson's monograph entitled, *The Book of Isaiah* (1994) is sub-titled more accurately, *Deutero-Isaiah's Role in Composition and Redaction*.[12] What he envisions by 'the book of Isaiah' is actually two or more 'books': those written by Isaiah himself and that produced by Deutero-Isaiah. Williamson bases this reconstruction on evidence that Deutero-Isaiah (chs. 40–55) depends directly on Isaianic tradition in chs. 1–39. The 'book' created by Deutero-Isaiah, of course, does not contain 'Trito-Isaiah' (56–66). Williamson states, 'It is assumed that Trito-Isaiah is a separate composition, later in date than at any rate the bulk of Isaiah 1–55' (p. 20). Williamson argues that his interpretation explains the independence of whole clusters of tradition on the theory that we find in 1–39 vestiges of 'a book' [or books] that Isaiah had once 'sealed' as a 'witness' for a later time (cf. 8.1-4; 8.16-17; 30.8-9). This 'book' was 'opened' (29.11-18) at a later time by Deutero-Isaiah, who revised it and added his own prophetic interpretations in direct dependence upon many of the themes and motifs found in the original book of Isaiah. The 'scroll' or 'book' that occurs in 34.16 is irrelevant to Williamson's vision of the book of Isaiah, since both chs. 34 and 35 already 'presuppose a form of the book in which the main parts of Proto- and of Deutero-Isaiah were present' and, consequently, chs. 34 and 35 'stand much closer to the world of Trito-Isaiah' (pp. 220, 243). Regardless of whether or not Williamson is convincing in his detailed historical assessment, his vision of the book of Isaiah aims at a speculative reconstruction of at least two 'books' which later editors of the scriptural book of Isaiah no longer sought to preserve with full independence or explicit distinction.

Much as in the case of Sweeney's detection of multiple redactional stages, we see the reasonableness of this vision of successive Isaianic books. But what is less evident is how one ought to interpret these differing pre-scriptural stages of redaction or 'books' collectively or in continuity with each other. If we allow fully for the difference and discontinuity between these various 'books', then we ought to be suspicious of any argument for continuity in the process of successive redactions—for example, either a theory of 'actualization' (Gerhard von Rad) or a 'canonical hermeneutic' (James Sanders)—that might claim to do justice to such a complex history of different traditions and books. Williamson wisely avoids this option, proposing simply that if his work is

12. H.G.M. Williamson, *The Book of Isaiah: Deutero-Isaiah's Role in Composition and Redaction* (Oxford: Clarendon Press, 1994).

compelling then we might be able to attempt 'a reading specifically from within the standpoint of Deutero-Isaiah' (p. 244). At a minimum, 'the book of Isaiah' is in this monograph only envisioned as two or more books that existed prior to a much later book of Isaiah in Jewish Scripture.

4. In his introduction to essays on *Reading and Preaching the Book of Isaiah* (1988), Christopher Seitz explains why the older historical approaches could not view the book of Isaiah as a whole.[13] In the older modern period scholars assumed that 'Unity of message demanded a consistent authorial voice', but times have changed, so, 'There may be newer critical attempts to describe the literary and editorial features that enable us to read a highly complex, multilayered Book of Isaiah as a unified whole' (p. 17). With further clarification, Seitz argues, 'Unity and coherence are sought rather in the "reciprocal relationships" between the literary blocks of First (1–39), Second (40–55), and Third (56–66) Isaiah' (p. 17). The most promising 'newer critical attempts' are 'the newer redactional studies' (p. 18). Their new goal is 'a clearer description of the intention behind the merger of these various literary strata, the result being our present Book of Isaiah' (p. 18). The resulting book 'requires a suspension of strictly historical-critical interest to try and read the sixty-six-chapter book as a coherent literary and theological composition' which is justified only 'once it is assumed that part of the intention behind the present growth of the tradition was not merely the result of *accident or historical expedient*' (my italics, p. 19).

Seitz also recognizes that the 'intent' of the whole book will be 'greater than the sum of all previous intentions of the text, as these have been reconstructed in modern historical analysis'. He calls attention, therefore, to two main key questions: '1) What is the source of the Book of Isaiah's unity? 2) How are we as readers to make sense of Isaiah as a sixty-six-chapter whole?' (p. 105) His description moves beyond older historical approaches to ask the question about the 'unity' or the 'present shape' of the book as a search for a comprehensive symbol or theme that weaves its way through each of the differing redactional levels in the prehistory of the biblical text. However, Seitz also wants to ask a question that sounds closer to reader-response criticism: 'But is there an internal, reader-oriented movement across the sixty-six-chapter length and breadth that we can perceive and that enables us to hear, see, and

13. C. Seitz, 'Isaiah 1–66: Making Sense of the Whole', in *idem* (ed.), *Reading and Preaching the Book of Isaiah* (Minneapolis: Fortress Press, 1988), pp. 13-22.

stand before this entire…"vision of Isaiah" (1.1), as the book calls itself?' (p. 106) Seitz finds this unifying feature in the concern with Zion in ch. 1 and throughout the book. The second question he asks is related naturally to how he answers the first, so that he then calls for a 'focus' on Zion's restoration throughout the book.

Despite Seitz's stated goals, I think much of his vision of the book of Isaiah both in his monograph, *Zion's Final Destiny* (1991), and in his commentary, *Isaiah 1–39* (1993) still remains mainly pre-scriptural, at the level of an intertextuality between different redactional levels of composition.[14] This vision of the book as an integration of redactional levels causes him to center the book by finding a solution to a particular 'theological' problem identified at all levels of redaction; namely, a continuing promise to Zion despite the experience of delay or the potential disconfirmation of exile. Various redactors' responses to this problem becomes the key to the book's unity and the 'focus' of the resultant text. Seitz can therefore conclude in his commentary for the book as a whole that 'Isaiah's particular view of Zion theology is vindicated' (p. 37). Such a view of the book of Isaiah as belonging to a particular moment of a longer theological debate in the history of ancient Israel is certainly one legitimate way to envision the traditions in the book. However, it may still fail to see the book fully as a book of Jewish Scripture or to describe adequately the book's participation within an even larger intertext of biblical books. Likewise, it misses other internal features in the organization of the book, such as the anticipation of a reversal of judgment and God's 'comfort' in Isa. 40.1-11 as found in the praise hymn of ch. 12 (cf. v. 2).[15] Similarly, what remains unclear in Seitz's description is how Isaiah's 'voice' can pertain to the whole book in his name and how this particular vision of the book informs its place among 'the Prophets', and as a part of a scripture that begins with the Torah of Moses.[16] From the standpoint of the later rabbinic concern with 'midrash' or a Christian emphasis on 'the literal sense' of

14. C. Seitz, *Zion's Final Destiny: The Development of the Book of Isaiah; A Reassessment of Isaiah 36–39* (Minneapolis: Fortress Press, 1991) and his *Isaiah 1–39* (Interpretation; Louisville: John Knox, 1993).

15. J.L. Mays (ed.), *Harper's Bible Commentary* (New York: Harper & Row, 1988), pp. 558-89.

16. See the defense of 'epireading' and a 'voice' conveyed by written texts, against Derrida and 'graphireading', in D. Donaghue, *Ferocious Alphabets* (Boston: Little, Brown & Co, 1981), pp. 95-148, esp. pp. 205-11.

Scripture, Seitz's analysis does not directly help us to see how this vision of the book meets or resists such different expectations by these historic religions.[17] Again, I do not assume that this concern is something every scholar must ask. I do think it becomes important to Seitz, since he wants to describe the unity of a scriptural book of Isaiah and demonstrates an impressive criticism of other criticisms in doing so.

2. Two Constructive Proposals on Isaiah as a Book of Scripture

With an appreciation for the validity and differences of these 'visions' of the text of Isaiah, I want to offer two constructive efforts of my own. My aim is to envision the book of Isaiah in both historical and literary terms as a book of Jewish and Christian Scripture. I will draw upon insights of continuity and discontinuity with various other texts of Isaiah within its scriptural prehistory. Most of the traditions now found in Jewish and Christian texts were not originally written to be 'Scripture' and, admittedly the moment when a text becomes scriptural is historically ambiguous. In my earlier work on 'canon-conscious' redactions, I sought to describe some of the signs of this semantic transformation from pre-scriptural to scriptural traditions.[18] In a later publication I will similarly

17. On the 'literal sense' in the Christian understanding of scripture, see H. Oberman, *Forerunners of the Reformation: The Shape of Late Medieval Thought Illustrated by Key Documents* (Philadelphia: Fortress Press, 1966), pp. 281-294; B.S. Childs, 'The Sensus Literalis of Scripture: An Ancient and Modern Problem', in H. Donner, R. Hanhart and R. Smend (eds.), *Beiträge zur Alttestamentlichen Theologie: Festschrift für Walter Zimmerli* (Göttingen: Vandenhoeck & Ruprecht, 1976), pp. 80-95; K. Froelich, '"Always to Keep the Literal Sense in Holy Scripture Means to Kill One's Soul": The State of Biblical Hermeneutics at the Beginning of the Fifteenth Century', in E. Miner (ed.), *Literary Uses of Typology from the Late Middle Ages to the Present* (Princeton: Princeton University Press, 1977), pp. 20-48; and H. Frei, 'The Literal Reading of Biblical Narrative in the Christian Tradition: Does It Stretch or Will It Break?', in F. McConnell (ed.), *The Bible and the Narrative Tradition* (New York: Oxford University Press, 1986), pp. 36-77; R.B. Robinson, *Roman Catholic Exegesis Since Divino Afflante Spiritu: Hermeneutical Implications* (SBLDS, 111; Atlanta: Scholars Press, 1988); and Sheppard, 'Biblical Interpretation after Gadamer' (see n. 9 above).

18. Cf. G.T. Sheppard, *Wisdom as a Hermeneutical Construct: A Study in the Sapientializing of the Old Testament* (BZAW, 151; Berlin: de Gruyter, 1980), and for other indicators of this transformation, see *idem*, 'Canonization: Hearing the Voice of the Same God through Historically Dissimilar Traditions', *Interpretation* 34.1 (1982), pp. 21-33. Also, see B.S. Childs's effort to describe historical

discuss the shift in the understanding of the pre-biblical and biblical understanding of these texts as 'witnesses' to revelation. Elsewhere I have discussed what I take to be some key internal features within the book of Isaiah itself.[19] Here I will focus only on two dimensions of the book of Isaiah in a way that might demonstrate my own orientation to the book as a part of Jewish and Christian Scriptures.

a. *The Distinctive and Central Message of Historical Isaiah's Prophecy, as Presented in the Book of Isaiah*

In two provocative essays, Rolf Rendtorff has called for fresh attention to the relation of the so-called 'call report' of Isaiah in ch. 6 to other parts of the book, including ch. 1 and especially ch. 40.[20] Without rehearsing all of his conclusions here, it will suffice to observe that he can show resonance both backward to ch.1 and forward to chs. 40–66, including such themes as 'seeing'/'hearing' (6.9b, 10b; cf. 1.3); 'knowing/discerning' (6.19; cf. 44.18, esp. v. 19); the metaphor of 'blindness and deafness' (cf. 42.16, 18-19; 43.8); and 'healing' (6.10; cf. 42.7; 50.4).[21] Melugin and Ackroyd had earlier paved the way by noting general similarities between Isaiah 6 and 40.[22] Rendtorff now concludes that the announcement of the stubbornness of the people in ch. 6 finds its logical resolution in the announcement of salvation in Isa. 40.1-11: 'der este Teil von Kap. 6 im Blick auf und in Wechselbeziehung mit Kap. 40 formuliert worden sein' ('the first part of ch. 6 has been formulated with a view toward and in dynamic relationship with ch. 40').[23] I want to push this discussion a step further by asking a

'trajectories' in the movement from pre-biblical to biblical traditions, in his *Biblical Theology of the Old and New Testaments* (London: SCM Press, 1992), pp. 97-207.

19. Cf. G.T. Sheppard, 'Isaiah 1–39', in Mays (ed.), *Harper's Bible Commentary*, pp. 542-70, and 'The Anti-Assyrian Redaction and the Canonical Context of Isaiah 1–39', *JBL* 104.2 (1985), pp. 193-216.

20. R. Rendtorff, 'Zum Komposition des Buches Jesaja', *VT* (34 (1984), pp. 295-320, and his 'Jesaja 6 im Rahmen der Komposition des Jesajabuches', in J. Vermeylen (ed.), *The Book of Isaiah* (BETL, 81; Leuven: Leuven University Press, 1989), pp. 73-72.

21. Rendtorff, 'Jesaja 6', pp. 76-79.

22. R.F. Melugin, *The Formation of Isaiah 40–55* (BZAW, 141; Berlin: de Gruyter, 1976), esp. pp. 177-78, and P.R. Ackroyd, 'Isaiah I–XII, Presentation of a Prophet', in *idem*, *Studies in the Religious Tradition of the Old Testament* (London: SCM Press, 1987), pp. 79-104.

23. Rendtorff, 'Jesaja 6', p. 81.

deceptively simple question about the relation of Isaiah 6 to the rest of the book: What is the message, according to the presentation of the scriptural text, that most people in Isaiah's day are too blind to see and too deaf to hear, a message which later generations will grasp? If Isaiah 6 and 40 represent what Rendtorff calls *'die "zentrale" Texte'*, then what is 'the central message' of the prophet as it is presented within the book as a whole?[24]

Clements allows for this question by interpreting the words of God to Isaiah in 6.9-10 as essentially a statement 'that God knew in advance that the people would not respond to his message'.[25] The question regarding the precise nature of the message rejected must be resolved by looking elsewhere in the book, a necessity Rendtorff has already seen when he asked other similar questions of ch. 6. One possible response would be to give attention to various 'themes' that run through the entire collection. What we find is a surprisingly complex inner-resonance among a great variety of themes throughout the book. I think especially of the work in this regard by Childs, Rendtorff, Seitz, Ackroyd, Clements and myself. These studies show that our problem is no longer that there are so few obvious connections between parts of the book, but that there are so many and that they may seem so independent and disparately related. The evidence is diverse and extensive. It ranges from the name for God, 'the Holy One of Israel', to plays upon a motif of 'briars and thorns', scored initially by the Song of the Vineyard in Isaiah 5 (Sheppard), to the 'plan' of God (H. Barth), to a major concern with the destiny of Zion (Seitz), and so forth. One key feature in the book is clearly the concern with former and latter things, with the implications for finding 'former things' in 1–39, as Childs and Seitz have shown. Without reviewing all of these contributions, I want to reduce my question to its most simple form: Does the book highlight a single message above others in the presentation of the prophet Isaiah, and how is it related to other demarcated parts of this book?

Granted that the first chapter is an introduction to the entire book, this question is a smaller one and must be linked to the presentation of the prophet and the response he gains. Similar to Rendtorff's work, Conrad likewise explores possible implications of the statement in Isaiah 6 that the people will be blind and deaf, unable to comprehend (6.9-11) until the devastation of the 'cities' and 'land' (6.11) and the exile (6.12).

24. Rendtorff, 'Jesaja 6', p. 76.
25. R. Clements, *Isaiah 1–39* (NCB; Grand Rapids: Eerdmans, 1980), p. 77.

Conrad thinks that 29.18—'On that day, the deaf shall hear the words of a scroll, and out of their gloom darkness the eyes of the blind shall see'—'echoes' ch. 6 and 8.16, and concludes, on further argument, that 'a scroll' mentioned here and as 'sealed' in 29.11-12 and 'the book' not 'read' in 30.8-11 is now found in Isaiah 6–39.[26] While I find this thesis contrived, it does show how Isaiah 6 raises this important question. By implication someone must be sent by God to deliver a message to the people, but after Isaiah volunteers to carry that message we hear only God's declaration that the people will not hear, see or comprehend it. We can still ask, 'Comprehend what?' If not, as Conrad suggests, an internal book of Isaiah 6–39, then what is the message which is like a sealed scroll to them until 'that day'?

I think that the answer is found clearly spelled out, initially, in the narratives that follow the call report. There we find a message that is essentially the same, repeatedly delivered with differing responses. So, the same message given to Ahaz in 7.4, who does not obey it, is given once more by God to Isaiah himself in 8.11-15, under the same circumstances of the Syro-Ephraimite threat. In both cases, the message can be summarized by the brief repeated formula, 'fear not' (7.4; 8.12), and summarized at the end of the word to Ahaz: 'If you do not stand firm in faith, you shall not stand at all' (7.9b). By implication, fear of anything but God will lead to human words and deeds which God will not approve. Likewise, taking an action based on that fear is forbidden. Ahaz does not obey this word, but the prophet and perhaps those closely associated with him do.

The narratives in chs. 36–39, about the later king, Hezekiah, confirm that exactly the same message is given to him during the crisis of Sennacherib's invasion: 'Do not be afraid', accompanied by a promise of deliverance (37.5). Instead of acting desperately in fear, Hezekiah prays and God rewards him with a salvation oracle and the deliverance of the city. Ackroyd has already shown impressively how Ahaz and Hezekiah are presented in these narratives as bad and good examples; my observation would add the prophet Isaiah himself as a positive example.[27] Certainly, this aspect of the book invites realistic mimetic interpretation on the subject of how one responds to God's word, 'Do not fear', or act out of fear, when enemies surround you.

26. Conrad, *Reading Isaiah*, pp. 131-34.

27. P.R. Ackroyd, 'Isaiah 36–39: Structure and Function', in *idem, Studies in the Religious Tradition of the Old Testament*, pp. 105-20.

Between the narrative where Ahaz rejects the prophet's message (ch. 7) and where Hezekiah accepts and acts according to it (chs. 36–38), the rejected message is written in a 'book' (8.16) and is to be a 'Torah' and 'testimony' for later generations, including those in exile (cf. 8.19-22). Here we find a situation like Ackroyd described in his important study, 'The Vitality of the Word of God in the Old Testament'.[28] The semantic density and reapplicability of the same word of God over time here in Isaiah correspond to Ackroyd's description of how the same prophetic words first given in 1 Kgs 14.11 recur in new applications and fulfill-ments in the mouths of other prophets addressing other persons in 1 Kgs 16.4; 21.19; and 21.24.

Finally, between the narratives about Ahaz, Isaiah and Hezekiah we also find several places that look forward to a time when people will no longer be deaf and blind, and will obey this word. The song in Isa. 12.1-6 plays a transitional role within the collection, after the section asso-ciated with the so-called Memoir of Isaiah (6–11) and before the oracles against the nations (13–23). Verse 1, as noted before, anticipates a reversal of God's judgment and the 'comfort' of 40.1, 'in that day'. But v. 2 is especially noteworthy for my current purpose. It similarly foresees a time when people will say, 'Surely God is my salvation; I will trust and *will not be afraid* for the Lord God is my strength and my might; he has become my salvation.' So too in 28.16 there is the reminder, 'One who trusts will not panic'. Again, Isa. 35.4 states, 'Say to those who are of a fearful heart, "Be strong, *do not fear*! Here is your God!" He will come with vengeance, with terrible recompense. He will come and save you.' The following verse assures us that at the same time the blind will see and the deaf will hear. Whether or not ch. 35 once formed a bridge to unite so-called Second Isaiah with a new edition of earlier tradition (O.H. Steck) or derives from 'a late stage in the composition of the book as a whole' (Williamson), it now plays an important summarizing role in the book, before the narratives about Isaiah in chs. 36–39 and in anticipation of the lengthy tapestry of oracles with no narratives in Isaiah 40–66.[29] In sum, what Ackroyd found to be

28. P.R. Ackroyd, 'The Vitality of the Word of God in the Old Testament: A Contribution to the Study of the Transmission and Exposition of Old Testament Material', in *idem, Studies in the Religious Tradition of the Old Testament*, pp. 61-75.

29. O.H. Steck, *Bereitete Heimkehr: Jesaja 35 als redaktionelle Brucke zwischen den Ersten und dem Zweiten Jesaja* (SBS, 121; Stuttgart: Katholisches Bibelwerk,

true of a prophetic word in 1 Kings illuminates what we find here. Clearly, such biblical prophecy is not governed by a narrowly modern idea of the author's intent or of 'fulfillment' in terms of a singular event which exhausts the vitality of the prophetic word. In the scriptural presentation at least, a prophetic word given to one audience can be saved and reread as a possible prophetic message to others. A fulfillment confirms the authority of the word without undermining its relevance to later times and events.

Above all, Conrad has most effectively shown that what he calls a war oracle formula, 'Do not fear', 'represents a clue to understanding the structure of the book as a whole'.[30] Conrad perceptively explores the use of the formula in the first part of Isaiah 40–55, especially in the 'trial scenes' (41.1-5, 21-29; 43.8-15; 44.6-8; 45.1-13, 20-25).[31] Conrad does not consider other recurrences of the same formula elsewhere in Isaiah 40–55 (i.e. 40.9; 51.7, 12; 54.4). Two observations beyond Conrad's study are as follows. First, 40.9 encourages Jerusalem, who is told 'do not fear' and instructed to tell the cities of Judah, 'Here is your God'. Again, the same message given to Ahaz, to Isaiah himself and to Hezekiah is now given to Jerusalem! Even the opening prophetic message to a devastated Jerusalem in 40.1, 'Comfort, O comfort my people', conveys the same idea. By contrast, the nations will be afraid (e.g. 13.8; 17.2; 19.16; 20.5; 21.4; 31.9), as will be the whole earth (e.g. 24.17; 25.3). Second, 51.7 directly recalls this message of Isaiah as conveying the same 'torah' (cf. 8.16, 20) of God: 'Listen to me, you who know righteousness, you people who have my teaching/torah in your hearts. *Do not fear* the reproach of others, and do not be dismayed when they revile you.' Similarly, v. 12 recalls ch. 40, the link between 'comfort' and the command 'do not fear', as well as the description of humanity as mere grass (40.7-8) in contrast to the word of God: 'I, I am he who comforts you; why then are you afraid of a mere mortal who must die, a human being who fades like grass?'

Beyond Conrad's treatment we need also to consider how the content of the formula is used in the last chapters, 56–66, the so-called 'Third Isaiah'. Acknowledging Rendtorff's emphasis on the importance of Third Isaiah as a means to hold 1–39 and 40–55 together, we ought to note especially 57.11 and 63.17. Isa. 57.11 challenges those who 'fear'

1985) and Williamson, *The Book of Isaiah*, pp. 212-14.

30. Conrad, *Reading Isaiah*, p. 37.

31. Conrad, *Reading Isaiah*, pp. 135-36.

others rather than God, echoing a counterpoint in the narratives (cf. Isa. 7.4b). In Isa. 63.17, in a prayer of penitence, we hear echoes of Isaiah's call report in the plea, 'Why, O Lord, do you make us stray from our ways and harden our heart, so that we do not fear you?' In the last chapter, the 'one to whom I will look' is in the eyes of God a person who is receptive, 'human and contrite in spirit who trembles at my word' (66.2b; see also 66.5). If those who receive comfort tremble at God's word rather than fear the nations, so the nations themselves 'tremble at [God's] presence' which threatens to devour them 'as when fire kindles brushwood' (66.2). Clearly, the hermeneutical nature of a prophetic word, its semantic density and capacity to speak to multiple audiences, including future readers of this book, sheds light on the 'structural' possibilities of this book as Scripture.

In sum, a thematic approach or an emphasis on connective motifs enters a dense thicket of inner resonances within the book of Isaiah. Many of these themes occur only in 1–39 while others continue throughout 40–66.[32] More important than a thematizing of the book based on evidence of one resonance or another will be the larger vision one has of the text and what questions we ask of it. Here 'fear not' is less a 'theme' than a historical prophetic message unleashed upon generation after generation of audiences. It points to one message among many that nevertheless becomes distinctive of the message of Isaiah at every level of the biblical text. It helps us hear the same prophetic voice, that of the Isaiah as presented in the book, throughout the whole composition in his name, without either reducing the words of the prophet to a small doctrinal statement or anchoring the prophetic word to only one audience in time and space.

b. *The Book of Isaiah and the Torah*
A preunderstanding that affects our search and perception of 'structure' implies that we have already asked a question about how the form of a text relates to a function or content that interests us. Premodern interpreters often answered this question by an appeal to a text's 'scope', a term referring both to the shape of the text itself as though it were a specific territory of land or a particular human anatomy and to

---

32. For example, R.E. Clements, 'Beyond Tradition History: Deutero-Isaianic Development of First Isaiah's Themes', *JSOT* 31 (1985), pp. 95-113, and Sheppard, 'The Anti-Assyrian Redaction and the Canonical Context of Isaiah 1–39', pp. 193-216.

its central purpose or argument.[33] In other words, what is the subject matter addressed by this text or, in a more nuanced manner, what are the idioms of that subject matter that correspond to the form and function of this text? Expressed in this way, the question is a historical one and is pertinent most clearly to the late resultant, effective or present text we have before us. Behind it lies the assumption that we do not want to impose our own views on this literature but want to see how its late 'shape' efficiently referred to a subject matter available to its readers, then and, perhaps, now. That subject matter, of course, may not have originally been intended by the sub-traditions that now belong to this book and may be due entirely to a semantic transformation occasioned by their new context within it.

In the simplest terms, we might at least wonder if Isaiah *as a book of Jewish Scripture* might not have the Torah as its principal subject matter and if there might not be signs of this assumption in the editing of the book itself. We are all aware of Jensen's study of *torah* in Isaiah and his conclusion that in eighth-century Isaiah's own tradition it conveys a wisdom sense of 'instruction' (1.10; 5.24; 8.16; 30.9).[34] However, we are asking a different question: What role does this same term, *torah*, come to play in the later, scriptural book of Isaiah? Later references to *torah* in Isaiah 1–39 may plausibly have the Mosaic Torah originally in mind (2.3; 8.20; 24.5), as do the references in 40–66 (42.4, 21, 24; 51.4, 7).

Sweeney articulates well these hermeneutical implications: 'In essence, the concerns of the latter part of the book dictated the final redaction of the first part', so that, 'the structure, genre, setting, and intent of the entire book must be determined in order to understand the overarching concerns which led to its formation and the role which its component texts play as part of the larger framework.'[35] One of Sweeney's most perceptive contributions, in my view, is his observation about Isa. 1.5, 'Why would you be smitten again that you continue apostasy?' He concludes that this verse, as part of the 'introduction' to the book of

---

33. See G.T. Sheppard, 'Between the Reformation and Modern Commentary: The Perception of the Scope of Biblical Books', in G.T. Sheppard (ed.), *William Perkins' A Commentary on Galatians: With Introductory Essays* (New York: Pilgrim Press, 1989), pp. xlviii-lxxvii.

34. J. Jansen, *The Use of Tôrâ by Isaiah: His Debate with the Wisdom Tradition* (CBQMS, 3; Washington, DC: Catholic Biblical Association, 1973), pp. 68-89.

35. Sweeney, *Isaiah 1–4*, p. 185, see esp. 198-201.

Isaiah, 'presupposes that punishment has already come, but it also implies that more punishment will come if the people do not correct their behavior' (p. 121). He elaborates, 'The presupposition here [v. 10] is that the people have sinned out of ignorance. That situation is corrected by YHWH's instruction [*torah*] so that the people may correct their own behavior, presumably to end the punishment mentioned in vv. 4-9' (p. 121). Since Sweeney dates 1.10 in the period of Hezekiah, he describes the original use of *torah* in this verse, as 'prophetic torah' (p. 128). However, Sweeney knows that a semantic shift takes place when this older reference to *torah* belongs to an 'introduction' presupposing *torah* as found in 2.1-4, which dates to the late fifth century (p. 163). As a redacted part of the 'introduction', 1.10-18 has a new context and altered import so that 'The oracle concerning cultic practice in 1.10-18 referred not [any longer] to Hezekiah's cultic reforms, but to those parties in the late fifth century who sought to continue cultic service to YHWH, but lacked the teachings which were the basis of His Torah' (p. 195).

Sweeney argues that *torah* and *word* in 2.3, along with many other parts of the book, convey a post-exilic tradition, perhaps fifth century in origin (p. 162), but at least by the early fourth century when Isa. 2.1-4 /Mic. 4.1-4 is quoted in Joel 4.9-12 (pp. 169-70). With further refinement, Sweeney concludes that it derives sometime 'after the time of Deutero-Isaiah' (p. 173), sometime 'much later than the completion of the Second Temple' (p. 174). Although Sweeney does not say more about the nature of the *torah* in 2.3, we may assume from his dating of the tradition that it would likely have the Mosaic Torah implicitly in mind. He compares the usage of Torah here to 'an earlier text from Deutero-Isaiah', 51.4, where *torah* is paired with *mishpat* unlike here. Likewise, 4.2-4 is post-Deutero-Isaiah and plays upon Exodus and wilderness traditions, which Sweeney thinks derive from 'the priestly traditions of the [pentateuchal] Torah' (p. 180). Redactionally, Isaiah 2–4, despite containing some older traditions, is late sixth or early fifth century (p. 192) and ch. 1 is still later, 'toward the end of the fifth century BCE, about the time of Nehemiah and Ezra' (p. 194).

Sweeney allows for older tradition to have new semantic import in the new context of this 'book' in the late fifth century; for example, '...the oracle in 1.29-31, originally delivered against the apostasizers of the late pre-exilic period, was just as appropriate at this time' (p. 195). An obvious question therefore concerns the nature of this *torah* which has *by the introduction* been made so prominent now for the book of Isaiah. Despite one aim of the book of Isaiah to 'convince people to choose righteousness, e.g., YHWH's Torah', Sweeney concludes that 'there is no indication in Isaiah that Torah refers to the Five Books of Moses or any specific body of teaching'. He speculates that the openness to 'foreigners (56.1-8; 66.18-23)' suggests that 'the party which produced the final form of the book did not fully agree with Ezra's program' (p. 196).[36]

In sum, as I have also argued elsewhere, the identification of 'the *word* of Yahweh' with 'the *torah* of our God' (1.10; cf. 2.3) points to the principal subject matter of the book of Isaiah as a whole. Here we find a post-exilic usage in the sense of 'laws...the statutes...everlasting covenant' (24.5). Against Sweeney, I do not think that anything in Third Isaiah precludes the possibility that the Torah here is complementary to the Mosaic Torah of Ezra. The relation of foreigners to reconstituted Judah is not a simplistic rejection. Moreover, Clements cautiously concludes on 24.5 that 'it is not impossible that the Mosaic covenant with Israel is meant, as the glossator at least seems to have understood by his reference to *laws*'.[37]

I want to call attention to one other redactional shift in the semantic understanding of *torah*, at a crucial place immediately after Isaiah is told to 'bind up' 'the testimony' and *the torah* in 8.16. I agree with Clements and others who see 8.19-20, as 'a comment on vv. 16-18 from the exilic age'. We therefore find in vv. 19-20, as well as in vv. 21-22, the darkness and gloom of exile into which the following Emmanuel prophecy casts a great light (9.1-6 [RSV 9.2-7]). In this exilic note we find a warning to avoid the false hope of other prophetic sources (v. 19), wedded to a positive alternative: 'No! Turn instead to the *torah* and the testimony.'[38] What is this *torah* in the exilic period? I think it clearly is identified here as the book of Isaiah, recalling 8.16, but implies a Scripture and a subject matter larger than merely this book. It is concerned with the Torah itself, not merely the book of Isaiah which is one testimony to that Torah.

Finally, a perplexing question raised by this treatment may be why the

36. For my further arguments with Sweeney's position on the identification of the Torah, see Sheppard, 'The Book of Isaiah as a Human Witness to Revelation within the Religions of Judaism and Christianity', p. 275.

37. Clements, *Isaiah 1–39*, p. 202.

38. Clements, *Isaiah 1–39*, pp. 101, 102.

book of Isaiah does not, in contrast to the Deuteronomistic History, have more overt signs of direct and less subtle dependence on the Mosaic Torah, the first five books? If such a relationship to the Mosaic Torah, promulgated by Ezra, is dominant in the period when Isaiah attains its main contours as a book of Scripture, then why do we not find more overt cross-references in Isaiah to the Mosaic Torah? I have two responses: 1) observation of a similar reticence in other books, and 2) the multivalent character of the relation of these books to the subject matter of Torah.

1. The late adaptation of older prebiblical tradition to become part of a later 'biblical' context in relation to the Torah can be illustrated in various books, but I want to focus only briefly on the Psalms. The work of James L. Mays, as well as that of my own have given special attention to the role of Psalm 1 as a introduction to the larger book of Psalms.[39] It is identified variously as a Torah and/or wisdom psalm. Perdue observes that with the removal of v. 2 and, I would add, the non-metaphorical last phrase of v. 3, it would be a pure wisdom psalm, with a proverbial message at the end (v. 6).[40] Without solving the redactional problems I want to call attention to these potentially additional words:

> Conversely, their delight is in *the torah* of Yahweh;
> On his *torah* they shall meditate day and night. (v. 2)
> In all that they do, they prosper. (v. 3b)

Without restating here the arguments regarding how these words now orient the following Psalms to the subject matter of Torah, I want to call attention to what has been noticed but unappreciated. The textual notes in *BHS*, for good reasons, suggest that the phrase in v. 3b is perhaps a gloss from Josh. 1.8. In fact, what is remarkable is that we can find in Josh. 1.8, and no where else in the Hebrew Bible, virtually all the words found here in Ps. 1.2 and 1.3b: 'This book of *the torah* shall not depart out of your mouth; you *shall meditate on it* [cf. 'on his Torah' in Ps. 1.2] *day and night*, so that you may be careful to act in accordance with

39. J.L. Mays, 'The Place of the Torah-Psalms in the Psalter', *JBL* 106 (1987), pp. 3-12; W. Brueggemann, 'Bounded by Obedience and Praise: The Psalms as Canon', *JSOT* 50 (1991), pp. 63-92; and G.T. Sheppard, 'Theology and the Psalms', *Int* 46.2 (1992), pp. 143-155, and *idem*, 'The Preface to the Psalter (Ps. 1 and 2)', in *Wisdom as a Hermeneutical Construct: A Study in the Sapientializing of the Old Testament*, pp. 136-144.

40. L.G. Perdue, *Wisdom and Cult* (SBLDS, 30; Missoula, MT: Scholars Press, 1977), pp. 269-73.

all that is written in it. For then your way ($d^e r\bar{a}kek\bar{a}$) *shall prosper* and then you shall be successful.'

In the formation of the Mosaic Torah, Deuteronomy was wrenched away from the rest of the Deuteronomistic History and combined with other old Jerusalemite priesthood traditions in Genesis to Numbers to form a single Mosaic Torah (Genesis to Deuteronomy).[41] The remaining portion of the Deuteronomistic History (Joshua–2 Kings) became part of 'the Prophets', distinct but related to the principal manifestation of the Torah in Jewish Scripture. The note in Josh. 1.8 points to this new relationship as Fishbane and others have observed.[42] The same device has therefore been employed in Psalm 1. My point is that a very significant moment in the semantic transformation of Scripture may not necessarily be registered with a heavy hand. In the case of the Deuteronomistic History, the book of Psalms, and here in the book of Isaiah, the same intertextual relationship between various parts of Scripture to the Torah is underscored. If one asks what Isaiah is about, a logical answer is now, 'the Torah'. Any structural analysis that ignores that identification of the subject matter ignores the late form and function of the book *as a book of Jewish and Christian scripture.*

2. While making this point about the Torah and Isaiah, I have not ignored the fact that there is little if any direct reference to the laws of the Mosaic Torah in the book of Isaiah. The same may be said for the Psalms and even, to a remarkably similar degree, for the Deuteronomistic History. These biblical books are not filled with obvious examples of later Jewish *halakah*. From the lack of this evidence, it is plausible to argue, as Sweeney has done, that the Mosaic Torah may not yet be accepted by everyone as the Torah at the time of some of these late redactions, perhaps for both Psalms and the book of Isaiah. This lack of consensus might explain the reticence in the editing of these books. At a minimum, we know these books came to belong within Jewish Scripture in a relationship with the Mosaic Torah, perhaps in a secondary manner similar to how the Letters of Paul became related through the Pastoral Epistles to the written Gospels in the formation of the New Testament. Regardless of the solution to this historical problem, we see that the

41. S.D. McBride, 'Prophetic Vision and Mosaic Constitution', in J.L. Mays (ed.), *Harper's Bible Commentary* (San Francisco: Harper & Row, 1988), pp. 22-23.

42. M. Fishbane, *Biblical Interpretation in Ancient Israel* (Oxford: Clarendon Press, 1985), pp. 384-85.

effect of the editing of biblical books has been to leave us with a clear demand for their interpretation as biblical books in terms of the Torah and accompanied by other biblical books that remain, to a remarkable degree, unharmonized. The Scripture in social scientific terms might be seen as a social contract between disparate groups of Jews who share some degree of consensus and must seek through the interpretation of their common Scripture to justify how they share, in fact, the same Torah in the future. The Scripture sets in motion moments of simple agreement alongside glaring and potentially unresolvable paradoxes of faith.

One highly significant effect of such a scripture, beyond its common orientation toward 'the Torah', is the offering of certain sub-idioms of the Torah by which these texts are read. I would identify these as chiefly 'prophecy', 'wisdom' and 'torah' (as *haggadah* and *halakah*). In brief, Isaiah could be read as commentary on the same Torah as that given to Moses. It could also be read as a resource for Solomonic wisdom, as the ending of Hosea suggests for that book (Hos. 14.9) and as is implicit in Isa. 1.2-3 and even in the retention of sapiential elements from the book's prehistory as seen in the work of Whedbee, Jensen and others.[43] Furthermore, the obvious identification of the book as among 'the Prophets' within Scripture, invites an interpretation in terms of promise /judgment and fulfillment. It is precisely this multivalent nature of the text as a scriptural text that allowed Christians, for better or for worse, to give preference often to the prophetic and sapiential reading of the text over its role as a guide to the law. Still, Christians often did acknowledge the primacy of the Torah as law for this book, even if they thought of that law apart from Jewish oral tradition and the traditions of the rabbis. The preface to Isaiah in the Geneva Bible of 1560, in a translation from Theodore Beza's annotations, states emphatically that

> God, according to his promes Deut. 18, 5. that he wolde never leave his Church destitute of a Prophet, hathe from time to time accomplished the same: whose office was not onely to declare unto the people things to come, whereof thei had a special revelation, but also to interpret and declare the Law...and principally in the declaration of the Lawe they had respect to thre things, which were the grounde of their doctrine: First to the doctrine contained briefly in the two tables: secondly to the promises

43. Cf. W. Whedbee, *Isaiah and Wisdom* (New York: Abingdon Press, 1971).

and threatenings of the Law: and thirdely, to the covenant of grace and reconciliation greeted upon our Saviour Jesus Christ, who is the end of the Law.[44]

What Christians knew they inherited from Judaism was a book in which the Gospel had to be formulated in conversation with the Jewish scriptural idioms of law, prophecy and wisdom. What should be clear from these observations is that the main force of this book of Isaiah, *as a book of Scripture*, is determined neither by isolating a few connective 'themes' throughout the book nor by an anti-Semitic view of Jewish Scripture as crushing the life out of richer pre-exilic tradition through a legalistic orthodoxy. Neither view can do justice to Judaism, or to such a remarkable book of Jewish Scripture and its retention, as well as some contextual reorientation, within a later Christian Scripture.[45]

44. *The Geneva Bible (1560): A Facsimile Edition, with an Introduction by Lloyd E. Berry* (Madison: University of Wisconsin, 1969), p. 282.

45. On the question of messianic interpretations of Isaiah, see P.D. Wegner, *An Examination of Kingship and Messianic Expectation in Isaiah 1–35* (Lewiston: Mellen Biblical Press, 1992), and *idem*, 'The Book of Isaiah as a Human Witness to Revelation within the Religions of Judaism and Christianity', pp. 277-80.

Figurative Speech and the Reading of Isaiah 1 as Scripture

Roy F. Melugin

Twenty to twenty-five years ago the prevailing practice in the analysis of prophetic books involved a reconstruction of the earliest forms of the literature and an attempt to reconstruct the history of growth of each prophetic book. Small, originally self-contained units were typically isolated by means of form-critical method, and the discipline of redaction history was employed to reconstruct the growth of a prophetic book and to recover the setting of each stage of redaction.

Whether we should continue to rely on such an approach is a question which is now very much open. Although few would dispute the claim that many prophetic books grew into their final form over a considerable span of time, it is quite another question to ask how successfully we can reconstruct that history of growth. Isaiah 1 illustrates the problem admirably. While there has been rather general agreement that vv. 4-9 may be dated sometime after the invasion of Sennacherib in 701,[1] it has proven much more difficult to speak with precision about other units in the chapter. Marvin Sweeney thinks that vv. 2-3 were composed as an introduction to vv. 4-9 because both focus on 'sons' and 'offspring' and because ignorance is mentioned in v. 3 ('Israel does not know...') and is implied in v. 5, presumably in the 'sons' who have no better sense than to continue to be smitten.[2] But Sweeney overlooks the differences in the portrayal of the 'sons' in vv. 2-3 and vv. 4-9. Although he has undoubtedly touched upon reasons for the *redactional* association of vv. 2-3 and

---

1. See the commentaries. Of particular significance are two works: B.S. Childs, *Isaiah and the Assyrian Crisis* (SBT, Second Series, 3; Naperville, IL: Allenson, 1967), pp. 20-22; R.E. Clements, *Isaiah and the Deliverance of Jerusalem* (JSOTSup, 13; Sheffield: JSOT Press, 1980), pp. 34-36.

2. M.A. Sweeney, *Isaiah 1–4 and the Post-Exilic Understanding of the Isaianic Tradition* (BZAW, 171; Berlin: de Gruyter, 1988), p. 126.

4-9, he has not presented strong arguments as to whether both units were *composed* in the same time period. Attempts to date other units in Isaiah 1 also suffer from analogous difficulties: If one argues that the so-called 'cultic torah' in vv. 10-17 is to be dated in the period of Hezekiah's reforms because they 'presuppose a stable political situation and prosperous economic climate in which the cult could function regularly without interruption', one wonders how persuasive such arguments actually are.[3] To be sure, these verses make no mention of national emergency, but does the mere lack of specific reference to the threat of national disaster necessarily indicate that no such emergency might have occasioned the utterance? Is it not imaginable that an invasion might have been considered the result of Yahweh's judgment because of the neglect of justice for the powerless and that the exhortations, 'Wash yourselves, make yourselves clean...judge the orphan, plead for the widow' (vv. 16-17), might have been offered to encourage the righteous behavior which could prevent the continuation of 'being smitten' (v. 5) in the context of a serious threat to the nation (see vv. 7-9)? Or how can we be certain that the language of vv. 19-20 ('If you are willing and obedient, you will eat the good of the land...') is clearly Deuteronomistic and thus later than most of the material in Isaiah 1?[4]

The problem of reconstructing setting is compounded by the poetic character of the text and its metaphorical depiction of reality. Let me illustrate. Verses 4-9 might well presuppose the invasion of Sennacherib. We are told that the land lies desolate, that cities have been burned. And there is reference to some sort of limitation on the catastrophe: if Yahweh had not left a few survivors, 'we' would have been like Sodom and Gomorrah; that is, completely destroyed. If vv. 4-9 do indeed refer to the circumstances of Sennacherib's invasion, we are not explicitly told that this is so. We are told almost nothing literal about the situation to which the text refers because the portrayal of events is metaphorical. The prophet's audience is portrayed as if it consisted of rebellious sons

3.   Sweeney, *Isaiah 1–4*, p. 128.

4.   Sweeney (*Isaiah 1–4*, p. 129) mentions the similarity between Isa. 1.19-20b and Deut. 1.26 and 1 Sam. 12.14-15. Admittedly, 1 Sam. 12.14-15, 'if you will fear Yahweh...it will be well, but if you do not hear...and rebel...' and Isa. 1.19-20 display a certain resemblance. But the language in 1 Sam. 12.14-15 is strongly Deuteronomistic ('if you will *fear* Yahweh and *serve* him and *hear his voice* and not rebel against the *commandment* of Yahweh), while such stereotypical Deuteronomistic terminology is absent in Isa. 1.19-20.

who had behaved badly, even as *offspring* of evildoers. Exactly what
they have done is not clear; they stupidly keep on being smitten, but we
are not told precisely what they have done. Their suffering appears to be
described partly literally and partly in metaphorical terms. They are
portrayed as wounded from head to foot, as if the calamity were a
bodily wound. The depiction becomes more literal, or so it seems, when
it speaks of the devastation of the land, the cities burned with fire. But
even here metaphor is present: the daughter Zion is said to be left 'like a
booth in a vineyard, like a lodge in a cucumber patch'. How literally
should this comparison be taken? Should we take it as a referent to the
historical event of Jerusalem in the midst of surrounding destruction by
an invading army? Or does the metaphor refer to some other kind of
historical reality? Metaphors, after all, are characteristically open to more
than one interpretation. The figurative picture in vv. 4-9 is manifestly
easier to describe than to comprehend the precise historical situation to
which the metaphorical language refers.

Let me be clear: I am not arguing that historical inquiry has no value.
Indeed, Isaiah 1 has very much to do with history. The prophet exhibits
an intense concern with what was happening in the history which lies
behind the text's figurative language. But I am profoundly skeptical of
our ability to recover with much precision the history which lies behind
the text. Furthermore, the form of the text itself suggests that our
preoccupation with reconstructing a setting for each pericope and with
recovering the history of redaction of the text flies in the face of the
concerns which the text's redactors seem to have had. The text's
redactors made no attempt to identify different stages of growth; they
did not distinguish the diverse settings which underlie the various
pericopes. They appear to have believed that the texts which they
received, combined and even supplemented with new material could
speak with power without the necessity of identifying original settings.

Although the redactors of Isaiah undoubtedly realized that the words
which they preserved had earlier been used in historical settings different
from their own,[5] they understood those words as living speech which
could speak to *them*. Words from the past could be combined and added

---

5.   A fascinating study by Christopher Seitz ('The Divine Council: Temporal
Transition and New Prophecy in the Book of Isaiah', *JBL* 109 [1990], pp. 229-47)
proposes that the composers of Isa. 40–55 understood quite self-consciously that the
era of the historical Isaiah had drawn to a close and that his words would be used for
the purposes of a different epoch in history.

to, as was the case with Isaiah 1, without any explicit concern to locate each pericope in a clearly-identified historical setting. Various pericopes could be juxtaposed and read together dynamically as sacred word.

How could this happen? How might various 'Isaiah' traditions be read *together* as living word of God? How might individual pericopes, which may have originated as oral speech, be read in a larger context as written 'scriptural' word?[6] The functions of oral and written discourse are quite different, as Paul Ricoeur has taught us.[7] Oral discourse is situation-bound, he argues, whereas written discourse is not. In oral discourse, speaker, audience and message are tied together because all three partici-pate in the same communication event. The spoken word has meaning for its hearers in the context of the situation in which it is uttered. With the written word, however, author and reader are removed from each other in space and time. Thus the word is no longer limited to a particu-lar situation. This means that the reader's capacity for understanding is not limited to that of the original audience.

In oral discourse, what is said characteristically refers to something which speaker and hearer share in common. While written texts usually refer to something, they typically do not refer to something in a situation directly shared by author and reader, for they are separated from one another in space and time. What a written text can do, says Ricoeur, is to portray a 'world' which may be appropriated by the reader,[8] such as the 'world' constructed by a particular Shakespearean play or by the book of Job. Ricoeur is particularly interested in texts which make manifest a symbolic world in which the reader may dwell and make a home. Generation after generation in diverse situations, religious commu-nities may be given identity by living in symbolic worlds constructed by reading their Scriptures.

One does not have to be a full-blown Ricoeurian (and I am not) to profit from these observations. Isaiah 1, although undoubtedly composite in nature, displays no interest in identifying the setting for each layer of tradition contained therein. Indeed, utterances from different circum-stances of origin are juxtaposed in such a way that we may see a

6.   Even before Israel had developed anything like a full canon of Scripture, composite works such as Isaiah were used *as a whole* to function as authoritative literature for the communities which treasured them.

7.   P. Ricoeur, *Interpretation Theory: Discourse and the Surplus of Meaning* (Fort Worth: Texas Christian University Press, 1976), pp. 25-44.

8.   Ricoeur, *Interpretation Theory*, pp. 36-37.

symbolic unity by reading the text synchronically. In contrast with Jeremiah and Ezekiel, and their identification of events according to date formulas, Isaiah 1 (indeed, most of Isaiah) makes no such explicit historical identifications but rather organizes the text, as I shall presently argue, first as a trial of Yahweh's foolish and rebellious sons (vv. 2-20) and then as a word of doom and hope which proceeds from a portrayal of Jerusalem as a once-faithful bride turned harlot (vv. 21-31). Indeed, the presiding images of Israel as foolish and rebellious sons and Jerusalem as whore, together with other tropes, can be used to construct a frightening yet hopeful figurative world in which a community of faith might live, hear itself addressed by God and experience both judgment and anticipation of renewal.

I

Isaiah 1 is marked off as a unit by the superscription at its beginning (1.1) and by the superscription (2.1) which introduces chs. 2–33. Although Isa. 1.1 undoubtedly serves as a superscription for the book of Isaiah as a whole, it also introduces the body of text which extends from Isa. 1.2 to 1.31.[9]

Isa. 1.2-3 may be divided into two parts: vv. 2-20 and vv. 21-31.[10] Verses 2-20 open and close with the inclusion *kî yhwh dibbēr* (v. 2)/*kî pî yhwh dibbēr* (v. 20). Moreover, vv. 2-20 begin and end with legal speech. Verses 2-3, as Whedbee argues, reflect the legal situation in which a father brings disobedient sons before a court of law (cf. Deut. 21.18-21).[11] And vv. 18-20 open with the invitation, 'Come, let us plead together', which as invitation to legal dispute begins what Sweeney calls a 'prophetic announcement of Yahweh's appeal to begin a legal proceeding'.[12] Whether the second part (vv. 21-31) should be interpreted as the portrayal of a legal speech of Yahweh as judge, as Sweeney contends, remains to be seen.[13] However that may be, the dominant

9. Sweeney, *Isaiah 1–4*, pp. 27-32.

10. Sweeney, *Isaiah 1–4*, pp. 119-23.

11. J.W. Whedbee, *Isaiah and Wisdom* (Nashville: Abingdon Press, 1971), p. 21

12. Sweeney, *Isaiah 1–4*, p. 114. See also H.J. Boecker, *Redeformen des Rechtslebens im Alten Testament* (WMANT, 14; Neukirchen–Vluyn: Neukirchener Verlag, 1964), pp. 68-69.

13. Sweeney, *Isaiah 1–4*, pp. 122-23.

image in vv. 21-26 is that of a once-faithful bride now turned harlot. Yahweh announces punishment upon Jerusalem, portrayed metaphorically as a bride-turned-whore, because her officials have taken bribes and neglected their legal responsibilities toward widow and orphan. Yet Yahweh's punishment is at the same time a process of purification in which the dross is removed; that is, the corrupt officials are purged and the city becomes once again faithful bride—a city once again governed by just officials. The promise of redemption of Zion in vv. 27-28 is dependent on the oracle about the bride-turned-harlot in vv. 21-26 and elaborates on that oracle. Verses 29-31 further elaborate on the foregoing text and thereby continue the compositional unit which revolves around the image of the harlotrous bride.

The first part of Isa. 1.2-31 (vv. 2-20) consists of several parts (vv. 2-3, 4-9, 10-17, 18-20)[14] which function as an artistic unit. Verses 2-3 open the composition by conjuring up in the reader's imagination the scene of a trial.[15] There is a call to witnesses: 'Hear, O heavens; give ear, O earth, for Yahweh has spoken.' Then follows the accusation: 'Sons I have reared and brought up, but they have rebelled against me.' The reader envisages a trial, with Yahweh as father and Israel as his rebellious sons. The accusing father speaks to witnesses, but they are not ordinary witnesses as in a real historical trial. This divine father speaks to heaven and earth, declaring that his sons have broken with him. The sons' rebellion is folly; the contrast of Israel with ox and ass who know their owner and their master's crib shows the depth of the sons' folly. It is no accident that Yahweh's speech contains this contrast, for its closing words, 'Israel does not know, my people does not understand', characterizes the kind of sons who are brought to trial.

Verses 4-9 represent a new formal unit.[16] Yahweh is no longer the speaker but is rather spoken about. Indeed, the speech is a woe-utterance which describes the lamentable circumstances brought about by the behavior of the people portrayed in the text.[17] Formally the unit

14. R.E. Clements, *Isaiah 1–39* (NCB; Grand Rapids: Eerdmans, 1980), pp. 30-35; H. Wildberger, *Isaiah 1–12: A Commentary* (trans. T.H. Trapp; Minneapolis: Fortress Press, 1991), pp. 8-58; Sweeney, *Isaiah 1–4*, pp. 102-14.

15. Whedbee, *Isaiah and Wisdom*, pp. 29, 42-43; Sweeney, *Isaiah 1–4*, pp. 102-30; Wildberger, *Isaiah 1–12*, pp. 9-11.

16. Childs, *Isaiah and the Assyrian Crisis*, pp. 20-22; Clements, *Isaiah 1–39*, pp. 30-32; Sweeney, *Isaiah 1–4*, pp. 104-108.

17. Childs (*Isaiah and the Assyrian Crisis*, pp. 20-22) shows that the pattern of the 'invective-threat' (or 'announcement of judgment' and its accompanying

is a 'prophetic admonition speech to the people concerning their continued apostasy'.[18] The woe-saying in v. 4 characterizes the people as
apostates, but the question in v. 5 is designed to precipitate reconsider-
ation of their behavior and its accompanying consequences: 'Why will
you still be smitten, continue to turn aside?' Given what has happened
to them in the devastation of their land, do they want to be smitten still
more? After all, had Yahweh not left a few survivors, would not this
people be completely destroyed like Sodom and Gomorrah?

Not only does this prophetic admonition speech represent a different
genre from the accusation speech in vv. 2-3, the terminology applied to
the people in vv. 4-9 is somewhat different from that used in vv. 2-3.
Verses 4-9 speak of 'sinful nation', people 'heavy with iniquity', 'seed of
evildoers', 'destroying sons'. Admittedly, concern with 'sons' is central
to vv. 2-3, but in vv. 4-9 'sons' is only one of the appellations. Thus vv.
4-9 are not directly a continuation of the speech of call to witnesses in a
trial (vv. 2-3).

The juxtaposition of vv. 2-3 and vv. 4-9 is nonetheless of significance.
Even though 'sons' is but one of the appellations in vv. 4-9, it is the last
in the series in v. 4. As last in the list, it lingers in the mind most
strongly. Moreover, it parallels 'seed', with the result that the entire last
half of the sequence portrays the people as offspring, or 'sons'. Thus
vv. 4-9, especially when juxtaposed with vv. 2-3, is an utterance about
'sons'. And, like the foolish sons of vv. 2-3, the sons in vv. 4-9 behave,
not only in apostate fashion, but also without sense. They go on being
smitten despite the punishment they have suffered. They fail to
understand the significance of what has happened to them; they do not
grasp the meaning of their having been granted a few survivors.

Thus far I have spoken largely in prosaic terms. I turn now to
imagery. Verses 2-3 picture Yahweh putting his foolish and rebellious
sons on trial. Unlike the ox and the ass, they do not know; they do not
understand. Verses 4-9 elaborate. The character of the sons' disobedience
is made more explicit: they are not only 'sinful people', they are also
'heavy' with iniquity. They are 'destroying' sons. Their sin is so weighty
that they are described metaphorically as the biological offspring of
sinners; that is, the 'seed of evildoers'. If taken literally, the metaphor,
'seed of evildoers', would appear to conflict with the metaphor of Israel

'reason') has been modified by the substitution of a lament for the more conventional
announcement of judgment.

18. Sweeney, *Isaiah 1-4*, pp. 107-108.

as *Yahweh's* sons (vv. 2-3). But 'seed of evildoers' is in poetic paral-
lelism with 'destroying sons'. Thus 'seed of evildoers' and 'destroying
sons' work together to emphasize the evil, destructive character of these
persons called 'seed' or 'sons'.

The speaker calls into question the good sense of these persons: 'Why
will you still be smitten, continue to turn aside?' (v. 5). As I said before,
this fits with the accusation that the sons are foolish (v. 3). The idiocy of
continuing rebellion is made manifest through a series of word-pictures:
the whole head is sick; from top to bottom there are wounds, festering
still through lack of treatment. Why continue to be smitten? Their land is
desolate, their cities burned with fire. Aliens eat their land and the
daughter Zion is left alone, like a booth standing in a vineyard or a lodge
by itself in a cucumber patch, like a city standing alone when under
attack. Why continue to be smitten? Why be so foolish as not to
recognize that, had Yahweh not left a few survivors, they would be
totally destroyed, like Sodom and Gomorrah?

To sum up thus far: Yahweh puts on trial foolish, rebellious sons, who
know not when they have been wounded enough, who keep on being
smitten. Unlike the ox and the ass who know their owner and the crib
where they feed, these sons have experienced their land being eaten by
foreigners. These foolish sons, who lack the wisdom of the animals who
know who provides what they eat, ironically suffer the eating of their
land. And they stupidly keep on being smitten.

A new formal unit begins in v. 10.[19] It may be distinguished from its
context as a prophetic torah speech, opening as it does with a call to
hear *torah* (v. 10) and continuing with a torah speech in the mouth of
Yahweh (vv. 11-17).[20] Yahweh claims to be sated with their sacrifices,
indeed, does not delight in them. Yahweh instructs them to bring no
more empty offerings; he hates their feasts and will not listen to their
prayers (vv. 11-15). Then Yahweh instructs his audience as to what they

---

19. Clements, *Isaiah 1–39*, pp. 32-34; Sweeney, *Isaiah 1–4*, pp. 108-12;
Wildberger, *Isaiah 1–12*, pp. 36-39.

20. E. Würthwein considers this genre to be a 'prophetic cult declaration'
('Kultpolemik oder Kultbescheid?', in E. Würthwein and O. Kaiser [eds.], *Tradition
und Situation: Studien zur alttestamentlichen Prophetie* [Gottingen: Vandenhoeck &
Ruprecht, 1963], pp. 115-31). I doubt that this is so. Most of the passages which
Würthwein discusses are not presented in the text as answers to petitions (as they
should be if Würthwein is correct). Instead, both Isa. 1.10-17 and Amos 5.21-24
function as *exhortations* for change of behaviour.

should do: 'Wash yourselves, make yourselves clean...seek justice, correct oppression...' (vv. 16-17).

Verbal similarities connect vv. 10-17 with its context: 'Sodom and Gomorrah' (vv. 9, 10), *tôsîpû sārâ* and *lōʾ tôsîpû hābîʾ minḥat śāwʾ* (vv. 5, 13). But the connections are yet more profound. Addressing the audience as if they were Sodom and Gomorrah intensifies the portrayal of Israel as sinful. Yet it is the very piety of these sinners which Yahweh hates. He is indeed utterly sated with what they have brought him to eat (note that imagery of eating appears once more). These rebellious sons, unlike the ox and the ass who know the crib where they eat, suffer the eating of their land as a consequence of their sin (vv. 2-9). *Now* they try to feed Yahweh a meal he refuses; 'bring no more', he says (v. 13). Thus the image of eating continues to tie the redactional composition together.

The admonition to bring no more vain sacrifice has its counterpart in the positive instructions in vv. 16-17. The words, 'wash yourselves, make yourselves clean', fit well in a text which speaks of a cultic meal. The people have profaned that meal and the prayers made by their uplifted hands because their hands are defiled with blood (v. 15). They must therefore wash and become clean. And, in becoming clean, they would come to behave properly in the legal sphere—by 'judging' the orphan and 'pleading' for the widow. Note that vv. 10-17 have combined imagery from eating and language from the legal sphere. And in so doing, the torah speech in vv. 10-17 takes the imagery of the composition a step further. Yahweh, who makes legal accusation against sons whose folly is contrasted with animals who know from whence their food comes (vv. 2-3), now instructs his cultic-meal-profaning sons as to their legal responsibilities concerning orphan and widow.

As the first major division of the composition comes to an end in vv. 18-20, the language of the lawcourt and the metaphor of eating continue to be joined. The unit begins with a summons to begin a legal proceeding: 'Come, let us plead together' (v. 18a), and it ends with language about 'eating the good of the land' versus being 'eaten by the sword' (vv. 19-20).[21]

The picture is purely fictive; the legal dispute between Yahweh and people is an artistic invention. But in the context of vv. 2-20, it amplifies the metaphorical portrayal. Yahweh the accuser disputes with his sons:

21. Boecker, *Redeformen*, pp. 68-69; Sweeney, *Isaiah 1-4*, p. 114; Wildberger, *Isaiah 1-12*, pp. 54-58.

'If your sins are as scarlet, can they be as white as snow? If they are red as crimson, can they be as wool?'[22] Certainly not; those whom Yahweh disputes must answer. In that case, the following alternatives must be accepted as valid: 'If you are willing and obedient, you will eat the good of the land; but if you refuse and rebel, you will be eaten by the sword.'

The figurative picture of vv. 2-20 is coherent. From beginning to end, Yahweh is involved in legal controversy with ignorant and rebellious sons. Unlike animals who know where their food comes from, they have no knowledge. Indeed, their rebellion leads to a bruising punishment so thorough that they are afflicted from head to foot; aliens make a meal of their land, while the sons foolishly continue being smitten. Moreover, their sacred sacrificial meals Yahweh rejects; he refuses their prayers because their hands are filled with blood. But all is not lost; they are instructed to wash themselves, to cease doing evil, and to carry through on their legal responsibilities to orphan and widow. Finally, Yahweh contends that there is no profitable alternative to obedience. Scarlet sins cannot be white, just as their reddened bloody hands will not be ignored by Yahweh in the context of their cultic meals and their hands uplifted in prayer. No, there are but two choices: obedience and eating the good of the land or rebellion and being eaten by the sword. It is with this choice that Yahweh the accuser leaves his rebellious sons.

The second major part of the composition (vv. 21-31) revolves around the image of the once-faithful-bride turned harlot. The nucleus of this unit is a partly-transformed prophetic oracle of judgment (vv. 21-26), containing both announcement of judgment (vv. 24-26) and reason for judgment (vv. 21-23).[23] Yet the typicalities of this genre are modified by incorporation of the language of funeral lament into the reason for judgment and by expression of the judgment as an act of purification which results in restoration. The compositional unit opens with the conventional language of the funeral dirge: 'How the faithful city has become a harlot...' (v. 21).[24] A funeral lament is sung over a city metaphorically portrayed as a once-faithful wife turned harlot. The dirge is sung, not over a woman who had literally died, but over a formerly-faithful bride who had turned to a life of harlotry. The transition from faithfulness to God to unfaithfulness is depicted metaphorically as a change from marital faithfulness to harlotry, which is in turn expressed

22. See the arguments of Wildberger, *Isaiah 1–12*, pp. 56-57.
23. Wildberger, *Isaiah 1–12*, p. 61.
24. See 2 Sam. 1.19, 27 and Lam. 1.1.

metaphorically as the transition from life to death. Metaphor within metaphor indeed!

Then the metaphor shifts. We no longer have a sexual metaphor but rather metaphors about pure metal becoming impure and drink made impure by dilution with water. The metaphors of impurity and harlotry are of course related. They both involve the transition from a 'good' or proper state of being to a 'bad' one. But the metaphors differ in emphasis. The sexual metaphor points to faithfulness or lack of faithfulness in a relationship, whereas the metal and wine metaphors emphasize the impurity of the substances involved.

Now the text turns to the actual situation toward which the metaphors point:

> Your princes are rebels and companions of thieves;
> Everyone loves a bribe and runs after gifts;
> The orphan they do not defend, and the widow's
> cause does not come to them.

The princes of society fail to carry out their social responsibilities. They associate with thieves; they take bribes. They do not uphold the cause of the widow and the orphan. They use their ruler status to enrich themselves. And so the social order is not what it is supposed to be; it is like silver made impure or wine mixed with water. Notice that such a claim is never directly made, but it is implied in the use of the metaphor. Nor is it actually said that the relationship with God has been impaired by thievery and the taking of bribes. But the metaphor of marital infidelity points to unfaithfulness in the most intimate kind of relationship and it seems likely that the city is the bride of Yahweh. The sexual and purity metaphors, when joined together, show the change from justice to injustice as both unfaithfulness and corruption.

The misdeeds have been made clear. Now comes the announcement of judgment (vv. 24-25):

> Therefore the Lord says, Yahweh of hosts, the
> Mighty One of Israel:
> Woe! I will comfort myself[25] on
> my enemies,
> and avenge myself on my foes,

---

25. The use of the niphal of *nhm* + *min* seems to mean to 'console oneself' in the sense of being consoled by taking vengeage on enemies (see BDB).

> I will turn my hand against you (fem. sing.)
>> and will smelt away your dross as with lye,
>> and will remove all your alloy.

This announcement proclaims bad things to come, as is characteristic of prophetic announcements of judgment. But the metaphor of impure metals made pure qualifies the message of judgment. The punishment is itself the means of renewal, for the attack upon the dross is the very means by which the metal is purified. And through purification the city is restored to its former 'good' state:

> And I will restore your judges as at first,
>> and your counselors as at the beginning.
> Afterward you shall be called city of righteousness,
>> faithful city.

No longer is the city a harlot; she is once again a faithful bride. The restoration to purity, the restoration of just leaders, the restoration of the faithful bride—all belong together as a vision of a restored relationship with God.

The poem about the once-faithful bride restored again to faithfulness comes to an end with v. 26. Once she is restored to her original state, the poem is over; the beginning and the end form an inclusion.[26] Verses 27-28, then, represent a literary supplement (probably a redactional addition), which as third-person *prophetic* speech interprets the restoration announced in vv. 21-26.[27] The restoration is called a 'redemption' in vv. 27-28, and it is said that 'Zion will be redeemed in justice and her returners in righteousness'. This interpretive supplement distinguishes between the fortune of those who 'return' and the fate of sinners. Verses 27-28 are indeed dependent upon vv. 21-26, specifying further the character of the purifying judgment. Verses 29-31 in turn elaborate upon the destiny of sinners in v. 28 by means of tree and garden imagery. The shift to second-person address, coupled with the drastic change in imagery, suggests still another stage of redaction.[28] Nevertheless, the text, read synchronically, presents the shame concerning the nature cult (v. 29), together with the proclamation that the sinners themselves shall burn like a withering tree and an unwatered garden (vv.

---

26. Sweeney, *Isaiah 1–4*, pp. 114-15.

27. The Yahweh-speech in vv. 21-26 turns into speech *about* Yahweh in vv. 27-31.

28. See, for example, Wildberger, *Isaiah 1–12*, pp. 75-76.

30-31) as further description of the fate of the sinners depicted in v. 28.

Verses 21-31 connect with vv. 2-20: Zion's once having been 'filled with justice' (v. 21) and the promise of redemption in justice (v. 27) are related to the instruction, 'judge the orphan' (v. 17). And the repetition of the roots $p\check{s}^c$ (vv. 2, 28), $ht^?$ (vv. 4, 28), and ^czb (vv. 4, 28) join vv. 21-31 with vv. 2-20. But let us be more precise about the relationship. Do vv. 21-31 present Yahweh speaking as a judge, as one who (according to Sweeney) 'decides who is righteous and who is not'?[29] The absence of clear trial *language* in vv. 21-31 is worthy of note. Indeed, Sweeney understands it as a speech of the judge only because vv. 2-20 portray Yahweh as accuser of his sons; vv. 21-31, he reasons, continue the metaphor of trial.[30]

I consider it quite reasonable to construe vv. 21-31 as continuing the metaphor of trial. Yet I myself am somewhat reticent about making such a claim; I shrink from doing so because of the lack of specific legal language in these verses. Moreover, vv. 2-20 and 21-31 may be contrasted in that the former directly exhorts change of behavior, whereas the latter encourages repentance only indirectly. Verses 2-20 directly exhort the people to 'wash themselves...' and to 'judge the orphan, plead for the widow' (vv. 16-17). Indeed, in vv. 2-20, the foolish sons whom Yahweh accuses in court are encouraged to stop the behavior that has caused their continuing to be 'smitten', to arrest the rebellion which has already led to the eating of their land by aliens. Furthermore, as vv. 18-20 indicate, Yahweh 'pleads' with them to choose between obedience which leads to 'eat(ing) the good of the land' and the rebellion which results in being 'eaten by the sword'. The trial in vv. 2-20 attempts to alter Israel's behavior in order to bring *past* punishment to an end; vv. 21-31, by contrast, depict judgment *to come*, albeit a judgment which is in essence an act of purification and restoration.

These two pictures cannot easily be harmonized. Yet in their differences there is also unity. Both anticipate altered behavior: The first *exhorts* it ('wash yourselves...'); the second *prophesies* it by proclaiming redemption for those who repent. The first directly instructs the people to change their behavior and *warns* of the consequences of rebellion; the second *prophesies* the future—a future that encompasses repentance as opposed to continuance in sin.

29. See Sweeney, *Isaiah 1–4*, p. 122, for additional connecting features.
30. Sweeney, *Isaiah 1–4*, pp. 122-23.

In sum, the symbolic world of the entire redactional composition hangs together. Yahweh's trial of his foolish sons is intended to lead them to cease rebelling, to begin to practice justice and thereby to bring an already-inflicted punishment to an end and to 'eat the good of the land' in the future rather than be 'eaten by the sword'. At the same time, future catastrophe apparently cannot be avoided. The future for Jerusalem includes punishment of that faithless bride for the sake of purifying and restoring its officials. But the fate of those who repent and those who continue in sin differs significantly (vv. 27-31). For the entire composition, changed behavior leads to 'redemption' and 'eat(ing) the good of the land', while continued rebellion results in continuing to be 'smitten', being 'eaten by the sword', and in being 'ashamed' of the nature cults together with being burned up, like dry gardens or like trees whose leaves wither.

This symbolic world which I described above is clearly a depiction of history. Yet the acts of judgment and restoration depicted in Isaiah 1 are not 'literally' or 'realistically' portrayed. We encounter a figurative picture instead—more accurately, a 'mosaic' of portraits of Israel's past, present and future. And it is these carefully-arranged *pictures*, rather than the 'real' history which supposedly lies behind the text, which the redactors preserved for us. It is this sequence of figurative representations of history which is 'scriptural' and which is the material from which a faith community can construct a symbolic world in which to live and to hear itself addressed by God. Indeed, that faith community can make Isaiah 1 its own by understanding itself as participating in a centuries-old community in which Isaiah plays a paradigmatic role as Scripture. The portrayal of history in Isaiah 1 can then function as a part of the sacred story in which the community of faith still participates and experiences judgment and salvation.

II

Isaiah 1, rich as it is, does not stand alone. It opens the entire book of Isaiah. Just as we have taken the several pericopes in Isaiah 1 and read them together in synchronic fashion, so also must we read Isaiah 1 as a part of the book of Isaiah as a whole. Christopher Seitz has argued forcefully for reading the book of Isaiah as a whole: The superscription in 1.1, he contends, is a superscription for the entire book. There is only one narrative of the commissioning of a prophet (Isa. 6); Isa. 40.1-8 does not represent the commissioning of a prophet. The boundaries between so-called First Isaiah and between Second and Third Isaiah are not indicated in any special fashion. Indeed, the transition from Isaiah 55 to 56 is no rougher than, for example, the transition between ch. 12 and the oracles against nations in chs. 13–23 within 'First Isaiah'.[31] Furthermore, he argues that Isaiah 40ff. is bound to 'First Isaiah' by the narrative of the delay of punishment from the period of Assyria to the time of Babylon (Isa. 36–39) and by references to 'former' and 'latter things' in chs. 40–55 to distinguish between words of judgment uttered in the Assyrian period and the words of comfort for the time of Babylonian exile.[32]

The judgments against Israel/Judah in the Assyrian period, against Zion/Jerusalem/Judah in the Babylonian period, against Israel's neighbors, against the entire cosmos and the visions of Zion's restoration and new creation are not distributed neatly into the conventionally-accepted three-part structure of the book.[33] The theme of judgment of the nations, says Seitz, is scattered in various places in the book. The judgment, exile and restoration of Israel appears in all three parts of the book. Indeed, Seitz argues, the book opens with a comprehensive perspective. The story of Israel encompassed by the book of Isaiah is already well underway as we begin our reading with ch. 1: cities have already been destroyed; already only Zion remains. The sparing of Zion is to be seen as a warning rather than as a signal for rejoicing. There will be judgment. Yet Zion will be restored and those who repent will be redeemed. Thus both judgment and restoration are already made manifest in Isaiah 1.[34]

A. Isaiah 2–4 seem to carry forward what began in ch. 1. The judgment and restoration of Zion expressed in ch. 1 is the central theme of chs. 2–4. Yahweh's people are put on trial (3.13-15), as in ch. 1. And 'elders and princes' are put on trial for oppressing the poor (3.13-15), just as 'rulers' take bribes in ch. 1 (1.23). Indeed, both Isaiah 1 and 2–4 depict well-being in terms of a just and stable social and political order. When 'rulers' or 'elders and princes' take bribes or otherwise oppress the poor (1.23; 3.13-15), society is destroyed. Isaiah 2–4 elaborates this theme by means of an extended portrayal of a time of judgment in

31. C. Seitz, 'Isaiah 1–66: Making Sense of the Whole', in *idem* (ed.), *Reading and Preaching the Book of Isaiah* (Philadelphia: Fortress Press, 1988), p. 109.

32. Seitz, 'Isaiah 1–66', pp. 110-11.

33. Seitz, 'Isaiah 1–66', pp. 113-14.

34. Seitz, 'Isaiah 1–66', p. 113.

which social order collapses because Yahweh removes mighty man, warrior, judge, prophet and other societal leaders and replaces them with babes and women (3.1-12). Furthermore, language in ch. 1 about cities burned with fire (1.7) and being eaten by the sword (1.20) is enlarged upon in chs. 2–4 by depiction of a loss of warriors so massive that each of the few remaining men will be seized by seven desperate women of the once-proud daughters of Zion (3.16-4.1).

The image of the removal of impurities from Zion (1.25) and the announcement of the redemption of those who repent (1.27) seem to be enlarged upon in the juxtaposition of chs. 1 and 2–4. In 4.1-5 we are told explicitly that there will be a remnant and that the remnant will be holy (compare the more ambiguous status of the remnant in 1.9). Indeed, the holiness will be achieved through the washing away of the filth of the daughters of Zion. And Yahweh will create over Mt Zion a cloud by day and a flaming fire by night, as well as a shelter from heat and storm.

Especially distinctive is the opening of chs. 2–4: Mt Zion becomes the place toward which all nations will make pilgrimage and be taught torah, with the result that they will change swords into plowshares and spears into pruning hooks.[35] Isaiah 1 also speaks of Zion's restoration (1.25-27) and of Yahweh's torah (1.10). But, if one reads chs. 2–4 in the light of ch. 1, the picture of the restoration of Zion and those within it who repent is extended into a vision of Zion as a teaching centre for the nations. The torah which was addressed to Israel (1.10) now instructs all peoples (2.1-4).[36] The warfare which threatened Jerusalem (1.7-9, 19) comes to an end (2.4). And the social order which is to be restored in Jerusalem (1.25-26) will be extended into a world order in which all nations participate (2.1-4). Indeed, the deliverance of the nations, which is a prominent theme in chs. 40–55, is first introduced in ch. 2.[37]

The theme of the legal accusation of Israel for acts of injustice (see ch. 1) continues on in chs. 5–12 (see especially the legal imagery of 5.1-7).[38] The earlier connections between justice and the behavior of community leaders (1.21-26; 3.13-15) are refocused in chs. 5–12 on the role of the

---

35. See especially C. Seitz, *Isaiah 1–39* (Interpretation; Louisville: John Knox, 1993), pp. 38-40, for intriguing comments about the relationship of 2.1-5 to the book of Isaiah as a whole.

36. Seitz (*Isaiah 1–39*, p. 38) argues that 2.1-5 clearly takes the destiny of Zion beyond the judgment of Isaiah's own days in the preceding text (1.2-31).

37. Seitz, *Isaiah 1–39*, p. 40.

38. Boecker, *Redeformen*, p. 82; Whedbee, *Isaiah and Wisdom*, p. 46.

king in a restored order of social justice (9.1-7; 11.1-9). Furthermore, the themes of the devastation of the land (1.7-9) and remnant (1.9; 4.1-6) continue in chs. 5–12 in the narrative of the prophet's commissioning (6.11-13), in the announcements of the future at the end of ch. 7 (7.18-25) and at the end of the woe-speech against Assyria in 10.5-19 (10.20-27). Yet in chs. 5–12 these themes are recontextualized into a framework of the hardening of hearts (6.9-10), the punishment of Zion/Jerusalem by Assyria and Assyria's subsequent fall (10.5-19), and the return of a remnant dispersed in 'Assyria, Egypt, Pathros, Cush, Elam, Shinar, Hamath and the coastlands of the sea' (11.11). Indeed, the return of a remnant from Assyria (11.16) employs the image of a highway—surely anticipating the use of that same image to describe the return from Babylon in 40.3-5.[39]

In chs. 13–33 the emphasis of the second half of the book on the deliverance from the 'coastlands' (Babylon in particular) is anticipated by the utterances against Babylon and various other nations (chs. 13–23); and the themes of the laying waste of the cosmos (51.6) and new creation (41.17-20; 43.16-21; 48.1-11; 65.17-25; 66.22-23) in chs. 40–66 are prepared for in the portrayal of cosmic punishment and restoration in chs. 24–27. But in chs. 28–33 the judgment and restoration of Jerusalem, so prominent in Isaiah 1 and 2–12, reappears (see especially the specific references to Jerusalem in 28.16; 29.1-8; 30.19; 31.4-5, 6-9; 33.5, 14, 20). In contrast with ch. 1, however, the references to Zion/Jerusalem in chs. 28–33 occur in contexts in which (1) drunkenness and blindness of leaders are emphasized (28.7-13; 29.9-24), (2) alliances with Egypt are criticized (30.1-7; 31.1-3), (3) judgment by Assyria and subsequent punishment of Assyria are of major concern (30.27-33; 31.6-9) and (4) royal rule in righteousness and justice is of great importance (32.1-8; 33.13-24).[40]

B. As the first half of the book (chs. 1–33) comes to a close, the second half (chs. 34–66) begins. Chapters 1–33 anticipate the judgment and subsequent restoration of Jerusalem, Judah and Israel, whereas chs. 40–66 presume that the heavy punishment of exile has ended and that Yahweh's worldwide sovereignty at Zion is coming about.[41] Much

---

39. Seitz, *Isaiah 1–39*, p. 109; Wildberger, *Isaiah 1–12*, p. 497.

40. Some of these themes, e.g., drunkenness and blindness, judgment by Assyria and punishment of Assyria, and messianic renewal, first emerge in chs. 5–12.

41. I am indebted to Marvin Sweeney's essay, 'The Book of Isaiah as Prophetic

in chs. 1–33 (especially 5–12 and 28–33) focuses explicitly on the time of the Assyrian threat while Isaiah 40–66 deals with the Babylonian exile and its aftermath.

Such generalizations need qualification. First of all, Isaiah 36–37 continues to speak about salvation in terms of deliverance from Assyria. Hezekiah trusts in Yahweh as savior of Jerusalem, hoping that the 'remnant' which remains will be delivered (37.3-4). Hezekiah seems to be the counterpart to the faithless Ahaz. Indeed, the utterances about the punishment *by* Assyria and the subsequent havoc heaped *upon* Assyria in chs. 5–12; 28–32 appear to be quite self-consciously connected to the historical epoch from Ahaz to Hezekiah. The expectation of the rule of a just and righteous king (9.1-6; 11.1-9; 32.1-8; 33.17-22) and of the deliverance of Zion from Assyria (10.24-27; 31.6-9) seems to find fulfilment in the righteous Hezekiah and the slaughter of 185,000 Assyrian soldiers (Isa. 37). Yet the messianic promise in 11.1-9 contains elements too utopian to be seen as completely fulfilled in the events narrated about Hezekiah's rule (chs. 36–39);[42] the same appears to be true also of Isaiah 2.1-4. Moreover, sandwiched in between chs. 1–33 and the Hezekiah narrative are chs. 34–35, which anticipate the material concerning the Babylonian exile and its aftermath (chs. 40–66).[43] And Isaiah 39 connects the Isaianic vision concerning the Assyrian period with the larger fulfilments associated with the exile and beyond.[44] Thus chs. 34–39 serve as a 'bridge' between 1–33 and 40–66.[45]

In Isaiah 40–66 imagery first introduced in ch. 1 reappears and becomes important for 40–66 as a whole. Yahweh commissions the

Torah', in this volume for this view of the macrostructure of the book of Isaiah.

42. C. Seitz's analysis of 11.1-9 is well worth reading (*Isaiah 1–39*, p. 102) because of the sensitivity with which he interrelates Isaianic understanding of prophecy fulfilled and prophecy far too utopian to be seen as already fulfilled in even a modest sense.

43. Scholars have long seen parallels between chs. 34–35 (especially ch. 35) and chs. 40–66.

44. R.F. Melugin, *The Formation of Isaiah 40–55* (BZAW, 141; Berlin: de Gruyter, 1976), p. 177; P. Ackroyd, 'Isaiah 36–39: Structure and Function', in W.C. Delsman *et al.*(eds.), *Von Kanaan bis Kerala* (AOAT, 211; Neukirchen–Vluyn: Neukirchener Verlag, 1982), pp. 3-21.

45. Seitz (*Isaiah 1–39*, pp. 239-42) argues that the placement of chs. 34–35 *before* chs. 36–39 allows the destruction of the destroyer Assyria (ch. 33) to function as a type of the nations (34.1-4) and to surround chs. 36–39 with Second-Isaiah-type material.

comforting of Jerusalem (40.1-2),[46] which is portrayed (as in 1.21-26) as
a woman ('cry to her...'). Indeed, Zion is often depicted as a woman
whose 'sons' will be restored to her (49.20-21, 24-26; 51.18; 54.1-3;
60.4).[47] Yahweh's stubborn and rebellious sons (1.2-9; 48.8) suffer the
punishment of exile and must be restored to their mother once the exile
is over. Moreover, the image of Jerusalem as a harlotrous wife (1.21-26)
anticipates the subsequent portrayal of her as a widowed wife whom
Yahweh forsook in wrath but now takes back in compassion (54.4-8).[48]

Despite the promise of the restoration of Zion after the Babylonian
exile (see chs. 40–55), the imagery of judgment and restoration found in
ch. 1 re-emerges in chs. 56–66. References to 'sons of the sorceress and
offspring of the adulterer and harlot' (57.3) and to wicked sons who
'burn with lust among the oaks...' (57.4b) remind us of language in 1.4-
9, 29-31. Indeed, in the recounting of Yahweh's relationships with
rebellious Israel (63.15–64.11), the father-son metaphor continues to
depict disobedient Israel (63.16; 64.7; see also 63.8). Yet Zion's sons will
be restored to her (60.4). And, as in 1.19-20, 27-31, only part of the
community will be saved (65.8-16; 66.1-4, 17, 24). In Isaiah 1, only
those who repent (1.27), who are 'willing and obedient' (1.19), and who
seek justice (1.17) will be delivered; in the latter part of the book, only
those who are just will survive (66.1-4).

Thus the book of Isaiah closes with a symbolic world reminiscent of
its opening. At both beginning and end what remains is a community of
survivors. And at both beginning and end we find both *exhortation* for
righteousness (1.16-17; 56.1-2) and *prophecy* of salvation for the
righteous and punishment for the wicked (1.27-31; 65.1-7, 8-12, 13-16;
66.1-5, 12-17, 22-24). The end of the book is admittedly more complex
in this regard than the beginning: There is communal confession of
injustice and proclamation of wrath upon God's adversaries and
redemption for those who turn from sin (59.1-21); there is petition for

46. R. Rendtorff connects the 'comforting' of Jerusalem in 40.2 with the psalm
in 12.1 ('The Composition of the Book of Isaiah', in *idem*, *Overtures to an Old
Testament Theology* [trans. and ed. M. Kohl; Minneapolis: Fortress Press, 1993],
pp. 146-69, especially pp. 149-50). The entire essay is of utmost importance as an
argument for the unity of the book of Isaiah as a whole.

47. See the important work on child and female imagery by K.P. Darr, *Isaiah's
Vision and the Family of God* (Louisville: Westminster/John Knox, 1994).

48. Darr (*Isaiah's Vision*, pp. 30-35) understands reading as something which
takes place sequentially, so that earlier passages take on additional significance as the
text moves forward.

God no longer to remember the community's iniquity (63.7–64.11, especially 64.7-11). But Yahweh's answer to 63.7–64.11 specifies different destinies for the obedient and the disobedient (see chs. 65–66).[49] The fate of each group, however, is not fixed; the prophecies show that the destiny of each group depends upon the response of each to the exhortations for repentance and righteousness.[50] The book closes as it opens, then, with a promise for a wondrous recreation of Zion, to be peopled by Yahweh's obedient children, while those who disobey will die by means of Yahweh's stormwind, flame and sword.

III

This essay's focus on figurative language and the construction of a symbolic world is directly related to the task of reading Isaiah as Scripture. As I argued above, the 'mosaic' of figurative constructs in Isaiah 1 and also throughout the entire book is a rich resource for a community of faith to employ for reading the text as judging and saving

49. If one reads synchronically, chs. 65–66 answer the petitions in 63.15–64.11, even though Yahweh's response to the petitions for deliverance of a sinful *people* (64.7-11) makes a distinction between those who will be saved from those who will not.

50. D. Carr ('Reaching for Unity in Isaiah', *JSOT* 57 [1993], pp. 61-80) argues that chs. 65–66, unlike ch. 1, do not exhort change in behaviour but presume instead that the destinies of sinner and righteous have have already been determined (pp. 73-75). Carr is quite right that chs. 65–66 announce the future without explicit exhortations for repentance. Indeed, readers might well expect that the portrayal of possibilities for the future at the very beginning of Isaiah would not be exactly the same as the picture of the future painted at the book's end; after all, the book itself moves the reader through the epochs of both Assyria and Babylon and envisages a new (and possibly different) future than that with which the book began. Nevertheless, I believe that Carr has overstated the case for the *inevitability* of consequences for sinners and the righteous in chs. 65–66. Even after Jerusalem has been 'comforted' (40.1-2) the implied audience is still exhorted to repent (44.22), to seek Yahweh and forsake wickedness (55.6-7), and to do justice and righteousness (56.1). Moreover, there are abundant promises that the nature of the future is dependent upon decisions about behaviour; that is, that righteous behaviour will lead to favorable consequences *if* such behaviour is chosen (58.6-14). And unrighteous deeds will lead to punishment (59.18-19). Thus the depiction of the different destinies of sinners and righteous persons (chs. 65–66) following the prayer for forgiveness of the community (64.7-11) may credibly be understood as portrayals of the different consequences of behavioural choices which can still be made.

word for its own life. Indeed, the formation of communities' identities in
relationship with Yahweh clearly involves the use of figurative language:
Jews and Christians understand themselves as children of God (see, for
example, Isa. 1.2-3), as creatures of God who are formed by God much
as a potter shapes clay (Gen. 2.7), or as persons who are knitted by God
in the mother's womb the way one makes clothing (Ps. 139.13).[51]

The use of such tropes for the shaping of persons in relationship with
God has to do with the *force* of language in the enterprise of personal
transformation. Explanation of a text's original meaning is not in itself
sufficient for using it to form and transform relationships with God in
communities of faith generation after generation. Using Isaiah to confront
Yahweh's rebellious children with a word of judgment is not the same as
explaining how and why a prophet more than twenty-five centuries ago
spoke a word of judgment. Using Scripture to exhort doing justice for
the orphan and other powerless persons is not the same as explaining
the circumstances in which Isaiah uttered such a word. The distinction
between *performative* and *explanatory* uses of language is well established indeed in the philosophy of language.[52] The most basic purposes
for the use of Scripture in communities of faith, I believe, should be
performative; the community's most sacred texts should be powerful
agents for judgment and healing. Explanation should be supportive
rather than primary.

Scholarship, however, necessarily involves explanation. My interpretation of Isaiah 1 is admittedly explanatory. But its explanations are
designed to prepare the way for performative use; my explanations of
figurative speech are intended to prepare users of the text to be its
audience—to prepare them to find themselves judged, exhorted to
repent and given a word of hope for the future. In short, I have sought
to produce a kind of scholarly explanation which can facilitate
performative use.

George Lindbeck appears to move in a similar direction. He argues
that taking on identity as a Christian (and similarly as a Jew, I should
think) involves learning the appropriate symbol system; that is, learning
the Bible well enough to interpret oneself and one's world through that

51. W. Brueggemann, *Texts Under Negotiations: The Bible and Postmodern
Imagination* (Minneapolis: Fortress Press, 1993), pp. 30-31.
52. J.L. Austin, *How to Do Things with Words* (New York: Oxford University
Press, 1962); J.R. Searle, *Speech Acts: An Essay in the Philosophy of Language*
(Cambridge: Cambridge University Press, 1970).

tradition.[53] The shaping of identity is a performative undertaking (even if supported by explanations). And learning the appropriate symbol system surely involves (among other things) the use of metaphors and other tropes for the shaping of the identity of the community.

Whoever reads Isaiah 1 as Scripture may find its tropes to be a powerful force in the construction of a symbolic world in which a community may hear and respond to God. Whether ancient Israelite audiences would have understood these tropes in precisely the way I construe them is difficult, if not impossible, to ascertain, for we know precious little about ancient Israelite conventions for *interpreting* figures of speech. Indeed, no generation of interpreters can escape bringing its own conventions of interpretation to the reading of Scripture. Nevertheless, in the formation of a symbolic world in which to live, we can participate in a centuries-old community which employs Isaiah (and other scriptures) to shape its experience of God as judge and savior.

Edgar Conrad's work may be suggestive for the task I have in mind. Instead of reconstructing how the Isaianic text was understood by actual communities of Israelite readers, Conrad focuses instead on an 'implied audience'; that is, a fictive audience which the text leads real readers to imagine.[54] Conrad construes the book of Isaiah in terms of a three-part structure: an opening section reflecting an implied community of survivors (chs. 1–5), a lengthy section involving that same community of survivors (chs. 40–66) and a testimony to a past community of survivors embodied in Isaiah the prophet and his community (chs. 5–39).[55]

The implied audience at the beginning of the book is portrayed as a remnant community that would have perished like Sodom and Gomorrah had Yahweh not left them a few survivors (1.9).[56] They speak in first person, as is also frequent in the third part of the book (chs. 40–66); for example, 'Behold, you were angry and we sinned...' (64.4); 'you hid your face from us and delivered us into the hand of our iniquities' (64.6); 'Oh Yahweh, why do you make us err from your ways and harden our heart...?' (63.17).[57] Both beginning and end (chs.

53. G.A. Lindbeck, *The Nature of Doctrine: Religion and Theology in a Postliberal Age* (Philadelphia: Westminster, 1984).

54. E.W. Conrad, *Reading Isaiah* (Minneapolis: Augsburg-Fortress, 1991), pp. 30-31.

55. Conrad, *Reading Isaiah*, pp. 117-18.

56. Conrad, *Reading Isaiah*, pp. 88-89.

57. Conrad, *Reading Isaiah*, p. 107.

1; 65–66) speak of the implied audience as a community of survivors (1.9; 66.18-21) who have already experienced calamity—a 'Sodom-and-Gomorrah-like judgment' in which Yahweh has already manifested judgment against Babylon.[58] The implied community, characterized by deeds of injustice (see, e.g., 1.21-31; 59.2-15), nevertheless waits for the justice which is presently absent (59.11)[59] and 'for the final manifestation of the Lord's plan to establish peace in all the world and to restore Zion to its promised glory'.[60] Isaiah and his community are depicted as the first survivors (chs. 6–39).[61]

I lack space here to deal with the complexities of Conrad's book, nor can I adequately articulate whatever reservations or disagreements I might have. But I do believe that his kind of hermeneutic is fruitful for reading the text as Scripture. If one, like Childs, wants to read Isaiah in such a way that it can speak to communities of faith in a variety of historical periods and diversity of social circumstances,[62] he or she might learn much from Conrad's approach. The text of Isaiah begins with addresses for (and by) an implied community whose historical features are not precisely delineated. That is also the case with Isaiah 40–66. To be sure, Isaiah 40–66 seems to presuppose a community sometime after Jerusalem was defeated and exiles were taken to Babylon. But a variety of Israelite communities over a period of hundreds of years could conceivably have identified themselves with the implied audience of the book of Isaiah as a whole. They could have seen themselves as a divided community, a community broken by injustice, a community suffering punishment but living in the promise of restoration and healing. Even today a community might see itself as participating in the implied community of the book of Isaiah. A conventional historical-critical reading of Isaiah, however valuable it might be, is surely not as suitable as a Conrad-like approach to facilitate the participation of readers in the text's implied community and for the potential transformation which might occur in the lives of those readers.

My intent here is not to endorse all of Conrad's arguments, for I differ with him in a number of ways. But I do recommend that, in Conrad-*like*

---

58. Conrad, *Reading Isaiah*, p. 102.
59. Conrad, *Reading Isaiah*, pp. 103-106.
60. Conrad, *Reading Isaiah* p. 102.
61. Conrad, *Reading Isaiah*, pp. 110-13, 118.
62. B.S. Childs, *Introduction to the Old Testament as Scripture* (Philadelphia: Fortress, 1979), p. 326.

fashion, the book of Isaiah be read in such a way that present-day interpretive communities can find themselves addressed as participants in its 'implied audience'. My own proposal has focused on figurative speech because I am convinced that communities of faith must participate imaginatively in the Isaianic symbolic world in order to be transformed profoundly by that prophetic book. While this is by no means the only move to make in the interpretation of Isaiah as Scripture, I consider it to be of great value.

Precisely what might be involved in participating in an Isaianic 'implied audience' needs further exploration. Is the implied audience almost entirely the product of the text itself? Or is the implied audience shaped by both text and reader? I believe the latter to be the case. If I am right about this, we might well expect, for example, Jewish and Christian readings of Isaiah to be somewhat different. Indeed, the ways in which Jewish and Christian communities might find their futures prefigured and their lives accordingly transformed by reading Isaiah would surely be influenced by the total context in which each community interprets its scriptures.

Greater specificity on this last question lies beyond the scope of this essay. But it is a question which deserves further scrutiny. If it is the case, as I have argued, that tropes in Isaiah can be fruitful in shaping the lives of its Jewish and Christian audiences, it is also important to reflect upon what kinds of hermeneutical moves might be appropriate for each community to make. For the moment, I can only hope that the present essay begins a discussion which at some later time can be extended.

PROPHET, REDACTOR AND AUDIENCE: REFORMING THE NOTION OF ISAIAH'S FORMATION

Edgar W. Conrad

Introduction

In the Seminar on the Formation of Isaiah, we have tended to talk past each other on some occasions because members within the group are working with fundamentally different notions of what 'the formation of Isaiah' means.[1] This division is complex. Our conflicting notions about formation concern the following questions: (1) How do we speak about textual meaning? (2) How do we speak about history? and (3) To what communities of interpretation do we belong? Since my own view represents the minority one, and since it is my responsibility to make my own view clearer, I offer the following essay as an edited version of the original paper I delivered in New Orleans in 1990.[2]

Textual Meaning

We have tended to characterize the split within the group as a division between diachronic and synchronic approaches, between approaches that seek to understand the development of the text through time and approaches that seek to read the text as it is in its final form. Indeed, we have downplayed these differences as if the two approaches can be easily melded and as if there is little at stake in choosing one or the other. The difference that stains the discussion will in the end, to continue the

1. I wish to express my thanks to W. Brueggemann and to my Australian colleagues, N. Habel, H. Spykerboer and P. Bedford who have read and offered insights on earlier drafts of this article.

2. The original paper was titled, 'Prophet, Audience, Redactor: The Reception of the Book of Isaiah', and was delivered at the Formation of the Book of Isaiah Consultation at the Society of Biblical Literature Meeting, New Orleans, November 1990.

metaphor, 'come out in the wash'. This appears to be the position of Rolf Rendtorff in the paper he delivered to the seminar in 1991. While giving priority to synchronic analysis, he suggests toward the end of his paper that the results of these two different kinds of studies might be blended fruitfully in a study of Isaiah's unity:

> The first and main question is no longer, What was the 'original' meaning of this text? and also not, When and how had this text been incorporated into its present context? but, What is the meaning of the text in its given context? This does not exclude the first two questions to be asked for additional information and clarification. But the priority is now clearly given to the interpretation of the text in its given context.[3]

The unity of Isaiah is, according to Rendtorff, a complex unity, an understanding of which can be enhanced by diverse methodological approaches.

While the call for 'hermeneutical pluralism', the combined use of synchronic and diachronic approaches,[4] may lessen the friction that now exists in biblical studies between final-form and genetic readings of Isaiah, any resulting harmony may be at the expense of ignoring a fundamental dichotomy between these two kinds of reading. The movement in Isaianic studies from understanding the text in terms of its beginnings (a search for sources, including the original words of the prophet) to understanding it in terms of its end (attention to the final form of the text) has radically altered the way in which the redactor is understood. The redactor, who was once thought to be a collector, has increasingly come to be understood as creative and the redactor's activity as less mechanical. For example, R.E. Clements says, 'the overall structure of the book [of Isaiah] shows signs of editorial planning and...at some stage in its growth, attempts were made to read and interpret the book as a whole'.[5] Clements suggests that the movement in Isaianic studies is from viewing the book as an unreadable collection to seeing it as a readable whole. In *Reading Isaiah*, I argued that such a change is a

3. R. Rendtorff, 'The Book of Isaiah: A Complex Unity. Synchronic and Diachronic Reading', *Society of Biblical Literature 1991 Seminar Papers* (SBLSP, 30; Atlanta: Scholars Press, 1991), p. 13. A revised and updated version of this essay appears in this volume.

4. The term 'hermeneutical pluralism' to refer to the combined use of synchronic and diachronic readings is used by M. Brett. See his *Biblical Criticism in Crisis? The Impact of the Canonical Approach on Old Testament Studies* (Cambridge: Cambridge University Press, 1991), p. 41.

5. R.E. Clements, 'The Unity of the Book of Isaiah', *Int* 36 (1982), p. 121.

challenge to the whole enterprise of redaction.[6] What has occurred in
Isaianic studies is what John Barton has called 'the trick of the disap-
pearing redactor':

> The trick is simply this. The more impressive the critic makes the
> redactor's work appear, the more he succeeds in showing that the redactor
> has, by subtle and delicate artistry, produced a simple and coherent text
> out of the diverse materials before him; the more also he reduces the
> evidence on which the existence of those sources was established in the
> first place. No conjurer is required for this trick: the redaction critic
> himself causes his protégé to disappear...Thus, if redaction criticism
> plays its hand too confidently, we end up with a piece of writing so
> coherent that no division into sources is warranted any longer...[7]

However, like every other magic trick, this illusion is less awe-inspiring
when one knows how the trick is done. The redactor has not disap-
peared but is in reality an author.[8] The 'author' of Isaiah is not
equivalent, of course, to a contemporary author. Ancient authors
engaged in scribal activity and utilized sources at hand changing them
and adapting them in the creation of something new.[9] They freely
practiced what we would refer to as plagiarism. But if the 'author' of
Isaiah is no longer a compiler of traditions, involved in collecting rather
than in creating something new, the whole project of so-called redaction
has changed.[10]

That the redactor has become an 'author' is not an indifferent change
but has fundamental implications for notions about the formation of

6.	I have discussed this change elsewhere. See my *Reading Isaiah* (Overtures
to Biblical Theology; Minneapolis: Fortress Press, 1991), pp. 12-20.

7.	J. Barton, *Reading the Old Testament: Method in Biblical Study* (London:
Darton Longman & Todd, 1984), p. 57. Barton, however, does not believe that the
redaction critic will ever succeed in making the redactor disappear (pp. 57-58).

8.	M. Sweeney has recognised this change in the perception of the redactor. He
says, 'Past scholarship viewed redactors in opposition to authors. Their basic task
was not creative, like that of authors, but mechanical, merely to collect and transmit
older literary works.' See his *Isaiah 1–4 and the Post-Exilic Understanding of the
Isaianic Tradition* (BZAW, 171; Berlin: de Gruyter, 1988), p. 2.

9.	For a discussion of this point see J. Barton, 'Reading the Bible as Literature:
Two Questions for Biblical Critics', *Literature and Theology* 1 (1987), pp. 135-53.
The distinction I am making between contemporary and ancient authors cannot be
pushed too far. Many structuralist and post-structuralist theorists have argued that no
author is original and that all writing is a pastiche of other works (intertextuality).

10.	I have discussed this in more detail in my *Reading Isaiah*, pp. 84-87.

Isaiah. The involvement by the 'author-redactor', as one who re-works sources, makes the recovery of sources much more problematic. When understood in this way, it is difficult to see how synchronic and diachronic readings of Isaiah can be easily combined. The more the Isaianic text is viewed as unified or readable, the more our study is moving in the direction of understanding a text that is 'authored' rather than 'compiled'.

In a recent article,[11] John Noble described diachronic and synchronic readings of biblical texts as relating to 'two different kinds of source analyses: Quotation- and Resource-Theories'. He defines Quotation Theory as 'a theory of composition in which the final text has been formed through (parts of) the original documents being incorporated into it verbatim'. Resource Theory is a theory 'of composition in which the author has used his source(s) as a resource from which he can freely draw ideas for plot, character, themes, etc. without being tied at all closely by the treatment that they receive in his sources'.[12] These two theories form a continuum but the more one moves toward a Resource Theory of composition the more one moves toward understanding the text as produced by an author rather than a redactor. Furthermore, 'a successful synchronic interpretation of a text renders a "sources-and-redactor" account of its prehistory highly improbable'.[13] It is my contention that our synchronic readings of Isaiah represent a change in the theory of the book of Isaiah's formation away from a 'Quotation Theory' to a 'Resource Theory'.[14] In such a situation, our ability to

11. J. Noble, 'Synchronic and Diachronic Approaches to Biblical Interpretation', *Literature and Theology* 7 (1993), pp. 130-48. This article by Noble has contributed substantially to my understanding of synchronic and diachronic reading of biblical books. In the article Noble critiques both Brett's and Barton's attempts to combine synchronic and diachronic readings (pp. 144-46).

12. Noble, 'Synchronic and Diachronic Approaches', p. 137.

13. Noble, 'Synchronic and Diachronic Approaches', p. 146.

14. Clement's observation that the creative role of the redactor has made it increasingly difficult to locate the original words of Isaiah is an indication that Isaianic studies has moved from a 'Quotation Theory' to a 'Resource Theory' of Isaiah's formation. He says, 'Duhm, with his analytical method, was entirely, and almost obsessively, concerned with the problems of original meaning. Such would be in order if the books of prophecy were merely collections, or anthologies, in which the original sense has been retained and the role of the editor, or editors, reduced to a minimum. On the other hand, if the work of the editors has been substantially more than this, then we may expect that they will themselves have

rewrite a pre-history of the text of Isaiah is becoming more and more unlikely. The creative use of sources by an 'author' (or 'scribe') underscores the difficulty in our determination, for example, of what might once have been the original ending of First Isaiah, or even whether there was a First Isaiah.[15] To be sure the 'author' of Isaiah used sources, but they were creatively used to construct something new, making their recovery not only improbable but also the accomplishment of that goal increasingly unimportant. From the point of view of a Resource Theory of text production, the book of Isaiah is like a literary collage. Formation is understood as occurring at a point in time rather than as transpiring over centuries through continuous growth. What is available for study is not the history of a tradition nor the intention of an 'author-redactor' but the literary creation itself, the book of Isaiah.

Those who attempt to do a diachronic analysis of the book of Isaiah traditionally have done so by understanding the process as beginning with the oral words of Isaiah, which in the course of time were expanded as Isaianic tradition grew, perhaps by the input of his disciples.[16] More recently, some scholars have begun to imagine the history of the book quite differently. Rather than being associated with the origin of the poetry in the book of Isaiah, the prophet is understood as an addition in the last stages of the book's development.[17] The possibility of imagining the book in two such fundamentally different ways underscores the fact that the book's sources have been obscured in the course of its

injected a great degree of their own understanding into the work. Even at a *prima facie* level it would certainly appear that the very complexity of the final shape given to the book of Isaiah points us to this latter conclusion. The later, redactional, stages in the formation of the book have contributed more to an understanding of what it means than can be gleaned by modern attempts to reconstruct the story of the "life and times" of Isaiah of Jerusalem in the eighth century BC' ('Beyond Tradition History: Deutero-Isaiah's Development of First Isaiah's Themes', *JSOT* 31 [1985], p. 100).

15. Seitz, in his recent book, *Zion's Final Destiny: The Development of the Book of Isaiah: A Re-Assessment of Isaiah 36–39* (Minneapolis: Fortress Press, 1991) argues that Isaiah 36–39 belongs essentially to First Isaiah. If Isaiah is seen as 'authored' from sources, then he is raising a question that is ultimately unanswerable for we do not have the data for determining the Book of Isaiah's prehistory. We only have the final form of the text; we know nothing about the history of its parts.

16. See *Reading Isaiah*, pp. 12-13.

17. See, for example, G.A. Auld, 'Poetry, Prophecy, Hermeneutic: Recent Studies in Isaiah', *SJT* 33 (1980), pp. 578-81, and R.P. Carroll, 'Poets Not Prophets', *JSOT* 27 (1983), pp. 25-31.

construction. Resources have been used to construct something new and are no longer available for study. The book of Isaiah's origins can be imagined in a variety of ways, but the data for identifying its roots are inaccessible.

History

To view the book of Isaiah as a literary construction at a point in time rather than to picture it as a text encoding a history of its development fits in clearly with the changing ways in which historians are talking about the history of Israel. With the demise of the Albright School, and with that the demise of biblical archaeology, the Syro-Palestinian archaeology that has taken its place has presented us with a picture of Israel in Iron Age Palestine that is considerably different from that portrayed in the biblical narratives.[18] It appears that 'ancient Israel' belongs to a world that has been constructed by the 'biblical'[19] literature.[20] That the 'ancient Israel' of the 'biblical' text is itself largely fictive has important consequences for our current diachronic studies of Isaianic tradition because our diachronic readings can now be seen to be plotted not against a 'real' world but against a literary Israel, a construction of a later age projected into the past.

Diachronic notions about how a text such as Isaiah evolved through time are also put in question by our sketchy view of the community from which it was supposedly emerging. It is no longer clear to what community or locality one can appeal as the society that produced the Hebrew literature which in due course came to constitute the biblical

18. See P.R. Davies, *In Search of 'Ancient Israel'* (JSOTSup, 148; Sheffield: JSOT Press, 1992), pp. 1-22.

19. I have placed 'biblical' in quotation marks because I am talking about the time of the origin of the literature, not the time when it became biblical. 'Biblical' refers to the time when a collection of literature is ratified by a community of faith, not the time of its having been written. See P.R. Davies, 'Sociology and the Second Temple', in *idem* (ed.), *Second Temple Studies. I. Persian Period* (JSOTSup, 117; Sheffield: JSOT Press, 1991), p. 11.

20. This thesis has been argued and defended recently by Philip R. Davies in his book, *In Search of 'Ancient Israel'*. See this page, note 17. For a similar position on the absence of archaeological data for uncovering the Israel of the biblical texts, see Giovanni Garbini, *History and Ideology in Ancient Israel* (trans. J. Bowden; London: SCM Press, 1986). Garbini's notions of historical reconstruction, however, differ significantly from those of Davies.

books of the Tanakh/Old Testament. However, to turn to a study of a 'biblical' text such as the book of Isaiah as literature is not to abandon an interest in history. But the terms of the relationship between history and literature have been reversed. Rather than history being understood as essential for explaining the development of the literature, literature itself may be used as data for understanding history.[21]

Biblical studies can gain insight into the role of literature in historical inquiry from theoretical discussions in a sub-discipline of history sometimes labelled 'the new cultural history'. What characterizes this theoretical approach 'is the pervasive influence of recent literary criticism, which has taught historians to recognise the active role of language, texts, and narrative structures in the creation and description of historical reality'.[22] Such discussions understand the historian, as a reader of the past, to be like the writers of the past, actively involved in the construction of history.[23] According to this understanding of historiography, literary theory does not stand in opposition to historical inquiry but offers an important insight into the task of the historian. A literary approach to prophetic texts, then, is not necessarily another 'nail in the coffin' of historical investigation but an alternative avenue into 'doing history' for those communities of interpretation where historical criticism and biblical archaeology are called into question.

Two prominent theorists who have taken an active lead in promoting the importance of literary criticism for historiography are Hayden White and Dominick LaCapra.[24] Kramer summarizes the significance of their approach in the following way:

> The concern that this White-LaCapra perspective brings to contemporary historians...concerns the complex problem of opening the essentially nineteenth-century historiographic paradigm of reality and representation

---

21. That literature contains a side of history not often found in history books is a point that D. Jobling makes. See his 'Text and the World—An Unbridgeable Gap? A Response to Carroll, Hoglund and Smith', in Davies (ed.), *Second Temple Studies*, I, p. 176.

22. L.S. Kramer, 'Literature, Criticism, and Historical Imagination: The Literary Challenge of Hayden White and Dominick LaCapra', in L. Hunt (ed.), *The New Cultural History* (Los Angeles: University of California Press, 1989), p. 98.

23. Kramer, 'Literature, Criticism, and Historical Imagination', p. 100.

24. For a definitive list of their works see Kramer, 'Literature, Criticism, and Historical Imagination'.

to the critical insights that have transformed nineteenth-century attitudes in literature, art, critical theory, and science.[25]

This summons to move away from nineteenth-century strategies of interpretation means that White's and LaCapra's challenge to historians is similar to Robert A. Oden's recent challenge to biblical studies—with one major exception.[26] While biblical studies perpetuated the notion of the nineteenth-century German historiographic tradition that 'the hand of God' was a stabilizing influence giving coherence and unity to the history of ancient Israel, 'secular' historians have long since abandoned such a metaphysical notion and substituted for it, 'the historical context', a unifying factor in historical investigation that they understood to be more concrete and therefore more 'real'.[27] Kramer summarizes LaCapra's notion of how God has been replaced by Context in historiography:

> The widespread tendency of historians to see the context as the essential and often unified causal force in history suggests to LaCapra the continuing influence of the Western metaphysical tradition in even the most secular and positivistic works of modern historiography. Historians want to describe a reality that exists beyond interpretation or outside of texts in ways that recapitulate the ancient metaphysical desire for pure being, and their 'contextualism' carries the 'Platonism' of a tradition that rests on 'an idealised notion of full, essential meaning'.[28]

White's and LaCapra's arguments against the historical context as 'the real' rest on their understanding of language as a construction, not a reflection, of reality. This observation is related to what literary theorists have said about the construction of textual meaning. Just as

25. Kramer, 'Literature, Criticism, and Historical Imagination', p. 100.

26. See his, *The Bible without Theology: The Theological Tradition and Alternatives to It* (San Francisco: Harper & Row, 1987). I will consider Oden's position in more detail below.

27. Of course the concern for historical context is also reflected in biblical studies. Many handbooks on exegesis stress the importance of establishing the historical context for interpreting biblical texts. This demonstrates the complexity of communities of interpretation. Interpreters belong to a variety of interpretive communities, and biblical scholars who have preserved the German historiographic tradition have also incorporated into their interpretive strategies conventions from the larger community of historians.

28. Kramer, 'Literature, Criticism, and Historical Imagination', p. 115. He is quoting from LaCapra, *Rethinking Intellectual History: Texts, Contexts, Language* (Ithaca: Cornell University Press, 1983), p. 115.

readers construct meaning rather than extract meaning embedded in the text so also when historians write about the past, they create it. The textual creation of the past applies, of course, not just to contemporary texts about the past but also to past texts which historians use in their research. Historians cannot simply read these past texts as reflections of reality because past texts are as much a construction of reality as are contemporary historical accounts of the past. To use texts from the past, then, to discover something that is more real—the divine or the historical context—is to require of texts from the past, such as the biblical text, something that they cannot deliver. Texts from the past are not reflections of history; they are artefacts of its construction. The past is available to us only as text; that is, as language that is always removed from whatever was.[29] 'The fictive, imaginary dimension in all accounts of events does not mean that the events did not actually happen, but it does mean that any attempt to *describe* events (even as they are occurring) must rely on various forms of imagination.'[30] To search for the 'real' as if we can get beyond the text, is to fail to see that what we find is our own construction of the past. We make ourselves the judges who determine what the real world is. White and LaCapra argue that texts can only point to the past and that we cannot know in a full and coherent fashion the real world of the past.

The distinction between history and fiction, then, is not as clear as historians often assume. For example, White says, 'In point of fact, history...is made sense of in the same way that the poet or novelist tries to make sense of it, i.e., by endowing what originally appears to be problematical and mysterious with the aspect of a recognisable, because it is a familiar, form.'[31] When contemporary historians write about the past, they construct it according to the interpretive strategies that prevail in their communities of interpretation. But what is true for contemporary histories is also true for past texts, which are also constructions designed to make the problematical recognizable.

What does all this mean, then, for us as readers of biblical books,

---

29. In *Reading Isaiah*, pp. 5 and 25-27, I also spoke about the problem in which historical-critical studies continued the naive notion of the relationship between language and the reality to which it supposedly referred.

30. Kramer, 'Literature, Criticism, and Historical Imagination', p. 101.

31. Kramer, 'Literature, Criticism, and Historical Imagination', p. 101. He is quoting from White, *Tropics of Discourse* (Baltimore: Johns Hopkins Press, 1978), pp. 126 and 98.

whose interest in them has been prompted by an interest in history? It means, as I said at the end of *Reading Isaiah*, that the past of the Isaianic tradition is not something to which we can return. Instead, that past has come to us in textual form and can be encountered only textually and only in the present.[32] The past is not available to us in some pristine sense that we can capture in a fuller or more coherent form than the past texts we read.

To be aware of our own textual constructions of the past as well as the textual constructions of the past texts we read has important consequences for us as interpreters interested in history. Past texts now stand more clearly at the centre of our interpretive concerns. They are no longer seen as resources for getting at something else, the historical context, but are our only links with what was. We can choose to be omnipotent readers re-writing the past texts, making them fit into our own canons of understanding, or we can choose to read them as 'other'; that is, to encounter them as alien or unfamiliar. Although as readers we are actively engaged in making meaning, we are making meaning out of something; we are not simply reading blank pages. LaCapra's suggestion for interpreters in such situations is to carry on a dialogue, rather than a monologue, with texts understood as voices from the past.

> The historian's task, then, is to develop a 'dialogue' in which the autonomous past is allowed to question our recurring attempts to reduce it to order. 'It must be actively recognised that the past has its own "voices" that must be respected', LaCapra writes, 'especially when they resist or qualify the interpretations we would like to place on them. A text is a network of resistances, and a dialogue is a two-way affair; a good reader is also an attentive and patient listener.'[33]

Often biblical scholarship has obliterated the 'other' voices of biblical texts by making them speak a familiar language, reducing a dialogue with past texts to a monologue about them. Fundamentalists do this when they make biblical texts speak in a present idiom; for example, when they familiarize Genesis 1 and read it as science or when they contemporize a prophetic text and read it as a political commentary on the present. Canonical critics do this when they make books like Isaiah speak the later and more familiar languages of Judaism or Christianity. Historical critics do this when they make a biblical text reveal the history

32. Conrad, *Reading Isaiah*, pp. 154-55.
33. Kramer, 'Literature, Criticism, and Historical Imagination', p. 104 citing LaCapra, *Rethinking Intellectual History*, p. 64.

of its own formation, often guided by the familiar language of divine guidance.[34] In fact, all of us as readers employ strategies to make texts familiar and that is why we must recognize all of our readings as limited and subject to the qualifications of subsequent readings. Genuine dialogue will take place by reading texts in such a way as to allow them to call our former constructions into question. Reading past texts is not a matter of devising quasi-scientific equations to master them but of encountering them as other human voices.

When reading past texts as 'other', however, neither the texts nor the reader should be given an omnipotent status in the dialogue. The voices of the past, as in any good dialogue, need to be questioned. Past voices construct reality just as we do in our own textual construction of the world.[35] In such situations our ideological perspectives will limit what we see and the way we tell it. We never will tell it 'like it is'; we will always tell it the way we see it. As readers we need to be alert to the fact that because a past text says something does not mean that it is necessarily so.

Historical context is important for understanding past texts, but here context should not be understood with a capital 'C'; that is, as essential reality. Here again LaCapra's position, as summarised by Kramer, helps to clarify the point I am developing:

> ...the context does not simply exist as a prelinguistic reality that language faithfully describes. On the contrary, reality is 'always already' situated in or shaped by textual processes that historians prefer not to examine. 'The context itself is a text of sorts', writes LaCapra; 'it calls not for stereotypical, ideological "descriptions" but for interpretation and informed criticism'. The historian should therefore read the context with sensitivity to the literary process of 'intertextuality' rather than with the causal notion of reflection. Common beliefs about the opposition between texts and reality simply do not hold up, because 'the past arrives in the form of texts and textualized remainders—memoirs, reports, published writings, archives, monuments, and so forth'. Yet this textual base of all knowledge about context is often 'obscured or repressed' among historians who rush headlong toward the stable ground of reality.[36]

34. This point is developed below.

35. On this point see M. Bal, 'Introduction', in M. Bal (ed.), *Anti-Covenant: Counter-Reading Women's Lives in the Hebrew Bible* (JSOTSup, 81; Sheffield: Almond Press, 1989), pp. 11-24, especially the section on 'Reading and Responsibility', pp. 13-15.

36. Kramer, 'Literature, Criticism, and Historical Imagination', pp. 114-15. Here

Historical context, then, exists only as a plurality of textual voices, each of which requires engagement. Reading prophetic books in their historical context necessitates dialogue with archaeological studies, which in turn are encountering archaeological remains of the past as texts requiring interpretation. It means dialogue with historians of ancient Palestine, many of whom are stressing the need to understand the social dimension of history rather than focus strictly on religious or theological matters.[37]

How we speak about history, then, is important for our notions about the formation of the book of Isaiah. Diachronic studies require our ability to move behind the text and trace its development through various contexts defined by time. However, the role of language in the construction of reality makes a move from text to context highly problematic.

Communities of Interpretation

Communities of interpretation play a major role in envisaging the formation of Isaiah. Whether we are speaking from theologically oriented settings of inquiry, or settings where the study of religion is dealt with more broadly, is important for the way we read. Robert A. Oden in his book, *The Bible without Theology: The Theological Tradition and Alternatives to It*, has helped us to see how moving from theologically oriented academic communities to departments of religion requires us to rethink the strategies of interpretation that have characterized biblical studies. Oden observes that 'the institutional setting for

he is quoting from LaCapra, *Rethinking Intellectual History*, pp. 95-96, and *History and Criticism*, p. 128.

37. This is a point made by R.A. Horsley in 'Empire, Temple and Continuity— But No Bourgeoisie! A Response to Blenkinsopp and Peterson', in Davies (ed.), *Second Temple Studies*, I, p. 163. He says, 'I find myself pleading with colleagues in biblical studies that our subject matter is not primarily "religious". That is, biblical literature and history are not "religious" and do not deal with "religious" matters in a way separate or separable from other dimensions of life, such as the "political" or the "economic". "Religion" is embedded with kinship and/or local community life and/or "the state" in virtually any traditional agrarian society, and hence is inseparable from political and economic matters. Our scholarly habit of pretending that we are dealing with primarily religious texts or institutions, which means basically imposing modern presuppositions and concepts on historical materials that had neither concepts nor terms for religion, blocks rather than enhances understanding.'

the majority of biblical scholarship has long been that of the Christian seminary or of universities committed to the training of Christian ministers'.[38] Such an 'intellectual or institutional setting' is an unusual one for it situates

> Biblical study within the context of preparing students for the professional task of serving in a particular confessional, most often ecclesiastical, role. Though this is an entirely legitimate and proper context, its unusual status has perhaps been too little considered. Most academic disciplines train people to be students of a phenomenon, not apologetic advocates of a particular system of rituals and beliefs.[39]

Oden's thesis is that this peculiar location of biblical studies has given shape to the historical-critical approach to the Bible. He argues that what undergirds the conventions of biblical interpretation in theological settings is called into question by scholars who study the Bible in other settings such as departments of religion or departments of English.

Oden has overstated his case here by ignoring the role played by other ideologies such as Marxism and feminism in the university. He has also failed to see that his own positivistic reading is no more objective than historical criticism but is in fact another form of confessional reading. However, Oden's argument that historical-critical strategies of interpretation have preserved a German tradition of idealism with its inception in the nineteenth century, a tradition that has long since been abandoned by other disciplines, is a helpful one. He provides a useful summary of the characteristics of 'the German tradition of historiography', which 'began to take shape at the end of the eighteenth century, had its peak just before 1850 and then after periods of doubts and competition from other models of understanding was revived in the decades around 1900'. This particular tradition of historiography 'influenced biblical scholars in the nineteenth century and...continues to influence biblical study in the twentieth century'.[40] Oden describes the key themes of this historiographic tradition as follows:

38. Oden, *The Bible without Theology*, p. 4.
39. Oden, *The Bible without Theology*, p. viii.
40. Oden, *The Bible without Theology*, pp. 50-56. He sees the origin of this thinking in Herder (1744–1803) and traces its continuation in von Humboldt (1767–1835), Ranke (1795–1886) and Droysen (1808–1884) (pp. 8-15). He also makes the case that this tradition influenced biblical scholars who, from Wellhausen to Gunkel, shaped the historical-critical approach characteristic of biblical scholarship throughout this century (pp. 20-37).

1. *Nations are to be treated as individuals*, as living organisms, and therefore, like individuals, are to be understood as unique. The emphasis on individualism also means that the best society is one in which each person is permitted to develop individual characteristics most fully.

2. *All phenomena are to be understood in terms of development* and, in the case of nations, as human development. Change is viewed positively because 'some idea—a world spirit or the hand of God or the ethical world—was progressing through history, to a higher end'.

3. *There is a rejection of all abstract thought and theorising* since this would deny the individuality of the nation. The historian, like a poet, is to appeal to imagination and intuition rather than rational analysis.

4. *History is understood as a special or autonomous discipline* because it provides us with 'a glimpse of the guiding hand behind all human development. From historical investigation alone comes revelation'.[41]

According to Oden, this German historiographic tradition has been preserved by a community of theological readers because it is easily adaptable to apologetic purposes. Biblical history is seen as unique and, by tracing its origin and development, biblical scholars are able to see the 'hand of God' at work in the course of Israel's development.[42] Argumentation appealing 'to concepts like "the mysterious" or "the workings of the divine will" is quite common' in such contexts so that in the practice of biblical study 'reference to the inexplicable is hardly unusual'.[43]

As I see it, the problem with the German historiographic tradition for communities outside the theological community of biblical scholarship is its contradictory premises, not its easy adaptability to apologetics. As Oden points out, its concern to understand nations as individuals is related to its concern for objectivity, and overarching theories or abstractions are suspect because they may distort the uniqueness of the nation. At the same time, however, the historical-critical approach imposes an ideology on the study of history. The 'ultimate keys to historical thought turn out to be some quite "elusive abstractions", concepts like "spiritual principle" or "the hand of God"'. These things 'are beyond discovery by any ordinary means of investigation'.[44] In

41. Oden, *The Bible without Theology*, pp. 15-16 (italics mine). He understands the historiographic tradition to be representative of the German tradition of idealism in general.

42. Oden, *The Bible without Theology*, pp. 36-37.

43. Oden, *The Bible without Theology*, p. viii.

44. Oden, *The Bible without Theology*, p. 17.

short, the historical-critical argument to avoid theoretical abstraction for the sake of objectivity is itself based on a theoretical abstraction about the meaning of history.

The idealist setting of biblical scholarship permits its adherents to proclaim with Martin Noth that in ancient Israel 'we encounter phenomena for which there is no parallel at all elsewhere'.[45] Nations are understood as individuals, as living organisms, and as such are understood to be unique. Furthermore, this very uniqueness is best observed when we are attentive to the creative individuals in a society, such as individual prophets. According to this view, the development of a prophetic book can be understood as governed by 'the hand of God', who is guiding this unique phenomenon from the time of its origin to its completion in its final form. Biblical scholarship can be seen as being tied together more than pulled apart by diversity of methods since from source analysis to canonical criticism God himself is coming to expression in the process of textual development.

This last point can best be illustrated by quoting from a series of historical-critical scholars who speak about what they have accomplished in their particular methodological approach to the text. Source analysis of prophetic books sought to locate the *ipsissima verba* of the prophet because, in historical-critical studies governed by the idealistic tradition, the prophet in ancient Israel was the person who most fully expressed his own unique, individual characteristics. This can be seen in Georg Fohrer's attempt to locate a prophet's authentic words.[46] More importantly, however, locating the words of the prophet is seen as leading toward God, the source of those words. Fohrer says,

> The first stage [in the development of a prophetic oracle] is a moment of personal experience of God, in which God's 'spirit' or 'word' comes to the prophet...or in which he is transported to another sphere... What he experiences or perceives he is constrained to put into words and to proclaim... This much can generally be said: the less mediation and rational revision a prophetic oracle betrays, the more tersely and unconditionally it proclaims God's will, the more clearly it preserves as its nucleus a primitive complex of sounds...the closer we are to its origin.[47]

45. M. Noth, *The History of Israel* (trans. P.R. Ackroyd; New York: Harper & Row, 2nd edn, 1960), p. 3.

46. G. Fohrer, *Introduction to the Old Testament* (trans. D.E. Green; Nashville: Abingdon Press, 1965), pp. 349-50.

47. Fohrer, *Introduction*, pp. 349-50.

However, when historical-critical scholarship began to encounter problems with locating the original words of the prophet, there was a move toward study of the redaction of a prophetic book. Here the chief concern was to show the continuity of the development of God's revelation. This is evident in the comments of Ronald Clements in his study of the redaction of Isaiah:

> To trace the process of literary growth by which the Book of Isaiah came to assume its present shape is a task which cannot yet be regarded as completed. The useful essays into tracing the redactional history of such a large and primary work have not yet achieved anything approaching a consensus regarding the relative dating of each of its component parts and sayings. Nevertheless, it must be claimed that the recognition that such a redactional history was undertaken by ancient scribes and interpreters for profound spiritual and interpretive reasons is an important factor for us to bear in mind. The prophetic word of God is essentially a divine message concerning his actions and intentions toward his people, and it should not be surprising for us to discover that it has been the continuity and connectedness of this divine purpose which provides the proper basis of unity in the four major prophetic collections.[48]

When canonical critics began to despair of the possibility of tracing the development of prophetic books and sought rather to concentrate on the final form of the text, they did not abandon the notion of the book as the expression of the divine that ensured continuity. This is clear, for example, in the comment of B.S. Childs in an essay on the canonical shape of prophetic literature:

> The purpose of this essay is to suggest a different approach to the biblical material, which I shall try to illustrate in terms of the prophets. It begins with the recognition that a major literary and theological force was at work in shaping the present form of the Hebrew Bible. This force was exerted during most of the history of the literature's formation, but increasingly in the post-exilic period exercised its influence in the collecting, selecting, and ordering of the biblical traditions in such a way as to allow the material to function as authoritative Scripture for the Jewish community. In the transmission process, tradition, which once arose in a particular milieu and addressed various historical situations, was shaped in such a way as to serve as a normative expression of God's will to later generations of Israel who had not shared in those original historical events. In sum, prophetic oracles which were directed to one generation were fashioned into Sacred Scripture by a *canonical process* to be used

---

48. Clements, 'The Unity of the Book of Isaiah', p. 129.

by another generation... The shape of the biblical text reflects a history of
encounter between God and Israel.[49]

What all this indicates is that the various historical-critical methods are
unified by a common perspective: at every stage in the process of
Israel's development or the development of a book such as Isaiah,
unique phenomena are seen as bringing to expression the revelation of
God.

In light of the German historiographic tradition, then, it can be seen
that what is giving unity to the phenomena being studied is not empirical
data but the abstract notion of God: 'God's "spirit" or "word"...
[proclaiming] God's will' (Fohrer), 'the continuity and connectedness
of...divine purpose' (Clements), or 'a canonical process...[reflecting] a
history of encounter between God and Israel' (Childs). The incorporation of such theoretical abstractions is compatible with the interpretive
strategies of communities in Christian seminaries or universities
committed to training Christian ministers. However, for those whose
academic worlds are in departments of religion (or for that matter
departments of English or departments of history), continuing to read
'biblical' literature in historical-critical ways (including canonical-critical
ones) is to read as an outsider in a world of academic discourse that
moves in quite different directions.[50]

What does not sit well in academic communities outside the theological seminaries and departments where historical criticism has its
home is the German tradition of idealism. Ferdinand R. Deist has
explained the movement away from an idealist position as one in which
'it is not ideas that shape a people's socio-political destiny, but socio-
political realities that shape ideas (ideology)'.[51] This movement from an
idealist to a materialist notion of reality is, among other things, a consequence of the impact of the social sciences. To understand 'ancient Israel'
from the perspective of the social sciences is a matter not of tracing the

49. B.S. Childs, 'The Canonical Shape of the Prophetic Literature', *Int* 32 (1978),
p. 47 (italics mine).

50. In many instances historical-critical methods have become technologies
separated from their philosophical base. For this reason historical-critical techniques
continue to be applied in some departments of religion because their rationale has
been obscured.

51. 'The Prophets: Are we Heading for a Paradigm Switch?', in V. Fritz *et al.*
(eds.), *Prophet und Prophetbuch: Festschrift für Otto Kaiser zum 65. Geburtstag*
(Berlin: de Gruyter, 1989), pp. 10-11.

history of an idea but of understanding how social realities shaped ideas (ideologies), including the idea of 'ancient Israel'. If Israel comes to be seen as an 'idea' (ideology) shaped by social realities, then it is important to investigate the social realities that gave it this shape. The text itself and our reading of that text can provide vital clues to the social world out of which the text arose.

Re-forming the Notion of the Formation of Isaiah

From the idealist perspective, the Isaianic tradition is imagined as an individual conceived in the oral words proclaimed by the prophet, maturing through a number of written stages of redactional development, and reaching adulthood in the final form of the text. Diachronic and synchronic readings are seen as complementary. When Isaiah is understood in these terms, there is little discontinuity in the formation of Isaiah. Prophets and redactors, including the final redactor, are all part of a harmonious world in which 'the hand of God' is coming to expression in the literary history of the book.

When one moves away from such idealist underpinnings and imagines a book like Isaiah emerging out of the social world of some ancient community whose origins are obscure, a different notion of formation applies. No longer can we be assured of a smooth line of divine trajectory from beginning to end. We have come to see that when communities write about the past they re-member it; they construct it.[52] Archaeology has highlighted an Israel constructed by the 'biblical' literature to be very different from that of Iron-Age Palestine. Such a situation forces us to rethink notions about the formation of Isaiah. Was there ever a prophet called Isaiah who lived in eighth-century Israel? Did an Isaiah of Jerusalem, a Second Isaiah or a Third Isaiah ever declaim any of the poetry attributed to them? Are the superscription to the book of Isaiah and the prophetic narratives a late veneer on a book whose poetry originally had nothing to do with prophetic speech? Did the book of Isaiah ever pass through a series of redactions, or did it have its origin as a scribal creation from bits and pieces of literature available to the scribe? Indeed, if it were possible, would it be important to trace the origins of the literary fragments used in the production of the book of Isaiah?

---

52. In this regard see K.W. Whitelam, 'Between History and Literature: The Social Production of Israel's History of Origin', *SJT* 2 (1991) pp. 60-74; and 'Recreating the History of Israel', *JSOT* 35 (1986) pp. 45-70.

I am suggesting that we need to read Isaiah as literature, as it is, divorced from uncertain notions of prophets or redactors and their intent, and from our dubious understanding of historical background. Contemporary literary theory can be a resource here for it has helped us to understand how textual meaning is independent of authorial intention or historical background. To read a text of Isaiah as literature means that our notion of the book is not dominated by questions of origin or development; but we do not necessarily ignore questions about the past. The Isaianic text creates a literary world that gives us insight into how an ancient society constructed its reality. The book of Isaiah can be seen as presenting Isaiah as a prophet from the past—a past constructed by a later community in order to make sense of its present. That literary construction of a past is important for our own reconstruction of a past that makes sense from the perspective of our present.

Isaiah's Audiences

Our notions of prophet and redactor, then, will be different depending on how we conceive of the formation of the book of Isaiah. If we think of formation in idealist terms, then there is continuity between prophet, redactor and final form because there is a continuity within the community of Israel, conceived as an individual growing up from ancient Israel to post-exilic Judaism, guided by the divine insuring its singular formation. If we think of the formation of Isaiah as a social construction growing out of the social realities of a post-exilic community, then we tend to see discontinuity between the original prophet (if there was an original prophet) and the community responsible for the book of Isaiah as a literary creation. In this kind of reading we will also see a discontinuity between the ancient community that produced the literature and the later communities of Judaism and Christianity that incorporated this literature into their respective canons of Scripture.[53]

---

53. Jacob Neusner makes the point in a number of his publications that at the time of the formation of the literature of the Old Testament/Hebrew Scriptures, there was a plurality of Jewish groups. He says that 'while the world at large treats Judaism as "the religion of the Old Testament", the fact is otherwise. Judaism inherits and makes the Hebrew Scriptures its own, just as does Christianity' (*Judaism and Scripture: The Evidence of Leviticus Rabbah* [Chicago: The University of Chicago Press, 1986], p. xi see also his *Torah: From Scroll to Symbol in Formative Judaism* [Philadelphia: Fortress Press, 1985], pp. xi-xii and 1-12).

But as present interpreters of the book of Isaiah we are also its audience, and our different notions of how to conceive of the book's formation indicate that we come from a plurality of communities. I will conclude here with the point at which my paper in 1990 began. Following some insights from the literary critic Stanley Fish,[54] I argued that the meaning of a text is dependent on the reader. Meaning arises when readers bring to the text interpretive strategies, which themselves are conventions employed by the community of interpretation to which the reader belongs. In the Formation of Isaiah Seminar, we need to become aware of the different communities in which we work as scholars. There is a significant difference between those of us who work in theological seminaries or departments of theology, whose task it is to speak theologically, and those of us in departments of religion whose task it is to speak about religion as a human phenomenon. The former operate in communities where discussion of the uniqueness of the biblical witness for a community of faith is an item high on the agenda. The latter operate in communities where all religions are taken as data for the construction of religion as an important element in what it means to be human.[55] These differences are not insignificant for how we speak about the formation of Isaiah. Historical-critical methods with their origin in the German historiographic tradition appeal to readers in theological settings; other methods are appropriate for those readers studying the humanities in secular settings.

The distinction I am making between theology departments and religion departments may be more heuristic than actual. Communities of interpretation are highly complex, and no one can ever be placed solely in one community. There are many scholars, not just biblical scholars, in departments of religion who construct religions along idealist lines (e.g. Mircea Eliade), and there are many theologians in departments of theology who take seriously the social dimension of reality (e.g. Walter Brueggemann). It is not my intention to draw a sharp and unbridgeable distinction between religion and theology. However, if biblical

54. S. Fish, *Is There a Text in this Class? The Authority of Interpretive Communities* (Cambridge, MA: Harvard University Press, 1980), pp. 13-16.

55. For a discussion of differences between these communities of interpretation see P.R. Davies, 'Do Old Testament Studies need a Dictionary?', in D.J.A. Clines *et al.* (eds.), *The Bible in Three Dimensions: Essays in Celebration of Forty Years of Biblical Studies in the University of Sheffield* (JSOTSup, 87; Sheffield: JSOT Press, 1990), pp. 321-35, especially pp. 323-26.

scholarship seeks to speak theologically at the end of the twentieth century, it should utilize notions of literature and history prevailing at the end of the twentieth century rather than those extant at the end of the nineteenth century.[56] David Gunn makes a similar point when he says,

> The life-force of modern historical criticism was a determination to deal with the biblical text in the same way as secular texts were treated, even if that should lead to the shaking of some dearly held verities. And that assumption, ironically, is at the heart of the current challenge which historical criticism faces—a challenge to both its notion of history and its notion of text.[57]

This, of course, is the argument of third-world and feminist biblical scholars who are calling on biblical theologians to respond more effectively to the needs of the contemporary world as they see them from their different perspectives.

---

56. For a discussion of this shift and its implications for theology see W. Brueggemann, *Texts Under Negotiation: The Bible and Postmodern Imagination* (Minneapolis: Fortress Press, 1993), pp. 1-25.

57. 'New Directions in Hebrew Narrative', *JSOT* 39 (1987), p. 66.

INDEXES

INDEX OF BIBLICAL REFERENCES

OLD TESTAMENT

INDEX OF AUTHORS